A CRITICAL HANDBOOK OF CHILDREN'S LITERATURE

FOURTH EDITION

Rebecca J. Lukens

MIAMI UNIVERSITY
OXFORD, OHIO

SCOTT, FORESMAN/LITTLE, BROWN HIGHER EDUCATION
A Division of Scott, Foresman and Company
Glenview, Illinois   London, England

Acknowledgments on page 299 are an extension of the copyright page.

Library of Congress Cataloging in Publication Data
Lukens, Rebecca J. 1922-
  A critical handbook of children's literature / Rebecca J. Lukens. — 4th ed.
     p.   cm.
  Includes bibliographies and index.
  ISBN 0-673-38773-9
  1. Children's literature—History and criticism.   I. Title.
PN1009.A1L84   1990
809'.89282—dc20   89-36063
                                                      CIP
ISBN 0-673-38773-9

1 2 3 4 5 6–KPF–94 93 92 91 90 89

Preface

Only the very rarest kind of best in anything can
be good enough for the young.

WALTER DE LA MARE

A Critical Handbook of Children's Literature, now in its fourth edition, has grown out of my conviction that literature for children differs from literature for adults in degree, not in kind, and that writing for children should be judged by the same standards as writing for adults. Children, like adults, read to explore the world, to escape the confining present, to discover themselves, to become someone else. Since children are helped in choosing books by adults—in the role of teachers, librarians, or parents—we hope to put into their hands the best literature for these purposes.

How can we choose the rarest kind of best from the approximately 3000 children's books published each year as well as from the many books that remain in print year after year? What are the standards we can confidently apply in evaluating writing for children? We may have felt amused and touched when we read *Charlotte's Web* by E. B. White, but how do we discuss or decide its literary worth beyond these vague feelings?

Why train students to make critical judgments? Because, although the techniques of judgment may in themselves be ordinary, such increased consciousness of them is in itself valuable training.

When we say a hearty "I like it!" we may be responding to believable and interesting characters or to something we know is true about people. When we are disappointed in a book—"I don't like it!"—we may be rejecting the story's action as too coincidental or its dialogue as too stilted. Learning to recognize such literary elements as character and plot and theme helps us understand the effects a writer achieves and appreciate the reasons for his or her choices. After all, Peter Rabbit and Rabbit in *Winnie-the-Pooh* are not the same, nor does the setting for *The Wind in the Willows* have the same effect upon us as the setting in *Island of the Blue Dolphins.* We could say fairly easily *how* they are different, but we need to go beyond that and say *why* they are different. Why did the authors make the choices they made and what are the effects of those choices upon us as readers? This knowledge helps us discover the reasons for our emotional responses. It sharpens our perceptions and increases our enjoyment of reading. To use a familiar analogy, do we go to the football game merely to find out who won? Or also to enjoy the plays and ploys that put the winning score on the scoreboard? In the same way, do we read only to find out how the story comes out? Or do we also take delight in the people, in the shifts and turns of events along the way, in the words that tingle our spines or quicken our pulses, or in discovering something about ourselves?

This fourth edition includes a new chapter on picture books and a revised chapter on the major genres of literature. The chapter delineates the common elements of literature and demonstrates how each genre may emphasize or rely upon one element more than others. Main points are provided in a chart to help readers more easily spot possible shortcomings of a story and pinpoint particularly significant elements. Some readers may find the chart useful; others may find it too simplistic, a common problem when one tries to quantify or make an abstraction concrete. Use the chart with caution.

Chapter study questions highlight the relationship of the element being considered to each of the genres cited in that chapter. The Glossary, of course, reflects literary terms. The updated Appendices include lists of current award-winning titles, children's magazines, and publications that review children's literature.

Other revised chapters focus on the elements common to all imaginative literature—character, plot, theme, setting, point of view, style, and tone. These terms are explained simply and clearly and are illustrated with new or lasting examples from all genres of children's literature. Although these terms are the critical tools and basic vocabulary we use to discuss and evaluate any piece of imaginative literature, writing for children presents some special concerns and problems; each chapter concludes with a discussion of such matters.

The chapter on informational books contains updated examples but does not deal with periodicals or reference materials. As for reading levels, they are also available in the reviewing media. No substitute exists for awareness of individual differences in the interests or capabilities of children. As we know, children are different, not only at different ages but also because their consuming interests one month may be succeeded by new fascinations the next. The bored child called uneducable by a third-grade teacher may be reading *Kon Tiki* behind a spelling book, while tales of illiterate high-school graduates continue to surface.

To fail to apply critical standards to children's literature is to imply that children's literature is inferior to adult literature, that children will not benefit from good literature or be harmed by poor literature. This handbook takes the opposite view: children's literature *should* be judged by the same standards as adult literature, with some small differences, and children *can* benefit enormously now and for a lifetime by exposure to writing of high quality. The approach to children's literature offered in this handbook, along with wide reading in children's books and serious practice of the evaluative skills discussed here, will develop critical thinking and increase understanding of and pleasure in literature. This knowledge provides a firm basis for discriminating among the good and the poor in children's books. This handbook will help to identify the rarest of the best—and to pass it on to a new generation of readers.

One final note—instructors might wish to assign reading of *Charlotte's Web* early in the term, perhaps even before assigning Chapter 3. Other books frequently mentioned throughout the text as examples might be assigned at appropriate times: for study of character, *Roll of Thunder, Hear My Cry;* for plot, *The Borrowers;* for setting, *The Witch of Blackbird Pond;* for point of view, *The Incredible Journey;* for theme, *A Wizard of Earthsea;* for tone, *The Slave Dancer;* for style, *Island of the Blue Dolphins*. A multitude of other possibilities exists.

For indefatigable assistance, I thank the staff of the children's department of Lane Library, Oxford and Hamilton, Ohio. For reviews and suggestions, I thank John A. Rutherford, Radford University; Alleen Pace Nilsen, Arizona State University; Robert Wiggins, University of California at Davis; Bette Peltola, University of Wisconsin at Milwaukee; Wilma Jean Hargrave, New Mexico State University; Chandler Barbour, Towson State University; Joan Nist, Auburn University; Sam Sebesta, University of Washington; and Julie M. Jensen. For their suggestions and frequent letters of support, I am also grateful to my many colleagues whom I call friends, those who have used earlier editions of *A Critical Handbook of Children's Literature*.

Rebecca J. Lukens
Miami University
Oxford, Ohio

ontents

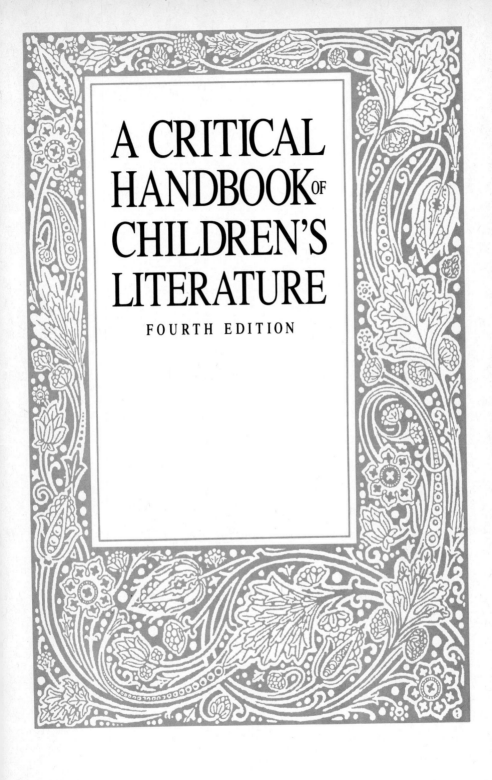

A CRITICAL HANDBOOK OF CHILDREN'S LITERATURE

FOURTH EDITION

From *Charlotte's Web* by E. B. White, illustrated by Garth Williams. Copyright 1952, renewed 1980 by E. B. White. Illustrations copyright 1952, renewed 1980 by Garth Williams. Reprinted by permission of Harper & Row, Publishers, Inc.

Literature: What is it?

We pick up *McCall's* magazine at the drug store, *TV Guide* in the super-market, *National Geographic* in the doctor's office, and pore over *Europe on $30 a Day* to give us information and vicarious experience, but they are not literature. Literature *may* give us information and vicarious experience, but it also gives us much more. What sets a chapter in *The Wind in the Willows* apart from a *National Geographic* article on the plant and animal life of the English countryside? Many things, and they are at the heart of our defini-tion of literature. Sometimes called *belles lettres,* literature is traditionally described as the body of writing that exists because of inherent imaginative and artistic qualities. The fine line drawn between literature and writing that is primarily scientific, intellectual, or philosophical often wavers.

Why do we adults pick up and read a novel or a collection of poetry? For pleasure—not to find a lesson in ecology, not to be taught about the natural habitat of the cobra or about sailing in Colonial America. We choose literature that promises entertainment and, sometimes, escape. If other discoveries come to us too, we are pleased and doubly rewarded. However, our first motive for reading a novel or a poem is *pleasure*. We may lay the book aside with mixed feelings, but if there is no pleasure, we reject it completely or leave it unfinished. For adults who have had a variety of experiences, who have known success and failure, who have had to decide what is "good" and what is "bad," who have had to face their own shaky standards of morality, the nature of pleasure in literature may be different from that for children.

Because we are all different, the pleasures we seek as well as those we may encounter may be very personal. But what is required of us as critical readers is that we examine the pleasure the work aspires to give, the real subject of literary criticism. To paraphrase critic Frank Kermode, it is the function of the writer to make sense out of life, but the function of the critic to evaluate the writer's efforts to make sense out of life. We may restate that argument to say that we as critical readers do not stop with our personal pleasure: "I like it, and that's so personal that it cannot be debated." We go on, instead, to find in the work the sources of that personal enjoyment. To our surprise, they may lie in a painful recognition of ourselves, a satisfying verification of our humanness, or in variations of the great questions of philosopher Immanuel Kant: What must I know? What should I be? What can I hope? But some kind of pleasure is essential, whether the reader is nine or thirty-nine years old.

Literature provides a second reward: *understanding*. This understanding comes from the exploration of the "human condition," the revelation of human nature, the discovery of humankind. It is not explicitly the function of literature, either for children or for adults, to try to reform human beings, or to set up guidelines for behavior; however, it is the province of literature to observe and to comment, to open individuals and their society for our observation and our understanding. If there is any question about what we are to understand, notice that our terms are "human" and "humankind," synonyms for "people."

As for information, it may or may not contribute to understanding. We may know a person's height, weight, hair color, ethnic background, and occupation. This is information. But until we are aware of temperament, anxieties, joys, and ambitions, we do not *know* that person. Information is not a person; spirit is.

When information is part of the story, we expect it to be accurate, of course, and relevant. The following passage from Johanna Spyri's *Heidi*, for example, contains much information, both summarized and detailed:

> Heidi began to tell her about life up on the mountain, and about the days spent in the pasture, and the winter life indoors. She told how her grandfather could make anything out of wood—three-legged stools, benches and chairs, and mangers into which hay could be put for Schwanli and Bärli. He had just finished a big new tub for summer bathing, and a new porringer and some spoons. Heidi became quite excited as she recounted the wonderful things his skillful hands fashioned from the wood.

The purpose of this passage, however, is not to supply information about Swiss handcrafts. Here are simplicity of life, skill in handiwork, and pride in creation—the spirit of a people and a way of life. Information alone without its contributing to understanding is not, by our traditional definition, literature.

Then perhaps a narrative of people acting in a way we can understand is all that is necessary. No, that is not the case. We may have a short account with understandable action called "Stevie Visits the A&P," and yet it may not qualify as literature. While Stevie's visit might conceivably tell us something about the nature of childhood, it just as easily might not. The grocery store situation provides vivid details about prices and cuts of meat and varieties of vegetables, and the action may be credible because Mother chooses a ripe cantaloupe and pays at the checkout counter. However, the significance of the experience in terms of the characters' lives may be lacking—significance that helps us, whatever our age, to understand a little more about ourselves and others. In the most general terms, then, literature is reading that, by means of imaginative and artistic qualities, provides pleasure and understanding.

To return to the comparison of the *National Geographic* article and *The Wind in the Willows:* We can feel fairly certain that we read the *National Geographic* article primarily for information, and we can also be reasonably sure that we read *The Wind in the Willows* primarily for pleasure; our second reward is understanding.

Literature has many other more specific appeals for us as readers. Literature *shows human motives* for what they are, inviting the reader to identify with or to react to a fictional character. We see into the mind of the character, or into the subconscious that even the character does not know. Through the writer's careful choice of details from the past, the current environment, and the imaginary world of the character, we come to see clearly the character's motivation for action. If in these chosen details we see some similarity to our own lives, we nod our heads and identify with the character, feeling that we understand the motives and can justify the deeds. Or seeing the error in judgment that the character fails to see, we understand. Seeing motives we disapprove of, we condemn, or seeing a reflection of our own mistakes, we are compassionate.

Our *touchstone*[1] book, E. B. White's *Charlotte's Web,* the story that will serve us as a critical standard and a frequent example, shows one character, Wilbur, at one moment crying out: "I don't want to die! Save me, somebody! Save me!" However, months later his motive for action is selfless concern:

> "Templeton . . . I will make you a solemn promise. Get Charlotte's egg sac for me, and from now on I will let you eat first, when Lurvy slops me. I will let you have your choice of everything in the trough and I won't touch a thing until you're through."

Charlotte's motives are born of pure sympathy and a desire to help Wilbur's suffering. She says briskly that Wilbur will not die, and she weaves words into her web until late at night. Our identification with each response to Wilbur's life-and-death crises varies as our experience varies.

Literature may also *provide form for experience*. Aside from birth and death, real life has no beginnings nor endings, but is instead a series of stories without order, each story merging with all other stories. Fiction, however, makes order of the chaos by organizing events and consequences, cause and effect, beginning and ending. When we look back on our lives, we notice the high spots: "the first time we met," or even "the day we sold the old refrigerator." What once seemed trivial, now, with the perspective given by distance in time, seems important. When we look back, we do not look at sequence, since chronology is merely the random succession of life's disordered events. Literature, however, by placing the relevant episodes—"and the next time we met"—into coherent sequence, gives order and form to experience.

In *Charlotte's Web* White selects events which, among other things, demonstrate the purpose in Charlotte's life. When she says, "By helping you, perhaps I was trying to lift up my life a trifle," we see more clearly the pattern of Charlotte's behavior. While she accepts the inevitability of death, she does not accept the prospect of passive waiting. Charlotte chooses instead to fill her days with order and purpose. As White directs our thoughts and alters our feelings in a chosen course, he gives form to the experience of the ongoing cycle of life.

Literature also may *reveal life's fragmentation*. Not a day goes by without our being pulled in one direction after another by the demands of friendship—"Please help." Of obligation—"I promised I would." Of pressure—"It's due tomorrow." And of money—"I wish I could afford it." Life is fragmented, and our daily experience proves it. However, literature, while it may remind us of our own and society's fragmentation, does not leave us there. Literature sorts the world into disparate segments we can identify and examine; friendship, greed, family, sacrifice, childhood, love, advice, old age, treasures, snobbery, and compassion are set before us for close observation. Little, if anything, is outside the province of literature.

While literature may be saying or revealing that life is fragmented, it simultaneously *helps us focus on essentials*. Adult fiction writer May Sarton says that her books are born of questions she needs to answer for herself. "Art is order, but it is made out of the chaos of life." This chaos reordered, experience given form, permits us to experience with different intensity but with new understanding the parts of life that we have known: We exclaim, "That's how it happened to me, too!" Or parts we have yet to meet: "Do you suppose I'll ever get my diploma?" Or experiences we may never have: "What must it be like to live in a housing project or on a reservation?" In the process of giving order to life, the writer sorts out the essential details from the nonessential. Undistracted by irrelevant experiences or minor anxieties, the reader focuses upon the essentials of action, people, events, and stresses. In retrospect, we see that life does not distribute events in order of their mounting intensity or their accumulative effects upon us. Literature, however, because it ignores the irrelevant and focuses on the essentials, makes significance clear. As we read, our detachment helps us to see events and their possible influences. We can know the challenge of making choices, feel the excitement of suspense, and glow with the warmth of accomplishment. Literature *says* that life is fragmented. What it *does* is something else: Literature provides a sense of life's unity and meaning.

Literature can *reveal the institutions of society.* Every week we become aware of a new regulation on our personal lives—a higher tax on gasoline, a no-left-turn sign where we have always turned left, or the disappearance of our favorite Tuesday night TV show. A group of people called an institution, something bigger than we are, makes a judgment, and a form of institutional control determines for us something we would like to determine for ourselves. The institutions of society—like government, family, church, school, as well as forces that shape our jobs—urge and coerce us to conform to standards. Institutions occasionally seem so threatening, in fact, that we fear they will close in on our lives, restricting us completely. Yet we know that some restrictions establish the order needed for a group to survive. In this way necessary institutions are born and grow. Literature clarifies our reactions to institutions by showing appropriate circumstances where people give in to or struggle against them.

In the institution called farming, for example, it is unprofitable to keep a runt pig, because fattening him will not pay a good return on the dollar. In *Charlotte's Web,* within Wilbur's conflict with an institution, we see what a life-and-death struggle does to an immature innocent. We may not literally identify with Wilbur—since it is highly unlikely we will ever be commodities on an exchange market—but his struggle for life is nonetheless somewhat similar to our own. Wilbur soon discovers who his friends are, how resourceful they can be, how hard they will work for another's safety, and even, in Templeton's case, what a person's price may be. Through Wilbur's struggle with profitable farming we discover in a small way the impersonal nature of society. In other stories we may discover that racism is institutionalized, or that although we individually hate war, it is ordered by a body larger than we are. The variety of such conflicts seems infinite.

Not only do institutions affect our lives, but nature does, too. Some literature *reveals nature as a force* that influences us. Tornadoes on the summer plains, avalanches in the springtime Rockies, hurricanes in the tropical Caribbean, blizzards on the Dakota prairies—we read of them each year, season by season, region by region. Nature constantly reminds us of its effects upon our lives. People's natural environment influences them, whether it be the stress of wind that wearies nerves, intense heat that produces lethargy, or extreme cold and sunlessness that depress spirits. Literature, by presenting human beings involved in conflict with such forces, makes us see their effects upon human life.

In *Island of the Blue Dolphins* Scott O'Dell shows tenacious Karana clinging to the cliff as she clings to life, battling nature as it sends a tidal wave upon the island:

> The wave struck the cliff. It sent long tongues streaming around me so that I could neither see nor hear. The tongues of water licked into all the crevices, dragged at my hand and at my bare feet gripping the ledge. They rose high above me.

Nature is a force affecting human beings, sometimes demanding that they exert all their powers against it. Although struggling cannot conquer nature, human beings may struggle heroically and yet not be conquered. In such a conflict, the reader can applaud the human will.

Literature provides vicarious experience. It is impossible for us to live any life but our own, in any time but our own life span, or in any space or place but our own. But literature makes it possible for us to live in the time of the French Revolution, in the period of the Vikings, or during the days of the American colonies. Through a good story, we can live in a small river town on the Mississippi, in the hold of a slave ship, in the hills of Appalachia, or even in a castle turret. The possibilities for us to live lives other than our own are infinite, as numerous as the books on the library shelves.

Finally, literature forces us, leads us, entices, or woos us into *meeting a writer-creator* whose medium, words, we know; whose subject, human nature, we live with; whose vision, life's meaning, we hope to understand. We are the student-novice before the artist. In the hands of a gifted writer, we turn from passive followers into passionate advocates calling new followers. The writer's skill with words gives us a pleasure we want to share, and an understanding we have an urge to spread.

We might say that literature, because it is not an accurate duplicate of life, is lies, all lies. But through "lying," a story may express great truth; through refusing to recount life as it is, the fiction transforms and adds something to life, remaking, embellishing, or opening it for examination. Events translated into words, life written not lived, constitute a profound modification, and become a momentary substitute for life, an experience of life different from our own. As novelist Mario Vargas Llosa says, fiction, "by spurring the imagination, both temporarily assuages human dissatisfaction and simultaneously incites it."[2]

LITERATURE FOR CHILDREN

Children are not little adults. They are different from adults in experience, but not in species, or to put it differently, in degree but not in kind. We can say then of literature for young readers that it differs from literature for adults in degree but not in kind. We sometimes forget that literature for children can and should provide the same enjoyment and understanding as does literature for adults. Children, too, seek pleasure from a story, but the sources of their pleasure are more limited. Since their experiences are more limited than those of adults, children may not understand the same complexity of ideas. Since their understanding is more limited, the expression of ideas must be simpler—both in language and in form. Related to the necessity for simplicity in the expression of ideas are vocabulary and attention span. Stories are more directly told, with fewer digressions and more obvious relationships between characters and actions, or between characters themselves. Children are both more and less literal than adults. They may find discrepancies between two descriptions of a setting and hold the writer accountable for error. On the other hand, children may accept the fantastic more readily than many adults. As long as the world itself is so remarkably complex and incomprehensible, one more fantastic experience in story form presents no impossible hurdle. Often, for example, the personified animals and toys of the child's world, by behaving like human beings, may show what human beings are like. Children are frequently more open to experimenting with a greater variety of literary forms than many adults will accept—from poetry to folktales, to adventure, to fantasy.

The many discoveries that children can make through literature might be sought in other ways by adults. Adults might discover human motivation through a study of psychology, or the nature of society and its institutions through a study of sociology, or the impact of nature upon human behavior through a study of anthropology. However, literature can do all of these things for children. Literature is more than a piece of writing that clarifies; it gives the child pleasure as well as understanding. Throughout the pages that follow we will refer to literature as "a significant truth expressed in appropriate elements and memorable language." As we shall discover, the ideas expressed in poetic form, the truths of theme and character explored through the elements of fiction, and the style of the artist with words constitute literature.

SUMMARY

Literature at its best gives both pleasure and understanding. It explores the nature of human beings, the condition of humankind. If these phrases seem too pompous and abstract for children's literature, rephrase them in children's terms:

What are people like?
Why are they like that?
What do they need?
What makes them do what they do?

The answers, or the mere glimpses of answers to these questions, are made visible in poetry or in fiction by the elements of plot, character, point of view, setting, tone, and style of an imaginative work; together they constitute literature. Words are merely words, but real literature for any age is words chosen with skill and artistry to give the readers pleasure and to help them understand themselves and others.

Illustration from *The Tale of Peter Rabbit* by Beatrix Potter. Copyright 1902 by Frederick Warne & Company. Reprinted by permission of Penguin Books Ltd.

NOTES

1 A touchstone is a test, criterion, or standard; the meaning is derived from the use of a stone as comparison to detect the purity of silver and gold. Matthew Arnold, using the term in literary criticism, wrote: ". . . there can be no more useful help for discovering what poetry belongs to the class of the truly excellent, and can therefore do us most good, than to have always in one's mind lines and expressions of the great masters and to apply them as a touchstone to other poetry."

2 Mario Vargas Llosa, "Is Fiction the Art of Lying?" *The New York Times Book Review,* October 7, 1984, p. 40.

From *Alice's Adventures in Wonderland* by Lewis Carroll, 1865, illustrated by John Tenniel.

Genre in Children's Literature

Like adult literature, children's literature offers variety. It is not uniform, created with cookie-cutter sameness. We recognize rhymes and fairy tales, fantasies and lyrics, and realistic stories about other countries as well as our own. These and other kinds of literature we sometimes call "genres."

A discussion of genre in literature must begin with an effort to define the term—not a simple task. A *genre* is a kind or type of literature in which the members share a common set of characteristics. As soon as we have said this, however, we face the fact that we can identify as many differences and variations among those members as we can find similarities. Classification is easiest when each class or group possesses clear-cut, unchanging characteristics. The chemist's chart of the elements provides a helpful analogy. In fact, when an element is found that lacks the qualities to fit it into any category, or possesses additional qualities, a new class must be added. While this may work for classification in chemistry, it does not work so clearly in literature. If, for example, we divide literature into prose and poetry, where do we place rhythmic but non-metrical writing spaced on the page in "poetic" line length? Is this work poetic prose because it lacks meter? Or prose-poetry because it is filled with sensory appeals and figurative language? Furthermore, if we decide that a work is poetry we might go one step further since, for example, both lyric and sonnet are themselves genres. Yet both are poetry. Must we subdivide?[1] Genres are not always clear-cut and easily distinguished; the terms are often used loosely. Today genre distinctions, although helpful, are often seen as arbitrary.

Opinions differ about classifications, although each of us may have several reasons for our opinions. Some people may find it unnecessary even to mention genres; others like the sense of order that genre classification provides. For our purposes, the term "genre" can be useful in organizing our discussion of children's literature. First, it helps us to be aware that there is more literature for children than one finds in the familiar genres of stories and nursery rhymes. Second, the literary elements we will be talking about in the following chapters—tone, setting, and others—function differently in different genres. And third, we should be sensitive to the broad and rich variety of literature available to children so that we can help them sample it.

For our purposes we will try to use "genre" in a way that is clear and useful, discussing here the kinds of literature that are most commonly written for or read to children and that are complete art forms when read. Since drama is complete only when staged and viewed, it is not discussed here. In Chapter 10, "From Rhyme to Poetry," we note kinds of poems from folk rhyme to lyric, but in this chapter we look at the kinds, types, or genres of fiction: realistic fiction, with subgenres of problem and social issues realism, historical, animal, and regional realism; fantasy with subgenres of fantastic stories, high fantasy, and science fiction; and traditional stories with subgenres of folktales, fables, myths, legends, and folk epics.

All elements of literature are included in each of the major genres of fiction, but within each type one element may be more significant than another. In some cases the genre demands that a particular element be strong or well developed; without the strength the credibility of the story may be in question. For example, animal realism requires an objective point of view, for we cannot know what an animal—a real animal, not a personified one—is thinking. Historical fiction, to cite another example, relies for credibility upon a clear sense of setting in a past time. And again, since folktales have been told orally by one generation to another, descriptions of setting or details of a character's past or a character's thoughts merely delay the telling. When we listen to a folktale, flat characters seem appropriate, because we recognize them immediately and can move quickly into the action.

The genres, then, are both distinct and overlapping; they contain all elements but in varying combinations and degrees. The chart at the end of this chapter may be a helpful guide, showing how elements relate to the specific genres. Refer to it cautiously, however, knowing that literature is not governed by inflexible rules.

REALISM

Realism means that a story is possible, although not necessarily probable. Effect follows cause without the intervention of the magical or supernatural. In *Did You Carry the Flag Today, Charley?* by Rebecca Caudill, Charley is rewarded because he helped out in the library, not because a fairy godmother intervened. The outcome seems reasonable and plausible; the story is a representation of action that seems truthful. Realistic stories have in common several characteristics: they are fictional narratives with characters who are involved in some kind of action that holds our interest, set in some possible place and time. Once again, keep in mind that if we divide realistic fiction into subgenres the divisions may at times seem overlapping.

Problem Realism and Social Issues Realism

Problem realism and social issues realism, which are similar in their focus upon problems, are relatively recent subgenres; their situations are realistic or possible. The problems in problem realism are not universal, like searching for friendship, but personal and particular, like being a foster child in *The Great Gilly Hopkins* by Katherine Paterson, or having a retarded sibling as in *Summer of the Swans* by Betsy Byars. Novels about social issues show the character, usually the protagonist or central character, encountering a kind of problem engendered by society, like discrimination because of race, gender, or social position.

In these kinds of realism the protagonist's problem is the source of plot and conflict, and that conflict may be with self, society, or another person. In a well-written book, character and conflict are both well developed and interrelated. In a poorly written novel, the character may either be stereotyped or may seem to be made up only of problems. The physical handicaps, the problems with drugs or sex, the divorce situations, and the minority or gender issues become so overwhelming that they may blot out the credibility of the character as a whole human being made up of a mixture of feelings and thoughts, emotion, and intellect. Furthermore, in poor fiction of these kinds, the protagonist's problems may be solved in too pat a manner. Such fictional solutions can be not only simplistic and sentimental, but they are also lacking in reality and justice. In real life, difficulties are not solved so quickly or easily. Readers who identify with the characters may find false hope for their own solutions; readers who observe the problem-ridden character may become condescending. "What's bothering my friend? Look how easy it is in this book!" Such simplistic solutions may then result in false themes or ideas like "Any problem is easily solved," or "Work hard and everything always comes out all right." Difficulty, after all, is natural to a complex problem. *A Hero ain't nothin' but a Sandwich* by Alice Childress, in which Benjie struggles with drug addiction, provides an example of a more credible truth: "Despite love and care, a big problem is not easily solved."

As the genre has matured, the stories seem to be better written, with characters who do have special problems but whose lives are not so problem-ridden that the characters lack full dimensions. Cynthia Voigt's *Dicey's Song,* for example, tells of children whose problems are significant and, in a less well-written novel, might seem insurmountable. Dicey has led her four siblings to Maryland from Massachusetts, where they have left their mother in a mental hospital, to seek the grandmother about whom they have just learned. Without money or parents, they settle in with Gram, who reaches out for the help that is available for food, clothing, tutoring, part-time jobs, and even old memories that become useful rather than bitter. The reality of the family and their friends convinces us of the seriousness of their problems, and the difficulty with which the problems are handled and solutions found convinces the reader. Tough questions have no easy answers.

Tone or attitude are also affected when the novel is poorly written. Works become sensational when, to hold readers' interest, the writer so loads the story with problems that the situation is incredible, and the realistic novel becomes sensational and unbelievable.

While all elements are important in problem realism and social issues realism, we notice particularly the elements of theme, character, and conflict. If such fiction is to help us understand ourselves and others, we must find soundly developed characters and believable conflicts.

Animal Realism

Nonfiction should deal accurately with animals, telling the details of their appearances, their habitats, and their life cycles. Animal realism as fiction adds another dimension by giving continuity and conflict or adventure to the story. The setting includes details of the seasons, the geographical regions, and the influence of the elements on the animals. Within the restrictions of scientific accuracy, the fictional portrayal of animals shows them in conflict of some kind. Some are the most important characters in the story, like the three pets of Sheila Burnford's *The Incredible Journey* which determinedly battle with nature to return to their masters through the wilds of Canada. While they may be thought of as characters, they are not given human traits or anthropomorphized. Such novels as *Rabbit Hill* by Robert Lawson or *The Wind in the Willows* by Kenneth Grahame cannot then be considered animal realism, because the animal characters behave, think, and talk not like animals but like human beings. Accuracy about animal life requires an objective point of view when the principals are animals, but a human character who is telling the story, like Billy telling about owls in Farley Mowat's *Owls in the Family,* may report interpretations of the animals' behavior. If the point of view falters, and we "get into the mind" of the animal, the story may become not only unrealistic but also sentimental in tone, as is Felix Salten's *Bambi,* where we know not only Bambi's thoughts but even those of the autumn leaves. In the course of an adventure in animal realism, we make some discovery about animals or about their relationships to human beings.

Historical Realism

Historical fiction is placed in the past, and the time and place in the past determine setting. Details about vehicles, clothing, or food preparation, for example, must fit the time and the place. Sometimes little is known of the period, and at other times much is known; it is possible to write historical fiction about the Vikings, like *Hakon of Rogen's Saga* by Erik Haugaard, as well as about the American colonies, like *The Witch of Blackbird Pond* by Elizabeth Speare. The integral setting demonstrates how the characters live and how families support themselves. Often the setting is a period when living was markedly different, as in the pioneer days of *Caddie Woodlawn* by Carol Brink, or the Revolutionary War era of *Johnny Tremain* by Esther Forbes. Since characters, and particularly the central character, are caught in the events of the time, setting influences plot. When the writer exaggerates the bad or the good of the times, the resulting historical fiction may suffer from sensational or sentimental tone. Although themes are often universal, they may relate clearly to a particular time; a story might easily be united by themes about how in times of civil war brothers fight brothers and families are torn apart, as *Across Five Aprils* by Irene Hunt exemplifies, or how in pioneer days the family unit was important to survival, as it is in the *Little House* stories of Laura Ingalls Wilder. Style may focus particularly upon descriptions that draw for us time and place, the dress and homes, the work and recreation of the day. Language should be appropriate to the time; obviously our current slang would be out of place in dialogue of Americans during the Revolution.

History presents facts. To turn facts into fiction, the writer must combine imagination with fact, bringing about an integrated story with a fictional protagonist in a suspenseful plot. As the twentieth century draws to a close, matters that not long ago were current events become the materials of a historical period. Today, for example, writers are seeing with increased objectivity the events of World War II, as does Bette Greene in *Summer of My German Soldier,* and of the Great Depression as does Mildred Taylor in *Roll of Thunder, Hear My Cry.* Such novels show the impact of the times upon the people living in them.

Sports Stories

Once a kind of formula fiction, sports stories have become increasingly individualized, with well-developed characters struggling with personal issues and discovering the forces and choices they must confront. Characters play, watch, or live on the fringes of all kinds of sports, although team sports such as baseball, football, and basketball are most common. Emphasis on team play and sportsmanship is frequently the theme, but in the past decades, with demand for more stories about integrated schools and nonracist themes, many stories involve acceptance of players of other races. Another shift has occurred with the appearance of sexually integrated sports. Once a genre of undistinguished stories, sports fiction is much improved. Because children take gym classes, watch televised sports, and are involved in organized sports after school, sport is part of their lives; their reading interests may move naturally toward such stories. A recent sport story of excellent quality is Bruce Brooks' *The Moves Make the Man.* Writers of sport stories whose work is worth noting are Matt Christopher, Scott Corbett, Alfred Slote, R. R. Knudson, and Mel Calabash, who wrote of Ruth Marini's struggles to become a professional baseball player.

FORMULA FICTION

Some kinds of stories follow distinct patterns and are therefore called *formula fiction.* Although following a formula does not necessarily eliminate the writer's originality, it may, however, restrict it.

Mysteries and Thrillers

One popular type of formula fiction is the mystery story, a story in which mystery and often terror play controlling parts. Mystery stories are set in any time, historical or futuristic, as well as the present. They rely for suspense upon unexplained events and actions which are sometimes, by story's end, resolved or explained by reasonable and carefully detected discoveries. Within the genre we include the detective story, as well as novels of crime, suspense, and espionage. The Gothic novel, traditionally filled with magical or mysterious happenings, occasionally with chivalry, and frequently with horror and terror, perhaps rides the borderline between realism and fantasy.

Plot carries most mysteries and thrillers, although those more carefully crafted also show strong characterization. The mood is almost inevitably suspenseful, and setting may include such intriguing places as vacant houses or abandoned buildings. On the other hand, mystery stories may also occur in the most ordinary or everyday settings. One of the traditional qualities of effective mystery stories is the clever planting of foreshadowing; those who read the genre over time acquire skills in putting together the bits of foreshadowing to predict outcome.

Every schoolchild knows Nancy Drew and the Hardy Boys, the most clearly representative of formula mysteries. A number of qualities make this type of fiction appealing. It is easy to read and understand, it moves quickly with little description and much dialogue, and it comes to satisfying conclusions. Although these novels may present little challenge, their sameness provides comfort and their predictability is reassuring to young readers.[2]

Many mysteries are not formula fiction. Many are not only carefully plotted, but they also have strong themes, characters we come to know well, and a style that is distinctive of the writer. British writer Philippa Pearce writes such mystery stories; one of her more recent books is *The Way to Sattin Shore*. Kate Tranter fits together, piece by piece, the evidence that leads to her other grandmother—her father's mother—and to the mystery of her missing father. Had he really died on the day of her birth? Why was her mother's mother so grimly secretive? Why was her father never mentioned in the household? Kate puts the puzzle bits together and with her father's return—back from Australia where he had fled under a cloud of false accusation about the mysterious drowning of his brother—the re-united family leaves the vindictive grandmother and begins a new life together. Mystery, a common element in many well-written stories for children, can hold us in suspense related to character and theme as well as plot. Mystery novels that have been popular for some time include those of Scott Corbett, Robert Newman, and Donald J. Sobol's *Encyclopedia Brown* books. Sobol's *Angie's First Case* promises a new series about a girl detective.

Romance

A recent development for young readers has been the burst of popularity of the romance novel; millions have been sold since the 1960s. The romance is not a new kind of realism, however, but has been around for generations; heroines in Victorian novels, for example, were often absorbed in them. Under the guise of realism, the romance oversimplifies and sentimentalizes male-female relationships, often showing them as the sole focus of young lives. The most thorough study of romances and their market suggests that these "fairy tales of desire" consistently show deeply feminine yet feisty females involved with the male paragon of tender-tough qualities, a combination that both verifies and contradicts the rise of feminism.[3] Romances, since they follow highly similar patterns of plot development and their characters seem to differ merely in hair color or name rather than in personality, lead a perceptive reader to comment, "Read one, you've read them all"—an exaggeration, of course, but containing some degree of truth.

FANTASY

Fantasy, in the phrase of Coleridge, requires "the willing suspension of disbelief." The writer of *fantasy* (sometimes called "literary fantasy" to distinguish it from folk fantasy which is of unknown authorship) creates another world for characters and readers, asking that readers believe this other world could and does exist within the framework of the book. The acceptance of this other world requires of the writer an ability to make the imaginary universe so credible, "so solidly grounded in reality" as Madeleine L'Engle says, that we wish it were all true; for sheer pleasure, we believe. Fantastic stories, high fantasy, and science fiction are identifiable subgenres of fantasy; often they seem to overlap, and thus make clear distinctions irrelevant.

Fantastic Stories

We might call one subgenre of fantasy *fantastic stories,* stories realistic in most details but still requiring us to willingly suspend our disbelief. Clear examples of such fantasy are the Borrowers books of Mary Norton, showing the daily lives of tiny people who face everyday problems like our own and make discoveries about fear of the unknown and about the disruption of family life through greed. To cite another example, the magical and fantastical govern *The Wish Giver* by Bill Brittain; when the Magic Man sells cards with luminous red dots and promises that each will make one wish come true, three children doubt him. But each of their wishes does come true: Polly's ugly tongue keeps her from friendships; her words are bullfrog croaks. Rowena wishes the traveling salesman would put down roots; he turns into a tree. Adam wishes the farm had water all over so he didn't have to haul it from the "crick"; the farm is flooded. Characters and setting are realistic, but happenings fantastic.

Perhaps the fuzzy line between realistic and fantastic stories can be exemplified by Virginia Hamilton's *Sweet Whispers, Brother Rush,* in which everything seems realistic except the appearance of ghostlike Brother Rush. Tree is convinced he is the ghost of her uncle, and that he takes her into the past to reveal details about her father and mother. All else seems real—the mother's work, her denial of her retarded son, Tree's responsibility for keeping the home—and we are prepared to believe in the ghost as fantasy. Or, on the other hand, to regard it as Tree's imagination.

Other fantastic stories are about characters that are not people but are represented as people because they talk or live in houses like ours, have feelings like our own, or lead lives like those of human beings; these we might call fantastic stories of personification. In some, characters are personified animals like Hans Christian Andersen's "The Ugly Duckling," E. B. White's *Charlotte's Web,* or Kenneth Grahame's *The Wind in the Willows.* Their themes are about human life: Growing up is fraught with trauma; no one appreciates the humble; a community supports its members, no matter how foolish. Another subgenre of personification is that of personified objects, like Andersen's "The Little Fir Tree," or his story about the darning needle.

In any of the subgenres of fantastic stories, we are drawn to willing suspension of disbelief primarily by character and theme.

High Fantasy

The *high fantasy* genre is primarily characterized by its focus on the conflict between good and evil. If it is successful, it captures our belief in two major ways: first, by the internal consistency of the new world, like the categories or classes of small, nonhuman beings in *The Lord of the Rings* by J.R.R. Tolkien; and second, by the protagonist's belief in his or her experience.[4] High fantasy also portrays full and complete human beings like the hero of Otfried Preussler's *The Satanic Mill*, or like Aerin in Robin McKinley's *The Hero and the Crown*. Point of view influences our acceptance of the character and the experience. Setting varies, but is most often integral because credibility may depend upon a created world different from our own. Time becomes flexible; sometimes it "wrinkles" as in Madeleine L'Engle's *A Wrinkle in Time*. Sometimes it balloons out and returns, as it does in C. S. Lewis' Narnia books. At other times it may be globe-shaped, as Eleanor Cameron says, "holding in equilibrium all tenses" of past, present, and future.[5] Tone is serious, even awed. Themes encompass a broad concern for humanity, effectively objectifying and universalizing the greatest conflict of human life, that between good and evil.

Science Fiction

Science fiction is a type of fantasy, and it is often difficult to decide whether a particular work is pure fantasy or science fiction. Perhaps when we realize that our enjoyment of *A Wrinkle in Time,* for example, is neither increased nor diminished by our decision to call it fantasy or science fiction, we may decide that such distinctions are unimportant. Yet, for the sake of order when we think in genres, we might say that *science fiction* stresses scientific laws and technological inventions—like gravity and the speed of light and the contrivances with which to deal with these forces and limitations.

Descriptions and criteria ought to begin with definitions. Robert Heinlein, well-known author of science fiction, calls it "speculative fictions in which the author takes as his first postulate the real world as we know it, including all established facts and natural laws." Don Moskowitz, historian of science fiction, defines it as a "branch of fantasy identifiable by the fact that it eases the 'willing suspension of disbelief' . . . by utilizing an atmosphere of scientific credibility for its imaginative speculations in physical science, space, time, social science, and philosophy." Kingsley Amis, critic and author, says that science fiction treats a situation "that could not arise in the world we know, but which is hypothesized on the basis of some innovation in science or technology, or pseudo-science, or pseudo-technology." Unlike fantasy, it must "achieve verisimilitude and win the 'willing suspension of disbelief' through scientific plausibility." And critic Bruce Franklin contrasts the two, saying that while fantasy tries to imitate impossibilities, science fiction confronts possibilities.

Perhaps the definition that comes closest to our considerations is that proposed by the acclaimed writer of science fiction, Theodore Sturgeon. He maintains that "a [good] science fiction story is a story built around human beings, with a human problem, and a human solution, which would not have happened at all without its scientific content."[6] In contrast, poor science fiction often shows characters committed to the scientific process of investigation and invention, and may therefore be governed solely by intellect. Their concerns are the products of their minds; they may expend their physical energies and mental powers mainly upon inanimate objects and abstract theories. Intellect may also govern relationships between characters, whose source of cooperation seems a union of intellects controlling or using a force either natural or mechanical.

The genre often may rely heavily upon conflict rather than character to hold the reader's interest. Such conflicts are frequently with societies alien to us in form and in values, like the Tripods of John Christopher's *White Mountains* trilogy. When the conflict is person against nature, as it is in *The Time of the Great Freeze* by Robert Silverberg, the battle seems weighted on the side of the natural force. While early science fiction seemed to have few themes—the strong will to survive, for example—recent work is far more varied and complex. Tone, like tone in any kind of writing either for children or adults, may, but not necessarily, be didactic: "If we don't care for our environment . . . " Writers like H. M. Hoover, William Sleator, and Ray Bradbury, however, whose interest in human beings is as keen as their interest in scientific speculation, write with subtlety and understanding of human motives.

It has been suggested that science fiction's mechanical persons or robots may serve as the means by which today's children work out their psychological conflicts and fears, as Bruno Bettelheim believes that folk and fairy tales have for preceding generations.[7] From Frank Baum and his Oz stories on, anthropomorphized machines have explored relationships of persons and twentieth-century inventions, examining such questions as: Which is superior, human or machine? Does it matter how one is created? Are sophisticated robots truly alive? Might the computer, the thinking machine, pose serious threats to human beings and their lives? Young in comparison to many forms of literature, the best of the genre ultimately asks what it means to be related and connected and responsible for others. Such considerations are the substance and subject of imaginative and artistic writing of any genre.

No other genre or subgenre generates such a sharp division of
into those who love it and those who do not care for it. Awarenes
division as well as of the evolution of the genre is bringing to
increasingly complete characters and more varied themes. Science
has changed and continues to change, attracting growing num
readers.

While, for the most part, British writers with their roots dee
faerie and folklore of northern Europe have concentrated on
American writers have created their specialty—fiction that dep
conflict between technology and the laws of nature, and increasir
moral laws of human relationships. Such generalizations may n
hold, as American writers like Lloyd Alexander and Robin McKinle
high fantasy, and British writers move into science fiction, long the
be an American domain.

TRADITIONAL LITERATURE

The term "traditional" or "folk literature" implies that the form con
from the ordinary person, an anonymous storyteller, and exists oral
than in writing—at least until some collector finds, records, and p
the stories or rhymes, thus setting them into temporary form. Ther
no final and definitive version of a piece of folk literature. Folkta
been called the "spiritual history" of humankind, the "cement of
binding a culture together. They seem to express the universality o
wishes and needs. Five hundred versions of the same story, such as "
ella," occur in countless cultures and show almost infinite variations
similar in their focus on human yearning for social acceptance and
comfort. Because of scholarly collecting, folktales that once flouris
in communities where people did not read or write have bec
property of all people.

Folktales

In form the folktale relies on flat characters, bad ones and good one
recognized. Since *folktales* were heard by the teller and then retol
teller's own words, there was hardly time for subtle character devel
A brief phrase, which may be repeated often, serves to draw charact
the teller cannot risk losing the audience by departing from the fa
narration of action to describe thoughts and feelings.

Stock characters, like the fairy godmother and the wicked stepm
"Cinderella," frequently appear. Conflicts are often between pe
personified animals in person versus person conflict, like Jack and

in "Jack and the Beanstalk." Plots are progressive, with the climax coming at the very end and the closing as brief as "They lived happily ever after." Action, fast and lively, is at the heart of the folktale. In European tales, incidents can occur singly, in threes as they do in "The Billy-Goats Gruff," or occasionally in more repetitions; in stories from Native American and other traditions, the numbers vary. The setting is usually a backdrop for the action, a background that creates universality by its vaguely recognizable appeal. Point of view is rarely first person, since the tales are told about flat characters in fantastic situations. Tone varies; it may be sentimental as in "Beauty and the Beast," objective as in "The Little Red Hen," or humorous as in "The Squire's Bride." Themes also vary, but comment on human needs and wishes, like the theme in "The Fishermans's Wife": "People are never satisfied."[8]

For years Americans read and heard few tales other than those from Europe, although some read the Uncle Remus stories or saw them dramatized in animation. Now, with the collection, retelling, and publication of African tales by Harold Courlander, Ashley Bryan, and Verna Aardema, all children may meet them. Virginia Hamilton and Julius Lester effectively retell black American folk literature. Many are animal tales, stories of how the weak defeat the strong, as does Br'er Rabbit, for example. A particularly attractive edition in very readable language is Hamilton's *The People Could Fly: American Black Folktales*. American Indian tales are also published in collections and as single tales, like, for example, *Arrow to the Sun* by Gerald McDermott, who has published tales from several countries. With the arrival of people from Asia, we see more folktales from their countries as well.

Although themes may be explicit, they tend not to be didactic or preachy. Frequently good conquers evil in a short battle and the story concludes with the optimistic view that a just victory is possible. Justice is absolute; it is never sentimentalized. Good is rewarded and evil punished; the wicked witch goes into the oven with no regrets on our part. G. K. Chesterton's statement that adults are wicked and therefore love mercy while children are innocent and therefore love justice may throw light on the popularity of folktales with children. Adults' desire for mercy over justice may account for recurrent adult attacks on folktales and the violence done to the wicked in them. The style of the folktale relies upon recurring images like "no bigger than my thumb" and often includes short rhymes like those in "Snow White": "Mirror, mirror, on the wall/Who is fairest of us all?" The cadenced prose fits the rhythm of oral telling.

Sometimes folktales are subdivided into tales of magic, romance, cumulation, religion, sillies, talking beasts, tall tales, and realistic situations. These categories often overlap; the subgroups only emphasize the richness and variety of the genre, all of them ideal media for the picture book. In *Why Mosquitoes Buzz in People's Ears,* for example, Leo and Diane Dillon boldly

design a cumulative tale, one told differently from most because it reverses the cumulation (usually a series of additions like those in "The House That Jack Built") to unravel the question of how the owlet was killed.

Fables

The *fable* is a very brief story, usually with animal characters, that points clearly to a moral or lesson. The moral, an explicit and didactic or preachy theme, is usually included at the end of the story and is the reason for the existence of the fable. The fable makes visible and objective some lesson like that we see in "The Tortoise and the Hare": "Slow but sure wins the race." Brevity dictates that one or two characters each have a single trait. It also dictates that conflict is sharp and clear—as it is in "The Dog in the Manger." The setting is a backdrop for the action, and the action has no interpretive narrator telling extra details of characters' thoughts or feelings. Style is crisp and straightforward. Everything in the fable exists to make an abstract point, to make a lesson clear, as clear as the moral in "The Milkmaid" who dreamily drops her basket of eggs on the way to market: "Don't count your chickens before they hatch."

Myths

Myths are stories that originate in the folk beliefs of nations and races and present episodes in which supernatural forces operate. Because they, too, are handed down by word of mouth, they have no right or wrong form. Myths, like that of the god Thor and his hammer of thunder, are stories which interpret natural phenomena. Some myths try to make visible and concrete the ways that human beings see nature, like the division of the year into seasons: In the story of Ceres and her daughter Proserpina, the girl is abducted and kept for part of the year in the underworld of Pluto, an explanation for the disappearance of summer's warmth and growth. Myths may show people's relationships with each other, like the generosity demonstrated in the myth of Baucis and Philemon in which hospitality is rewarded by an eternally filled oil cruse and an endless supply of meal. Myths show the ways that human beings see the forces that control them, like the separation of day and night caused by Apollo's crossing the sky in his sun chariot. Myths explain creation, religion, and divinities; they guess at the meaning of life and death, or at the cause for good and evil as made clear in the myth of Pandora's box.

Characters represent very few qualities in the way that the goddess Ceres or Demeter represents fertility and thus is linked to the supernatural, or unexplainable, issues of seasons and growth. Plots are often single incidents or a few incidents linked by characters. "Long ago in ancient Greece" is sufficient for setting. Since the abstract issues or themes that myths explore are broad and universal, their tone is dignified and somewhat mystical. The effective telling of a folk myth has dignity and simplicity, for it tries to recreate the spirit and intention of the original. When myths are badly told, as they are by Nathaniel Hawthorne in *Twicetold Tales,* they condescend or even insult the efforts of earlier societies to find meaning in life. When myths are well told, they appeal to something deep and primitive in all humankind.

Legends

A *legend* is similar to a myth because both are traditional narratives of a people; sometimes the two subgenres are interwoven. Legends, however, often have more historical truth and less reliance upon the supernatural. When, for example, we read the legends of the Trojan War, we are aware of the actual siege of the city as well as of legendary heroes and actions. And there was a King Arthur, but most stories about him are legends and not historical truth. Robin Hood, too, was a historical figure, but some stories about him are legends and not historically accurate. Such figures as Abraham Lincoln, a national hero, accumulate legends that are rooted in the authenticity of the character but are fictional in detail.

Folk Epics

The *folk epic* is a long narrative poem of unknown authorship about an outstanding or royal character in a series of adventures related to that heroic central figure. This character or hero is, like Beowulf, larger than life, grand in all proportions, and superhuman in physical and moral qualities. The action may involve journeys and quests, and it may show deeds of great courage and valor coupled with superhuman strength; the forces of the supernatural intervene from time to time. The setting is vast, including a nation, a continent, or even the universe. Point of view is objective, for the story is so grand that a protagonist of such remarkable accomplishments seems to need no interpretive narrator. The tone is dignified, and the style is therefore elevated. Often the story, which begins in the middle of things, includes long lists or catalogs of such things as warriors, treasures, gifts, or ships. Extended comparisons called "epic similes" frequently occur. Like the best retellings of myth, those of epic do not condescend in any way; they show the values of the society and awe the reader with the possibility of great courage and moral strength.

POETRY

Poetry, a kind of imaginative and artistic writing, can also be called a genre of literature. And, as with many genres, there are subgenres. For the sake of simplicity, we might identify them here as ballads, narrative poetry, and lyric poetry, acknowledging, however, that these categories are not absolute any more than the genres of fiction are absolute. A lyric may have balladlike qualities—a refrain, for example—and a narrative may have lyric or songlike passages. Compactness exists in lyric poetry to make words say much more than literal or denotative meaning. Ballads, too, rely upon compactness; they are elliptical in their phrasing, often forcing the reader or listener to leap from inference to inference. Perhaps the narrative poem, at first glance, does not seem to demand compactness. The account of action and tension in a narrative poem, however, in all probability uses far fewer words than a prose account of the same action and tension.

We often make the mistake of calling any writing that has rhythm, rhyme, or short lines "poetry." Much of it, however, is rhyme or verse. Steeped as we are in the Mother Goose or nursery rhymes, we identify them easily, and do not call the rhymes poetry. But once the short lines written in rhythm become unfamiliar, or address a subject that lacks the familiarity of nursery rhymes, we think they might be poetry. A trace of uncertainty, however, may linger: Where does verse end and poetry begin? If we wish to answer that question, we enter into one of the age-old literary controversies not to be answered here, although some effort to address the issue is made in Chapter 10, "From Rhyme to Poetry."

NONFICTION

Purists might find the title of this volume inaccurate, perhaps even blasphemous, because within a handbook of children's literature we have the temerity to include nonfiction. What is the rationale? Returning to our definition of literature as imaginative and artistic writing, we see that nonfiction may be a questionable inclusion. True, some nonfiction is written with high artistry; we think of Loren Eiseley's descriptions of the working of the natural world, or of the philosophical discourses of Plato's *Republic*—to juxtapose modern and ancient writings. Where to draw the line? Rather than draw any line whatsoever, we might instead express the wish that all nonfiction, informational books as well as biography, were written with high artistry, and might then be called "literature" without sigh or concession. Nonfiction is included here because it is written and read by children for their pleasure and understanding. Under that umbrella we hope to discover how to recognize the best available.

Nonfiction, too, may be subdivided, but with little likelihood of satisfying all readers. We might look at the librarian's classifications and decide that we must address each of the categories, from natural and physical sciences, social sciences, history (if it is not seen as part of the social sciences), through the arts, then subdivided even further. In fact, we might go on and on with genres and subgenres. Once again, we must be practical. For that reason, we might subdivide nonfiction into informational books and biography, knowing full well that some would like finer distinctions. The standards for informational books of all kinds, however, are similar. And standards for biography, the account of the life of an individual, can be set with some degree of common sense.

ACROSS GENRE LINES

What is there left to consider?

There are some books which we cannot put neatly into genres because, although they have qualities in common, they cross genre lines. Some books we group together not because of subject matter, but because they rely upon pictures to extend the story—picure books, of course. (For a full discussion of picture books, see Chapter 11.) Other books are singled out for another reason; they are placed in a loose and overlapping group called "classics." These works come from all genres and are works that have lasted for some time.

Classics

Classics are books that have worn well, attracting readers from one generation to the next. They cross all genre lines; they are historical fiction, regional literature, and high fantasy. What seems to keep them in continuous circulation may be the significance of theme, the credibility of character, the continuing reality of the conflict, or the engaging quality of style. The classics often serve as models. The success of the mischievous Tom Sawyer, for example, has resulted in periodic spates of books about mischievous boys. What seems apparent, however, is that mischief is not what keeps *Tom Sawyer* alive. Instead, it is the far more complex and universal matters like Twain's perceptive portrayal of the adults in the community; his mixture of the experiences, emotions, rites, and yearnings of childhood; the significance of ideas like sacrifice and courage for the sake of other people, as well as Twain's lively variety of tones and the aptness of his language.[9]

A work may be popular for a time, as were *A Dog of Flanders* and *Seventeen,* and then fade. What seemed the height of ingenious wordplay at one time may at another time seem dull and trite. For example, the wit in the once-popular *The Peterkin Papers* now seems heavy-handed. *Alice's Adventures in Wonderland,* on the other hand, remains an incomparable work of nonsense; readers have never outgrown Carroll's wit, and his playful inventiveness remains unsurpassed. Similarly, even if the diversified family farm becomes extinct, E. B. White's finest novel, *Charlotte's Web,* will last. White's thorough portrayal of character and his choice of life-and-death conflict, his affectionately humorous tone, and his universal themes about friendship, satisfaction, and death are elements that identify classics. The classics of one

GENRE IN CHILDREN'S LITERATURE

REALISM

Genre	Character	Plot	Setting	Theme	Point of View	Style	Tone
Problem Realism and Social Issues Realism ex: *Roll of Thunder, Hear My Cry*; *The Great Gilly Hopkins*	Best novels have round central characters. Poor ones load protagonist with problems, or have flat or stereotyped characters*	Any kind of conflict, but problem is usually source. If problem is solved too easily, story is flawed	Any	Any, though usually related to solution of protagonist's problems. Sentimentality, sensationalism, didacticism are flaws*	Any	Uses all devices	Any, but sentimentality or sensationalism are flaws*
Animal Realism ex: *Incredible Journey*; *Owls in the Family*	Realistic portrayal of animals, without personification*	Conflict is usually animal versus nature	Usually integral*	Usually related to some discovery about animals or their relationships to human beings	Objective in respect to the animal character; human characters may be shown in other points of view*	Uses all devices	Any, but if point of view falters, tone may become sentimental*
Historical Fiction ex: *Johnny Tremain*; *The Witch of Blackbird Pond*	Protagonist has universal human traits, but is a product of the time and place*	Any, but conflict more often person versus society or self, as well as another person	Integral setting with focus on particular time and place, usually time of stress or crisis, or of social change	Any universal theme		Uses all devices. Relies for credibility on accurate descriptions of place—costumes, activities, etc.	Any, but flawed if past is recreated sentimentally or sensationally*
Regional Realism and Stories of Other Countries ex: *Where the Lilies Bloom*; *Heidi*	Protagonist has universal human traits, but is a product of the time and place	Conflict often related to the region, whether topography, livelihood, or mores of area*	Integral and essentially so*	Any universal theme	Any	Uses all devices	Any
Mysteries ex: *The Way to Sattin Shore*	Well developed	Usually carries story; some coincidence	Any; often spooky	Any	Any	Uses all devices	Mysterious

*Represents elements that have special importance in a genre, or elements that are frequent sources of inadequacy in a work.

Genre	Character	Plot	Setting	Theme	Point of View	Style	Tone
Sports Stories ex: *The Moves Make the Man*; *The Baseball Bargain*	Realistic	Involves sports	Any	Often personal growth	Any	Uses all devices	Any
Formula Fiction Romance ex: *Sweetheart* novels	Flat, stereotyped	Boy-meets-girl	Any, often exaggerated wealth	Often "Love conquers all."	Any	Trite*	Sentimental*
Formula mysteries ex: *Nancy Drew* *Hardy Boys*	Flat, stereotyped	Suspenseful	Any	Unimportant	Any	Trite	Factual, or mysterious

FANTASY

Genre	Character	Plot	Setting	Theme	Point of View	Style	Tone
Fantastic stories ex: *The Borrowers*; *Charlotte's Web*; *Winnie the Pooh*; "The Fir Tree"	Like or unlike human beings; magical qualities; personified toys, animals, objects	Any kind of conflict	Often realistic world with some fantastic qualities	Any	Any	Any	Any / Often humorous
High Fantasy ex: *The Hero and the Crown*; *The Hobbit*	Realistically portrayed	Any, but underlying conflict is good vs. evil	Often special world, an integral setting where time and place have special qualities of expansion or limitation	Universal, important themes of good/evil in conflict	Any	Usually highly sensory	Serious, awed
Science Fiction ex: *The House of Stairs*; *The Lost Star*	Flawed stories often have inadequately developed central characters*	Any kind of conflict; often mechanical or natural forces are antagonists. Plots usually progressive and suspenseful	Often distinguishes one story from another; set in future time sometimes on unexplored planets	May be subtle, implicit, but flawed stories have didactic theme*	Any	All devices; often much description in concrete forms	Often objective, factual, but flawed story may be heavily didactic

*Represents elements that have special importance in a genre, or elements that are frequent sources of inadequacy in a work.

TRADITIONAL TALES

Genre	Character	Plot	Setting	Theme	Point of View	Style	Tone
Folktale ex: *Cinderella*; *Beauty and the Beast*	Flat, even the protagonist; bad and good characters easily identified; stock characters like the wicked stepmother and the fairy godmother	Person versus person or person versus personified nature conflicts. Action moves rapidly to a climax and stock closing	Backdrop setting: "Long ago and far away . . ."	Either implicit or explicit. Often strongly focused on justice	Usually omniscient or limited omniscient	A few recurring images; often short verses; cadenced prose*	Varied. May be sentimental, humorous, objective, but is not often didactic
Myth ex: "Apollo's Sun Chariot"	Gods and heroes with traits linked to supernatural powers	An incident or incidents linked by character	Backdrop: "Long ago in ancient Greece . . ."	Explanations of natural phenomena or human relationships	Usually objective	Significant symbols, abstract terms, little or no dialog; brief descriptions of action	Myth: Dignified, perhaps mystical. Sentimentality is flaw
Legend ex: "King Arthur"; "Robin Hood"	Historical figures with fictional traits and situations	Any conflict featuring protagonists	Backdrop: "When Arthur was king . . ."	Fictional glorification of historical figures	Usually objective	Significant symbols, abstract terms, little or no dialog; brief descriptions of action	Often objective. Sentimentality is flaw
Fable ex: "The Boy Who Cried Wolf"; "The Fox and the Crow"	Flat and stock; often personified animals with single traits	Person versus person conflict; extremely brief; usually a single incident*	Backdrop	Explicit and didactic	Objective or dramatic	Terse, lacking imagery or connotative language	Straightforward, didactic, and moralizing
Folk Epic ex: *Beowulf*	Protagonist is heroic, superhuman*	Begins in middle of things (*in medias res*); conflict is person versus person, society, or nature. Usually three incidents showing hero victorious against supreme odds*	Undefined long ago, but set in the vast world or the universe	Good can be victorious over evil, but only after great struggle against superhuman odds and with assistance of gods*	Objective or dramatic	Long, cadenced lines of oral language; symbols and images; grandeur and simplicity; epic similes and elaborate comparisons; extended formal speeches	Dignified; grand; awesome

* Represents elements that have special importance in a genre, or elements that are frequent sources of inadequacy in a work.

RHYME TO POETRY

Genre	Form or Focus	Rhythm	Rhyme	Devices
Nursery Rhymes	Topics open to young children; usually brief; any tone; folk in origin	Regular	Regular	Personification, simile, metaphor, and others
Verse	Easily understood; for specific purpose; meaning less important than form; often trite, banal in form, subject, or phrasing	Highly rhythmic; rhythm often more important than meaning	Usually regular in scheme; often forced, or more important than meaning	Often ordinary images, predictable; less emotion, imagination, intensity than poetry
Narrative poetry ex: "The Highwayman"; "The Worm"	Storytelling, long or short	Suited to story	Any form	Any, though fewer than in lyrics
Ballad Folk Ballad: (author unknown) ex: "John Henry" Art Ballad: (author unknown) ex: "Rime of the Ancient Mariner"	Narrative of physical courage; incidents in lives of common people; supernatural; largely dialogue, little characterization; great simplicity; refrains, often incremental; abrupt transitions; single dramatic episode	Great variation, but usually lines 1 & 3 having four accented syllables, lines 2 & 4, three unaccented syllables; variations in number of unstressed syllables	Refrain often used; usually *abcb* rhyme; approximate rhyme very common	Any (See form)
Lyric	Brief, subjective; personal emotional response; single unified impression; "An end in itself"; intense, compact	Suited to topic and emotion evoked	Rhymed or unrhymed	All figurative and sound devices used to produce compactness

NONFICTION

Genre	Essential qualities	Organization & Scope	Style	Tone	Illustrations
Informational books	Gives information and facts; relates facts to concept; stimulates curiosity; "starter," not "stopper"	From simplest to most complex; from known to unknown; from familiar to unfamiliar; from early developments to later; chronological; may have slight narrative for younger reader	Imagery, figurative language, all devices; comparisons extremely useful; flawed if style is monotonous, repetitious, fragmented in statements*	Wonder, not mystery; respect; objectivity, occasional humor; fostering scientific attitude of inquiry. Flaws: condescension, anthropomorphism, oversimplification; facts not separated from opinions*	Diagrams and drawings often clearer than photographs
Biography	Gives accurate, verifiable facts, and authentic picture of period; subject worthy of attention	Assumes no omniscience; shows individual, not stereotype; does not ignore negative qualities of subject; focuses not only on events, but on nature of person	Storytelling permissible for youngest reader; too much invention destroys credibility	Interest; enthusiasm; objectivity; didacticism and preaching to be avoided	Authentic

* Represents elements that have special importance in a genre, or elements that are frequent sources of inadequacy in a work.

generation may be supplanted by later works, but the appeals of other books may remain for a surprisingly long time. To paraphrase Ezra Pound, a classic is "news that stays news." It is not the bribery of The Classics List graven in stone, but time, that will tell.

The charts in this chapter summarize the similarities and differences in the genres. If we keep in mind the dangers of generalizing about all the stories in a category, they may prove helpful. Literature, since it is not so easily classified as the chemical elements, will often be elusive, refusing to fit neatly into a genre, but the charts may keep us aware of the great breadth of fiction available to children.

NOTES

1 In Shakespeare's *Hamlet,* Polonius' speech praising the actors (Act II, Scene 2), makes fun of the genres of drama in such phrases as "pastoral-comical" and "tragical-comical-historical-pastoral."

2 Barbara Moran and Susan Steinfirst, "Why Johnny (and Jane) Read Whodunits in Series." *School Library Journal,* March 1985, p. 113.

3 Janice Radway, *Reading the Romance.* Chapel Hill: University of North Carolina Press, 1984.

4 For an enlightening discussion of the narrator and the reader/audience in fantasy, see "Some Presumptions About Fantasy" by Perry Nodelman in *Children's Literature Quarterly,* Summer 1979.

5 Eleanor Cameron, *The Green and Burning Tree.* Boston: Little, Brown, 1969, p. 72.

6 These definitions come from *Alternate Worlds: The Illustrated History of Science Fiction* by James Gunn. Englewood Cliffs, NJ: Prentice-Hall/A&W Visual Library, 1975.

7 Margaret Esmonde. "From Little Buddy to Big Brother: The Icon of the Robot in Children's Science Fiction," in *The Mechanical God,* Thomas P. Dunn and Richard D. Erlich, eds. Westport, CT: Greenwood, 1982.

8 Jack Zipes responds to Bettelheim's optimism regarding folktales, saying that "such focus on resolution and happiness only points to our tenacious capacity to avoid unpleasant insights into childhood experiences.... Perhaps the most therapeutic aspect of these stories is the reassurance they give *parents* that children survive the horrors they impose on them ...." "Child Abuse and Happy Endings," *The New York Times Book Review,* November 13, 1988, pp. 39, 60.

9 While critics call *Huckleberry Finn* the better novel, *Tom Sawyer* seems more clearly a book for children.

RECOMMENDED BOOKS CITED IN THIS CHAPTER

AARDEMA, VERNA. *Why Mosquitoes Buzz in People's Ears.* Leo and Diane Dillon, ills. New York: Dial, 1975.

AESOP. *Fables.* New York: Dutton, 1963

ANDERSEN, HANS CHRISTIAN. *The Ugly Duckling; The Little Fir Tree; The Little Tin Soldier.* New York: Macmillan, 1963.

BRINK, CAROL. *Caddie Woodlawn.* New York: Macmillan, 1946.

BRITTAIN, BILL. *The Wish Giver.* New York: Harper & Row, 1983.

BROOKS, BRUCE. *The Moves Make the Man.* New York: Harper & Row, 1984.

BURNFORD, SHEILA. *The Incredible Journey.* Boston: Little, Brown, 1961.

BYARS, BETSY. *The Summer of the Swans.* New York: Viking, 1970.

CARROLL, LEWIS. *Alice's Adventures in Wonderland.* New York: Dutton, 1954 (first published, 1865).

CAUDILL, REBECCA. *Did You Carry the Flag Today, Charley?* New York: Holt, 1966.

CHILDRESS, ALICE. *A Hero ain't nothin' but a Sandwich.* New York: Coward, 1973.

CHRISTOPHER, JOHN. *White Mountains.* New York: Macmillan, 1970.

FORBES, ESTHER. *Johnny Tremain.* New York: Dell, 1969.

GRAHAME, KENNETH. *The Wind in the Willows.* New York: Scribner's, 1953 (first published, 1908).

GREENE, BETTE. *Summer of My German Soldier.* New York: Dial, 1973.

GRIMM, JACOB and WILHELM. *Grimm's Fairy Tales.* New York: Grosset, 1962.

HAMILTON, VIRGINIA. *The People Could Fly: American Black Folktales.* New York: Knopf, 1985.

_____ . *Sweet Whispers, Brother Rush.* New York: Putnam, 1982.

HAUGAARD, ERIK. *Hakon of Rogen's Saga.* Boston: Houghton Mifflin, 1963.

HUNT, IRENE. *Across Five Aprils.* New York: Follett, 1964.

JACOBS, JOSEPH. *English Fairy Tales.* New York: Dover, 1898.

LAWSON, ROBERT. *Rabbit Hill.* New York: Viking, 1944.

L'ENGLE, MADELEINE. *A Wrinkle in Time.* New York: Farrar, 1962.

LEWIS, C. S. The *Narnia* Books. New York: Macmillan, 1951.

McDERMOTT, GERALD. *Arrow to the Sun.* New York: Viking, 1974.

McKINLEY, ROBIN. *The Hero and the Crown.* New York: Greenwillow, 1981.

MILES, BETTY. *The Real Me.* New York: Knopf, 1974.

MOWAT, FARLEY. *Owls in the Family.* Boston: Little, Brown, 1961.

NORTON, MARY. *The Borrowers.* New York: Harcourt, 1965.

PATERSON, KATHERINE. *The Great Gilly Hopkins.* New York: Crowell, 1978.

PEARCE, PHILIPPA. *The Way to Sattin Shore.* New York: Greenwillow, 1983.

PREUSSLER, OTFRIED. *The Satanic Mill.* New York: Macmillan, 1973.

SALTEN, FELIX. *Bambi.* New York: Grosset & Dunlap, 1929.

SILVERBERG, ROBERT. *Time of the Great Freeze.* New York: Harper, 1964.

SOBOL, DONALD. *Angie's First Case.* New York: Four Winds, 1984.

_____ . *Encyclopedia Brown.* New York: Nelson, 1970.

SPEARE, ELIZABETH. *The Witch of Blackbird Pond.* Boston: Houghton Mifflin, 1958.

TAYLOR, MILDRED. *Roll of Thunder, Hear My Cry.* New York: Dial, 1976.

TOLKIEN, J.R.R. *The Lord of the Rings.* Boston: Houghton Mifflin, 1974.

TWAIN, MARK. *The Adventures of Tom Sawyer.* New York: Macmillan, 1966 (first published, 1866).

VOIGT, CYNTHIA. *Dicey's Song.* New York: Random House, 1982.

WHITE, E.B. *Charlotte's Web.* New York: Harper, 1952.

WILDER, LAURA INGALLS. The *Little House* Books. New York: Harper, 1953 (first published, 1932–43).

CHAPTER 3

Character

Children sometimes say: "I like stories where the people are one way at the beginning of the book, and different at the end."

We often have the superior notion that children are too immature to recognize what makes a whole human being, or to see how people can be one thing at one time, and become something else with the passage of time or events. We also falsely assume that children have neither the experience nor the training to relate to fictional people and their differences. As a result of our assumptions, we may cheat children by choosing for them stories that merely recite daily routine like *About a Bicycle for Linda*, or that rely for interest almost entirely on excitement and suspense like *The Hardy Boys* or *Nancy Drew*.

Children can catch many of human nature's subtleties. They care about human beings and are sensitive to them. Even an infant responds to differences in people. The infant may hide in a protective shoulder to avoid a noisy stranger, lean out of a crib to be snuggled by a familiar friend. The smallest child, furthermore, knows and expects consistency in people. Try to persuade a child that the usually brusque and irritable Aunt Amy is—this time—friendly and kind. By turning away from what he or she regards as Aunt Amy's fakery, the child clearly demonstrates not only sensitivity to personality but also an expectation of consistency.

It seems to follow that if even the smallest children are aware of personality in the people around them and can detect their differences, children are able then to recognize personality in stories they read. It also seems natural that the child who responds to real people will respond to people in a story and will be sensitive to consistency in their actions. If the functions of literature include the giving of pleasure and the discovery and understanding of ideas and of other human beings, then character development in literature makes its own contribution to these ends.

Character as the term is generally used means the aggregate of mental, emotional, and social qualities that distinguish a person. In literature, however, the term *character* is used to mean a person, or in the case of children's literature, sometimes a personified animal or object. Each of the living beings in a story, play, or poem is a character.

When we add to the word *character* the word *development,* we have a literary term, *character development,* which also has a special meaning. In life the development of a person's character or personality is a matter of growth and change. In literature, however, character development means showing the character—whether a person or animal or object—with the complexity of a human being. Each of us in real life is three-dimensional; that is, we are a mixture of qualities. None of us is completely generous; we have our limits. None of us is completely selfish; we have other traits. In the full development of character in the literary sense, the writer shows the whole, composed of a variety of traits like those of real human beings.

The writer has privileges and responsibilities in this matter of character development. Since we are following a central character in a story, it is the writer's obligation to make this person's thoughts and actions believable. On the other hand, if the character is less important, the writer has the privilege of making the character two-dimensional or even a representative of a class—for example, the bossy older brother, or the impish little sister. The importance of a character in a story—primary, secondary, minor, or background importance—determines how fully the character is developed and understood. The closer the character comes to the center of the conflict—and therefore the more important the character is—the greater is our need to know the complexity of the character's personality. Conversely, the more the character functions merely as background, the less likelihood that the character needs to be developed.

REVELATION OF CHARACTER

In life we become acquainted with people in many ways. We see our new neighbors from a distance and draw tentative conclusions about age, occupation, and social status. We hear the diction of the Cockney, the twang of the Texan; even the precision or the explosiveness of short sentences indicates something about temperament. From their public actions we decide that the neighbors seem to be neighborhood assets, since they prune their shrubs and walk their dog in the proper places. Finally, if the new neighbors are known to our friends, we listen to their opinions. We have come to know these neighbors by how they look, what and how they speak, how they act, and what others say about them.

In literature the process of coming to know a character is comparable.

In literature, however, the writer has another alternative: the author may choose to tell what the characters are thinking. In this case, the writer may fill in details about the characters' innermost anxieties and dreams, the patterns of childhood behavior, and early home life.

By Actions

Templeton in *Charlotte's Web* is an example of a character whose actions help to define his nature. After Wilbur moves to the barn, we meet Templeton, who creeps up cautiously to the goslings, keeping close to the wall. Templeton's furtive manner arouses our curiosity; we are as suspicious as the barn animals. Twice in the story Templeton grins, first when Wilbur lands with a thud, hurt, crushed, and tearful after his unsuccessful web-spinning efforts. Templeton grins a second time as he takes Wilbur's tail and bites it as hard as he possibly can. Gleefully savage, Templeton delights in slinking about and nipping at his friend; he is surly, sneaky, and ill-tempered, pleased at others' discomfort. He is self-centered and gluttonous, going to the Fair only to scavenge in the garbage and litter. Templeton's actions create a picture of Templeton's character.

By Speech

Accompanying Templeton's actions are his predictable sarcasm and ill-tempered outbursts as he gripes to Wilbur in sneering tones. He crawls into Wilbur's crate as a stowaway and grumbles:

> ". . . kindly remember that I am hiding down here in this crate and I don't want to be stepped on, or kicked in the face, or pummeled, or crushed in any way, or squashed, or buffeted about, or bruised, or lacerated, or scarred, or biffed. Just watch what you're doing, Mr. Radiant. . . ."

At the fair when Wilbur is optimistic that he may avoid becoming bacon, Templeton cannot resist commenting that when Zuckerman hankers for smoked ham, he will take the butcher knife to Wilbur. Templeton boasts about every grudging action and every carefully bought favor; he even pretends his motives are kind when he bites Wilbur's tail or saves the rotten egg. Complaining, "What do you think I am, anyway, a rat-of-all-work?" Templeton resentfully orders the directors' meeting to break up because meetings bore him. He grumbles at his commission—finding words for the web; he is not spending all his time rushing over to the dump after "advertising material." Templeton characterizes himself by what he says, showing himself to be cynical and selfish, resenting any intrusion on his own pursuits.

By Appearance

Gluttony is one of Templeton's most obvious traits, and his appearance shows it. He returns after his night of gorging at the fair, swollen to double his usual size. Only an appeal to appetite will tempt Templeton to fetch the egg sac, and as he eats first at Wilbur's trough every day, he grows fatter and bigger than any other known rat. Templeton's appearance verifies and supplements what we know of his character; gluttony and self-interest are the essence of Templeton.

By Others' Comments

Templeton is characterized by what he does, what he says, and by the way he looks. However, there is more to be learned from the comments of others about him. The animals carefully watch his furtive actions since they neither like nor trust Templeton. The old sheep enlists Templeton's help in finding words, saying that the rat can be persuaded only by appeals to "his baser instincts, of which he has plenty." Since the sheep is on our side, the side of saving Wilbur, we trust his judgments. And we distrust those characters who are on the wrong side of our sympathies. We are less accepting of their judgments, just as we would doubt Templeton's opinions on any character because we know how deceitful he is. The comments of the other characters, like the comment of the old sheep, help to show character.

By Author's Comments

White's comments also add to the picture we have of Templeton's character. He calls Templeton a crafty rat who does as he pleases, even his tunnel showing his cunning. White's thoroughly negative description of Templeton verifies the goose's and gander's feelings about the rat who:

> . . . had no morals, no conscience, no scruples, no consideration, no decency, no milk of rodent kindness, no compunctions, no higher feeling, no friendliness, no anything. He would kill a gosling if he could get away with it.

Templeton becomes a character we know so well that we know what to expect of him in almost any situation; he is consistent.

UNITY OF CHARACTER AND ACTION

The writer creates the whole cast of characters for the story—some important, some minor, some complex, some relatively simple—through the use of these techniques. As we come to know these characters, we respond to them.

Most of us respond to other human beings as we see similarity to ourselves, or if not similarity, recognizable traits and responses. We may say we "identify with" someone. Reading a story, we make the same demands of character—not that every character be exactly like ourselves, but that a character be credible.

In real life we know that change occurs in ourselves and in those we know well. We recognize that change only if we see a person before and after. We say that a child has grown, but even that statement implies a comparison between what *was* his or her height and what is *now* that height. If we must know both the *was* and the *is* to see growth, so it is with a character's change. If the impact of the events shapes or reshapes the personality of the character, the author is obligated to show how that change has come about.

Implicit within the acceptance of change is, of course, the idea of cause, and cause involves the story—its action. Given this complex character and adding these events, the combination may result in change. In life we say, "Just what you'd expect of her," or "It could only happen to him," and by these words we admit that character and action are inseparable. The phrase "unity of character and action" may not mean much to you at first glance, but it expresses an important idea, one of the most important in understanding any fiction. In the best fiction, according to Henry James, "What is character but the determination of incident? What is incident but the illustration of character?"[1] *This character* because of *this personality* provokes *this action;* this action by its nature demonstrates this character. In literature the skillful writer shows characters by means of actions and speeches so that character, incident, and outcome seem interwoven—and, at the end, inevitable. Think of Hen Wen in *The High King* or Karana in *Island of the Blue Dolphins* or Claudia in *From the Mixed Up Files of Mrs. Basil E. Frankweiler.* Can you think of these characters apart from the actions they take part in? (When we say "actions," we are also talking about plot, of course, the subject of the following chapter.)

Look at Hans Christian Andersen's "The Ugly Duckling" as an example of James' view on the unity of character and action. Notice how we come to know the central character. The Duckling's *appearance* seems of primary importance, since that is the basis for his being excluded. He is big and ugly, clumsy and grayish black throughout the story. However, at the end of the story his strong wings, white ruffled feathers, and slender neck have replaced his earlier awkwardness with beauty and grace. As for the dejected Duckling's *actions,* he does not look up when he is bitten and ridiculed in the duckyard. In the old woman's cottage, his panic sends him into the milk dish, the butter trough, and the flour barrel. But at the end of the story he floats gracefully upon the water, his head tucked modestly under his wing. What the Duckling *says* is equally revealing of his character; several times he says sadly, "I'm so ugly," or "even the dogs won't bite me." The Duckling is sure that he is an inferior nothing, and he never resists his enemies. At the end of the story, the Duckling shows by his speech that he is still modest when he says joyously, "I never dreamed of so much happiness when I was the ugly duckling."

As for what *others say* about the Ugly Duckling, his mother says he is not pretty, his brothers and sisters that they will not put up with him for he is too big, and some wish that the cat would get him. The old woman's hen calls him a fool and finds him no fun. However, at the end of the story, the children call him the prettiest, "so young and lovely!" Finally, Andersen the *writer* has kept us informed about the Duckling not only by describing appearance and actions and reporting speeches, but also by his writer's comments, the result of his knowing everything. Andersen calls him a poor duckling, tells us he is miserable, exhausted, unhappy, terrified, the laughingstock. He calls the Duckling "poor thing!" and informs us of the Duckling's strange desire to float on the water, of his mysterious yearning to join the migrating swans. Finally, at the end of the story, Andersen tells us of the Ugly Duckling's beauty that combines with his shyness, his happiness without pride as the Duckling speaks "from the depths of his heart."

Through all the means at his disposal, Andersen has shown us the character of the Ugly Duckling. The result is that we know this character well, and know that the story is the result of the character's traits combined with the actions that occur. The two are inextricably intertwined; together they demonstrate the unity of character and action. The character of the Ugly Duckling lives because the trials and harassments he goes through in the course of growing up determine his personal change and are his character; the story identifies the reality of maturing. Family rivalry, rejection, fear of failure, inability to find friends, or to relate to others, even the feelings of ugliness and wishing one were dead are included in Andersen's story of the self-doubt of childhood.

Leon Garfield's *Fair's Fair* moves at a rapid pace, but we still gain a clear picture of Jackson and Lillipolly from the brisk dialogue in this short illustrated story. Two homeless children meet over dinner. Both are street children led to the fine old house by the fearsome black dog with whom they had shared food. They show not only patience as they go from door to door looking for the one that the key fits, but also honesty as they care for the splendid empty house, and generosity when they share their meat pies with dogs and carollers. As reward, they become the children of lonely Mr. Beecham Chambers and live comfortably ever after. They've earned it; fair's fair.

> "What's your name?" asked Jackson, sharing some beef with the dog.
> "They call me Lillipolly, down Shadwell way. What's yours?"
> "They call me Jackson, down Bluegate way."
> "I cleaned all the silver and polished the table," said Lillipolly, "so it'll be nice for 'em when they come home."
> "Fair's fair," said Jackson. "I'll do the grate and the kitchen floor."

The plot of *Like Jake and Me* by Mavis Jukes demonstrates clearly the principle of unity of character and action. Alex isn't quite at home with his stepfather, the former cowboy. But the experience each has with being afraid—everybody's afraid of something—helps them to appreciate each other. Alex is afraid to pull his loose tooth, but as the son of an entomologist, he is fascinated by the wolf spider on Jake's collar. As he appreciatively describes the mother spider carrying her babies, Jake, looking out at his pregnant wife Virginia, thinks he is describing her. Suddenly the spider disappears, and Jake panics. Like their mutual love of Alex's mother, their shared admission of fears brings them together.

On the other hand, not all writers are as successful in integrating or unifying character and action. Perhaps one of the biggest disappointments to a perceptive reader of Judy Blume's novels is the inadequate portrayal of characters: even the main characters in such novels as *Then again, maybe I won't* seem shallow and unbelievable. Speaking in cliches, possessing little self-understanding, and acting in stereotypical fashion, the young people and the adults contribute little to our understanding of human motivation or to the integral nature of human beings and their actions. Judy Blume's popularity seems to lie in her selection of situations common to children rather than in portrayal of believable characters.

TYPES OF CHARACTERS

There are certain terms that describe the degree of character development and that refer to change or lack of it in a character in the course of a story. Briefly, a *round character* is one that we know well, who has a variety of traits that make him or her believable. A *flat character* is less well developed and has fewer traits. A *dynamic character* is a round character that changes, while a *static character* does not change in the course of the story.

Flat Characters

Let us begin with the less important characters. They are essential to the action, but since they are not fully developed, we call them *flat*. In most stories, we must have these flat characters to help carry the action, to show how the central character behaves or relates to others, to make the setting a believable place because in this setting live these people. Flat characters are quickly made known to the reader, and they quickly assume their necessary places in the narrative so that the story can then focus on the central characters.

For example, in *Charlotte's Web*, Fern is a relatively flat character, a child with an intense interest that absorbs her for a time. She treats Wilbur like a doll, listens to the animals' conversations, and reports them to her incredulous parents. She plays and quarrels, and she loves the Ferris wheel and the freedom of the Fair. However, Fern has few traits that distinguish her from other little girls; she remains a believable little girl but not a special one. Wilbur's relationships and worries are the focus of the story, and the conflict goes on without Fern's being totally aware of all that spiders and pigs mean to each other. Because this is Wilbur's story, not Fern's, she needs no greater development. Dr. Dorian and Mr. Arable are more obviously flat characters.

When a character has very few individual traits, the character does not seem to exist as an individual human being. When the character seems only to have the few traits of a class or of a group of people, the character is called a *stereotype*. Each of us has a few mental stereotypes—those of politicians, mothers, athletes, or poets. When we examine these mental pictures and compare them to individuals we know well, we find that each stereotype is inaccurate and unjust. In literature, however, the stereotype, like the stock character who appears in many stories, is useful, since he or she quickly settles into a background position and performs there in an easily understood role.

In *Charlotte's Web* Lurvy is an example of a stereotype—in this case of a hired man. Lurvy has only the expected traits and does only the expected things. He nails down the loose board on Wilbur's pen, he slops Wilbur, he discovers the exploded dud. Lurvy is neither eloquent nor imaginative:

> "I've always noticed that pig. He's quite a pig." "He's long, and he's smooth," said Zuckerman. "That's right," agreed Lurvy. "He's as smooth as they come. He's some pig."

As Lurvy's speech shows, stereotypes describe themselves by what they say as well as how they say it.

Occasionally the writer may use a **character foil,** a minor character whose traits are in direct contrast to a principal character, and thus highlight the principal. The snobbish lamb is as young and naive as Wilbur, but she is smug instead of humble. Pigs are little or nothing to her. Since the lamb is consistently disdainful, her behavior contrasts sharply to Wilbur's, and in this way she acts as a foil.

Stereotyping, or compressing people into flat caricatures that eliminate individual differences, is useful in literature for particular background figures that fill narrow roles. Flat and stereotyped characters, however, are not suitable protagonists; we should be particularly watchful for them in literature about minorities, because they do great injustice. (We will discuss the flat characters of folk literature shortly.) We have noted the necessity for character and action to be unified. However, flat and stereotyped characters do not truly grow out of action, and action cannot grow out of their less-than-full human natures. It seems more descriptive of flat characters and action to say that they coexist; flat characters and stereotypes move over the surface of the action, rather than being integrated with the action. Flat characters, furthermore, make little contribution to our understanding of human nature. In fact, if we read only about stereotypes, our perceptions about people may be narrowed rather than expanded. While stories for adults do occasionally make their points by careful stereotyping, these protagonists are reaching a more sophisticated readership, one that is capable of seeing a point by contrast to what is already known of the complexity of human nature.

Round Characters

A *round character* is one that is fully developed; we know this character well, because the many traits are demonstrated in the action of the story. We know appearance and actions, speeches and opinions, what others say and think about the character, and oftentimes what the writer thinks about him/her. The character is so fully developed that we may even be able to predict actions and reactions. Yet, like a real person, the character may surprise us or respond impetuously on occasion. It is as though we know the character so well that the character has become a real person, one we wish we could meet or might enjoy knowing.

In children's literature there are a great many round characters that we may feel we know. However, in order to help us see clearly what is meant by a round character, compare the many traits of Wilbur, for example, to the few traits of Mr. Arable, or the stereotype Lurvy. From the first words of the first page when Fern asks where her father is going with the ax, we are anxious about Wilbur's fate. We soon discover that Wilbur's struggle is the conflict, and that he is therefore the *protagonist,* or central character. Tiny, dependent Wilbur has almost no life of his own at the opening of the story, except to amuse himself like a toddler, finding the mud moist and warm and pleasantly oozy. When he goes to live in the barn, he is bored, unable to dream up anything exciting to do. Friends must introduce themselves to him. When he squeezes through the fence and is pursued, he has no idea what to do with freedom; and his constant appetite makes him captive again, since Lurvy's pail of slops is irresistible. Wilbur plans his day around his body: sleeping, eating, scratching, digging, eating, watching flies, eating, napping, standing still, eating. On the day that Wilbur wants love more than comfort and food, he has grown. But now he wonders uncertainly about friendship, which seems such a gamble. After Wilbur makes a friend, life becomes more exciting and he becomes confident enough to try spinning a web. Cheerfully, he tries and fails; humbly he admits that Charlotte is brighter and more clever. Wilbur's innocence and dependence are clear when he pleads for a story or a song, for a last bedtime bite, a last drink of milk, and calls out the series of quiet good-nights to Charlotte. Panic is Wilbur's reaction to news of his destiny—the Arables' dinner table. But once he is assured that Charlotte can perform miracles, he calms down to be patient, trusting, and humble. The congratulatory words in Charlotte's web make Wilbur an exemplary pig; he decides that if he is called "radiant," he must act radiant, and in his way he becomes radiant. Despite all the admiration Wilbur attracts, he remains modest. Happy and confident, he honestly admires Charlotte's peach-colored egg sac and gazes lovingly into the faces of the crowd. He looks both grateful and humble. Wilbur has enough traits to classify him as a round character.

CHANGE IN CHARACTER

If there is a unity of character and action such as James speaks of, then the character is not only affected by the events, but his or her nature may bring about various events. Frequently, the events of the story may change a character.

When the word *dynamic* is used in ordinary conversation, it may mean forceful, or perhaps exciting. However, in the context of literature, the word has special meaning, since a **dynamic character** is one who changes in the course of the action. He or she may change from being shy to being poised or even domineering; or from cowardly to brave, from selfless to selfish. The character may demonstrate a new realization about himself or herself, or about his or her personal values. He may show that he is now able to take care of himself, or she may show that she has become able to care for others as well as herself. Somehow, the events of the story and qualities of the character have effected some basic character change. The variety of possibilities for change is huge.

The character, of course, may grow older by an hour or by a decade in the course of the novel's action. However, the mere passage of time is not sufficient evidence of character change. Some people are as immature at thirty-five as they were at seventeen. On the other hand, we know some people who have been changed by a single event—a traumatic experience or a simple and joyous one that has brought a realization of some kind. It is not then the passage of time that is important in character change, but the impact of events on the character—the unity of character and action—creating new traits to supplant or alter the old. The character may not necessarily be aware of his or her own change, just as looking back we may see that we are different from what we once were, but cannot necessarily account for the *where* or *when* of our change. The essential matter is that we are different.

Wilbur changes. He is a believable character early in the story, although he is young and immature. The experience of receiving selfless friendship makes him able to give selfless friendship. Slowly, as we watch this change occurring, Wilbur is altered by his part in the action, by his receiving so much. Now he is the same Wilbur, and yet not the same. To his early qualities of humility and naiveté are added dependability and steadfastness, sacrifice and purpose. Even Wilbur's vocabulary matures. When first he hears the bad news, he is a panicky child:

> "I can't be quiet," screamed Wilbur, racing up and down. "I don't want to die. Is it true . . . Charlotte? Is it true they are going to kill me when the cold weather comes?"

By the end of a summer of maturing, Wilbur responds to news that his dearest friend will die, and he knows that he must save the egg sac. Notice how his vocabulary has changed to adult words, and his tone has changed to reasonable persuasion:

> "Listen to me! . . . Charlotte . . . has only a short time to live. She cannot accompany us home, because of her condition. Therefore, it is absolutely necessary that I take her egg sac with me. I can't reach it, and I can't climb. You are the only one that can get it. There's not a second to be lost . . . Please, please, please, Templeton, climb up and get the egg sac."

Wilbur does not scream; he uses "please" liberally. His desperation does not arise from his own need, but from the need of another. Once Charlotte had said to the screaming Wilbur that he was carrying on childishly; the new Wilbur tells Templeton to "stop acting like a spoiled child." Wilbur—who once planned his day around his slops—can now, out of deep concern for Charlotte, promise solemnly that Templeton may eat first and take his choice of all the goodies in the trough.

During winter Wilbur warms the egg sac with his breath in the cold barn. By the end of the story, it is Wilbur who offers the first mature greeting, a cheerful Hello! for the baby spiders. The change is significant, and it occurs slowly. It is convincing. Little by little events have molded a self-centered child into responsible maturity; we believe in Wilbur's maturity just as we believed in his childishness.

Since less important characters are not so closely focused upon, and may even remain on the fringes of the action, their change is unlikely to be important or to grow out of the events of the plot. Furthermore, their changing could even be distracting.

A *static character* is one who does not change in the course of the story. The conflict does not affect the character to make any impact upon personality or outlook. Flat characters—including stereotypes and foils— would not change; they are not known well enough for us to recognize changes or to care. A round character, too, may be unchanged by the conflict, and, in fact, even the protagonist may be unchanged by the action.

Although Charlotte is not the center of Wilbur's story, we know her consistent nature very well. Charlotte is not only motherly, but hard-working, and her web words prove it. She is the same wise and selfless character at the end of the story that she was at the beginning, and we therefore call her a static character.

It is not necessary that a story have a dynamic or changing character. In one story the round central character may change, and in another may not. The change or lack of it does not constitute a judgment about the quality of characterization. However, the static or dynamic nature of the protagonist does help the reader to see the action and to understand the idea behind it.

In life a person rarely changes overnight, and in literature we find such a change unbelievable. In Victor Barnouw's *Dream of the Blue Heron*, Wabus, an Indian boy, must choose between his own culture and the white man's. Wabus sees brutality, rigidity, depersonalization, and the substitution of material goals for spiritual ones, all epitomized in the character of Mr. Wickham, the disciplinarian in the government school, who hustles Wabus roughly, rips and tears his clothing, seizes him by the hair, and jams a hat on his cropped skull. When he finds the Indians ceremonially burying Wabus' grandfather, however, close to the end of the story, he suddenly changes. In minutes he flashes a smile, makes an offering, reassures Wabus, springs to carry the body, seizes a shovel, and leaps into the grave to dig furiously. Then, although he is convinced of the innocence of Wabus' father, he turns him in to the law. In the final pages of the story, he offers books to the father in prison and promises to help Wabus become a lawyer. Wabus' choice to follow the culture of the white man is unbelievable and insufficiently motivated. Nothing in the white society he has experienced is appealing. The source of *our* dissatisfaction is the sudden change in Mr. Wickham's character.

In another story contrasting Indian and white cultures, note the experience of Matt in Elizabeth Speare's *The Sign of the Beaver* compared to that of Wabus. Left to keep the new cabin in Maine when his father leaves to bring the family north, Matt must live alone by means of fishing line, rifle, and garden, experience enriched by his friendship with the Indian boy, Attean. During the seven months of waiting, Matt matures, learns to live in solitude, to find his way through the forest, to adapt to the Indian culture, and to triumph in his independence.

In Allan W. Eckert's novel *Incident at Hawk's Hill*, we follow the slowly and cautiously developing relationship of interdependence between Ben and Badger, and we grow certain that Ben can survive living like an animal underground. Notice, too, how slowly Gilly in *The Great Gilly Hopkins* by Katherine Paterson changes from her early defiance as she drives with the social worker toward Gilly's new foster home. Slowly, in incident after incident, she grows more appreciative of Trotter, more accepting of W. E., more understanding of Mr. Randolph, until she no longer needs her illusions about her own mother.

The number of round characters depends upon the complexity of the plot, and thus there can hardly be a firm rule about number. Katherine Paterson, for example, draws a variety of characters, many of whom we know rather well considering their places in the story *Jacob Have I Loved.* Best of all, of course, we know the narrator, jealous Wheeze, but we also see quite clearly her irrascible grandmother, the elderly retired Captain, dull and honest Call, and secure Caroline who knows she is loved. Certainly it is not feasible that every character be round. It seems evident, furthermore, that a large number of fully developed characters becomes highly distracting in a story for children. Even *Charlotte's Web,* which has three round characters, focuses more fully on Charlotte and Wilbur than on Templeton, important as he is. Some writers, in speaking of the writing process, say that a too fully developed minor character can get out of hand and become so round as to lose his or her place as subordinate and take over, thus changing the plot. For the sake of unity in the story, it then becomes the writer's choice between flattening out the character once again, or giving him or her new importance in what must now be an altered plot.

EVALUATING CHARACTER IN CHILDREN'S LITERATURE

While character study alone may be enough for some adults, it is not enough for most children, and for several reasons. First, the younger the child, the more limited is his or her awareness of alternatives. Young children are often prevented by their elders from making discoveries about "what happens if"; they often hear instead "Do this, so that may happen," or "Don't do this, or that might happen." Chances for exploring outcomes and discovering alternatives on their own are often denied them. A related problem for the young reader is a limited understanding of motivation. Children rarely see motives for behavior beyond what they would like to see happen. Furthermore, to the young, choices are black and white, yes and no; unaware of their own mixed motives, they rarely see those of others. With maturity—which the experience of literature increases—children become aware of unselfish motives, or of subtle and self-serving motives disguised as unselfish.

Although children may have keen interest in character, they want character involved in action and in making decisions. Children, like adults, are intent on the peace or uproar that results from the characters' decisions. Children, too, like to follow characters and their motives through their emotions and their reasoning, as they face decisions and make choices. Children are also excited by the possibility of the accidental, and perhaps even more by the inevitable. The likelihood of success or the chance of defeat keeps readers of any age involved in a story's action. While character, then, is essential, there are other considerations.

A discussion of character in children's literature is incomplete without reference to various kinds of protagonists, since characters are not only people or animals, but may also be inanimate objects. Winnie-the-Pooh and Piglet may once have been stuffed toys, but now they are believable characters. Paul Hazard pays high tribute to Hans Christian Andersen when he comments on Andersen's skill in characterizing the inanimate—from tiny soldiers to willow trees, from shirts to darning needles.

> [The collection of countless objects] that the indifferent call "things," stirs, moves, speaks and fills the air with its complaints or its songs. Everything is alive. . . . The arithmetic problem fidgets about on its slate, the letters grow restless in the copy book and complain at having been badly traced.[2]

Andersen, like many other writers for young children, makes characters of things, endowing them with few or many traits, depending upon the length of his story and the theme he is exploring; he can give to the old lantern will power and intelligence, to the starched collar pride, to the teapot arrogance, and to the silver shilling imagination. In the many tales Andersen has told and that are still frequently read, it is the unity of character and action that makes each story live. The Steadfast Tin Soldier and the Fir Tree, although inanimate objects, are convincing characters in their stories.

Traditional Literature

Traditional literature has been handed down orally from generation to generation and finally been set into print. Perhaps because of the necessity to keep the spoken story moving with suspense, the folktale relies upon stock characters. The jealous fairy, the foolish youngest son, and the girl as good as she is beautiful are all useful stock characters. "A beautiful daughter" calls from the listener the same set of responses each time the phrase is used. Since suspense and action carry the folktales, and the usually optimistic ending makes its comment upon life, characters need only be mentioned by a class-name to be known. In a sense, this is one of the pleasures of traditional literature; we enjoy meeting characters we have met before, and whose actions are thoroughly predictable. We are free then to concentrate on action and idea as it all moves along quickly. Our discovery of the nature of human beings comes then from the relationship of theme to action, often a discovery about universal human yearnings.

Animal Realism

In fantasy like *Charlotte's Web* and *Wind in the Willows,* the animals are people, but in a realistic story we expect animal characters to behave like real animals, to be true to their natures. Sheila Burnford, in her award-winning novel *The Incredible Journey,* knows the qualities of her animal characters and depicts them as true to family and breed. In a story filled with suspense and conflict, she has made us care what happens to her three central characters as they struggle for survival against the Canadian wilderness.

First, there is Luath the Labrador retriever, a one-man dog who is slow to warm up to anyone but his first master. A hunting dog, Luath is at home in the wilderness. Trained to retrieve and not to eat game, he nearly starves rather than violate his generations of breeding. The most determined of the three animals, Luath leads the trek through the wilds of Ontario. Though his soft, protective mouth is not good for fighting, he can ford a river and encourage the cat and the terrier to swim.

The two followers are the Siamese cat and the English bull terrier, an independent loner and a sociable clown. The feline aristocrat also is true to family and breed: she races straight at her friends and then darts away, opens doors with a leaping twist, cries the childlike wail of the Siamese, prefers heights as vantage points, and reverts easily to predator. The English bull, always the pet, seeks out people along the way; he smiles at Indian and hermit, expecting like any pet that their dinner time is his own. While shy Luath seeks the trail, the bull terrier seeks human habitation along the way.

Our intense interest in *The Incredible Journey* results from our involvement in the struggle of these characters as they trek across the wilderness. We believe the story because we are convinced that these characters—these pets acting true to their breeds—can and would seek their masters in any way they can. We know from occasional news accounts that pets in the real world do make such loyal journeys; here in the fictional world of animal characters we come to believe that this is how such a journey is possible.

As we shall note in a later chapter (Point of View), animal realism is at its best when the animals act only like animals. The temptation for the writer is to guess and to report what thoughts and feelings the animals are having. However, the writer, who does not really know what animals think or feel, must draw conclusions from observing appearance and behavior. And, of course, when the writer permits the animals to talk with one another in human speech, realism is destroyed. Burnford, however, has developed the characters of her animals primarily through observation, and we therefore believe in their reality.

Science Fiction

Examining literature by genre sets up a collective set of expectations derived from our experiences with the particular genre. Science fiction has been called the fiction of change, "future history." Although some historians of the genre credit Heraclitus and Aristophanes with the seeds of it all, others credit H. G. Wells and Jules Verne with its beginnings. Wells and Verne are still much read, but more frequently readers use the term *science fiction* to cover the work of more recent authors. Historian James Gunn notes that it springs from naturalism, or the view of man as animal, but dominant animal that must be tough and aggressive although using innate human qualities to temper animal qualities with love, self-sacrifice, and creativity, combined with a concern for the race. In the changing of science fiction from natural-ism toward more mainstream contemporary literature, science fiction now has greater concern for character, for a subjective reality, and for subtlety in language; it is now reaching a larger audience. As critic Kingsley Amis says in verse, "These cardboard spacemen aren't enough,/ Nor alien monsters, sketched in rough,/ Character's the essential stuff." Although such broad-ening of concern to encompass character may extend science fiction's audience, it also causes regret among some writers and critics because they see science fiction as growing virtually indistinguishable from mainstream fiction.

Look at a group of four works of science fiction. First, *The Robot and Rebecca and the Missing Owser* by Jane Yolen—some might call them science gadgetry—provides an example for young children. Rude and aggressive Rebecca fancies herself a detective and with the help of her robot Watson solves the mystery of stolen owsers, three-legged empaths sold at the Pettery. The story relies on the invention of nonsensical characters: canti-loopers shaped like cantaloupes with a vinegar smell that makes a person feel drunk or "looped"; Iris and Iri, vividly colored children who leave colored smudges; copbots who drone their investigative questions; marbeliters, pets shaped like ball bearings; a bookworm like a snake; and from the planet Chameleon III, a gray, mop-shaped crook, a "mopster" of course. The story, populated with Rebecca and the odd beings, none with recognizable human qualities, is pure invention without theme or characters to know or care about.

For older children, note the stereotyped scientists in Ben Bova's *The Flight of Exiles*. First the situation: 20,000 exiled scientists have been en route for fifty years to another planet in a deteriorating space ship. While the ship is in the hands of amateurs, the one all-knowing scientist is killed. Who is the murderer? By page 45 we have met thirteen characters of almost equal development, names rather than people. Unable to identify the protagonist, we can scarcely be expected to identify the murderer. Specialists—psychotechs, cryogenists, molecular geneticists, and one astronaut—are all known only by their technical jobs. In Henry James' terms, characters and action are not fused but described only from the outside.

Frank Bonham's *The Forever Formula* deals somewhat more effectively with futuristic themes regarding the prolongation of life. Characters, although rather flat, at least hint at a yearning for love and family. The United States, in its preoccupation with longevity, is overpopulated with the old destined to live useless lives for over 200 years. Ancient Guppies, Gold Seniors with translucent flesh, drink pink gin and play endless cro-quet. Evan Clark, son of the scientist who discovered Rejuvenal, is thawed from cryogenic state for a brain probe: What is the formula for Substance 1000, the substance that will restore youth to the aged population? One theme—that anything one does too long, even living, gets useless and boring—is reenforced by our awareness that worlds overpopulated with superannuated people suffering from Terminal Boredom will also suffer shortages of everything. The ending anticipates a return to normal life span for people who, like us, will worry about who they are and what they must do with their lives.

A more satisfying work, perhaps, is William Sleator's *Interstellar Pig,* the account of Barney's involvement with three mysterious neighbors who draw him into a new board game in which a player draws pieces and instruction cards that change the player into the monster described: lichen, giant spider, gill-breathing waterman, for example. The goal of the game is to find The Piggy, the source of power. Through fearful transformations of nightmare proportions, Barney battles the three stranger/monsters and finds that The Piggy, the prize, is really powerless. The novel abounds in themes, the most significant being that power merely for its own sake corrupts. Since the game has never been played to the finish, no one really knows how it will come out; similarity to the arms race is hinted at but never defined. If we did not become caught up in caring for a very real Barney, it would not matter. Another of Sleator's novels, *The House of Stairs,* in which the power of human love conquers the inhuman machine, carries our concern for the outcome because the believable human qualities of the characters give the action significance.

If we apply the axioms of character development, we realize that believing in the reality of character makes us believe in the experience. If the experience is fantastic, as it is in science fiction, a believable character can make us feel that the discoveries within the story have significance. Shallow character delineation limits our discovery about ourselves; action alone is left to hold our interest. When action does not grow out of the nature of character, the plot seems contrived and unimportant. The failure of such a story is often one of failure in character development.

Clearly some science fiction suffers from inadequate character development, but such inadequacy is not necessary to the genre and is becoming less frequent.

Classics

A *classic* is a book that lasts—not because it is continually enshrined on lists and because people talk about it, but because it continues to be read. The most memorable stories, those that like *Peter Rabbit* we take with us from childhood to adulthood, are those that create solid and believable characters. Frequently, what characters did—or the plot—has faded from memory, but we recall with vividness the characters themselves.

Look at two classics read perhaps by more girls and boys than any other two. They are two very different novels: Louisa May Alcott's *Little Women*, which has very little action or plot, is primarily a story of daily activity, even routine, and the thinking and doing of five females. Mark Twain's *The Adventures of Tom Sawyer* has many chapters of seemingly unrelated episodes, but it still has action and suspense leading to an exciting climax and discovery.

It is the character of Jo March that carries *Little Women* and has made it one of girlhood's favorites.[3] In her family, composed of vain Amy, saintly Beth, proper Meg, and worn but cheerful Marmee, Jo is the center. Jo is alive—aggressive and tomboyish, awkward and clumsy. She invents, acts, directs, complains and teases, sings off-key, and resents any restriction that would turn her into a stereotyped girl. She makes up games, dreams of heroism in active roles, and without guilt or gloom drops her bread on the carpet, butter side down.

Tom Sawyer is a second classic example of memorable character—as innumerable followers tend to prove. Tom, seeking freedom, goes off pirating; fear-stricken, observes a murder; ingeniously hunts treasure; smugly attends his own funeral; level-headedly finds the way out of the cave; contritely does favors for Muff Potter; and courageously gives evidence in court. We remember Tom for the variety of character traits, each demonstrated in episodes of action throughout a long and absorbing story.

Not all characters are as memorable as Tom Sawyer or Jo March, but there are others. The Ugly Duckling and Peter Rabbit have been tested and have endured. Perhaps Wilbur will live as long as Tom and Jo. However, other characters are so real to us that we feel we would recognize them on the street—characters like the three pets of *The Incredible Journey* and Laura of *The Little House* books. Our pleasure in our earliest introduction to the characters is renewed each time we recall an event from the plots involving them. Because we have known these characters, we have not only experienced vicariously their exciting adventures, but we have come to understand something about ourselves and others. Furthermore, one generation is pleased to find that the next enjoys the same stories and is disappointed to learn that a favorite does not speak with the significance it once did. In a sense, the characters of true classics are a social cement, joining one generation to another by common exploration of human beings.

SUMMARY

In life and in books children can sense differences in human beings and are capable of recognizing and responding to well-developed characters. Even in the simplest stories it is possible to find characters that verify truth about human nature. We meet these characters in action that seems part of their natures. We learn to know them—whether they be personified objects, real or personified animals, or human beings—by their appearances, words, actions, and thoughts, and the opinions of others about them. Round characters have many traits, while flat characters have limited development. Two kinds of characters that serve as background figures or contrasts are stereotypes and foils. Central characters in the action are round, so that by believing in their reality we are led to discover something about humanity, and we are thereby convinced that the conflict in the story, like conflict in life, is significant. The round characters may or may not change, but if they do, we expect such change to be convincing.

We find great pleasure in reading about people like ourselves or people we know, beings both wise and foolish, brave and cowardly, frightened and confident, lonely and secure. It is this pleasure of recognition that leads to understanding. Children as much as adults, or perhaps even more than adults, need the discovery of themselves as part of humanity. Conversely, they need the pleasure of discovering that humanity exists in themselves. If literature is to help children understand the nature of human beings, we need reality in the portrayal of character. Nothing—not style, nor conflict, nor adventure, nor suspense, nor vivid setting, nor laughter, nor tears— nothing can substitute for solid character development in creating a pleasurable and lasting literature for children as well as adults.

READING AND EVALUATING

1. **Historical Fiction**   Read or reread one of the Laura Ingalls Wilder *Little House* books. Is the protagonist a round character? Compare the character of Laura with that of another child from a story of pioneers. Is the protagonist round? If dynamic, can you follow the process of change throughout the action?

2. **Social Issues Realism**   Read a novel about a member of a minority group, one witten in the last fifteen years. If the protagonist changes, is the change convincing? Is the protagonist round or flat? Does it matter whether the change is convincing? Might the reader's guilt about Americans' treatment of minorities interfere with judgment about literary quality? How?

3. **Problem Realism**   Read a recent book about a character with a problem of some kind. Is the protagonist a round character, or merely a composite of traits that make the character seem flat? Can the reader follow the change—if there is change—throughout the action as it unfolds? Is there a second character, less well-developed, who seems to change? Is it a believable change? Why or why not?

4. **Science Fiction**   Read a science fiction story by William Sleator, Eleanor Cameron, Andre Norton, Frank Bonham, or H. M. Hoover, and examine the development of the protagonist as a credible human being. Is he or she a round character? Flat? Dynamic or static? If the protagonist changes, is the change convincing? What is the effect?

5. Realistic Novel   Read either a novel you remember from later childhood or a classic you missed. Evaluate the characters. Who are flat, round, foil, stereotype, dynamic, and static? How do you come to know them? Do you discover anything about human nature that seems true or worth discovering? Do you believe this discovery has any relationship either to your remembering the novel or to its continuous popularity with your friends? Was its popularity a matter of temporary circumstances or of universal character interest?

6. Fantasy   Read a high fantasy by one of the writers mentioned in the chapter or by another writer. Is the character fully developed? Does the character believe in the reality of the fantasy world created in the story? Are you willing to suspend disbelief? Is the portrayal of character one source of your willingness?

NOTES

1 Henry James, *The Art of Fiction.* New York: Oxford University Press, 1948, p. 13

2 Paul Hazard, *Books, Children, and Men.* Boston: The Horn Book, Inc., 1960, p. 98.

3 As we will note in the chapter on theme, the strengths of *Little Women* lie in theme as well as character.

RECOMMENDED BOOKS CITED IN THIS CHAPTER

ALCOTT, LOUISA MAY. *Little Women.* New York: Dutton, 1948 (first published, 1868–69).

ALEXANDER, LLOYD. *The High King.* New York: Holt, 1968.

ANDERSEN, HANS CHRISTIAN. *The Fir Tree.* New York: Harper, 1970.

_____ . *The Steadfast Tin Soldier.* New York: Atheneum, 1971.

_____ . *The Ugly Duckling.* New York: Macmillan, 1967.

BONHAM, FRANK. *The Forever Formula.* New York: Dutton, 1979.

BURNFORD, SHEILA. *The Incredible Journey.* Boston: Little, Brown, 1961.

ECKERT, ALLAN. *Incident at Hawk's Hill.* Boston: Little, Brown, 1971.

GARFIELD, LEON. *Fair's Fair.* New York: Doubleday, 1981.

GRAHAME, KENNETH. *The Wind in the Willows.* New York: Scribner's, 1953 (first published, 1908).

JUKES, MAVIS. *Like Jake and Me.* New York: Knopf, 1984.

KONIGSBURG, E. L. *From the Mixed-Up Files of Mrs. Basil E. Frankweiler.* New York: Atheneum, 1974.

O'DELL, SCOTT. *Island of the Blue Dolphins.* Boston: Houghton Mifflin, 1960.

PATERSON, KATHERINE. *The Great Gilly Hopkins.* New York: Crowell, 1978.

_____ . *Jacob Have I Loved.* New York: Crowell, 1980.

SLEATOR, WILLIAM. *The House of Stairs.* New York: Dutton, 1974.

_____ . *Interstellar Pig.* New York: Dutton, 1984.

SPEARE, ELIZABETH. *The Sign of the Beaver*. Boston: Houghton Mifflin, 1983.
TWAIN, MARK. *The Adventures of Tom Sawyer*. New York: Macmillan, 1966 (first published, 1876).
WHITE, E. B. *Charlotte's Web*. New York: Harper, 1952.
WILDER, LAURA INGALLS. The *Little House* Books. New York: Harper, 1953 (first published, 1932–43).

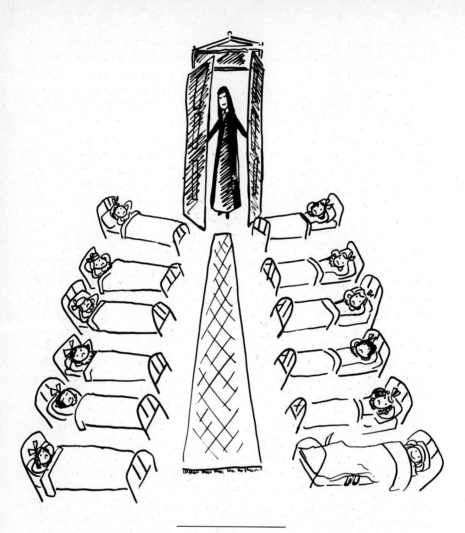

lot

While some adult readers may be more interested in character than in any other element in the story, most of us—and most children—cannot get involved with stories that are only character studies. We want things to move and things to happen; we call this order *plot*. Plot is the sequence of events showing characters in action. This sequence is not accidental but is chosen by the author as the best way of telling his or her story. If the writer has chosen well, the plot will produce conflict, tension, and action that will arouse and hold our interest.

The child wants what most adults want in literature: action, happenings, questions that need answers, answers that fit questions, glimpses of happy and unhappy outcomes, discovery of how events grow and turn. For the very small child there is pleasure in finding recognition of daily routine within the pages of a book, but many people think that *all* a child needs in a narrative is the recognition in printed words of an everyday happening they call action—an action as prosaic as going to bed at night or waking up in the morning. It is surprising that adults who would never find pleasure in a literal, hour-by-hour account of their own daily routines expect such accounts of children's daily lives to satisfy them. No matter how content the young are with daily order, children very soon expect that they should find life more exciting in a story than in their own experience. Here, in a book, children and adults alike can lose themselves in possibility as they pose the big question of all literature: What if? This element of possibility, of possible action and reaction that confronts character, builds the plot.

TYPES OF NARRATIVE ORDER

One of the writer's privileges is to reorder existence, to rearrange events, or in other words, to create plot. The writer may focus on one moment of a day and ignore all others, or he or she may charge one hour with significance and portent that influence months or years of a life. The writer may either ignore the segments of time that have little significance or may simply summarize those moments. The writer makes alterations and deletions that our memories are unable to make for us in our own lives. The writer's selectivity and purposeful reordering and highlighting create plot.

Narrative order in fiction, the order in which events are related, may follow several patterns, but the most common pattern in young children's literature is the chronological arrangement.

Chronological Order

As we all know, our lives are one 24-hour period followed by another. This time order is simple chronology. If a story relates events in the order of their happening, the story is in *chronological order,* perhaps moving with the characters from one place of action to another and yet chronological. The writer may make the story line more complex by showing action that occurs with one character in one place, then turning to action that occurs to another simultaneously, but in another place: "Meanwhile, back at the ranch . . ." The accounts of simultaneous action follow one another in the story, but the events have occupied the same point in time; therefore, the action is still chronological.

Plot in historical fiction occasionally condenses for us centuries of chronological time unknown except by examination of history's artifacts. Jill Paton Walsh has written such a story in *Toolmaker*. Following the story of Ra, we find condensed into the life of one fictional man the change from nomadic hunting to settled agrarian society, from weapon maker to toolmaker. Specialized labor results when Ra, finding himself a better maker of flint weapons than hunter, trades weapons for game. When game is scarce and the tribal market saturated with his weapons, Ra tries hunting again, but has lost his skills. Now a useless member of a hunting tribe, he is abandoned by the forest people and wanders alone and hungry. In his journey he finds a settled farming village which does not need to move with the migration of game. Now he trades tools for food and a wife, and prospers as a settled artisan. The simple, brief plot with little character development gives a sense of prehistoric life and a society's change.

Flashbacks

In fiction for mature readers, narrative order may involve a *flashback.* Many readers can recall their first experience with a flashback; it was puzzling. "What happened? How come?" The writer disrupts normal time sequence to recount some episode out of the character's past, showing how that event influences the character's response to an event in the present. Or the writer shows in flashback a past event that has brought on the present one. In either case, the writer chooses to juggle time to make a point about the character and the character's story. The small child, however, may find it difficult to follow such movement back and forth in time.[1]

The child relies on his or her own experience of time for understanding when and how events occur. Since the child knows from experience, for instance, that one falls asleep and dreams, he or she understands Maurice Sendak's *Where the Wild Things Are*. The child knows that such a marvelous adventure could happen to Max while he sleeps or daydreams, since the child has had similar dreams. As the child grows in sophistication, he or she comes to comprehend the possibility in literature of mixing memory, imagination, dream, daydream, and flashback. As the child matures, the experience of literature provides growing recognition of time in its infinite variations. Jean George, for example, uses flashback effectively in *Julie of the Wolves*. She plunges into the story of Miyax's or Julie's dependence upon the wolves for survival on the Arctic tundra, then, in a flashback Part II, "Miyax, the girl" tells us of her early life. Finally, Part III returns us to Miyax's struggle and safe arrival at her father's house. Television probably increases children's exposure to flashback and dream techniques, and this experience could help them to recognize the techniques in literature.

CONFLICT

Plot is a more inclusive term than narrative order or its synonym, story line, since it involves not only sequence of events, but also *conflict*. In this discussion of books for the young, tension, friction, force, alternatives, excitement, suspense, discovery, and resolution are parts of conflict. Conflict occurs when the protagonist struggles against an *antagonist* or opposing force. In short, it is conflict which, added to narrative order, makes plot.

In the following subsections we will discuss four kinds of conflict in literature: person-against-self, person-against-person, person-against-society, and person-against-nature.

Person-Against-Self

Consider, for example, the classic *Tom Sawyer*—not Twain's best, but his most popular for children—which has a plot of such complexity that we can discover several types of conflict. Mark Twain shows Tom as he faces an internal conflict, a tension within Tom that pulls him toward either of two courses of action. Tom happens to see Injun Joe—a pejorative term that is unacceptable today—murder the doctor. He makes a pact not to reveal what he has seen, and signs it with his blood, but Tom cannot forget that the town has condemned innocent Muff Potter while Joe goes free. Tom takes tobacco and matches to Muff in jail. He often speculates about how to free him. Afraid of Joe's revenge, but guilty about keeping Muff's innocence secret, Tom cannot sleep. When he does, he talks in his sleep. Fearful lest he tell what troubles him, Tom ties his mouth shut. Such an internal struggle is between Tom's fear and his conscience, and there is no mistaking its intensity. When Tom's conscience—his keen awareness of his moral responsibility even in the face of danger—wins the battle, he goes to the judge to tell the truth about the murder. Such an internal conflict of feelings within the protagonist is called *person-against-self*. This kind of conflict also exists for the narrator in *My Brother Sam Is Dead* as he struggles with his anger and bewilderment—to be a Tory, or to be a Rebel like his brother.

In the struggle between good and evil within himself, Ged, of the high fantasy *A Wizard of Earthsea* by Ursula K. Le Guin, must first recognize his own flawed nature, represented by the shadow.

> Aloud and clearly, breaking that old silence, Ged spoke the shadow's name, and in the same moment the shadow spoke without lips or tongue, saying the same word: "Ged." And the two voices were one voice.
> Ged reached out his hands, dropping his staff, and took hold of his shadow, of the black self that reached out to him. Light and darkness met, and joined, and were one.

Ged neither wins nor loses the battle, but by seeing that the shadow and he are one, he makes himself whole: "a man: who, knowing his whole true self cannot be used or possessed by any power other than himself." He will from now on live his life for its own sake, not for hatred, pain, ruin, or the darkness of evil.

Internal conflict also occurs in *A Solitary Blue* by Cynthia Voigt. Jeff, whose mother left him and his father when Jeff was seven, goes several years later to visit her and falls in love with her spontaneity and beauty. During the next year, his letters unanswered and his second visit a lonely failure, Jeff struggles to free himself from what he thinks is an unreasonable love for his mother. Only when, at 17, he can tell her honestly that he neither loves her nor wants to live with her does his honesty win over his guilt.

In *On My Honor* by Marion Dane Bauer, Joel's internal conflict arises from his guilt. He is afraid to tell anyone that he has disobeyed and gone into the polluted and dangerous river, and he is afraid to tell that after he dared Tony to swim to the sandbar, Tony drowned. The guilt is so strong that he wishes he could sleep, run away, or even die. Only when his father understands Joel's anguish is Joel in any way able to deal with his internal conflict.

Tensions and conflicts in stories vary; some seem more likely to occur in the lives of children and may, therefore, seem more real, but others may give readers glimpses of important moral issues.

Person-Against-Person

Tom Sawyer must face still another conflict. Muff Potter is freed only because Tom has the courage to testify—in court and in Joe's presence—that Joe is the murderer. From the moment of his testimony, Tom's life is in danger. Joe disappears, and then, disguised as a deaf and dumb Spaniard, he comes back to prey upon the town and to steal the buried treasure. Once again Joe is a very real threat to Tom's life. As the boys hide breathlessly in the haunted house, they know that Joe will turn on them viciously if he finds them there. Later, lost in the cave with Becky, Tom catches a glimpse of Joe and knows that his murderous enemy is close by, hiding from the law. Here we have a *person-against-person* conflict.

The terms in which we describe the conflict are not so important. What does matter is that we see clearly the protagonist and the antagonist. The strain between the two forces is what holds our continuing interest and our intense curiosity about the outcome. It is Tom's internal, growing awareness of justice opposing his fear for his life that finally forces him to take action, and this action confronts Tom with the vengeance of a villainous man. Children's literature is filled with suspenseful examples of person-against-person conflict: In *Peter Rabbit,* Peter evades Mr. McGregor; in *The Hundred Penny Box* by Sharon Bell Mathis, Michael and his mother conflict on letting his grandmother keep her precious box; and in Madeleine L'Engle's *A Wrinkle in Time,* Meg defeats IT, the disembodied brain.

Television cartoons, too, are filled with examples, as Woody Woodpecker frantically opposes the owl or Popeye opposes Brutus. In folktales, where protagonists are usually stereotypes, the person-against-person conflict is very common. Jack climbs the beanstalk and defeats the giant. Hansel and Gretel shove the wicked witch into the oven and all is well. Both Red Riding Hood and the Three Little Pigs face wolves. In some folktales the person-against-person conflict moves quickly and vigorously to conclusion, and in others conflict travels with gentle humor to an equally satisfactory resolution, as it does in "The Squire's Bride," or in "The Old Woman and Her Pig." *The Time Ago Tales of Jahdu* and *Time Ago Lost: More Tales of Jahdu,* Virginia Hamilton's stories with their traditional motifs of African and black American folklore, show Jahdu running, in conflict with Trouble, as he helps Trouble's victims and as he shows the creatures how to manage against adversity and puzzlement.

Person-Against-Society

Conflict and an unknown outcome keeps us reading *Charlotte's Web.* Wilbur's struggle is serious: life and death. Although we may define the struggle as a *person-against-society* conflict, the child knows it simply as "Will Wilbur live? Will Charlotte save him from being made into bacon?" In this case we may regard society as the farming business, which, after all, is based on profit. A runt pig is not worth keeping. Although the child reading *Charlotte's Web* gets involved in the conflict of Wilbur-versus-dinner-table, the conflict is actually Wilbur against good business. The conflict begins immediately, page one, line one: "Where's Papa going with the ax?" Whether or not Wilbur will be saved from death commands our interest. This conflict of Wilbur against the business of farming keeps our interest from start to finish.

Person-against-society conflict is much more easily understood by adults than by children. When we read, for example, of Hester Prynne's conflict with the Puritan society in *The Scarlet Letter,* we see society's instrument of degradation—the stocks. We know the society by bits of dialogue as the crowd shouts its taunts at Hester's back, or plots to take Pearl from Hester. To children, however, society as antagonist is clearer if it is representative of society. In Tien Pao's conflict with society in *The House of Sixty Fathers,* the airplanes and the devastation they bring to sampans and thatched huts represent the antagonist society. The enemy lookouts and the horsemen on patrol are identifiable human fragments of the war-making society. They serve to make the conflict understandable.

Person-Against-Nature

Julie in Jean George's novel *Julie of the Wolves* experiences *person-against-nature* conflict. Having run away from her village to the wild frozen Arctic lands, Julie faces possible death by freezing and starvation. The wolves who befriend her save her life, leaving her to continue her search for her father. *Island of the Blue Dolphin* is believable because Scott O'Dell spends considerable time describing nature and makes it a complex antagonist. First of all, Karana's people have always lived with nature, using its bounty, conserving its offerings, and preparing for its dangers. However, when Karana is left alone, she is forced to violate the taboo of the tribe in order to survive; Karana, a young woman, must make weapons to defend herself against nature, and we fear that the spirits will punish her. Around her cave she must build a whale-rib fence to keep out the wild dogs. She must fight infection from injury caused by falling on the rocks; she is defeated by the sea when her canoe is too leaky for a voyage into the morning sun. The protagonist is threatened by one element after another, each one a component of nature, the antagonist. Karana's conflict is dramatic, building up to the earthquake and its following tidal wave:

> I stood facing the rock, with my feet on a narrow ledge and one hand thrust deep into a crack. Over my shoulder I could see the wave coming. It did not come fast, for the other wave was still running out. For a while I thought

that it would not come at all because the two suddenly met beyond the sandpit. The first wave was trying to reach the sea and the second was struggling toward the shore.

Like two giants they crashed against . . .

Conflict of any kind grows out of character. Peter Rabbit's character—his mischievous nature, combining curiosity with greed—brings him to Mr. McGregor's garden and keeps him eating long enough to be discovered. Karana's womanhood and the traits it implies in her culture make her struggle against nature suspenseful. In *The House of Sixty Fathers* Tien Pao's innocence and youth highlight his conflict with a society at war. Tom Sawyer's inner conflict of conscience results from his sense of loyalty and justice.

There are stories with minimally developed characters in which conflict carries all of the reader's interest; some are mysteries like *Nancy Drew,* with plots so coincidental that children are finally bored. On the other hand, the traditional stories from folk origins do not depict fully developed protagonists, but they do rely upon universal human traits and dreams expressed in their themes. These themes seem to take the place of character as the origin for conflict.

Intent upon conflict, television often neglects to create a fully drawn protagonist; as a result children do not learn to see the relationship between conflict and character. Plot incidents seem merely to happen *to* protagonists, rather than to be brought about by the protagonist's personal traits; the result is a dramatic story that makes little contribution to the viewer's understanding of human beings.

PATTERNS OF ACTION

Plot is more than the sequence of actions or conflict. It is also the pattern of those actions. If we oversimplify plot patterns by diagrams, we might describe them with these shapes:

1.   2.   3.

The first of these patterns moves from one incident to another related incident, building upon discoveries and changes toward a final climax that brings the action to its peak. Such a pattern is most clearly demonstrated in Mary Norton's *The Borrowers,* a story with a *frame,* since it begins and ends with Mrs. May relating the events to Kate. The frame encloses the developing plot and within it occur the events that involve the Clock family. The borrowers change from people with simple needs to a family ruled by their possessions. Homily's materialistic grab for more and more leads to discovery, to the ratcatchers, the fumigators, and the high suspense surrounding the family's escape. In the final chapter, a return of focus to Mrs. May and Kate, we know only that the borrowers might have established a new home by the hawthorne hedge, or, perhaps, that the family might have been a figment of a small boy's imagination. The plot line of development has moved steadily upward to leave us in uncertainty.

The second of these patterns of action can be demonstrated by *Jennifer, Hecate, Macbeth, William McKinley, and Me, Elizabeth*. Action moves with tension that does not mount to a breaking point, but keeps us interested in the growing friendship between Jennifer and Elizabeth. The conflict—and there is conflict despite minimal suspense—exists as concern, curiosity, and pleasure in the narrator who is unraveling her story as she wonders and worries, tries or refuses to conform to witch-Jennifer's demands. In *Little House in the Big Woods,* Laura Ingalls Wilder shows Laura's life as eventful and filled with pleasure; the security of Laura's home keeps the reader interested in day-to-day happenings, but without building anxiety. This kind of action follows a straight line plot pattern.

The third pattern of action is more complex. The story rises to some climax and then clearly concludes. *Rising action* begins with a situation that must be shown and explained; we must know what has happened before the story opens, what has created the current situation. This explanation of the situation and the characters' condition is called *exposition.* In most stories for children, it is woven into early action so that attention is caught immediately and held. When, for example, on page eight of *Roll of Thunder, Hear My Cry,* Little Man is nearly run down by the school bus loaded with white children, we are aware of the situation, of the feelings between blacks and whites.

Exposition in *Jacob Have I Loved* by Katherine Paterson is spread throughout the first two chapters in which we read of Wheeze and Caroline, twin sisters with different personalities, talents, and dreams. We learn that Wheeze resents sickly Caroline for having taken so much of her parents' care and attention when they were little, and for having musical talent that sets her apart from all others on the island. Since children's stories are usually short and must move quickly, *complications* begin very soon. The elements of a story that deal with rising action are: suspense, the cliffhanger, foreshadowing, sensationalism, the climax, denouement, and inevitability. Each of these terms will be treated separately in the following subsections.

Suspense

From the first line in the first chapter of *Charlotte's Web*—"Where's Papa going with the ax?"—we know that Wilbur's fate is uncertain, and from that initial moment White holds us in *suspense*, a state that makes us read on. By tears, sobs, cries, and yells, Fern wins temporary reprieve for Wilbur, who becomes Fern's baby. Wilbur's brothers and sisters are all sold and it is Wilbur's turn. There goes Wilbur. But, see if Uncle Homer Zuckerman will buy Wilbur so Fern can visit him at the nearby farm. Wilbur is lonely, finding his life boring without Fern as constant companion. When he finds a friend, loneliness vanishes. Then, electrifying news comes: An old sheep spitefully tells Wilbur he is being fattened for Christmas slaughter. Charlotte to the rescue. She weaves the words "Some Pig" into her web; people come from miles around to see Wilbur. Mr. Zuckerman now admires him, and no celebrity was ever made into sausage.

As the excitement wears off, our worries revive. Charlotte, however, sends Templeton to the dump for more words. When each of the woven words miraculously appears, we have new hope. Then Wilbur's protector announces regretfully that she cannot accompany Wilbur to the Fair. Catastrophe looms again, but a ray of hope glimmers: "We'll leave it this way: I'll come to the Fair if I possibly can." Our security lasts only until we overhear Arable and Zuckerman talking about the fine hams and bacon he'll make. A huge pig called Uncle is stiff competition: "He's going to be a hard pig to beat." Wilbur's doom is sealed. Suddenly, an unprecedented award, but Wilbur faints and "We can't give a prize to a *dead* pig.... It's never been done before." No prize. Then Templeton bites Wilbur's tail, and Wilbur revives and wins the prize.

But Charlotte is languishing. Can Wilbur survive without Charlotte? Charlotte spins her final Magnum Opus and dies, and Wilbur, now mature, takes responsibility for Charlotte's egg sac. When spring comes, Wilbur is still alive and hearty, and life continues.

Suspense, the emotional pull that keeps us wanting to read on, involves us in conflict up to the climax in the final pages. These moments of suspense are not panic points in the story, nor at any time do we know the outcome with certainty. White controls the suspense to keep it peaking and leveling, and at every point we remain not only curious but concerned for the outcome, because either success or failure looms and we cannot be completely certain which will prevail.

Suspense has kept us reading, but White has carefully led us with optimism, never despair. The author skillfully builds the story so that nowhere is the ending too predictable, lest we lose interest, nor too frightful, lest we give up. At the end of the book, the reader feels that the ups and downs of "perhaps he'll win, perhaps he'll lose" are finally settled. Suspense does not go beyond the story's ending. White, as he pulls us to the satisfactory end of the story, makes us heave a final, relieved sigh. The feeling that all will be well, even after the final page, results from White's skill in handling suspense. Our optimism has been justified. To cite another example, the authors of *Where the Lilies Bloom* keep readers in suspense by implied questions: Will Roy Luther die? Will his death be discovered? Will the children be sent to the county home? Will Kiser honor his bargain about the house? Will they have to move into a cave? Such suspense keeps us reading.

The most interesting books for early readers also have suspenseful plots, and their mystery format seems most intriguing. For example, Marjorie Weinman Sharmat's *Nate the Great and the Fishy Prize* tells, in simple vocabulary, how Nate's dog Sludge solves the puzzle of the missing prize. Nate checks out all the possibilities, going from one master and pet to the next, all of them entering the Smartest Pet Contest. The thread line of Nate's biking to the store for ingredients to make pancakes, his stop at each entrant's house, and Sludge's curious sniffs at the grocery bag lead to the missing trophy, a tuna fish can lettered "Smartest" in gold. Of course, Sludge is the winner. The brief story has all of the elements of a progressive plot, from exposition to final climax and denouement. *Sebastian (Super Sleuth) and the Bone to Pick Mystery* by Mary Blount Christian and *Judge Benjamin: Superdog* by Judith Whitelock McInerney also have detective dogs as protagonists. These dogs solve mysteries successfully, the latter in first person point of view and a humorous tone. In *Tac's Island* by Ruth Yaffe Radin, a successful episodic story is unified by the action of six-year-old characters. Here, friendship grows as the boys do all of the fun things available to islanders.

There is no shortage of suspense in Gary Paulsen's *Hatchet,* as Brian, the protagonist, meets a black bear, an attacking moose, and invasion by a porcupine.

> . . . slithering. A brushing sound, a slithering brushing sound near his feet—and he kicked out as hard as he could, kicked out and threw the hatchet at the sound, a noise coming from his throat. But the hatchet missed . . . and his leg was instantly torn with pain, as if a hundred needles had been driven into it.
>
> Now he screamed, with the pain and fear, and skittered on his backside up into the corner of the shelter, breathing through his mouth, straining to see, to hear.
>
> The slithering moved again, he thought toward him at first, and terror took him, stopping his breath. He felt he could see a low dark form, a bulk in the darkness, a shadow that lived, but now it moved away, slithering and scraping it moved away and he saw . . . .

The Cliffhanger

A form of suspense that White does not use is the *cliffhanger,* the exciting chapter ending that makes it hard to lay the book aside. Unlike the chapters in *Charlotte's Web,* wherein each contributes to the development of central conflict in the total plot, each moving to its own peak and yet managing to end quietly, the cliffhanger chapter ends with such suspense that the plea for "just one more chapter" is irresistible. The cliffhanger is most obvious in the series novels like *Nancy Drew* and the *Hardy Boys,* and in today's soap operas, as well as in newspaper, magazine, and Saturday movie serials of the past. Each child left the darkened theater for the afternoon sunlight, worried about the hero, left, perhaps literally, hanging by the fingernails from a sheer cliff. The hero was in mortal danger and might not survive until the following Saturday matinee.

This dramatic device for building suspense is exemplified clearly in *The Borrowers.* These tiny people live in constant fear of being seen, and many chapters end with this fear expressed. Chapter 4 ends with Arrietty's parents talking:

> "She doesn't know about Eggletina. She doesn't know about being 'seen.'"
> "Well," said Pod, "we'll tell her. We always said we would. There's no hurry."
> Homily stood up. "Pod," she said, "we're going to tell her now."

And Chapter 8 ends: "Startled, she caught her breath. Something had glittered. Arrietty stared." When the climax is close, the housekeeper says at the conclusion of Chapter 17, "The police, that's what this means—a case for the police." Note, too, the cliffhangers of Lloyd Alexander's *The High King* which conclude with such lines as "Wicked Queen is gone!" or "Magg's jaws will close on them as tightly as they are closed on us," and "'Smoke,' he gasped." The intensity of the suspense varies from chapter to chapter, but the hook that catches us at the end of one section carries us relentlessly into the next, since we must know what happens.

Foreshadowing

The writer for children must decide how much suspense the child can sustain, and how much reassurance is needed to balance suspense. To relieve the reader's anxiety and to produce a satisfying sense of the inevitable, the writer must see that there are clues about the outcome—without the suspense being destroyed. Such clues must be planted artfully and unobtrusively within the action. Not all readers will be alert to all dropped hints, it is true, but White in *Charlotte's Web* uses them to hint at Wilbur's ultimate safety and Charlotte's death, and to reassure us that finally all will be well. These planted clues indicate outcome and are called *foreshadowing*.

In Wilbur's first conversation with Charlotte, we learn that gentle Charlotte lives by eating living things, and friendship looks questionable.

Seeing a need to reassure, White adds that "she had a kind heart, and she was to prove loyal and true to the very end." The first clue suggests friendship; the second, "to the very end," has a prophetic ring.

Foreshadowing and suspense balance throughout the narrative. When in "Bad News" Wilbur hears he is being fattened for slaughter, he wails. However, his safety is foreshadowed when Charlotte asserts calmly, "I am going to save you."

Another event for which we must be prepared is Charlotte's death. If her death had been unforeseen, we would be justified in accusing White of playing with our emotions. But Charlotte's acceptance of her life span foreshadows her approaching death and prepares Wilbur and the readers. The song of the crickets foreshadows death of all kinds. "Summer is over and gone. . . . Over and gone. . . . Summer is dying, dying," they sing. Charlotte, whose life like the crickets and the seasons has a predictable cycle, "heard it and knew that she hadn't much time left." Of the word "humble," she says, "It is the last word I shall ever write." When she says that she is "languishing," she is peaceful and contented, and we are as resigned as she. *Charlotte's Web* concludes with a sense of inevitability, and even, because of the 514 baby spiders, with a sense of optimism.

Clear examples of foreshadowing occur throughout good children's stories. For example, in William Armstrong's *Sounder*, the father has been sent to prison for stealing food for his family. When at long last a figure appears in the red dust of the road, Sounder the coonhound revives. Once near death from the sheriff's gunshots, now, before the approaching figure is identifiable, Sounder pants, whines, wags his tail, and paces the dooryard. His agitation foreshadows the father's limping return. In *Dicey's Song* we very early see Jeff hanging around after school with his guitar. When he stops Dicey to talk with her, their eventual friendship is foreshadowed.

Foreshadowing is clear in Marion Dane Bauer's *On My Honor*. Tony wants to swim, and although Joel has promised his father not to, Joel, goaded by Tony, finally challenges Tony to swim out to the sandbar. As the boys walk into the dangerously fast Vermillion River, Joel calls out, "Watch out for the current." Tony grabs his throat with both hands: "The current! It's got me. It's going to suck me under . . . swallow me up!" When Tony jumps into the water, he thrashes about, and Joel mutters, "Doesn't look like he even knows how." As he fights the current, Joel sees similar significance in Tony's earlier false claims about his hang-gliding experience. (Good swimmer that he is, Joel remarks that the current frightens him.) When he calls back without looking, his voice bounces off the bluffs, and when he steps into a bottomless hole, he realizes that Tony really couldn't swim. We are prepared for Tony's drowning in the strong current.

Even in a suspenseful story with a well-developed protagonist, however, plotting problems can occur. In *Jasmin* by Jan Truss, for example, we miss adequate foreshadowing of events, like a violent storm and the arrival of the social workers to take retarded Leroy away to a special home and school.

Sensationalism

The author must drop hints about what is ahead, if the reader is to feel satisfaction as the story unfolds. In the strong life and death conflict of *Charlotte's Web,* unrelieved suspense might be too much for the small child. The skill of the writer lies in balancing two elements—suspense over the action and hints at the outcome.

Unrelieved suspense, however, makes a story *sensational;* it plays us like instruments, keeping us holding our breaths in crescendoes of anxiety. The writer for adults has greater latitude in the creation of anxiety, since adults can tolerate it; with persistent enthusiasm, some adults read *sensationalism:* mystery stories, murder thrillers, and survival adventures. The suspense absorbs them; they breathe horror and terror with the protagonist. However, they are never deceived, since they never forget that it's just a story. Other adults find themselves bored with the unrelieved suspense because they, too, know that it's just a story, and, wanting more than sensationalism, they seek some discovery of real people in suspenseful action. They demand the significance of well-developed character in a conflict that reveals something about human beings.

A situation of unrelieved suspense, on the other hand, may be more than a child can bear. Take, for example, the folktale "Snow White and the Seven Dwarfs." The storyteller, watching the expressive faces of the listeners, relieves the suspense with reassuring hints about outcome. In making the movie, however, Walt Disney turned suspense to sensationalism and many children were upset by it. The ugly witch with clawlike hands and viciously evil features roused sheer terror. Many children hid their faces and suffered nightmares long after they had seen "the great children's story come alive on the screen."

Any action may be made sensational, but important and even violent events can be described with accuracy and sensitivity, yet without sensationalism, as, for example, the Colliers' description of Sam's execution before a firing squad at the end of *My Brother Sam Is Dead* manages to do. Sensationalism results when the writer focuses on the thrilling or startling at the expense of character and idea.

The Climax

The peak and turning point of the conflict, the point at which we know the outcome of the action, is called the *climax.* Throughout the development of plot, from initial recognition of the conflict through the critical turns and irregular progress, past reversals and discoveries, up to the point where we know who wins the conflict, we follow the plot to the climax. While we speak of the climax as the turning point in the conflict, children call it "the most exciting part," or "where I knew how it would come out." No matter which term is used, the climax is inextricably related to conflict.

Paula Vinson's story *Willie Goes to the Seashore* lacks a climax because it lacks conflict. Instead of plot being resolved, it merely peters out. Instead of coming to a decisive conclusion, the narrative just quits. The result is disappointment.

Climax of some kind exists in any story with conflict (Hooray! Peter Rabbit made it through the gate!), although the climax may come with varying degrees of intensity or varying closeness to the end of the story. For example, in the three parts of *Beowulf*, there are dramatic confrontations and triumphant battles between Beowulf and Grendel, Beowulf and Grendel's mother, and finally, between Beowulf and the dragon.

However, look at the quiet climax of *Charlotte's Web*. Here, in the conflict of person-against-society, Wilbur is in a life-and-death struggle. The climax logically comes when we know that he will live. Checking on suspense, we find that the high point, brought on by frequent minor crises and excitement peaks, finally comes when Wilbur revives and wins the prize—the handsome bronze medal for "attracting so many visitors to our great County Fair." The runt pig has defeated good business, since Wilbur has taken the final round of the contest. By his additional award—the special prize of twenty-five dollars—Zuckerman is rewarded with money and Wilbur is a good business investment after all; this is the climax. From here on Wilbur has nothing to worry about; the conflict is resolved.

In *The Borrowers,* where the conflict pits the family of tiny people against Mrs. Driver the housekeeper, the climax comes within a few exciting pages of the end. Mrs. Driver's discovery of "the little varmints," living amidst their borrowed luxuries below the floorboards, brings on the rat-catchers. They board up the gratings and seal the space below the floor. Then they start the gas and the fumigating bellows, hoping to kill the creatures, whatever they are. But the borrowers, with whom we have worried about emigrating since Chapter 1, have a friend in the Boy who sets out to give them ventilation:

> Pick-ax in hand [he] ran out of the door.... Already, when he reached it, a thin filament of smoke was eddying out of the grating . . . a flicker of movement against the darkness between the bars. . . . behind him the crunch of wheels on the gravel and the sound of horse's hoofs.... [W]ith two great blows on the brickwork, he dislodged . . . the grating. It fell....

Although we do not see the borrowers fleeing from the gas, we think they may have escaped. With the airtight grating gone, their path to fresh air and freedom is open.

The Witch of Blackbird Pond poses a conflict of a young woman who emigrates from the Barbados to the witch-hunting Puritan society of New England. Elizabeth Speare shows us how Kit's independence, her compassion, her defiance of ridiculous rules, and even her luxurious wardrobe and her swimming ability work against her to prove to the Puritans that she is a witch. Accusation and trial bring us to the climax. At the hearing, filled with the accusations of the townspeople, rising suspense keeps the reader hoping for the climax. The accuser, faced with evidence that Kit has not bewitched his child but has taught her to read, drops charges, and Kit is now free and innocent. Throughout the story we have followed each indication that Kit is different, that she is willful, and that she will not conform; we have seen the frowning and suspicious community and concluded that witchcraft charges will be brought. But it has not all been so pat. Will Prudence be brave enough to prove that Kit was teaching and not bewitching her? Will Nat's ship be in port? Will he be able to help Kit? He has been forbidden to enter the town; how can he help? Will he be able to convince the villagers of the truth? When all these questions have been answered, the climax is reached.

The final chapter of *A Wrinkle in Time* is filled with Meg's thoughts, and yet Madeleine L'Engle maintains suspense to the climax. When Meg the protagonist finally gathers her courage to return to Camazotz and to confront the monster brain that holds her brother prisoner, we know that the climax approaches. Meg discovers that she has love and IT has not; she adds all the love of those who surround her with all she feels for them, and love and will together defeat evil and bring joy. Only when Meg's battle with IT frees the last hostage are we satisfied about the final outcome. Conflict and suspense have been intense until the last two pages. For one final example, look at the keen suspense built in the conclusion of H. M. Hoover's *The Shepherd Moon*, where the struggle between two dying cultures comes to its climax when the alien Mikel dies and the great house which represents Merry's corrupt culture collapses.

In looking back over these examples of climax, we note that each involves the final battle of the protagonist with an antagonist. Each results in victory for the protagonist, and this victory seems right in children's literature. Anti-heroes, or badly flawed protagonists, and defeated protagonists are for adults only, or more accurately, for some adults only. The child has been involved in the life of a protagonist and wanted the protagonist to win. However, the winning has not happened without a struggle. There is a difference between the climax that says with sticky sweetness, "The world is good, since right always wins," and one that says, "The forces of evil are powerful, but courage and justice together can defeat them." A conflict brought to a climax makes the idea of the story clear through plot that has tension and resolution.

Denouement

Children who are following an exciting story may have trouble pinning down what for them is the climax. Agreeing on that, however, is not as important to the success of the story as agreeing that the story ends with a sense of completeness or **resolution.**

The **denouement** begins at the climax, at the point where we feel that the protagonist's fate is known. From here the action of the plot is also called the *falling action.* In the denouement of *Charlotte's Web*, Templeton and Wilbur, the two survivors of the original trio, reach a bargain about who eats first at Wilbur's trough. Wilbur returns the egg sac to the barn, and its presence sustains the feeling that Charlotte is still there. Finally, warmed and protected by Wilbur's breath, the eggs hatch. Joy, Aranea, and Nellie, three of Charlotte's tiny progeny, stay on in the barn to keep Wilbur company, and to learn from him the ways of barn life. The seasonal cycle continues; everything is resolved. There is no question left unanswered. We say there is a resolution.

When the reader is assured that all is well and will continue to be, we say that the denouement is closed, or that the plot has a *closed ending.* In this case, the tying of the loose ends is thoroughly optimistic and satisfactory, a good conclusion for a small child's story. There is no anxiety for reader or listener on the last page of *Charlotte's Web.* The sigh is not a breath of anxiety, but one of regret that so good a story is over.

In an *open ending,* an occasional thing in adult fiction, we are left to draw our own conclusions about final plot resolution. Among enduring examples of children's literature, there seem to be few with open endings, although stories do appear from time to time. The realistic stories of the seventies, particularly those problem realism stories for the older child, occasionally leave the end open. In *Guy Lenny* by Harry Mazer, for example, we are not certain whether Guy will choose to live with mother or with father, although we are left feeling that he is mature enough to make his own decision. At the end of *A Hero ain't nothin' but a Sandwich,* we are left with an urgent question: Will Benjie show up for the drug counseling session?

Although some adult readers are intrigued by such inconclusive mystery, others find such endings frustrating. Just as some adults find the open-ended story unsatisfactory, many more children are left dissatisfied and unsure by unsolved mystery. Depending upon the gravity of the conflict and the maturity of the readers, they may even be left frightened. Without the experience and perspective needed to supply their own endings, some children may turn away from the story with a disturbing sense of anxiety. If tension has been high and the possible outcome serious, the unresolved plot and the open ending seem far less suitable for a children's story.

Inevitability

By White's use of the device called foreshadowing, we are well prepared for Wilbur's salvation and Charlotte's death. Her life is complete, and her mission accomplished. She has saved her dearest friend and produced her egg sac to carry on another spider generation. There is no other way for the story to end. Although there may be a shadow of sadness, there is a more profound sense of the quality called *inevitability,* or "it had to be." "It was inevitable" is high praise for a writer's skill in bringing plot to conclusion.

Properly motivated action that grows out of character provides inevitability, just as Peter Rabbit's curiosity and greed bring about his inevitable squeezing into Mr. McGregor's garden, his flight, and his stomach-ache. At the other end of the literary spectrum, Beowulf, "mightiest yet mildest of men," is the organizer and leader of the band who sail to Hrothgar's country to liberate it from Grendel's scourge. Since Beowulf is pure valor, unsullied by any past defeat or any selfish motive, and since his motive is love for his fellow beings, Beowulf cannot lose his battle with personified evil. Despite the suspense of the epic story, we are sure that such goodness will conquer evil. The battle must be to the death, since too easy a victory demeans the godlike hero. The struggle is satisfying in its intensity, but the outcome is inevitable.

The plot that depends for resolution of conflict upon sudden and incredible changes in character fails because it lacks inevitability. In *Dream of the Blue Heron,* Mr. Wickham, the cruel disciplinarian, strangely and without foreshadowing becomes kind and sympathetic to Wabus, who will someday be a lawyer because he can count on the assistance of the unbelievably reformed Wickham. Since the resolution of the conflict depends upon unbelievable character change, the plot lacks inevitability.

TYPES OF PLOTS

The plots of *Charlotte's Web* and *A Wrinkle in Time,* with their central climaxes followed quickly by denouement, are called *progressive plots.* Apparently people have always liked suspense and climax because the progressive plot is common in traditional literature. In "The Shoemaker and the Elves," for example, we move directly into the action from a few short phrases—"once upon a time," and "the couple was very poor." The first short paragraph also includes the elves' first visit and the work they leave behind. By the end of the second paragraph, the shoemaker is rich and we are halfway through the story. The couple hides to watch; their grateful gift of clothes for the elves brings on the climax—the dance of the delighted elves who then disappear. In "The Wolf and the Kids" the climax comes three lines from the end; filled with stones, the wolf falls into the well and drowns. The Bremen Town Musicians raise a furor that frightens the robbers away; the musicians stay forever. When the Fisherman tells the fish that his greedy wife wishes to be God—they are returned to their vinegar jug. The teller of oral tales knows that once the climax comes, he may lose his audience; he must finish the story quickly and conclusively.

Some book-length stories for children have another type of plot, an *episodic plot* in which one incident or short episode is linked to another by common characters or by a unified theme. A diagram of this plot might look like this:

A clear contrast to the progressive plot of *Charlotte's Web*, which we have already discussed in some detail, is the episodic one of *The Wind in the Willows*. Like White, Kenneth Grahame uses personified animals as characters in his fantasy. In the twelve short chapters, each a separate story and each a part of the whole, Mole meets Rat, they picnic, and they meet Toad, who can think only of motor cars; Mole, lost in the Wild Wood, is found by Rat and they visit Mole's home. Toad "borrows" a car and is jailed, but he escapes and returns to Toad Hall.

The events of *The Wind in the Willows* are quiet in total effect, although many chapters have their own suspenseful conflict. Each chapter is an episode in a community of kindly animals whose lives are intertwined by loyalty and mutual concern. The suspense within each chapter is usually resolved within that chapter. Although there are twelve chapters, only the last two contribute to the conquest of Toad Hall.

Instead of a central conflict, what holds our interest are the relationships of the group of developed characters. Rat is consistently kind and reliable; Toad is consistently inconsistent, but Mole, as his self-confidence increases, changes from follower to leader. The community life of these diverse beings, living their leisurely and unselfish lives, is the discovery of *The Wind in the Willows*. In the unhurried progress through chapters that focus alternately on Rat and Mole, then on Toad, we are further warmed by discovering among other things that one loves one's home where one's belongings are, and that even the most contented find faraway places alluring.

Winnie-the-Pooh supplies another example of episodic plot, and its form is well suited to its young listeners. One episode follows another, each with its own high point and resolution, and with a natural stopping place at the end of chapter and episode. The episodic plot relies upon characters, theme, and tension within each chapter, rather than upon suspenseful progress to the climax, to keep readers reading and listeners listening. Books with episodic plots make excellent bedtime stories.

There are many other examples of episodic plot development. For example, *Pippi Longstocking*, Astrid Lindgren's nonsense story of the independent girl who does as she pleases, including rolling cookie dough on the floor, is one nonsensical episode after another. Robert McCloskey's *Homer Price* amuses children with the story of the runaway doughnut machine, or Miss Terwilliger's huge ball of string that she unwinds in County Fair competition. Each chapter is a story, and many of the same characters appear throughout—Uncle Ulysses and the Sheriff, for example. Other books, like Beverly Cleary's *Henry Huggins,* show a boy's mischief in a series of episodes.

Yearly, new stories in episodic form, both fantasy and realism, are written for children. However, without conflict building to a climax in a progressive plot, the writers of these stories with purely episodic plots rely upon other devices to carry the reader's interest. In one case the greater emphasis is upon characters; in others, upon humor or nonsense.

There is great possibility for variation and combination in plot structure. *Alice in Wonderland* combines progressive with episodic plot. The underground setting, Alice's growing and shrinking, and her increasing self-confidence provide unity and progress. We recall the many ingenuities—the pool of tears, the caucus race, the caterpillar's advice, the mad tea party, and the croquet game—without being sure of their order. However, the story concludes in a flurry of excitement and a whirl of angry cards as Alice sees the ineffectual adults at the trial and finally asserts herself. *Tom Sawyer,* too, combines elements of episodic structure with progressive plot and climactic focus. Although there are a strong conflict and a final climax, there are also many chapters that are merely episodes in the life of a small-town boy and that make little contribution to the central conflict.

EVALUATING PLOT IN CHILDREN'S LITERATURE

Most of what we have said about plot up to this point applies to plot in adult literature as well as in children's literature. For the remainder of the chapter we will discuss some of the special problems in stories for children.

We have mentioned the dangers of sensationalism in our earlier discussion of patterns of action. While adults may choose such stories, children may find sensationalism is more than they can bear. Sensational suspense, furthermore, places the focus upon tension rather than upon human beings and ideas. If the functions of literature are pleasure and understanding, the latter is slighted by sensationalism—as well as by sentimentality.

Coincidence

The concurrence of events apparently by mere chance is *coincidence*. In real life, we well know that coincidence does occur. In literature, however, where the truths of human nature and human existence are explored, reliance on coincidence to resolve conflict weakens plot. One example in which excellence is flawed by coincidence is the *The Incredible Journey*. Here we follow the travels of three pets across the Canadian wilderness of deep woods, rushing rivers, and lonely lakes. In their conflict with nature, three chance happenings that are not in any way foreshadowed leave us troubled, doubting the credibility of the larger plot. First, part of a handwritten note blows into the fire and leaves the housekeeper baffled. Since she therefore does not realize that the two dogs and the Siamese cat have struck out on their own, she does not search for them. Later, an old and crumbling beaver dam by a "twist of fate" gives way at just the right moment to sweep the frightened cat downstream. Still later, a boy, hunting for the first time with his own rifle, with one remarkably accurate shot saves the Siamese cat from a lynx. Fortunately, however, the story of the pets' struggle against the wilderness is so strong in many other ways, from characterization to style, that perhaps we may choose to overlook coincidence.

Such fictional strength is not always the case, however, since inadequate foreshadowing leads the reader to doubt the credibility of an event. The test of coincidence, therefore, is foreshadowing. We are prepared to accept the concurrence of events if the incident does not seem to be mere chance, but a previously threatened or foreseen possibility.

White might easily have fallen into the coincidence trap in *Charlotte's Web*. If, for example, the enormous and healthy Uncle, the obvious choice for first prize, had happened to take sick at the Fair, that would have been coincidence. However, had Wilbur won the blue ribbon by mere default, our pleasure in the outcome would then have been a mixed pleasure over a far less satisfying victory. Furthermore, if Charlotte had by incredible coincidence eventually lived as long as Wilbur, she would have defied the natural laws of a spider's life cycle. Charlotte may talk and write words in her web, but she is a spider leading a spider life. White, by using foreshadowing and by rejecting coincidence, has given *Charlotte's Web* an inevitable, satisfying conclusion.

Sentimentality

Nor should another negative element, called **sentimentality**, mar a well-constructed plot. We term **sentiment** a natural concern or emotion for another person. When, for instance, our parents are hurt in a painful accident, our natural sentiment, called love, causes an emotional response. We are hurt with those we love. However, when our sentiments are used, or played upon as they are in soap opera, we have what we call a tear-jerker situation, or sentimentality.

We have all at some time left a movie theater surreptitiously wiping our eyes, knowing the movie wasn't worth tears. At other times we have been unashamed of our tears, even perhaps proud. It is the legitimacy of our emotional reaction that makes us feel honest. When we are honestly moved by art, we may weep because we suffer with the character, taking his or her sorrow upon ourselves. But sometimes the writer may cause us to weep or to exult, and we know our reactions are false, because we are asked for an emotional response in excess of what the situation requires.

Sentimentality takes varied forms. Character may be sentimentally drawn. For instance, a saintly sweet woman who never raises her voice, who is patient, kind, loyal, true, keeps a full cookie jar and a spotless kitchen is no reality. She is a cardboard, two-dimensional figure, a highly sentimentalized picture of Mother. Sentimentality may also occur in the plot. Sydney Taylor's *All-of-a-Kind Family* pictures growing up poor in an Orthodox Jewish family. However, the writer not only creates a sentimental picture of Mother, but sees family life as a continually joyful chain of events, or perhaps nonevents. Five identically dressed little girls going happily to the library in a group, living frictionless lives in a large family, accepting and making the happy best of poverty, inviting the librarian to dinner and causing a loving marriage to result from her meeting with another guest— these sentimentalized pictures challenge our knowledge of the reality of family life. Because we rejoice, or are dubious of, Taylor's sentimentalized view of family life, we may, unfortunately, reject the far more important discoveries about the practice of Jewish orthodoxy.

A typical story and a great favorite among children of the late nineteenth century was a supposedly realistic horse story called *Black Beauty*, Anna Sewell's novel told in first person by Black Beauty himself. As we look at it now, the book strikes us with its heavy sentimentality. The pathos of Beauty's own life is comparable to that of "Poor Ginger," as one chapter is entitled. Ginger tells Black Beauty her story, and the short chapter concludes with Black Beauty's observations:

> A short time after this a cart with a dead horse in it passed our cab-stand. The head hung out of the cart-tail, the lifeless tongue was slowly dropping with blood; and the sunken eyes! but I can't speak of them, the sight was too dreadful. It was a chestnut horse with a long, thin neck. . . . I believe it was Ginger; I hoped it was, for then her troubles would be over. O! if men were more merciful they would shoot us before we came to such misery.

While none of us would argue that people have a right to be cruel to any animal, Sewell's sentimentality is apparent. The graphic description of a lolling, bloody tongue, the frequent exclamation points, and even the basic idea of a realistic story of a horse being told in first person by the horse—all are tear-jerkers. Because of the sentimentality, the reader may sob more soulfully over Ginger's death than over that of a human being—although there is little confusion in our minds as to which misused creature is more deserving of grief.[2]

Rarely do we have sensationalism in folktales, and rarely does the storyteller stop to rouse our tears by false sentiment. The wicked wolf whose stomach is full of rocks falls into the well and is drowned; we waste no sighs. The unkind girl whose punishment is to spout toads creeps into the corner and dies. The rapid pace of the folktale plot seems to prohibit pauses for tears. We appreciate the celebration of a marriage "the very next day," and we are not anguished over the fate of Rumpelstiltskin, who stamped his two feet so hard that he split in two and "that was an end of him." Instead of being sentimental, the tale-teller resorts to humor.

Charlotte's Web does not resort to sentimentality. Lingering sobs and whimpers from Charlotte at her own death would have destroyed credibility. Charlotte is a spider and knows it. Her spider-defined life prepares us, Wilbur and the readers, for her dignified and inevitable death. Or again, Wilbur's fainting might easily have become sentimental panic, but is instead humorous. Or Templeton might have broken down, become a reformed rat, and committed some unselfish or heroic act. Such an incredible change would have been sentimentality. Our every response to each situation in White's story is legitimately roused, never exaggerated nor superficial, and therefore unsentimental.

What is wrong with sentimentality? A good cry never hurt anyone. Perhaps. However, there are dangers inherent in a steady diet of forced emotion. We have all had our turns at sneering at the soap opera, but perhaps we have not really considered why we sneer. One after the other, one dramatic occurrence, one crisis, and one tragedy pushes another out of our memories. We are like pumps primed to spout tears, and then just as we have settled down, primed again.

The most destructive element in the overuse of sentiment is not boredom, but the fact that the young reader, faced with continual sentimentality, will not develop the sensitivity essential to recognize what is truly moving and what is merely a play on feelings. The use of judgment and the sense of proportion grow and mature when we see honest emotion, whether it be joy or sorrow. If, after all, we regard the death of a pet mouse with the same degree of emotional intensity as the death of a brother, we have no sense of emotional proportion.

By contrast to *Black Beauty*, notice in Katherine Paterson's story *Bridge to Terabithia* the wide range of emotions that children wrestle with. They follow Jess from shyness with other children to rivalry with his sister Brenda, from pleasure over the secret bridge to the hideaway island, to numbness and grief at his friend Leslie's drowning. Or chart the genuine sentiment that a small child, reading or being read to, experiences during the relationship with Charlotte and Wilbur. Here he or she comes to know loneliness, friendship, sacrifice, tact, patience, loyalty, and maternity—as well as death and continuity; the child meets such negative human traits as selfishness, avarice, and gluttony. Furthermore, among the more surprising discoveries is the way in which such significant human traits and experiences are explored in both books—not with bathos or sentimentality, but with seriousness or deft humor. The total impact of White's book embodies respect for animals, yes, but more importantly, respect for people, as Wilbur and Charlotte personify human beings.

The child fed only on such surface sentimentality as soap opera and

Walt Disney—with their sterile and stereotyped pictures of human beings and their distorted sensationalism with simplistic solutions—this child risks developing emotional shallowness.[3] The child nourished through real literature in the breadth and depth and range of true emotion grows in understanding of human nature.

Lack of Conflict

Many of today's mass-produced storybooks, like those found on racks in supermarkets and drugstores, lack conflict. Events follow one another in chronological narrative. Without any struggle, the story lacks suspense, any hint of alternative outcomes, a sense that it had to happen, and, therefore, satisfaction. All that the reader can say at the conclusion of such a story is "So what does that prove?" Conflict, the tension that keeps a story interesting, has never appeared.

Inadequately developed conflict, like flat characterization, leaves us unconcerned about the outcome of a story. Conflict holds our attention if it presents some semblance of a fair fight, and if the question of outcome is open. In poor science fiction, the protagonist combats an irresistible natural force, or in person-against-person conflict, the ingenuity of the two intellects without emotions becomes a dry, academic struggle. When pure intellect does battle with itself in person-against-self conflict, the struggle is merely a problem with a rational answer. The reader who is uninvolved in either characters or conflict becomes apathetic; "I cannot conceive of it; I therefore cannot care."

Take once again, however, the example of *A Wrinkle in Time*, where conflict is person-against-person. Meg battles against a disembodied brain that controls the citizens of Camazotz, whose people are programmed to be identical. Meg and Calvin struggle against IT's magnetic persuasion, but Charles Wallace, whose allegiance to mind is stronger than it is to spirit, arrogantly gives in. Pure mind, however, cannot conquer stubborn Meg, whose believable flaws make her human enough for us to care about her. When Meg sees that her strength lies in her power to love, she overcomes IT and frees Charles Wallace. These human responses of will, dependence, and love oppose the antagonist IT. We are concerned about the outcome, yearning to help Meg in a fantastic plot based upon the possible reality of opposing forces in conflict.

SUMMARY

Character study alone rarely carries the child's interest, but character becomes inextricably woven into plot by the very natures, protagonist as well as antagonist, in the conflict. Order is easier for the child to follow if it is within his or her experience; chronological order is therefore more frequent, while flashback is used more rarely. In a progressive plot, suspense pulls the reader through the rising action to the central climax, where conflict is resolved in a manner foreshadowed and thus inevitable; the last questions are usually answered in a denouement with its closed ending.

By contrast, each chapter in an episodic plot has its own small tensions and is joined to the others by theme and character. Finally, a well-plotted story relies on neither sentimentality nor coincidence for action and resolution.

There is no right plot structure in a story for children. There are only variations of the two principal forms. The understanding of the child—reader or listener—may determine the length or structure of the story, whether that story be a single progressively arranged unit or an episode in a longer work. However, what does matter is that the piece of literature sustains interest and gives pleasure as it is read.

In considering the plot development, we are most aware that without sufficient conflict or tension, accompanied by suspense, foreshadowing, and inevitability, a story is just plain dull. Few adults want to read a dull story, and certainly no children will.

READING AND EVALUATING

1. **Animal realism**   What is the nature of the conflict in *The Incredible Journey*? Is the conflict well-defined? How is the antagonist made believable? Do you agree that the plot is marred by coincidence? Explain. Is the plot sufficiently strong in other ways to make the coincidence unimportant? Are there coincidental actions in the story other than those mentioned? Do they mar the story? How does the fact that the coincidence involves minor characters influence acceptance of them?

2. **Fantasy**   Read a time fantasy by Eleanor Cameron, Joan Aiken, Natalie Babbitt, Alison Uttley, or another writer, or a science fiction novel by Andre Norton, H. M. Hoover, or William Sleator. What is the conflict between the protagonist and the antagonist? Is there a chance of victory for the protagonist? What is the outcome of the conflict? Explain your reaction to the outcome.

3. **Other countries**   What is the conflict in *The House of Sixty Fathers* by Meindert DeJong? How does the writer manage to show the antagonist without turning the reader against a particular people? Is there coincidence? How does DeJong avoid sentimentality?

4. **Science fiction**   Read Ben Bova's *Flight of Exiles* or a science fiction novel by Eleanor Cameron or another writer. Does the book show the kinds of problems in plotting mentioned in this chapter? How are you as reader concerned about the outcome? What carries your interest in each story?

5. **Realism**   From your reading of literature for children, what examples of flashback do you recall? Of open-ended conflicts? Do the stories have sound character development and plotting? What levels of maturity do the examples seem to be written for?

NOTES

1 For a discussion of time in time fantasy, a subject in itself, see Eleanor Cameron, "The Green and Burning Tree," in *The Green and Burning Tree*. Boston: Atlantic Monthly Press, 1969, pp. 71–134.

2 Readers take opposite views on *Black Beauty*. Perhaps it is not the personification in a realistic story, but the injustice of his treatment and the justice of his feelings, that prompts their responses.

3. For a discussion of Walt Disney's work, see Frances Clarke Sayers, "Walt Disney Accused," in *Children & Literature: Views and Reviews*, Virginia Haviland, ed. Glenview, Illinois: Scott, Foresman, 1973, pp. 116–25.

RECOMMENDED BOOKS CITED IN THIS CHAPTER

ALEXANDER, LLOYD. *The High King.* New York: Holt, 1968.

ARMSTRONG, WILLIAM H. *Sounder.* New York: Harper, 1969.

BAUER, MARION DANE. *On My Honor.* Boston: Houghton Mifflin, 1986.

BURNFORD, SHEILA. *The Incredible Journey.* Boston: Little, Brown, 1961.

CARROLL, LEWIS. *Alice's Adventures in Wonderland.* New York: Dutton, 1954 (first published, 1865).

CHILDRESS, ALICE. *A Hero ain't nothin' but a Sandwich.* New York: Coward, 1973.

CHRISTIAN, MARY BLOUNT. *Sebastian (Super Sleuth) and the Bone to Pick Mystery.* New York: Macmillan, 1983.

CLEARY, BEVERLY. *Henry Huggins.* New York: Morrow, 1950.

CLEAVER, VERA and BILL. *Where the Lilies Bloom.* Philadelphia: Lippincott, 1969.

COLLIER, JAMES LINCOLN and CHRISTOPHER. *My Brother Sam is Dead.* New York: Four Winds, 1974.

DEJONG, MEINDERT. *The House of Sixty Fathers.* New York: Harper, 1956.

GEORGE, JEAN. *Julie of the Wolves.* New York: Harper, 1972.

GRAHAME, KENNETH. *The Wind in the Willows.* New York: Scribner's, 1953 (first published, 1908).

HAMILTON, VIRGINIA. *Time Ago Lost.* New York: Macmillan, 1973.

————. *The Time Ago Tales of Jahdu.* New York: Macmillan, 1969.

HOOVER, H. M. *The Shepherd Moon.* New York: Viking, 1984.

KONIGSBURG, E. L. *Jennifer, Hecate, Macbeth, William McKinley, and Me, Elizabeth.* New York: Atheneum, 1967.

LE GUIN, URSULA K. *A Wizard of Earthsea.* Berkeley: Parnassus, 1968.

L'ENGLE, MADELEINE. *A Wrinkle in Time.* New York: Farrar, 1962.

LINDGREN, ASTRID. *Pippi Longstocking.* New York: Viking, 1950.

MATHIS, SHARON BELL. *The Hundred Penny Box.* New York: Viking, 1975.

MAZER, HARRY. *Guy Lenny.* New York: Dell, 1973.

MCCLOSKEY, ROBERT. *Homer Price.* New York: Viking, 1943.

MCINERNEY, JUDITH WHITELOCK. *Judge Benjamin: Superdog.* New York: Holiday House, 1982.

MILNE, A. A. *Winnie-the-Pooh.* New York: Dutton, 1926.

NORTON, MARY. *The Borrowers.* New York: Harcourt, 1965.

O'DELL, SCOTT. *Island of the Blue Dolphins.* Boston: Houghton, 1960.

PATERSON, KATHERINE. *Bridge to Terabithia.* New York: Crowell, 1977.

————. *Jacob Have I Loved.* New York: Harper & Row, 1980.

PAULSEN, GARY. *Hatchet.* New York: Bradbury, 1987.

RADIN, RUTH YAFFE. *Tac's Island.* New York: Macmillan, 1986.

SERRAILLIER, IAN. *Beowulf the Warrior.* New York: Walck, 1961.

SHARMAT, MARJORIE WEINMAN. *Nate the Great and the Fishy Prize.* New York: Coward McCann, 1985.

SPEARE, ELIZABETH. *The Witch of Blackbird Pond.* Boston: Houghton, 1958.

TAYLOR, MILDRED. *Roll of Thunder, Hear My Cry.* New York: Dial, 1976.

TRUSS, JAN. *Jasmin.* New York: Atheneum, 1982.

TWAIN, MARK. *The Adventures of Tom Sawyer*. New York: Macmillan, 1962 (first published, 1876).

VOIGT, CYNTHIA. *A Solitary Blue*. New York: Atheneum, 1983.

———. *Dicey's Song*. New York: Random House, 1982.

WALSH, JILL PATON. *Toolmaker*. New York: Seabury, 1973.

WHITE, E. B. *Charlotte's Web*. New York: Harper, 1952.

WILDER, LAURA INGALLS. *Little House in the Big Woods*. New York: Harper, 1953 (first published, 1932).

Illustration from *The Borrowers,* copyright 1953 by Mary Norton and renewed
1981 by Mary Norton, Joe Krush, and Beth Krush, reprinted by permission of
Harcourt Brace Jovanovich, Inc.

Theme

We each have at least one friend who tells a story by linking one anecdote to another, using slender threads of association as continuity: "And later that day . . ." or "And then we . . ." We have heard a more artful storyteller whose stories are involved and who keeps us in suspense: "You'll never believe what she said then," or "And what should happen next . . .!" The first of these narrators can bore us quickly; the second can hold our interest longer. However, the storyteller we especially value is someone whose stories awaken us to awareness of new meaning—of the inconsistency of people, or the mixed joys of family living, or the pain of social exclusion, for example. This storyteller is aware of meaning and has reached for idea, or theme.

In storytelling "What happened next?" is a question about chronology and narrative order. "Why did it happen?" is a question about conflict and plot. But when we ask, "What does it all mean?" we begin to discover theme.

THEME OR UNIFYING TRUTH

Theme in literature is the idea that holds the story together, such as a comment about society, human nature, or the human condition. It is the main idea or central meaning of a piece of writing.

Ask a woman about the plot of *Little Women,* the story she loved as a child, and she looks baffled and perhaps chagrined that she cannot remember it. Setting, too, has faded from memory to become merely "in the past." Character, however, is still with her, because restless Jo, who has difficulty fitting into traditional female roles, seems to be Everywoman—or at least Manywomen. And chances are the adult's memory of the idea or theme of the novel is still strong; she can confidently say, "It's about a loving family of varied but accepting people." The characters of Louisa May

Alcott's story convince us of one of its themes—the love of family members for each other is real and enduring. Theme comes alive and becomes memorable as the characters act out the plot.

Our definition of literature, you will recall, is "a significant truth expressed in appropriate elements and memorable language." The "significant truth" is an element that is essential to turn a simple narrative into literature. This truth goes beyond the story and comments on human beings. This discovery holds the story together so that long after details of plot are forgotten, the theme remains.

This significant truth unifies and illuminates a story, giving the reader pleasure. The reader gains one pleasure from the discovery of the simplest of truths, and another from the discovery that truth is not simple.[1] Theme provides this discovery, this understanding, this pleasure in recognizing "Yes, that's the way it is!"

TYPES OF THEMES

Explicit Theme

Sometimes the writer states theme openly and clearly—an ***explicit theme.*** Once again we turn to *Charlotte's Web* for examples. The devotion between Charlotte and Wilbur suggests many ideas that make the reader say, "It's true"; their relationship reveals and defines friendship and suggests other themes.

Charlotte has encouraged, protected, and mothered Wilbur, bargained and sacrificed for him, and Wilbur, the grateful receiver, realizes that "Friendship is one of the most satisfying things in the world." And Charlotte says later, "By helping you perhaps I was trying to lift my life a little. Anyone's life can stand a little of that." Because these quoted sentences are exact statements from the text, they are called explicit themes. Consider this statement from Zilpha K. Snyder's *The Witches of Worm:* "We all invite our own devils, and we must exorcise our own." It, too, is an explicit theme, as is "Love is just the beginning" in Cynthia Voigt's *A Solitary Blue*. The explicit theme of *A Fine White Dust* is stated in its closing pages. Pete has worked through his disillusionment with The Man, the revival preacher who had left him, but remains forgiving. "It's a world where good guys ... are happy atheists, and nice folks ... don't care much about church and spiritual people like me wander around the earth wishing it was heaven." Explicit theme occurs in *There's No Such Thing as a Channukah Bush, Sandy Goldstein* by Susan Sussman, as the wise grandfather helps Robin cope with Christmas without a Christmas tree. We can share the holidays of other faiths without being disloyal to our own, Robin discovers. Such explicit themes are common in children's literature because the writer may wish to be sure the reader finds the unifying truth.

Implicit Theme

Underlying *Charlotte's Web* are certain implied or ***implicit themes,*** as important and almost as apparent as explicit themes. If two such different characters as a runt pig and a carnivorous spider can find friendship, others can; even a self-centered rat can be a friend of sorts. White thereby implies that friendship can be found in unexpected places.

Charlotte's selflessness—working late at night to finish a new word, expending her last energies for her friend—is evidence that friendship is giving oneself. Wilbur's protection of Charlotte's egg sac, his sacrifice of first turn at the slops, and his devotion to Charlotte's babies—giving without any need to stay even or to pay back—leads us to another theme: True friendship is naturally reciprocal. As the two become fond of each other, still another theme emerges: One's best friend can do no wrong. In fact, a best friend is sensational! Both Charlotte and Wilbur believe in these ideas; their experiences verify them. These themes are all developed through the characters, their action, and their thoughts as we see them throughout the story's conflict.

Throughout realistic *Jacob Have I Loved* runs the implicit theme that one is not deprived of love but finds what one is open for. Not only does Wheeze feel that Caroline has beaten her out of the family's love and the community's favor, but she has also taken from her what she was not even sure she wanted—Call's love. Grandmother, too, in her aged fantasies, feels that her daughter-in-law has stolen her son from her, and that in her youth another had stolen from her the Captain's love. And yet, no one steals love from anyone. No one is favored. H. M. Hoover's fantasy *The Shepherd Moon* is the story of a cold and privileged society attended by vast numbers of slaves. One implicit theme is that freedom is so important that it is worth even the threat of annihilation.

When we think of theme as "a moral" or "a lesson," or even as "a message," we are turned away by the idea that we must learn how or how not to behave. But a good story is not meant to instruct us. Its purpose is to entertain us by its action and characters; at the same time, it gives us insight into people and how they think and feel, and enlarges our understanding. However, when we think of theme as the unifying idea that holds the other elements of a good story together, we are pleased to find that we have not only been entertained, but have made a discovery of some kind.

Dicey's Song by Cynthia Voigt has a variety of themes that control the story without being preachy. As Dicey says, Gram's request that she reach out, followed by another that she let go, seems contradictory. The four children living with a newly found grandmother are proud and secretive, hiding from classmates the fact of their mother's mental illness and their welfare-maintained lives. Letting go—of Momma and of their pride—recognizing that others, too, have difficult times, that some things just have to happen and no amount of trying to prevent them will help, and finally that home has no geographical location but is where one is comfortably loved—these are ideas that permeate the story.

Themes, as we will note later, occur even in picture books. It follows, then, that easy-to-read stories may also have themes. *Harry's Mom* by Barbara Ann Porte manages, despite the narrative simplicity, to convey an important idea. Harry learns that "orphan" means someone who has lost father or mother. He tells his father, who lovingly sends him to Aunt Rose and his own dog Girl; there he hears stories about his mother. Then he talks with his grandparents about her. Memories can help to complete a family. *Blackberries in the Dark* by Mavis Jukes is a short story about a boy's visit to his grandmother's ranch; both are grieving the loss of grandfather, and together they relive his favorite activities, especially trout fishing, to their mutual solace; sharing grief helps.

It may seem unnecessary or even unwise to state theme in sentence form. Why not say, "The theme of *Charlotte's Web* is friendship"? Notice what happens if we do state the theme this simply. *Friendship* is too broad a term: "Friendship is fraudulent," or "Friendship is a useless luxury," or "Friendship is all giving and no receiving." Any of these statements concerns friendship and might reasonably be explored and proven in literature, but none is the truth of E. B. White's story. When we force ourselves to make a specific statement based upon the facts of the story, we define the theme more carefully.

Multiple and Secondary Themes

Each of us brings to a story a personal past, a present, and plans for the future. These elements shape our responses to the story. It seems absurd then to expect that diverse human beings must agree upon exactly the same ideas as being the most important, and must take from the story exactly the same themes, since the story speaks to us out of our own individual and varying experiences. It speaks a universal truth to us, but our own universal truth.

Although complexity and variety in themes may be one of the strongest proofs of the work's excellence, most literature for children seems to center upon a ***primary theme***. When a story contains a variety of themes, they are often linked.

Consistent with high fantasy's focus upon good-evil conflict, *A Wizard of Earthsea* explores the greatest of all struggles: that within one's self. Ged, in his flight from the shadow, heeds the advice of his mentor: "You must choose. You must seek what seeks you. You must hunt the hunter." When, after sailing for days, Ged confronts the thing that has sloughed off all human form, and recognizes it as the evil within himself, he is strong enough to win the battle. Internal conflict has illuminated theme. Other less personal themes abound. "Need alone is not enough to set power free: there must be knowledge." "To hear, one must be silent." "Danger must surround power." "As a man's real power grows and his knowledge widens . . . he chooses nothing, but does only and wholly what he must do." "The wise man is one who never sets himself apart from other living things." The novel is rich in thematic ideas.

If a story has multiple themes, some seem less important than the primary one. These we call *secondary themes.*

In *Charlotte's Web,* almost as important as the theme about the nature of friendship is a secondary one about death. It is the possibility of Wilbur's death that disturbs us; we would feel different if he were an old boar who had lived long and well. We recognize, just the same, that "Death is inevitable and not to be feared." Charlotte, knowing her life cycle, foresees her own death, but neither dreads it nor asks for pity. Others accept death too. Seasons die when they have run their terms. Maple trees, crickets, lilacs, baby spiders, and the harvest Fair all celebrate the inevitable cycle of birth, life, and death. There is no grief, only acceptance.

A wealth of minor themes also emerges in *Charlotte's Web:* "People are gullible"; "People don't give credit where credit is due"; "The meek may inherit the earth"; "Youth and innocence have unique value." Each character accepts and maintains the simplicity of his or her own particular style of living, so "Be what you are." As for nature, "There are beauty and wonder in all things, even the simplest," "Life in nature is constant and continuous," and finally, "Nature is a miracle," from the silver forest of asparagus to the waterproof egg sac.

In one story, value lies in the explicit yet nondidactic statement of theme. In another, the fact that the theme is implied and must be stated by the reader for himself or herself is value of another kind. The only general rule that can be made is that a theme should be there. On first reading a good story, we usually see one or a few thematic ideas, both explicit and implicit. We see more perhaps on second reading. However, the wealth in a book for children often lies in the continuous discoveries about theme.

Does the child see these ideas? If we ask the child, "What is the theme?" we can scarcely expect replies like those we have mentioned.

The story of Salty told by Ouida Sebestyen in *Far from Home* subtly explores a theme about love, one that children may know but never express. Salty, who has never been acknowledged by his father, goes with his great-grandmother Mam to live with the Buckleys, the kind former employers of his dead mother. There an odd assortment of irresponsible Hardy, pregnant Rose Ann, and homeless Jo reveal that people must live their lives in their own ways. Like Buckley, who cannot reveal himself without hurting his wife, some must go on loving on faith: people love because they want to, not because they have to, nor because love has been earned.

Children differ, and the variety of their capacities for discovery as well as for phrasing that discovery is almost infinite. The smaller the child, the less likelihood of a coherent statement. We realize, however, that although a small child cannot define "home" or "mother," the youngest knows what each concept is. Security and love, comfort and constancy, warmth and protection are abstractions they know, but abstractions beyond articulation. For children, knowing and saying need not be—and rarely are—the same.

EVALUATING THEME IN CHILDREN'S LITERATURE

Traditional Literature

Folktales have similar themes even though they originate in different cultures. Their presence in traditional literature passed on from one generation to another seems to be evidence that people create and respond to similar ideas about life and human nature. By noting just a few of these themes, we become aware that a simple, optimistic core of truth like "good can conquer evil" is explored in a great many of the tales. Some leave the theme as simple as that, but others explore ideas a bit more complex, clarifying the kind of good or the kind of evil. "The Goosegirl," a German tale, explicitly identifies the conquered evil as deception; the servant girl who threatens and impersonates the princess is punished. "Snow White," another German tale, defines the defeated evil more clearly as jealousy; the queen-witch tries ceaselessly to kill the one more beautiful than she. "Drakestail," from the French, identifies the particular good as humility; the modest hero calls upon the Fox, the Ladder, and the River to save him from a tyrant king.

Other folktales, like the Norwegian "The Three Billy-Goats Gruff," prove that keeping your wits about you can save you from danger. In the German tale "The Twelve Dancing Princesses," the soldier outwits the princesses and wins one for his bride. The Scandinavian "Boots and His Brothers" shows that if you have the wit to see its potential, curiosity can pay off. Both the Russian "The Little Humpbacked Horse" and the Norse "The Princess on the Glass Hill" praise the capacity of cleverness to bring success. Both "The Bremen-Town Musicians" from Germany and "The Ram and the Pig Who Went into the Woods" from Scandinavia offer proof that each creature can use its gifts to contribute to common success. Tales told over and over, tales told in one land or another, tales complex in structure for older readers or simple in outline for younger readers, most have themes that state a universal truth.

Like the conflicts in folk literature that so obviously set protagonist against antagonist, the themes are straightforward and easily seen. Although themes are often implicit, the conflict and the characters make them so evident that explicit statements are unnecessary. Good can conquer evil, hard work can bring success, intelligence is more valuable than physical strength, kindness brings rewards—these are basic issues that the vigorous action of the folktale makes clear. The prominence of theme in traditional stories seems to verify the human wish to know not only what happened, and how it happened, but also why it happened and what it means. According to Wayne Booth, one of the strongest of human interests is the "desire for causal completion." "Not only do we believe that certain causes do in life produce certain effects; in literature we believe that they should." This interest is distinct from the "pleasure of learning, of satisfaction of intellectual curiosity."[2]

But the themes of literature are not all optimistic. Human beings are not totally good nor completely successful; good does not always conquer evil. Hans Christian Andersen, although he uses the traditional forms of folktales, makes no effort either to be constantly optimistic or to preach about what people ought to be. He is too busy showing what people are. Many of his stories of humble people, animals, and inanimate objects demonstrate one of his most personal and optimistic themes, that of the Ugly Duckling: "Humble beginnings and painful trials can end in happiness." But Andersen's themes also frequently remind us that people are foolish; they value the artificial and the trivial more than the real, as "The Swineherd," "The Nightingale," and "The Princess and the Pea" tell us. People will do anything for vanity, as we see in "The Emperor's New Clothes." Whether we like it or not, the rogue sometimes wins the prize, as he does in "The Tinder Box." Andersen honestly admits that death is sometimes sudden and may leave children bereft; he explores serious themes and develops them into individualized and realistic comments on humankind. His stories prove that literature for children as well as for adults can make sad or even negative comments and still give both pleasure and discovery.

Didacticism

We often wish to help children by telling them what they ought or ought not to do. We give them little mottoes and short, preachy verses to hang on their bedroom walls. From our own past experience we tell them stories which really are instruction disguised as reminiscence. The result may be the child's comment, "I'm sick of hearing how my dad *loved* to walk to school every day. And according to him, it was uphill both ways." No one is fooled.

Or we admire the welcome hyacinths in the springtime flower bed, but instead of comparing their varied colors, smelling their fragrance, touching curled, waxy petals, we turn our admiration into a botany lesson on stamen, pistil, and corolla. The science lesson has its place, of course, but not every flower bed must stimulate it. A growing awareness of startling beauty and perfection in nature may sometimes be stifled by a lesson from "Botany 101."

Didacticism or instruction is the function of textbooks. Some literature gives a great deal of information without letting it take over from a suspenseful and exciting plot, or from well-developed characters. Other narratives are so filled with teaching details about a historical period, a geographical area, a social inequity, or a physical disability that conflict, character, and theme are lost in "what the reader ought to know." If the information displaces the understanding, then didacticism has won out. Literature, on the other hand, does not teach; it helps us understand.

Nor does literature preach. "Eat it; it's good for you," never persuaded anyone. Adults who choose stories for children that force morals upon them think that a story is good only if it contains obvious lessons. However, knowing our own adult dislike for "do this, but don't do that," we can scarcely expect children to enjoy such preaching, and we may be preventing the child from making discoveries personally. We may be impeding growth rather than fostering it. Furthermore, sugar-coating a moral by surrounding it with a shallow story deficient in plot, character portrayal, and style does injustice to children. They come to a story excited by the promise of pleasure only to discover they have been tricked into a sermon. The preached-at child may come to reject all reading and thus to close off the vast discoveries about human beings and society available in literature.

The obvious purpose of some narratives, like *I Want to Be a Homemaker*, shows little imagination on the part of the writer and awakens little response from the reader; it may even stimulate resistance.[3] Because everything in this narrative is commonplace, the narrative itself is commonplace. We have a sexist view of what a homemaker does: she bakes and sews and tends the baby. Why? Because that is her job. But there is no word of what a mother *is*. A real mother loves her children and finds satisfaction in providing for them—like the mothers of Peter Rabbit and the Moffats, or the mothers of the troubled children in *Sounder* or *Roll of Thunder, Hear My Cry*. In a story exploring motivation in a real mother we might come to see the dimensions of such love.

A selfish, tit-for-tat approach to friendship that says, "Be nice to your friends and they will be nice to you," or "Make everyday occurrences into fun," would be preachy. Throughout a story, understanding of friendship may grow and ordinary experience may be joyful, but the stories need not be reduced to neat little mottoes suitable for framing.

Although the setting of science fiction is commonly future time and alternative worlds, it seems to have a "missionary" bent; often it urges upon readers a new set of morals and ethics, of religious views, of thinking patterns, a new way of living life, in fact. It has been called "the last refuge of the morality tale." In the changes over the years, we see a movement from exploration to colonization of the solar system. In order to colonize successfully, however, human beings must learn to conquer war, pollution, and overpopulation, and to conserve natural resources. If our children are to inherit a world worth anything, we must be careful conservators. To accomplish these goals, human beings must learn to control themselves. And to achieve such overwhelmingly difficult transformation, writers often take their characters to new and alien worlds. Moving from concern for survival of humankind to a sense of futility about changing human behavior, writers next create successors to human beings, new species that are less corrupt. Given missionary concerns, science fiction writers may be dedicated to proving that prejudice, and sentimental or romantic views of reality make no sense; the universe is indifferent and has concern for neither human life nor death. It is this indifference that seems to distance many readers from the genre. Some advocates of distance and objectivity regret the recent movement away from the common sense of logical outcome toward regarding human emotions as more "real."[4] Didacticism in science fiction seems, if not inevitable, at least difficult to avoid.

Nonsense

Such nonsense-fantasy stories as Kipling's *Just So Stories,* or *Pippi Longstocking,* and even *Alice in Wonderland* seem to lack theme, but each has as its core the idea of wonder and delight at the order and disorder of life. We marvel as the *Just So Stories* tell why whales have tiny throats and leopards have spots; *Winnie-the-Pooh* seems to say that people do strange and exciting things—and with such solemnity. Although adults find satire and social comment in *Alice,* Carroll in his opening poem speaks of:

> The dream-child moving through a land
> Of wonders wild and new . . .
> And half believe it true.

Nonsense as a whole seems to say, "The world and all its inhabitants—thank heaven—are illogical and inconsistent." Nonsense, in its own way, may develop a theme. If it doesn't, it finally palls.

Mature Themes in Children's Stories

Stories like those from Hans Christian Andersen may introduce children to ideas far more mature than we would expect to grasp, ideas we find difficult to explain in other ways. Fear, for example, is very much a part of childhood. However, what one is afraid *of* is often hard to pin down. Child psychologist Bruno Bettelheim writes of the capacity of folk and fairy tales to help the child "externalize" the fears that go on in the child's mind. Folktales confront and thus legitimate the universal fears like that of the death of a parent in "Hansel and Gretel," the attractiveness of evil in "Snow White and the Seven Dwarfs," and the fear of going out into the world in "Dick Whittington and His Cat." Stories like *The Borrowers* can carry the child through a variety of fears that may haunt the reader in real life and yet are rarely clarified. We fear the unknown: Homily fears what will happen to Pod on his cupborrowing expedition. Both parents keep Arrietty at home lest she be seen by a human being. They fear the fate of Uncle Hendreary, and what the Boy will do; they fear Mrs. Driver, her friend Mr. Crampfurl, and the exterminators. Most of all, Homily fears moving, emigration to the unknown world beyond the floorboards. Moreover, there is in *The Borrowers* another idea that adults find easy to understand but hard to put into words for children: Materialism is a destructive force. Homily admits, "My mother's family never had nothing but a little bone thimble which they shared around. But it's once you've *had* a tea cup . . ." Homily nags Pod for new blotting paper carpet, and sends him off for things to store away. Even when she is screaming with fright at the Boy's appearance, she wants more possessions. Homily's materialism sends Pod to his "club" upstairs, and brings on the exterminators. Materialism has disrupted the family and brought it to disaster—a big discovery for readers too young to know the word "materialism."

Such adult themes as the reasons for divorce can also be handled with sympathy by the skillful writer, as Beverly Cleary does in *Dear Mr. Henshaw*. Love alone cannot hold a marriage together; two adults also need to be able to rely on each other.

In recent years, situations and themes in stories for older readers have been changing. With society today more open in its discussion of the many problems of growing up, recent novels have confronted many subjects that were once taboo. Although there are boy-meets-girl romances, novels now explore the growth of sexuality and its effects. Stories for older children deal with impotence, premarital sex, pregnancy, forced marriage, and abortion. What has been called the perfect-parent syndrome has been broken. Books for young people now show parents as imperfect and human—unreliable, perhaps, or alcoholic, or simply shallow. Other stories deal with such problems as death, divorce, drugs, and disease. These subjects attract readers partly because of their taboo status, but also because these matters do concern today's youth.

Often these stories seem to have been written for the vast market that the pulp magazines once appealed to; often the quality of the writing seems comparable. Sometimes the young reader is carried along by sentimentality and coincidence; writing is drab in style and shallow in characterization; themes are didactic and oversimplified. On the other hand, some writers are dealing with the issues of today with sensitivity and skill, writing about the problems that confront the young in ways that create suspenseful stories and make the reader care about the protagonist's problem. Style and characterization show skill and perception, while the themes show the universal truths that arise from the conflicts.

Take, for example, the following stories about young people, each with a problem. First there is *Deenie* by Judy Blume. Deenie has scoliosis and wears a back brace. While we do feel sorry for Deenie, she is so close to being a stereotyped adolescent—interested only in boys and beauty—that we soon find her uninteresting. One theme of the book, that even girls with back braces can find friends, seems didactic and unconvincing because we have little interest in or understanding of the flat protagonist.

By contrast, look at Fran Ellen in *The Bears' House* by Marilyn Sachs. In her imagination Fran Ellen lives a completely happy life that becomes real to her whenever she sits at the back of the schoolroom to stare into the tiny house of The Three Bears. Here in her daydreams Fran Ellen is accepted and loved; she eats turkey and lemon pie and can have friends over whenever she wants to. In real life, Fran Ellen runs home at noon, and even at recess, to care for baby sister Flora who "loves her best." Meanwhile, her older sister is preoccupied with herself, and her alcoholic mother is too depressed to do anything. Since Fran Ellen, who tells her own story, is so believable in her feelings and in her way of expressing them, we care about her. We believe the theme: "Everyone yearns for a stable and loving home."

To cite another example, notice how the portrayal of Julius in *Luke Was There* by Eleanor Clymer convinces us of the truth of the theme. Julius, who has been abandoned, comes to depend upon his social worker Luke. When Julius finds a small child who depends upon him, he makes a discovery that we are prepared to accept: "Others depend upon us." In Katherine Paterson's *The Great Gilly Hopkins,* the protagonist is a resentful girl who enjoys keeping people around her stirred up and must move from one foster home to another. When she begins to respect Trotter, her new foster mother who will not be manipulated, and when she begins to appreciate the qualities of the blind man next door as well as to take pride in teaching W. E., the other foster child, Gilly has a new source of pleasure. The new Gilly is able to give up her fantasies about her real mother and to admit her disappointments. She then settles down to become her grandmother Nonie's child, knowing that there is satisfaction in making tough decisions and sticking with them.

Current stories that deal with realistic problems are a significant trend. They can show us real characters; they can explore the problems of today's youth. However, what is true for other literature seems to be true here, as well: When we believe in the character, we believe in the experience, and are then prepared to accept the theme. When, on the other hand, theme seems to have been the first motive for writing—"Now I'll write a story about the evils of smoking pot"—the stories may become didactic, as does *The Grass Pipe.* If we look beneath the surface of many recent realistic stories for young people, we find didacticism and sentimentality; such stories are likely to be a fad. The well-written stories, however, will convince us of the truth of the theme and thus contribute to the readers' growth and discovery. Mature themes can be explored in children's literature; they contribute to understanding when they meet the requirements of excellence.

SUMMARY

Theme, stated explicitly or implicitly, is essential to a children's story if it is to merit the name of literature. A narrative with action and people but without theme is a story without meaning that leaves the reader wondering at the close, "So what?" A piece of writing, a collection of words with plot, character, setting, style, and meaning (without preachment) is literature for children just as it is for adults. The theme we take to become part of ourselves is the one that enlarges our understanding and the one we discover for ourselves—not the one underlined and delivered didactically by the author.

Illustration by Louis Glanzman from *The Bears' House* by Marilyn Sachs. Copyright © 1971 by Marilyn Sachs. Used by permission of Doubleday, a division of Bantam, Doubleday, Dell Publishing Group, Inc.

READING AND EVALUATING

1. **Historical fiction**   Read a historical fiction book by Laura Ingalls Wilder, Rosemary Sutcliff, or another writer, and state the theme. Is it explicit? Implicit? Does the historical information seem more important to the writer than understanding of human beings? Are the historical details seen as important to our understanding of the story, or are they the purpose of the story? Is the theme relevant to today? To you? To today's society?

2. **Other countries**   Read a story about children from other lands by Meindert DeJong, Katherine Paterson, or another writer. What is the theme? How is it made known? Given the country and its customs, are the characters believable enough to make you believe in the theme?

3. **Problem realism**   Read a book written within the last 15 years that has a protagonist or central character with a physical, emotional, or social adjustment problem. Does the story convince you of its truth? Does the information seem more important than the characters and the theme they make you understand?

4. **Regional realism**   Read a regional realism book by William O. Steele, Joseph Krumgold, Esther Wier, Clyde Bulla, or another writer, and state the theme. Is the theme a truth only for these people in this part of the country, or is it a truth for all people? Explain your answer.

5. **Social Issues realism**   Read a story about a religious or ethnic minority by Virginia Hamilton, Natalie Carlson, or another writer. Is the theme about all human beings or does it prove that this group is singular and strange? Does the theme make this group more understandable to you? Compare *Bright April* (Marguerite DeAngeli) and *Jennifer, Hecate, Macbeth, William McKinley and Me, Elizabeth* (E. L. Konigsburg) for thematic value and didacticism. Or compare two other stories for their themes regarding minorities.

NOTES

1 Wayne Booth in *The Rhetoric of Fiction* (Chicago: The University of Chicago Press, 1961) makes this comment (p. 136).

2 *The Rhetoric of Fiction*, p. 126. The satisfaction of knowing causality in children's literature is most obviously demonstrated in the cumulative tales like the humorous "Old Woman and the Pig," or the verse story "This Is the House That Jack Built."

3 *I Want to Be a Homemaker* by Carla Greene (New York: Children's Press, 1961) in many libraries is shelved among the picture books as JE. Commenting on the book here reminds us of the difference between real stories and instructive narrative. Others in the series of 54 books describe jobs; *Homemaker* seems to be describing role.

4 See "The Shape of Things to Come" in James Gunn's *Alternate Worlds: The Illustrated History of Science Fiction*. Englewood Cliffs, NJ: Prentice-Hall, 1975, pp. 225–39.

RECOMMENDED BOOKS CITED IN THIS CHAPTER

ALCOTT, LOUISA MAY. *Little Women*. New York: Dutton, 1948 (first published, 1868–69).

ANDERSEN, HANS CHRISTIAN. "The Ugly Duckling," "The Swineherd," "The Nightingale," "The Princess and the Pea," and "The Tinderbox" in *The Twelve Dancing Princesses and Other Fairy Tales*. Alfred David and Mary Elizabeth Meek, eds. Bloomington: Indiana University Press, 1974.

———. *The Emperor's New Clothes*. New York: Harcourt, 1959, and others.

ARMSTRONG, WILLIAM H. *Sounder*. New York: Harper, 1969.

CARROLL, LEWIS. *Alice's Adventures in Wonderland*. New York: Macmillan, 1963 (first published, 1865).

CLEARY, BEVERLY. *Dear Mr. Henshaw*. New York: Morrow, 1983.

CLYMER, ELEANOR. *Luke Was There*. New York: Holt, 1973.

HOOVER, H. M. *The Shepherd Moon*. New York: Viking, 1984.

JUKES, MAVIS. *Blackberries in the Dark*. New York: Knopf, 1985.

KIPLING, RUDYARD. *Just So Stories*. Garden City, NY: Doubleday, 1946 (first published, 1902).

LEGUIN, URSULA K. *A Wizard of Earthsea*. Berkeley: Parnassus, 1968.

LINDGREN, ASTRID. *Pippi Longstocking*. New York: Viking, 1950.

MILES, MISKA. *Annie and the Old One*. Boston: Little, Brown, 1971.

MILNE, A. A. *Winnie-the-Pooh*. New York: Dutton, 1926.

NORTON, MARY. *The Borrowers*. New York: Harcourt, 1965.

PATERSON, KATHERINE. *The Great Gilly Hopkins*. New York: Crowell, 1978.

———. *Jacob Have I Loved*. New York: Harper & Row, 1980.

PORTE, BARBARA ANN. *Harry's Mom*. New York: Greenwillow, 1985.

POTTER, BEATRIX. *The Tale of Peter Rabbit*. New York: Warne, 1902.

RYLANT, CYNTHIA. *A Fine White Dust*. New York: Bradbury, 1986.

SACHS, MARILYN. *The Bears' House*. New York: Doubleday, 1971.

SEBESTYEN, OUIDA. *Far from Home*. Boston: Little, Brown, 1980.

SNYDER, ZILPHA. *The Witches of Worm*. New York: Atheneum, 1973.

SUSSMAN, SUSAN. *There's No Such Thing as a Channukah Bush, Sandy Goldstein*. Niles, IL: Whitman, 1983.

TAYLOR, MILDRED. *Roll of Thunder, Hear My Cry*. New York: Dial, 1976.

VOIGT, CYNTHIA. *Dicey's Song*. New York: Random House, 1982.

———. *A Solitary Blue*. New York: Atheneum, 1983.

WHITE, E. B. *Charlotte's Web*. New York: Harper, 1952.

Illustration by Margot Tomes reprinted by permission of G. P. Putnam's Sons
from *Homesick, My Own Story* by Jean Fritz, drawings copyright © 1982 by
Margot Tomes.

etting

Both depiction of character and working out of plot and theme occur, of course, in time and place. These latter elements we call *setting*. In an adult novel, action may occur anywhere, even in the mind of the protagonist, and may need little delineation of place or time. However, the story for children almost always occurs in a time and place described in some detail.

The possibilities for setting are endless. It is possible to write of a time when human beings lived in caves, and it is possible to write of a time when they may live in capsules adrift in space. As for settings in place, from cave to capsule, the spread is equally broad. When we consider all of the times and places known to us, and add to them all those we are capable of imagining, there is no limit to possibilities. Sometimes the writer wishes to make setting very clear, because the story depends upon our understanding and envisioning the particular setting. At other times, the writer deliberately refrains from closely examining and describing setting. Making the setting a specific time and place might for a particular story limit the universality of conflict, characters, or ideas the writer wishes to explore. It is the writer who determines the nature of the story, and thereby determines the setting.

Sometimes we must know the physical description of the setting, the details of what is present, how it all looks, smells, feels, and sounds. These are the relevant details that will directly influence character, conflict, and theme. Such details at other times—kinds of sounds and smells, kinds of buildings, quality of light and climate—may create the mood of the time and place and so create the atmosphere for the characters and the conflict.

You will notice from our discussion of character and plot that we found those two elements influencing and reflecting each other. This interdependence with other elements is true of setting, too. If, for example, *The Why's and Wherefore's of Littabelle Lee* by Vera and Bill Cleaver were to take place not among the rivers and valleys and cliffs of the Ozarks, but on the plains of North Dakota or in glittering Miami Beach, the story would change. Aunt Sorrow's fall over the cliff on her burro, for example, could not have happened; Littabelle's wonder about what to do with her life would have included options other than teaching or woods doctoring. Such settings would create totally different novels. The Cleavers did not hit upon their choice of setting accidentally; it was *the* setting for *this* story. In evaluating a piece of literature, we should be aware of the basic kind of setting, and then decide how it functions in the story. As we analyze this relationship, we evaluate the effectiveness of the author's selection.

TYPES OF SETTINGS

In any piece of literature, whether for child or adult, there are essentially two types of setting: (1) the *backdrop* or relatively unimportant setting and (2) the *integral* or essential setting.

The importance of setting—whether it is integral or backdrop— depends upon the writer's purpose. For example, in a story of internal conflict, the first-person narrator may tell the progress of the plot in narrative, dialogue, and action, or in diary form. The reader may not need to know where or when the character lives, since understanding depends upon interest in character and in the character's internal conflict as the narrator reveals the inner tension. Time and place are merely a backdrop. This kind of setting contrasts sharply with the significant integral setting in a nonfiction book such as *Anne Frank: The Diary of a Young Girl.* Although this autobiographical account, too, has internal conflict, where and when the action occurs are essential information if we are to understand conflict and character. In fact, setting working upon character is the essence of conflict in this book.

The writer makes the setting clear in descriptions. Each reader may have a personal catalog of mentally pictured settings—a beach, a farm, or a cabin—but the writer does not depend upon the reader's experience nor upon recollection of settings. If the writer wants to make the setting integral to this story, the writer must describe it in concrete details, relying on sensory pictures and vivid comparisons to make the setting so clear that the reader understands how this story is closely related to this particular place.

By contrast, if the unskilled writer insists that setting is significant, and yet creates a setting superficial in concept and shallow in depiction, the reader may then reject all of the story's reality, from character through action and unifying idea. A one-dimensional setting cannot be convincingly integral, and therefore little that happens seems believable.

The title *Willie Goes to the Seashore* suggests that the setting is an integral part of the action; the seashore must be so interesting that Willie will have an exciting time. The actual case is quite different. The little cottage and the sandy beach are the setting. Willie, moving in quick succession from one to another of the activities one expects at the shore, seems to move *over* the setting rather than *in* it, finding no conflict nor involvement in any of the activities the setting suggests. Setting does not come alive to involve character in plot. So what is exciting about a seashore? Why would Willie want to live there all the time? The setting has failed as an integral part of the story, since it does not influence character, conflict, or idea.

Backdrop Setting

The term *backdrop setting* comes, of course, from the theater. For example, some of the action in scenes from Shakespeare or from many musicals takes place on the apron of the stage before a featureless curtain, or before a flat, painted scene of an unidentified street or forest. Soliloquy, dialogue, action, or character confrontation concerns us; where the characters are positioned matters, but less than our seeing and hearing them, and following them in the developing conflict. Yet, while the street or forest is unidentified, it may have importance. It may have some subtle meaning that suggests the forest as a place of physical or spiritual darkness, and the busy street as a reminder of society.

A clear example of a children's story with backdrop setting is *Winnie-the-Pooh*. A. A. Milne's Christopher Robin might live anywhere at all—from England's Land's End to Lancashire, or from America's Bangor to Sacramento. Action occurs on the bank of a stream, or by a big oak tree with a honeybee nest. While time and place are not specific, they may suggest something about the action or characters when Pooh, Eeyore, Rabbit, and his assorted friends-and-relations set off on an "Expotition" to the North Pole. The Forest—with a capital *F*—is of course the proper place for Pooh and Piglet to track the fearful Woozle/Wizzle, but there is minimal description of the beech tree beyond its being in the middle of the Forest. It is the tension in the characters that matters and dominates.

Pippi Longstocking, Astrid Lindgren's heroine, might also live anywhere. Pippi's chaotic home, Villa Villekula, figures minimally in the story action as we admire Pippi's found treasure, or as she rolls out cookie dough on the floor. Our eyes and ears focus instead on Pippi as she shows her skills as a Thing Finder, plays tag with the policeman, or tops the ladies' gossip with her own nonsensical servant problems. Pippi's house is important to us only because it must be a remarkable place; Pippi does such ridiculous things there.

In both *Winnie* and *Pippi,* setting is generalized and universal; its vividness exists in our minds merely as the place where the interesting action occurs. We do not know, for example, what Rabbit's house looks like; what matters is the memorable view of Pooh's legs serving as towel racks.

Although time and place have importance, they do not influence the character and plot in the same ways that an integral setting does.

Integral Setting

We say a story has an **integral setting** when action, character, or theme are influenced by the time and place, since, as Eudora Welty says, setting has "the most delicate control over character . . . by confining character, it defines it."[1] These characters, given these circumstances, in this time and place, behave in this way.

When we open to Chapter 1 of Patricia MacLachlan's *Sarah, Plain and Tall*, we are immediately drawn into the integral setting. Caleb sits close to the fire, the dogs "beside him on the warm hearthstones," a pioneer home, apparently. Anna looks out the window to the prairie that reaches out and touches "the places where the sky came down. Though winter was nearly over, there were patches of snow and ice everywhere." A dirt road crawls across the plains, and there are "fields and grass and sky and not much else." The wind seems to blow Papa into the house. When Sarah comes in answer to Papa's ad for a wife, the family is relieved to find that she enjoys farm life, even to climbing up the ladder on "the mound of hay for bedding, nearly half as tall as the barn, covered with canvas to keep the rain from rotting it." Because the issue is whether Sarah, who loves the dunes and sea of Maine, can be happy as a prairie wife and mother, we must see her involved with and enjoying the prairie farm. The setting is integral.

Knowing the nature of the river in which Tony dares Joel to swim is essential to plot and theme in *On My Honor* by Marion Dane Bauer. We read of the red-brown water "slithering" under the bridge. Chemicals and sewage are not visible, but Joel knows they are there. Although the water flows past like "a refreshing massage," he doesn't want to put his face in it; "the river smelled of decaying fish," and divided in a sharp V at the boys' waists. We know not only the pollution but also the threat of strong current to an inexperienced swimmer like Tony.

Brian, the protagonist in *Hatchet* by Gary Paulsen, is the sole survivor of the crash of a single-engine plane in Alaska; his only survival tool is his hatchet. To believe in his struggle with isolation in the rugged surroundings he must make habitable, we must see the setting clearly. A stone ridge near the lake that the plane has crashed into yields a cave-like shelter.

> At one time in the far past it had been scooped by something, probably a glacier, and this scooping had left a kind of sideways bowl, back in under a ledge. It wasn't very deep, not a cave, but it was smooth and made a perfect roof and he could almost stand in under the ledge. . . . Some of the rock . . . had . . . been pulverized by the glacial action, turned into sand, and now made a small sand beach that went down to the edge of the water in front. . . .

Here, once he can build a fire, Brian finds protection from the black flies and mosquitoes that blanket his body.

Setting in *Charlotte's Web*

Our touchstone, *Charlotte's Web,* is an excellent example of integral setting literally described. This story could have occurred nowhere but on a farm, in fact only on a farm that has the traditional farm animals. This is not a sprawling ranch, nor a grain-growing industry, because such farms have concerns other than pigs and their barnyard friends. The Arable farm is near a country road, since Fern catches the school bus at her front door. There is a brook for playing in, with wonderfully oozy, sticky mud. This farm has a dump—or how could Templeton find essential words for the web? It has meadows that show seasonal changes, maples that redden with anxiety, and a big pasture that frightens a timid piglet. This farm, with an orchard where apples fall and the gander's family feasts, is no generalized farm; there is no other farm quite like it, where fog and rain, crickets and song sparrow are all parts of the place, the setting. However, most important of all, this farm has a barn that houses a variety of animals—or how could sheep, pigs, and geese become acquainted, advising, consoling, and taunting one another? White shows the Zuckerman barn as soon as Wilbur sees it. The reader, too, knows its smells, its sights, and its warmth:

> The barn was very large. It was very old. It smelled of hay and it smelled of manure. It smelled of the perspiration of tired horses and the wonderful sweet breath of patient cows. It often had a sort of peaceful smell—as though nothing bad could happen ever again in the world. It smelled of grain and of harness dressing and of axle grease and of rubber boots and of new rope. And whenever the cat was given a fish-head to eat, the barn would smell of fish. But mostly it smelled of hay, for there was always hay in the great loft overhead. And there was always hay being pitched down to the cows and the horses and the sheep.

No one could confuse this setting with any generalized backdrop, since each item in the description shows the singularity of this setting, home of Wilbur, Charlotte, and Templeton. We know this place as well as Wilbur does, and because its description is so vivid, we are alerted to its importance in the total story.

To know the exciting Fairgrounds, we must:

> . . . hear music and see the Ferris wheel turning in the sky. . . . smell the dust of the race track where the sprinkling car had moistened it . . . smell hamburgers frying and see balloons aloft. . . . hear sheep blatting in their pens.

At night the lighted Ferris wheel revolves in the sky, the gambling machines crackle, the merry-go-round makes music, and a voice calls numbers from the beano booth. In the morning we hear sparrows stirring, roosters crowing, cows rattling chains, and cars whispering on the roadway.

The Fair is an essential part of the story, and it is therefore necessary that the reader see, hear, smell, and even touch and taste it. Wilbur's character is fully revealed at the Fair, where, experiencing threatened failure and final success, he remains humble but radiant. Wilbur's conflict, furthermore, cannot be resolved without the Fair. Wilbur must have time to grow, and then must prove himself worthy of being saved; the fall Fair is a traditional proving time for farm animals. Charlotte's efforts to prolong Wilbur's life produce no certainty of success until the Fair—he wins the prize for attracting so many visitors.

White must also show temporal change, since character growth and conflict, as well as several of the story's thematic discoveries, are dependent upon the passing of time. White must make us see the seasons as they exist, merge, and change. As we hear, see, and smell, we are aware of time passing, and of weather and landscape changing.

Spring is the time for pigs to be born; rain drips from the eaves, runs crookedly between the pigweed, and gushes from the rainspouts. Summer is everyone's holiday; lilacs are blooming, bees are dropping in on the apple blossoms, and horses are pulling the noisy mower. Birds sing and nest. However, since summer cannot last forever, the crickets' song prepares us for fall and the important Fair time. Uneasy sheep break out of their pasture, and the gander's family invades the orchard. Although little of the story's action occurs in winter, even winter is not slighted. The pasture is frozen, the cows are standing in the sun beside the strawpile, the sheep are eating snow, and the geese just hanging about. Then to complete the year's cycle, and to prove that Wilbur has survived butchering time and that Charlotte's eggs have hatched, White returns to spring and its strengthening light, new lambs, nine goose eggs, and Charlotte's old web floating away.

The time element is important here. As the year passes, Wilbur matures from a panicky child to a responsible adult. In the passing of a full year we know that his victory over society is complete. We have had time to see the truth of such themes as the growth of friendship and of maturity, and the inevitability and acceptance of death. The integral setting has helped to make all of these clear.

FUNCTIONS OF SETTING

Setting That Clarifies Conflict

As *Charlotte's Web* demonstrates, an integral setting plays an important part in conflict. Time setting for a story can be any time, past, present, or future. In British writer Robert Swindell's *Brother in the Land,* time is a frightening future just after nuclear war. Danny, one of the few survivors, must bury his mother, see his father killed by marauders who steal his food stores, and watch while his little brother Ben dies of radiation sickness. We see the devastated land, the flattened city, and the individual homes and business places left without windows, walls, or furnishings. People drink from puddles of Black Rain, scratch for edible roots, and bed down where they find shelter in places that are dank with the odor of decay. As this book demonstrates, understanding setting is essential to understanding character and conflict as well as theme.

In *M. C. Higgins, the Great* by Virginia Hamilton, M. C. looks out from the mountain top over the land devastated by strip mining. The air is still and hot, without the sounds of birds or insects. He remembers how the scene once looked, with "ranges of hills with farmhouses nestled in draws and lower valleys." Now he sees a "gray-brown snake" curling in cuts and loops along the ridges, the hill summits "shredded away with rock and ruin which spilled down into cropland at the base of the hills." Soon he learns from the visitor Lewis that the waste heap is sliding on the oil, and that, given the right steep angle, the "pressure is going to build up until it crashes down" and buries his house. M. C.'s nightmare has come alive and dread sickens him. Once again, setting reveals character, suits plot, and influences theme.

In H. M. Hoover's *The Last Star,* although an alien world, setting is recognizable in many ways. Lian, who has spent much of her life in similar enclosures, finds the inside of the lumpies' quarters comfortable; gravel crunching beneath boots, she has proceeded to the enclosure through a vine-covered opening to a cavelike space, a wall of brilliant green with sunlit leaves, and around a curve, a doorway machine-tooled and circular as though it opened into a monstrous vault. As she knocks on the wall with her knuckles, it rings as though it is not rock but formed metal. These descriptive images and comparisons enable readers to see setting.

Turn to the austere Puritan New England setting of *The Witch of Blackbird Pond,* into which Kit Tyler is transported from her West Indies birthplace. Author Elizabeth Speare does not rely merely on our history book knowledge of that time and place when witchcraft was feared; she clarifies setting by her description of the austerity of life among the Puritans: the house with hand-rubbed copper, indicative of hard work; the heavy, fortress-like door; the dim little mirror; and the severe wooden bench. Speare weaves description of the house itself into a description of Kit's tasks in a typical day. Meat must be chopped, vegetables prepared, and the pewter mugs polished with fine sand and reeds. Throughout the day Kit stirs the kettle of boiling soap with a stick, the lye fumes stinging her eyes and the heavy stirring tiring her muscles. Even the easiest task, making corn pudding, keeps her leaning over the smoky fire which burns her watering eyes. Walking through the little town to church with Kit, we see severity in the straight, cold lines of functional buildings with punitive devices. The unpainted Meeting House, the whipping post, the pillory, and the stocks are frightening evidence that Kit is now in a rigid and uncompromising environment, one for which her carefree Barbados upbringing has scarcely prepared her.

Homesick: My Own Story is Jean Fritz's fictionalized memories of her first years in China, a country she loved, but loved less than her native United States. Each summer the non-Chinese spend away from the cities, either in the mountains or at the ocean, and despite the beauty of the summer setting, with its Rattling Brook and the multitudes of wild flowers, there is no setting like that of rural living near "Washington, PA," where she feels rooted. The grape arbor, the yard pump, the rooster that crows when the family laughs, the wonderful climbing trees, the garden peas waiting to be shelled, the hand-cranked washing machine—all these elements are new and exciting to China-born Jean. The contrast between the two settings accentuates the conflict Jean feels as she yearns for her homeland.

Sometimes we must know a mode of living or of making a living in order to understand the story's conflict. In such a case the setting may be integral. *Where the Lilies Bloom,* for example, shows setting as a power shaping the lives of those who live in the Smokies. The Cleavers create a setting beautiful enough to hold the characters' loyalty, and yet so wild that it offers Mary Call's family little on which to subsist. Weaving descriptions of setting into action, the writers show wildcrafting, a tedious labor with small rewards, action native to this particular lush wilderness. Mary Call's struggle to keep her family together is the more convincing because we see the setting with which she struggles.

Time, particularly in fantasy, has a way of lengthening or shortening, depending upon the make-believe world the writer creates. We know how time is relative: when we're entertained, time goes quickly; when we're bored, time drags endlessly. But the writer of fantasy takes other liberties with time, perhaps by making one event, or one life, last through centuries or be over in seconds.

Setting as Antagonist

Sometimes setting itself is the antagonist as it is in *Julie of the Wolves.* Even fog, one of nature's milder elements, frightens Miyax, who had never given it much thought. As it streams and rolls up the wolf slope, making the wolves invisible one by one, she remembers that fog imprisons people: In fog they cannot hunt. As noted earlier, the setting for Burnford's *The Incredible Journey* is an essential part of the story, since the Canadian wilderness is not only setting but antagonist. Without clear descriptions of the dense brush, forest land, and wilderness river, such a novel would have no believable conflict to hold the reader. However, on the opening page of the novel, Burnford prepares us for the conflict; the rugged country of north-western Ontario is introduced on line one of page one, and the description continues for a page and a half.

> . . . a vast area of deeply wooded wilderness—of endless chains of lonely lakes and rushing rivers. Thousands of miles of country roads, rough timber lanes, overgrown tracks leading to abandoned mines, and unmapped trails snake across its length and breadth. It is a country of far-flung, lonely farms and a few widely scattered small towns and villages, of lonely trappers' shacks and logging camps.

Since nature is the antagonist in Burnford's story, she must show nature as strong, even threatening, to the three pet characters. If their journey is to be credible, we must believe in the forces they battle. The Siamese cat, its ancestors bred originally for elegant court life; the comfort-loving bull terrier; and the Labrador, trained to be companion and servant, have to adapt to the wilderness to survive. Their persistent trek toward their masters becomes suspenseful as we realize what these three must contend with. The conflict holds our interest because nature is not benign, but an unyielding force that threatens them with possible failure. Nature as setting and antagonist is worthy of our respect.

Setting is also the antagonist in another book discussed earlier, O'Dell's *Island of the Blue Dolphins*. We must be aware of the passing of time and of the seemingly endless period of Karana's isolation as she waits for rescue. If we did not see the dangers that threaten her survival on the island, we might find the story a happy, escape-to-the-wilderness tale. Instead, because of the many vivid descriptions, *Island* is an account of a patient and determined young woman who struggles and survives against a powerful antagonist—nature, which brings hunger, thirst, injury, wild dogs, an earthquake, and a tidal wave. Setting, Karana's antagonist, is vivid. We see, hear, smell, and feel it in O'Dell's descriptions. Although Karana is not overwhelmed, her adversary is powerful.

Setting That Illuminates Character

In many examples we have been discussing, setting influences character. Notice the effect of isolation and crowding upon the protagonist's fear in that unusual autobiography *Anne Frank: The Diary of a Young Girl*. We must see the stiflingly cramped atmosphere of the Secret Annexe or we cannot experience the yearning for freedom and privacy that Anne expresses during the twenty-five months of the family's hiding from the Nazi soldiers who are rounding up the Jews for imprisonment. We must see Anne's surroundings as we follow her tensions with her parents and fellow prisoners, her awakening sense of self, and her curiosity about growing up. Just two days after the family crowds into the Annexe, Anne writes as though it is an adventure:

> Our little room looked very bare at first with nothing on the walls; but thanks to Daddy who had brought my filmstar collection and picture postcards on beforehand, and with the aid of paste pot and brush, I have transformed the walls into one gigantic picture. This makes it look more cheerful, and, when the Van Daans come, we'll get some wood from the attic, and make a few little cupboards for the walls and other odds and ends to make it look more lively.

But thirteen months later, we have another picture, this time of the efforts necessary when bedtime approaches:

> Nine o-clock in the evening. The bustle of going to bed in the "Secret Annexe" begins. . . . Chairs are shoved about, beds are pulled down, blankets unfolded, nothing remains where it is during the day. I sleep on the little divan. . . . chairs have to be used to lengthen it. A quilt, sheets, pillows, blankets, are all fetched from Dussel's bed where they remain during the day . . . creaking in the next room: Margot's concertina-bed being pulled out. Again, divan, blankets, and pillows, everything is done to make the wooden slats a bit more comfortable. It sounds like thunder above, but it is only Mrs. Van Daan's bed . . . shifted to the window.

The setting becomes overwhelming in its effect upon every aspect of the characters' lives. Bickering, quarrels, arguments, and rages result from the pressures of close confinement. Then, in Anne's description of her own actions, her responses to being so long confined in this setting, we see the impact of setting—time and place—upon the protagonist:

> I wander from one room to another, downstairs and up again, feeling like a songbird whose wings have been clipped and who is hurling himself in utter darkness against the bars of his cage. "Go outside, laugh, and take a breath of fresh air," a voice cries within me, but I don't even feel a response any more; I go and lie on the divan and sleep, to make the time pass more quickly, and the stillness and the terrible fear, because there is no way of killing them.

The people in Anne Frank's diary become more understandable, the conflict more credible, and the themes more convincing because, in this remarkable account by an extremely perceptive adolescent, we see the setting so clearly.

Setting and Mood

As several of the preceding examples demonstrate, setting affects mood. Take, for example, *The Eyes of the Amaryllis* by Natalie Babbitt. In order for the reader to experience the isolation of the little house on the New England seacoast and to see how its situation affects Gran and her visitor Jenny, we must know the essential setting. We see Jenny and Gran's regular walk along the tide-washed shore at midnight, notice how the smooth sand sucks their feet into its depths as they search for some sign of the grandfather's ship wrecked so long ago. On the night of the hurricane, however, the quiet beach changes, becoming savage and threatening:

> [The storm] wheeled slowly north. Its eye rode far offshore, but its sweeping arms of wind and rain clawed at the nearest beaches, and the sea rose up before it in great, spreading welts that raced for miles ahead, rolling to land in the measured waves. . . .
>
> But as it swung in an upward arc to the west and north, its indignation grew, the speed of its winds increased, until at last, arriving in mid-coastal waters, it had spun itself into a rage. It was small, not more than forty miles across, but deadly: round its eye the winds were whirling ninety. . . .

Only such violent turbulence could prepare us for the lost figurehead of the Amaryllis, the sign washed up on the shore, liberating Gran from the past. Had the figurehead floated in on a benevolent wave, its significance would have been less evident and its mysterious appearance less dramatic.

Epic style is grand style, vivid and resonant; and setting—like character and action—can be pictured in elevated language. In keeping with the heroic subject, the setting of Ian Serraillier's retelling of the epic *Beowulf the Warrior* has solemn majesty; its description produces a mood of great dignity. Serraillier sketches the setting briefly with phrases that ring with grandeur. Book One begins with a description of the vast and splendid hall Heorot, scene of Grendel's monstrous deeds and of Beowulf's selfless struggle:

> Hrothgar, King of the Danes, glorious in battle
> Built him a huge hall—its gleaming roof
> Towering high to heaven—strong to withstand
> The buffet of war. . . .
>
> The long hall . . .
> The floor paved with stone, the roof high-raftered.

As Beowulf battles with Grendel in a struggle of awesome violence, this huge hall shudders. The struggle is greater, and therefore the victory is greater, because of the mood created by the splendor of setting. Book Two opens with the mother of Grendel descending upon Heorot for vengeance. The mist, the gloom, the chill, and the vast emptiness set the ominous mood and prepare us for the monster's mission:

> Over the misty moor, under the dark
> Vault of heaven a shadow came gliding—a she-monster,
> Mother of Grendel. From the chill waters of the fenland,
> Brooding on her grief. . . .

Filled with foreboding and suspense, these brief phrases describing the setting prepare us for a story of a hero and monsters. They are more than backdrop; they are a setting which creates a mood integral to the story of heroic battles and grim victories.

Setting as Symbol

Symbols may operate in setting as they may in other elements of literature. A *symbol* is a person, object, situation, or action which operates on two levels of meaning, the literal and the figurative or suggestive. When we first become aware of symbols, we have a tendency to run wild, to read into stories all sorts of fanciful overtones not legitimately supported by the story. What seems important here is that only fairly obvious symbols will be understood by most children.

The simplest of symbolic settings are those that suggest that the forest is both a literal setting and a symbol for the unknown; the garden is both a literal setting and a symbol of natural but cultivated beauty; sunlight may symbolize goodness, while darkness is evil. In such a way some of the settings in folktales have symbolic meanings. Hansel and Gretel, as well as Snow White, are lost in the fearful and unknown—the forest. The forest is also the domain of ogres and giants, mysteriously frightening creatures. Despite their backdrop qualities, these symbolic settings often set the mood in traditional tales.

Symbols may be combined to create *allegory,* as they are in some stories for children. According to Northrop Frye, allegory translates into images.[2] To be a true symbol, the object must be emphasized or repeated, and supported throughout the entire story; it represents something quite differ- ent from its literal meaning. But stories for children operate on a fairly literal level. Ideas of good and evil may be translated into characters, actions, or setting, which then become symbols for ideas.

In this sense the Narnia series by C. S. Lewis is allegory. However, the Narnia books are also highly successful when read on a literal level; the young reader may or may not see the ideas symbolized by characters or setting. A child may read through the series with great excitement, think a bit, then exclaim "He's talking about good and bad!" and then reread them all, this time on an allegorical or symbolic level.

In contrast, the Forest seems a natural place for Pooh and Piglet to hunt a Woozle/Wizzle; to extend the meaning of the Forest to the point of calling it a symbol for evil is pretentious and pointless. Hannah, the supposed Quaker witch in *The Witch of Blackbird Pond,* does not live in the dark forest; a kind and harmless woman, she lives in the sunny meadows. Speare chooses this setting for Hannah's home to assist in creating conflict, but calling the setting symbolic seems heavy-handed.

EVALUATING SETTING IN CHILDREN'S LITERATURE

Like adults, children will accept as much or as little setting as the story seems to call for. Like adults, too, they expect that when a setting is important to understanding the story, they will be made to see, to hear, perhaps even to smell the setting—to sense the setting in any way relevant to the mood, conflict, and characters in the story. It seems reasonable, however, that younger children will be less likely to sit still for long descriptions that take them away from the conflict and characters. For them, and for many adults as well, setting interwoven with action is the most interesting and readable. Once this setting is established, any reader of any age expects the writer to be consistent. At times we all accept settings as escapes. The scene of an exotic ball or lavish banquet in a folktale undoubtedly was a satisfying escape for the poor and oppressed who heard these stories told in the past; today setting in some adventure and science fiction stories seems to function as escape. But once again, we return to the principle that the essential setting should be integrated with character and conflict, and that it not be a mere digression. Since folk literature and fantasy seem to be more common in literature for children than for adults, their special considerations may need examination.

Traditional Literature

In most folktales action and theme are the focus of interest and the setting is backdrop. The action is usually brisk and little time is spent describing time and place. The setting is a vague long-ago-and-far-away that avoids pinning down time and place. Such a setting also suggests magically one of the most pleasurable aspects of the folktale: maybe-it-happened-here, maybe-yesterday! Thus such a setting also anticipates the equally pleasurable possibility that perhaps-it-could-happen-again, perhaps-here! We have noted in our discussion of character that in a folktale the protagonists are so general and universal that what happens to them might hapen to anyone. Similar vagueness in setting reinforces the possibility of adventures for us, the readers.

Folktale settings often follow the "once upon a time" formula. A random sampling of tales from Grimm—the tales best known to a majority of Western readers—reveals the following settings, or lack of them, in their opening lines; little is added within the stories:

> Once upon a time there lived an old man and his wife who for a long time . . .

> Once upon a time there was a king who had twelve daughters.

> Once upon a time in deep winter, when the snowflakes were falling like feathers . . .[3]

Occasionally we read a simple variation: "At the edge of a great forest lived a woodcutter and his wife." Folktale settings from other cultures seem to vary little from the patterns of Grimm, with little more specific definition of time and place than the American Indian "My grandfather told me. . . ." It is the nature of the folktale—originally told to an audience who might become restless—to plunge into conflict and action. Such generalized settings can demonstrate more clearly a universal theme: the kindness of the daughter is rewarded; she lives happily ever after in the palace of the prince.

Other folk literature seems equally vague about setting. The fable omits setting altogether, going immediately into action and its didactic point:

> A certain Wolf, being very hungry, disguised himself in a sheep's skin.

> A mischievous Shepherd's Boy used to amuse himself by calling "Wolf! Wolf!"

Many of the fables are only a few sentences long, and, since they exist to point a moral, setting is quite logically unimportant. The lesson is universal, unlimited by time or place. Myths happened "in ancient Greece," or "in the days of Thor," and designation of time and place is barely relevant. What matters is not location of specific action, but pinning down the locale to the cultural world of Greece or Scandinavia. Here, too, simplicity in setting reinforces the universal qualities of the myths, their comments upon human vanity or greed.

Legends, those unauthenticated stories handed down from tradition and regarded by the public as figuratively possible or even true, are by their definition related to historical events or people. This relationship narrows somewhat their time and place. For example, Robin Hood's adventures occur in Sherwood Forest, since that is where Robin Hood, according to history, lived. Often, however, the legends refer to mystical events occurring centuries later than the lifetime of the character, and caused supposedly by the character's onetime presence. The oases of the Egyptian desert, for example, are said by legend to have sprung up wherever the fleeing Joseph, Mary, and infant Jesus stopped to rest.

Fantasy and Science Fiction

Setting in fantasy is a special consideration, since fantasy often begins in a setting of reality and moves to the setting of a fantasy realm, then back again. Such a book as *Alice in Wonderland* moves easily from the real to the fantastic by the device of a dream; *Where the Wild Things Are* does so by daydream. *And to Think That I Saw It on Mulberry Street* is a fantastic daydream, a parade framed by what the narrator actually saw on the way home from school. Other transitions are more complex. In Susan Cooper's *The Dark Is Rising,* the world that Will enters is filled with the mysterious and the supernatural—integral parts of the setting and essential to the story. The castle where Will meets the Old Ones, who for centuries have been battling evil, is the setting for Will's discovery that by the exercise of his willpower he can actually bring change. Reluctantly, he learns that he must accept his power in order to use it for good:

> [He looked] across the room at the light and shadow dancing side by side across the rich tapestries on the stone walls, and he thought hard, in furious concentration, of the image of the blazing log fire in the huge fireplace behind him. He felt the warmth of it on the back of his neck, and thought of the glowing heart of the big pile of logs and the leaping yellow tongues of flame. *Go out, fire,* he said to it in his mind, feeling suddenly safe and free from the dangers of power, because of course no fire as big as that could possibly go out.

The fire goes out. Next Will sees that each of the many tapestries on the castle walls has its own frightening image, some as terrifying as "the empty-eyed grinning white skull of a horse, with a single stubby broken horn in the bony forehead and red ribbons wreathing the long jaws." Threatened by the rising of evil, the Dark, Will sees clearly his responsibility to use the special power given him.

In *Alice's Adventures in Wonderland* Lewis Carroll sets all logic awry, including the logic of setting. A rabbit hole extends deep into a strange, unboundaried world, and time moves in all directions to create a setting essential to our experience of the story. To us as well as to Alice, time and place are illogical and confusing; they influence nonsensical behavior which defies every rule. In defiance of time and the related laws of growth, Alice grows and shrinks; the Mock Turtle's lessons lessen; the tea party murders time by going on forever; the White Rabbit tries fruitlessly to catch up with time. As for place, nothing seems to be where it is expected to be, and nothing can be counted upon to be in the same place at another moment. The great hall with glass table and tiny door vanishes, and Alice finds her way into a tidy little room. Turning her back on the tea party, Alice walks through a door into a tree—only to find herself back in the long hall with the glass table and the tiny door. Finally, cause and effect—which occur in that order and are logically related to time—defy time to appear in nonsensically reversed order: sentence first, verdict later.

SUMMARY

Setting is of two principal types. First, it may be a backdrop for the plot, like the generalized backdrop of a city, street, or forest against which we can see some of the action of a play. In traditional literature, setting is usually backdrop, so generalized that it becomes universal. Or setting may be an integral part of the story, so essential to our understanding of this plot, these characters, and these themes that we must experience it with our senses. Backdrop or integral—the choice is the writer's. The integral setting not only may clarify the conflict, but it also may help the reader understand character, may be cast as the antagonist, may influence mood, or perhaps act as symbol. Often the sense of place prepares the reader to accept the story and the writer's personal view of life and its significance.

Deciding that setting is integral or backdrop does not constitute a judgment for or against the quality of a piece of writing. What is important, however, is that understanding may develop only when we realize that this particular setting is essential to this story. And, if setting is essential to our understanding, the writer must make the reader see, hear, touch, and perhaps even smell the setting. It is as much the writer's task when writing for children as for adults to evoke setting, described either in paragraphs or in phrases woven into action, by the details of color, sound, figurative comparisons, and other stylistic means.

READING AND EVALUATING

1. **Other lands**   Read *The Master Puppeteer* by Katherine Paterson and examine the relationship of setting to story. How is the reader acquainted with life in Japan? What details make setting distinctive? Are setting and its resultant life patterns related to the story? How? Of what significance is historical period in the story? Must time be pinned down? Explain.

2. **Folktales**   Read four folktales from each of three cultures—for example, German, Japanese, and American Indian. Is it possible to generalize about the folktale's backdrop setting? What variations do you see in depiction of settings? Are there symbolic settings?

3. **Epics**   Read an epic like a child's version of the *Odyssey,* another version of *Beowulf,* or *Gilgamesh.* Is setting integral? Backdrop? Does it establish mood? Do more than that? Explain.

4. **Historical fiction**   Read a historical novel for children and check the data about setting against what you know of the period and place. Does action occur

in setting? Explain. Does the protagonist live in the setting, or does he or she move over it? Are action and character superimposed upon time and place?

5. **Fantasy/Nonsense** Read *Alice's Adventures in Wonderland*. Does Carroll make use of setting as an element of his fantasy-nonsense world? Explain. How does he define Wonderland? Is it part of the nonsense? Extraneous to it?

NOTES

1 Eudora Welty, *Place in Fiction*. New York: House of Books, 1957, p. 22.

2 Northrop Frye, "Theory of Symbol," in *Anatomy of Criticism*. Princeton, NJ: Princeton University Press, 1957, pp. 71-128.

3 *The Twelve Dancing Princesses,* Alfred David and Mary Elizabeth Meek, eds. Bloomington: Indiana University Press, 1974.

RECOMMENDED BOOKS CITED IN THIS CHAPTER

BABBITT, NATALIE. *The Eyes of the Amaryllis.* New York: Farrar, 1977.

BAUER, MARION DANE. *On My Honor.* Boston: Houghton Mifflin, 1986.

BURNFORD, SHEILA. *The Incredible Journey.* Boston: Little Brown, 1961.

CARROLL, LEWIS. *Alice's Adventures in Wonderland.* New York: Macmillan, 1963 (first published, 1865).

CLEAVER, VERA and BILL. *Where the Lilies Bloom.* Philadelphia: Lippincott, 1969.

————.*The Why's and Wherefore's of Littabelle Lee.* New York: Atheneum, 1973.

COOPER, SUSAN. *The Dark is Rising.* New York: Atheneum, 1973.

FRANK, ANNE. *Anne Frank: The Diary of a Young Girl.* Garden City, NY: Doubleday, 1967.

FRITZ, JEAN. *Homesick: My Own Story.* New York: G. P. Putnam's Sons, 1982.

GEORGE, JEAN. *Julie of the Wolves.* New York: Viking, 1972.

HAMILTON, VIRGINIA. *M. C. Higgins, the Great.* New York: Harper, 1974.

HOOVER, H. M. *The Lost Star.* New York: Viking, 1979.

LEWIS, C. S. The *Narnia* Books. New York: Macmillan, 1951-56.

LINDGREN, ASTRID. *Pippi Longstocking.* New York: Viking, 1950.

MACLACHLAN, PATRICIA. *Sarah, Plain and Tall.* New York: Harper & Row, 1985.

MILNE, A. A. *Winnie-the-Pooh.* New York: Dutton, 1926.

O'DELL, SCOTT. *Island of the Blue Dolphins.* Boston: Houghton Mifflin, 1960.

PAULSEN, GARY. *Hatchet.* New York: Bradbury, 1987.

SENDAK, MAURICE. *Where the Wild Things Are.* New York: Harper, 1963.

SERRAILLIER, IAN. *Beowulf the Warrior.* New York: Walck, 1961.

SPEARE, ELIZABETH. *The Witch of Blackbird Pond.* Boston: Houghton Mifflin, 1958.

SEUSS, DR. *And to Think That I Saw It on Mulberry Street.* New York: Hale, 1937.

SWINDELL, ROBERT. *Brother in the Land.* New York: Holiday House, 1984.

WHITE, E. B. *Charlotte's Web.* New York: Harper, 1952.

From *The Garden of Abdul Gasazi* by Chris Van Allsburg. Copyright © 1979 by
Chris Van Allsburg. Reprinted by permission of Houghton Mifflin Company.

CHAPTER 7

Point of View

When we hear the term *point of view,* we commonly think of opinion or attitude: "From my point of view, women's rights are . . . ." Sometimes we think of a personal angle or perspective: "That may be true for you, but I'm a student, and . . . ." But the term **point of view** has special meaning for literature. As we read a story we may be aware that we are seeing the events through the eyes—and mind—of one character. Or we may feel that we are objective observers watching the events unfold before our eyes. The writer wants to tell us this story. Whose view of the story the writer tells determines the point of view. Who sees the events determines how the story will develop.

As we all know, two people to whom the same incident happens simultaneously can have different versions of the event. Each responds out of past experience, or from belief in right and wrong behavior, as well as from the more obvious differences in the physical and emotional effects of the incident. Each version of the facts is a personal truth.

A similar situation exists in literature. As readers we describe point of view depending upon who sees and tells about the action. The same story is a different story, depending upon which side of the story we see. In the case of Louise Fatio's *The Happy Lion,* the story depends upon which side of the cage door the zoo lion is on. The Happy Lion thinks his visitors are pleasant, civil people. They nod, they bow, they greet him, and feed him—when he is inside the cage. But the day the keeper forgets to close the door, the Happy Lion walks out and meets his friends in their territory. One faints, one screams, and another throws a bag of vegetables in his face. Now the Happy Lion's friends have become puzzling strangers. Since the point of view is what we would call limited omniscient, and we know the Happy Lion's innocent thoughts, we are completely sympathetic to his puzzlement. When he calls the people foolish, we agree, since we know this lion is not vicious nor predatory. He's just taking a walk. However, if we didn't know the protagonist's thoughts, we'd be as frightened as the human citizens of the Lion's town. It is all a matter of point of view—whose thoughts we know, whose view of the action we follow.

TYPES OF POINT OF VIEW

Point of view is determined when the writer chooses who is to be the narrator and decides how much the narrator is to know. The first possibility a writer might consider is the *first-person point of view,* used when a story is told in first person "I." In such storytelling, the reader lives, acts, feels, and thinks the conflict as the protagonist experiences and tells it, just as Karana does in *Island of the Blue Dolphins* or the narrator Jessie does in *The Slave Dancer.* Occasionally the first-person narrator is not the protagonist, but a minor character who observes action and tells what the protagonist is doing.

The second possibility is the *omniscient point of view.* Here the writer, telling the story in third person (he, she, they), is all-knowning or omniscient about any and every detail of action, thought, and feeling—conscious or unconscious—in past, present, or future; if the writer chooses, he or she may recount any and all details. This omniscience is White's choice for *Charlotte's Web.*

A third possibility is the *limited omniscient point of view,* in which the writer, again telling the story in third person, concentrates on the thoughts, feelings, and significant past experience of only the central character or protagonist, as Wilder does in her *Little House* stories. Occasionally the writer may choose to be omniscient about a few characters; this choice, too, is sometimes called limited omniscient.

The fourth possibility is the *objective or dramatic point of view,* again using third person as, for example, Lenski does in *Cowboy Small.* The meaning of this term seems clear when we refer to the fictional reality of drama or motion picture. A camera seems to record—it cannot comment or interpret. There is no one there to explain to the reader what is going on or what the characters think or feel. The camera selects and we see and draw our own conclusions.

First-Person Point of View

The first-person narrator is limited; like us, he or she cannot tell what another character thinks unless told by that other character. Even though the narrator sees the action of another character, the narrator, again like us, can only speculate about what the other is thinking. A hasty tucking in of shirt or a nervous shaking of head gives evidence from which the narrator may draw conclusions, just as we draw conclusions. However, unless the second character says aloud what he or she thinks, the first-person narrator, again like us, can only guess.

The first-person narrator who tells the story may be either the protagonist or a minor character observing the action. The narrator in *The Slave Dancer* by Paula Fox is mortified to find that he is permitted to stare at the naked bodies of the slaves. As he stands amidst the crew on deck, he observes that they are dressed, shod, even armed. Then he notes the few ragged bits of cloth around the slaves' waists, and the crew staring fixedly.

> I felt fevered and agitated. I sensed, I saw, how beyond the advantage we had of weapons, their nakedness made them helpless. Even if we had not been armed, our clothes and boots alone would have given us power. . . .
> There was something else that held the attention of the men—and my own. It was the unguarded difference between the bodies of the men and women.

The narrator recalls his earlier childish curiosity, his window-peeking at women undressing; what he feels now that he can gaze "without restraint at the helpless and revealed forms of these slaves," is a mortification beyond imagining. With new sympathy, he dreads the coming of daylight, knowing he must bow to the screams of Cawthorne who would tie him to the topmost crosspiece of the mast if he refused to play his fife, to "dance the slaves." We are convinced that the story is true partly because the narrator maintains a consistent first-person point of view limited by what he can know.

Karana, the protagonist in *Island of the Blue Dolphins,* is also a first-person narrator. At no time does Karana pretend to know what is in the minds of others, not her brother, the hunters, Tutok the Aleut stranger, or the animals. Tutok comes out from the brush quickly; Karana says, "She must have been waiting nearby." That possibility is all that Karana can know about Tutok's motives. Tutok hugs Karana when she receives the shell necklace. Karana says, "She was so pleased that I forgot how sore my fingers were." From a hug—action from another character—Karana concludes that Tutok is pleased. Although Karana knows her dog Rontu very well, she describes only his actions, never his thoughts, concluding that the dying Rontu wishes to bark only because he always had:

> [Rontu] raised his ears at the sound, and I put him down, thinking that he wished to bark at [the gulls] as he always did. He raised his head and followed them with his eyes, but did not make a sound.

Had O'Dell violated the first-person point of view by telling us Rontu's feelings, we would have lost some of our concentration on Karana and the story would have been less real.

As we can see clearly from these passages, one of the strongest assets of first-person narration is its great potential for pulling the reader into what appears to be autobiographical truth. Because Karana's thoughts are interesting to us, we are sympathetic with her. Because she is believably limited in what she can admit to knowing, she is consistently credible. Because solitary Karana—like solitary Robinson Crusoe—tells her own realistic story, the vicarious experience of survival is a powerful reality, convincingly immediate to the reader. If the story had been filtered through an omniscient writer, the immediacy of the experience would be less intense. The intervention of someone who wasn't there but who still knows and can tell it all would create an intervening omniscience between the solitary protagonist and the reader. The story would then be more remote, less immediate, and less intensely real.

Clearly the danger in first-person narration lies in the possibility of "I" ignoring his or her limitations, reporting thoughts of others, and predicting, when such prediction would not naturally fall within "I's" ability to predict. Credibility is then lost.

In *Owls in the Family*, Farley Mowat helps us discover a great deal of natural history. In a story filled with information and appreciation of animal life, Mowat does not violate point of view to tell the thoughts of anyone but the narrator. Mowat has particular skill in combining believably youthful vocabulary with keen observation and meticulous attention to accurate detail. A very personal description of the prairie of western Canada fits easily into Billy's account of his hunt on the bluffs for a baby owl:

> The cottonwood trees shed a kind of white fluffy stuff that looks like snow. Sometimes it's so thick it comes right over the top of your sneakers and you get a queer feeling that you really are walking through snow, even though the sun on your back is making you sweat right through your shirt.

Through Billy's story of his pets, the reader not only discovers Saskatchewan's bluffs and cottonwood clouds, but also how an owl looks, when its eggs are laid, where its nest is built, how the bird attacks. All such objectively reported details come naturally into the narrative because they are relevant to the action. Mowat's young narrator is sympathetic to the many animals in his menagerie—white rats, gophers, garter snakes, pigeons and Mutt the dog—but he never becomes sentimental by telling what they feel and think. The effectiveness of the story is due in large part to a first-person point of view, which is clearly within the limitations and vocabulary of its young teenage narrator.

Matters of vocabulary and word usage are restrictions, as the person telling the story is limited to diction compatible with age and personality. Vicky Austin's view of events in Madeleine L'Engle's *A Ring of Endless Light* is shaped by her sixteen-year-old experiences. The story opens at the funeral of Leo's father, where Vicky comments: "I looked at Leo and his face was all splotchy as though he had cried and cried, but he hadn't cried, and he needed to." Later that day, she comments:

> I held Leo and he held me and we rocked back and forth on the old elm trunk, weeping. . . . And I discovered that there is something almost more intimate about crying that way with someone than there is about kissing, and I knew I'd never again be able to think of Leo as nothing but a slob.

And of Adam she says, "He wasn't particularly gorgeous . . . but he had a kind of light within that drew me to him like a moth to a candle." This is the diction of a sixteen-year-old speaking her feelings and thoughts, and not assuming to know what she cannot know: "I don't think Adam realized how nervous I was."

Cynthia Rylant uses first person point of view in her novel *A Fine White Dust*, showing Pete's thoughts and feelings as he is caught up in The Man's preaching. Mesmerized by the revivalist's preaching magic, Pete rejects his parents and his best friend and agrees to leave town secretly to become a boy minister. But, left behind, Pete struggles to purge himself of The Man's influence by telling his story; first person point of view reveals his rapt commitment, his disappointment at his parents and friend, who don't share his religious interest, and his pain at being left behind.

Occasionally a writer experiments successfully with different points of view, as does Alice Childress in *A Hero ain't nothin' but a Sandwich*. Using first person point of view, each of the characters tells the story from her or his own perspective of events and relationships. From the total of their stories, we see events, characters, plot, and theme, as well as setting. The story, set in the inner city, concerns Benjie's experience with drugs, and to be convincing, each of the speakers must reveal self through distinctively personal diction.

> *Benjie:* My block ain't no place to be a chile in peace. Somebody gonna cop your money and might knock you down cause you walkin with short bread and didn't even make it worth their while to stop and frisk you over.
>
> *Grandmother:* This house is my jail, only I pay rent. I'm afraid to go out in the street alone, day or night. Bad boys will beat [us] and take away our little money.
>
> *Nigeria Greene, teacher:* Bernard Cohen is not to be believed. His whole mission in teaching is to convince Black kids that most whites are great except for a "few" rotten apples in every barrel. It burns me.
>
> *Benjie's mother:* I try to keep the neighbors out of my business because every friend has a friend, and if I can't keep a secret, how can I ask them not to tell what I told?

Dear Mr. Henshaw, by using letter and diary format, makes following a first person story easy for younger readers. Even small children are aware of letters, and as letters shift to letters-in-a-journal to Dear Mr. Pretend Henshaw, then change to dated diary entries, the first person is maintained and the point of view remains clear.

So successful in maintaining point of view is Joan Blos in *A Gathering of Days: A New England Girl's Journal,* that we find ourselves searching for a footnote: Where did Blos discover this journal; it is no work of fiction.

Omniscient Point of View

A distinct change from the limitations of the first-person point of view occurs when the writer chooses the freedom of the omniscient point of view. The writer in this case may recount relevant information about any and every character, their thoughts, ideas, and feelings about themselves as well as others. The writer may flash back into past experiences, feelings, and thoughts, or forward into what will happen in the future. The omniscient writer may tell anything he or she believes is relevant to the story, moving around, in, and through the characters, knowing everything, explaining motives, and giving the reader helpful information. We see in *Sounder,* for example, how the boy feels when his father has been taken to jail. "The loneliness that was always in the cabin . . . was heavier than ever now. It made the boy's tongue heavy. It pressed against his eyes, and they burned. It rolled against his ears. His head seemed to be squeezed inward, and it hurt." In adult fiction, details may be more subtly and less obviously related to the conflict and characters, but in children's stories, the writer concentrates on what is essential to the reader's understanding.

White finds the omniscient point of view best for *Charlotte's Web.* The objective, third-person statement that Fern wore a very pretty dress to the Fair has little significance until the young reader has the omniscient writer's interpretation: because she thought she'd see boys. When Wilbur learns of Charlotte's bloodthirsty appetite, he thinks that although Charlotte is pretty and clever, she is everything he doesn't like—scheming and fierce. The reader is as uncertain as Wilbur until White adds that fears and doubts go with new friendships. We know why Templeton finds the dirty junkyard his favorite spot; he thinks it's a good place to hide. If we had merely heard speeches and seen actions, we might have interpreted the details quite differently. White knows and tells what is in the minds of all his characters: Fern thinks the world is blissful; Lurvy feels weak at the sight of the dew-covered words in the miraculous web; Wilbur can't bear loneliness; Templeton is miserable when his rotten egg breaks. And when Wilbur tries to spin a web, Charlotte watches him delightedly, pleased that he is no quitter. White is truly the omniscient narrator. The reader knows everything because of the point of view.

Limited Omniscient Point of View

Often a story is told from the limited omniscient point of view. Here the writer chooses to see action through the eyes of one character—occasionally several characters—and to report that character's thoughts. In children's literature, this character is usually the protagonist. The writer shows not only what the character sees and hears, but also what the character feels and believes. The writer is inside as well as alongside the character.

When Dicey of *Dicey's Song* is asked in her classroom if her portrait-essay of a person she knows is really her relative, Dicey stands accused of showing fiction as fact, and even of plagiarism. She lifts her chin, and deliberately concentrates on something else—the sailboat Gram has let her refinish.

> She didn't answer. There was no way anybody could make her answer. In her mind, she made a picture: the little boat, she'd have painted it white by then, or maybe yellow—it was out on the Bay beyond Gram's dock and the wind pulled at the sails. Dicey could feel the smooth tiller under her hand; she could feel the way the wooden hull flowed through the water.

This is Dicey's story, her mind and feelings.

Although most of the story is told from Sara's point of view in Betsy Byars' novel *Summer of the Swans*, the story occasionally tells what is in the mind of Charlie, her retarded brother, as well. When we find him waiting for Sara while she is visiting a friend, we see Charlie's still body hunched over his knees: "The whole world seemed to have been turned off when Sara went into the Weiceks' house." His ticking watch is his pleasure as he listens to it and watches the red second hand sweep around the dial. These are simple and credible glimpses of what is in Charlie's mind. In Wilder's *Little House in the Big Woods*, we know from limited omniscient narration what pioneer life was like to a child. First, however, Wilder shows us the universal child Laura. Laura had never had more fun than when she fell from a stump into the soft snow and made pictures shaped like herself. Like everything else in the Wilder series, the understanding of Santa Claus and the giving of Christmas gifts are suited to the child's view of reality. "Santa Claus did not give grown people presents, but that was not because they had not been good. . . . It was because they were grown up, and grown people must give each other presents." Through Laura's innocent point of view we get the literal interpretation of a Bible story. As Adam names the animals, Laura envies him his clothing:

> Adam sat on a rock, and all the animals and birds, big and little, were gathered around him anxiously waiting to be told what kind of animals they were. Adam looked so comfortable. He did not have to be careful to keep his clothes clean, because he . . . wore only a skin around his middle.

Because through limited omniscience we see Laura's simplicity and innocence, we accept her account of pioneer life. In detailed description Laura tells us what butchering was like to the frontier child. As one detail follows another, from playing with the pig's bladder to roasting the pig's tail, the modern city child who knows only that meat comes from the supermarket is prepared to believe the truth of butchering on the frontier. By recognizing the feelings of childhood, the reader accepts the particular and specific routines and actions of Laura's life—different though they are from the reader's own. Wilder is successful in large part because she chooses Laura's point of view.

Objective Point of View

In the dramatic or objective point of view the writer does not enter the minds of any of the characters. The action speaks for itself as it unfolds and the reader hears speeches and sees action. The term *dramatic,* of course, comes from the drama where characters reveal themselves by what they say, what they do, and what others say about them. Drama permits the audience to see and hear, but to draw inferences only from what it sees and hears. Inner thoughts or feelings must be revealed by visible action. In most plays there is no interpreter standing at stage left to tell the audience what thoughts run through the speakers' minds. The audience must sometimes figure out for itself the meaning of the actions and speeches, deciding from a character's voice inflections or actions what—beneath or in spite of the words—may lie in that character's mind.

The objective or nearly objective point of view in some stories makes heavier demands on the imagination and understanding of the reader. Adults guess that when a character looks at the floor, scuffs the dust with a toe, or twists a lock of hair, that person is shy or embarrassed, but the ability to interpret body language is a skill few children have. It is the writer's responsibility when using the dramatic or objective point of view to describe and report action which, since it is without interpretation, must be within the child's understanding.

The *Incredible Journey* is an example of the use of omniscience for the minor human characters and of relative objectivity for the major animal characters. Realistically, we can never know what, if anything, is in the minds of the three animals. Since we cannot know, we instead must listen to the sounds they make, watch the tension in their bodies, note their actions and movements:

> The old dog walked gingerly into the shallow water, shivering . . . turning his head away. Once more the Labrador swam the river, climbed out . . . shook himself, and barked. There was no mistaking the command. The old dog took another reluctant step forward, whining piteously, his expressive tail tucked under. . . . again the Labrador swam across. . . .

Because we see the reluctant step of the old terrier, hear the piteous whine, and note the tucked-under tail, we draw conclusions about how the dog feels. The terrier "swam in jerky rapid movements, his head held high out of the water, his little black eyes rolling." Burnford does better than most writers of animal stories, but even she steps over the objective line when she uses animal/human comparisons, calling the terrier a white cavalier, and describing his wild actions on reaching the shore as "transports of joy"; he is like a "shipwrecked mariner after six weeks at sea on a raft."

Allan W. Eckert, in his portrayal of the badger in *Incident at Hawk's Hill*, is perhaps more successful; his objectivity falters less frequently. Eckert mentions instinct and experience as aids to the badger as she digs a tunnel five feet into the earth to a point she chooses for a nesting chamber. He describes the digging, the earth moving and scattering, and the choosing of a spot fifty feet away to start a longer escape tunnel connecting with the chamber. An incredible engineering feat now accomplished with unerring skill, she wheezes with fatigue. We observe actions, but we do not know thoughts.

EVALUATING POINT OF VIEW IN CHILDREN'S LITERATURE

Maturity of the Reader

It is not possible, nor even relevant, to make authoritative statements about the best or most successful point of view for children's literature. We can make a few sensible inferences, however. The first-person point of view may present difficulties for the smallest child. Because the child is just learning his or her own "I" identity, he or she may have trouble identifying with the strange "I" of the story. Furthermore, first-person narration may be difficult for the young child to understand because the child is limited to knowing only what the narrator can know. "I" can transmit only limited interpretation or understanding.

The older child, on the other hand, may find first-person stories exciting proof of understanding, and of the capacity to project self into another "I." First-person seems to be an increasingly popular choice of point of view in stories for older children or young adolescents. When Twain wrote *Huckleberry Finn* in first-person, he probably had adult readers in mind, but when Robert Louis Stevenson wrote *Kidnapped* and *Treasure Island*, he must have wished to involve young readers in you-are-there adventures. Since that time we have had many more first-person stories for older readers, and currently there is an abundance of them; they seem to have proliferated since Emily Neville's *It's Like This, Cat*. Like David's conflict with his father in the book, conflicts in these stories often explore the growing-up tensions in child or adolescent. Paul Zindel's *Pigman*, for example, shows guilt over youthful thoughtlessness.

As for the objective point of view, children are inexperienced in draw-ing conclusions from speeches and from descriptions of actions; they may find the dramatic point of view hard to understand. This necessity for objectivity, therefore, presents a particular kind of challenge to the writer whose audience is the small child. If the story relies, however, on pictures showing the characters' feelings through facial expressions—as they may in picture books—the interpretive words about emotions and thoughts are not so essential.

Animal Realism

Animal realism is a popular kind of story for children that presents special problems in point of view. Look back at *Charlotte's Web*, a story in which the characters are animals. White's story is not a realistic story about pigs and spiders and rats that live in barns; we know that. Such a story would have to show characters living and moving like animals, making animal noises. It would have to be told from a point of view that does not imagine and report the thoughts of nonhumans acting human. White had no intention of being realistic; he chose to portray his animals living as animals and yet similar to people. So successful is White that we have a distinct feeling that they *are* people. In fact, since they all think and worry and love and hurt and laugh and needle one another as people do, White's animal story reveals human truths of friendship and continuity, death and maturity. His careful control of what is animal and what is human in each character, never confusing the two, is the source of his success.

The objective or dramatic point of view seems to be the logical choice for a realistic animal story. We have noted how successful Burnford is in maintaining an objective point of view in *The Incredible Journey*. But *Black Beauty* by Anna Sewell presents a distinct contrast. The book may give the impression of being a realistic story because the horses lead "horse lives." *Black Beauty's* first person narrator, however, is a horse, using human language to tell us his horse emotions and thoughts. Sewell inconsistently mixes and confuses Black Beauty's animal and human natures. The point of view destroys realism. The horse's feelings would be believable—if we assumed that animal feelings are identical to our own. It is, furthermore, inconsistent with realism that we should know the animal's feelings by anything but observation and speculation, although perhaps accompanied by a hearty dose of our sympathy. Black Beauty, speaking in the first-person "I," says:

> Day by day, hole by hole, our bearing reins were shortened, and instead of looking forward with pleasure to having my harness put on . . . I began to dread it.

Black Beauty decides to do his duty despite his harassment. But worse things come; the sharp bit cuts his tongue and his jaw, and he froths at the mouth. He feels:

> a pressure on my windpipe, which often made my breathing very uncomfortable . . . my neck and chest were strained and painful, my mouth and tongue tender, and I felt worn and depressed.

While perhaps it is true that the story makes us feel like a horse, as Frances Clarke Sayers says,[1] the reverse is more nearly accurate; this horse feels the way we would feel if we human beings were living in horses' bodies. In a realistic animal story we expect to find at least a relatively objective point of view, whether the story is for child or adult.

Choice of point of view, as we can see, affects the reader's acceptance of a story. Some writers of animal stories manage to avoid the temptation to sentimentality; they seek to convey the reality of animal life by picturing the animals' natural habitat, showing the relationships of predators, weather, seasons, and maturity cycles on animal lives. Such a writer is Felix Salten, author of *Bambi*. Sometimes Salten successfully evokes wonder; through the mind of Bambi, the deer, the reader watches the approach of winter, feeling the cold rain and hearing the shushing of falling leaves.

> [It pleases Bambi] to see the milk-white veils of mist steam from the meadow in the morning. . . . They vanished so beautifully in the sunshine. The hoar frost . . . with such dazzling whiteness delighted him too.

Salten clearly and believably carries the suspense through a winter in which Bambi's first enemy is starvation and his second is Man. However, when Salten depicts as human Bambi's affection for his doe, or his admiration for the wise owl, the other information—the accurate natural history—seems less reliable. Salten begins to falsify when he humanizes even the leaves, which are also speaking characters. They worry and reassure, are troubled and touched. Salten is totally omniscient; his assuming unlimited knowledge may make us question his otherwise accurate portrayal of nature and its forces. Such complete omniscience, perhaps some of it traceable to the translation, is sentimental; it creates doubts in the reader's mind about what is really true.

Fantasy

If fantasy is to be successful, we must willingly suspend disbelief. If the story's characters, conflict, and theme seem believable to us, we find it plausible and even natural to know the thoughts and feelings of animal characters or tiny people. In fact, the story may be so good that we wish it *were* true. We wish we knew Arrietty. This persuasion that the writer wishes to bring about—persuasion that "what if" is really "it's true"—is most successful when the writer is consistent about point of view.

Point of view is an essential part of our appreciation of Mary Norton's *The Borrowers*. Norton's central characters are diminutive; we see most of the action through the eyes of young Arrietty. The Clock family is only six inches tall, and everything in the story, from postage stamps to primroses, is seen in relationship to the characters' size. If we are to believe that Arrietty is so tiny, we must enter the dimensions and scale of her world. Pushing through the grass, she is startled by something glittering and discovers, "It was an eye. Or it looked like an eye. Clear and bright like the color of the sky. An eye like her own but enormous." While "human beans" find a walk across the carpet easy, to tiny Arrietty it is like pushing through a dense field of grain. She moves off the rug to the shiny floor beside the wall where she can run; She "loved running. Carpets were heavy-going—thick and clinging, they held you up." Beneath a table is a great expanse of the unknown, dark as a cave, "a great cavern of darkness. . . . Chair legs were everywhere and chair seats obscured her view." The yard and garden are huge; here is Arrietty's glimpse:

> A greenish beetle, shining in the sunlight, came toward her across the stones. She laid her fingers lightly on its shell and it stood still . . . when she moved her hand the beetle went swiftly on. An ant came hurrying in a busy zigzag. She danced in front of it to tease it and put out her foot. . . . Cautiously she moved . . . in amongst the green blades. As she parted them gently with her bare hands, drops of water plopped on her skirt. . . . pulling herself up now and again by rooty stems into this jungle of moss and wood-violet and creeping leaves of clover. . . . she sat down suddenly on a gnarled leaf of primrose.

No wonder we suspend disbelief and are convinced the Clock family lives. Not only do we know that safety pins and postage stamps have a way of disappearing, but we see everything from furniture to flowers from the point of view of Arrietty, who lives in our world, though seen from a six-inch height. The scale is relative to a tiny borrower, and point of view is thoroughly consistent.

The consistency in the point of view and the detail which is described from this point of view create a memorable miniature world in *The Borrowers*. It is this same strongly established point of view and its detailed development that helps to account for some of the greatest successes in children's fantasy. One thinks of Carroll's *Alice's Adventures in Wonderland* and many of Maurice Sendak's books.

Stories of Other Countries

Stories of children from other countries are a particular problem for the writer. Early in the twentieth century a series of books was published about children of other lands—*The Eskimo Twins, The Japanese Twins,* and others by Lucy Fitch Perkins. These stories stressed what seemed to be peculiarities of life in other countries. We read of flat and unreal children living in exotic and uninhabitable lands. Fascinating as it all was, stories about children eating whale blubber or octopus, or wearing wooden shoes or tatami sandals, may now seem condescending. We recall, however, at this point in our discussion of children's literature, that once we believe in the reality of character, we believe in the vicarious experience of the character's way of life. How can a story about other countries show how life is lived there without making the country and its people weird and wondrous, strange and unbelievable? People in other countries may, after all, eat different foods, live in homes unlike our own, or work at jobs unfamiliar to us.

One effective way in which the writer can picture the country accurately, make the story credible, and at the same time present the truth of human nature, is to make careful use of point of view. An objective point of view in a story about life in Morocco, for example, might leave a child puzzled by uninterpreted facts. Some degree of omniscience, however, achieves several results. First of all, since we can know thoughts, the character can more easily be shown as like us. Then, once we recognize these similarities, we accept the character as believable. From this acceptance of the character we can move on to believe the character's way of life is different but interesting, rather than strange or beneath us.

Children, like adults, see first the obvious differences in people: he has black hair and I have blonde; she is tall and I am short. From these outward physical traits, we shift our attention to more subtle differences, like names, houses, pets, and games—differences we all expect and look for. In *The House of Sixty Fathers* Meindert DeJong satisfies our curiosity on these scores; Tien Pao looks distinctively Chinese and wears clothing different from ours. He lives on a houseboat and has a pet pig. Once DeJong has established outward differences and similarities, he effectively uses his limited omniscient point of view to show more significant and subtle similarities. As we see the events of the conflict through Tien Pao's eyes and mind, we note that the protagonist's emotions and thoughts are like our own. Tien Pao loves and laughs, cries and fears. We are won to understanding what the people and their way of life are like, what it is like to be lost and wandering in a war-ravaged country, to be forced to find our parents on our own, to be cared for by strangers, and adopted by sixty fathers, then to be safe with our family once again.

Point of view also reveals other things about people from foreign lands.

Through DeJong's use of limited omniscient point of view, American readers not only discover experiences unfamiliar to themselves and to this Chinese child, but also how familiar parts of American experience must look to a child of another land. We, who automatically peel paper from chewing gum and pop it into our mouths to chew continuously and without purpose, find the action nothing unusual, but Tien Pao is mystified. Not every child has ridden in a jeep, and yet any reader can discover the experience, since here we ourselves ride for the first time in a jeep, a small, open carriage:

> The man behind the strange wheel did things with his hands and feet. The carriage suddenly roared, shot ahead. It hopped and jumped and bounced in swiftness over the little road. It went still faster.

In consistent, childlike point of view, each aggressive action Tien Pao sees is committed by impersonal war equipment, but every kind act is done by a human being whom Tien Pao comes to know.

An interesting corollary to consider beside *Sixty Fathers* is *Dragonwings,* Laurence Yep's story of a Chinese immigrant boy coming to California, "the Golden Mountain." As he approaches the California coast, he is disappointed; it is only "a brown smudge on the horizon," the wooden houses "like shells of wood which terrible monsters had spun about themselves." As the narrator tries to learn the new language, the "letters keep on rearranging themselves in the most confusing patterns." Because they can use their great powers for good or evil, the Chinese immigrants call the Americans "demons"—demons whose calendars, even, are not properly arranged, not based sensibly on the movements of the moon nor on the ten-day week.

Because we are aware of their feelings, we find ourselves breathlessly involved in the Chinese family's lives, and are fearful for their safety. Although their lives are different from our own, they are themselves like us. We see people, countries, cultures and ways of life—all through the point of view and wide eyes of a child—and are persuaded that a child is a child in any culture. The writer's use of the omniscient point of view has helped.

SUMMARY

Point of view, an integral part of storytelling, determines the view the reader gets of events, character motivation, suspense and climax, and theme. There are four major kinds of point of view: first-person with an "I" narrator, omniscient with an all-knowing writer, limited omniscient with focus on one or a few characters, and objective or dramatic with a report only of what can be seen and heard.

Since the limited experience of children makes it hard for them to draw their own inferences from objective description of action and speech, the writer often clarifies the story by use of some degree of omniscience. The pleasure of literature comes from style, character, plot—all of the literary elements. In literature for children, understanding of character and the other elements is aided by a sensitive choice of point of view adapted to subject matter, type of conflict, and expected maturity level of readers.

READING AND EVALUATING

1. **Animal realism**   Read *Blue Canyon Horse* by Ann Nolan Clark, or another animal realism story. What is the point of view? Is it suitable for animal realism? What is the effect? Compare point of view to this story to that in *smoky* by Will James or to that in *Black Beauty* by Anna Sewell. What are the relative effects upon the reader?

2. **Regional realism**   Read a novel by Rebecca Caudill or Ester Wier. What is the point of view? Does it affect tone? Does it produce sentimentality? Does it alter credibility? Explain.

3. **Fantasy**   Read and compare *Paddington Bear* by Michael Bond and *Winnie-the-Pooh* by A. A. Milne. What is the point of view in each story? What effect has point of view on each of the two stories? How does point of view affect tone? Characterization?

4. **Realism**   Read a *Moffat* book by Eleanor Estes and compare it for point of view with one by Betsy Byars or a *Ramona* book by Beverly Cleary. What impact has point of view on characterization in each case?

5. **Social Issues realism**   Read *Dorp Dead* by Julia Cunningham, or another first-person novel. Does the writer stay within the limitations of the chosen point of view? Describe the diction. Is it believable considering the narrator's age and character? What is the effect of first person on the conflict? On characterization? Setting? Mood and tone?

NOTE

1 "Walt Disney Accused," by Francis Clarke Sayers in *Children and Literature: Views and Reviews,* Virginia Haviland, ed. Glenview, IL: Scott, Foresman, 1973.

RECOMMENDED BOOKS CITED IN THIS CHAPTER

ARMSTRONG, WILLIAM. *Sounder.* New York: Harper, 1969.

BLOS, JOAN W. *A Gathering of Days: A New England Girl's Journal, 1830–32.* New York: Scribner's, 1979.

BURNFORD, SHEILA. *The Incredible Journey.* Boston: Little, Brown, 1961.

BYARS, BETSY. *The Summer of the Swans.* New York: Viking, 1970.

CHILDRESS, ALICE. *A Hero ain't nothin' but a Sandwich.* New York: Coward, 1973.

CLEARY, BEVERLY. *Dear Mr. Henshaw.* New York: Morrow, 1983.

DEJONG, MEINDERT. *The House of Sixty Fathers.* New York: Harper, 1956.

ECKERT, ALLAN W. *Incident at Hawk's Hill.* Boston: Little, Brown, 1971.

FATIO, LOUISE. *The Happy Lion.* New York: McGraw, 1954.

FOX, PAULA. *The Slave Dancer.* Scarsdale, NY: Bradbury, 1973.

L'ENGLE, MADELEINE. *A Ring of Endless Light.* New York: Farrar, Straus & Giroux, 1980.

MOWAT, FARLEY. *Owls in the Family.* Boston: Little, Brown, 1961.

NEVILLE, EMILY. *It's Like This, Cat.* New York: Harper, 1963.

NORTON, MARY. *The Borrowers.* New York: Harcourt, 1965.

O'DELL, SCOTT. *Island of the Blue Dolphins.* Boston: Houghton Mifflin, 1960.

RYLANT, CYNTHIA. *A Fine White Dust.* New York: Bradbury, 1986.

SALTEN, FELIX. *Bambi.* New York: Grosset & Dunlap, 1929.

STEVENSON, ROBERT LOUIS. *Kidnapped.* New York: Scribner's, 1913 (first published, 1886).

_____. *Treasure Island.* New York: Scribner's, 1911 (first published, 1883).

TWAIN, MARK. *Huckleberry Finn.* New York: Dutton, 1955 (first published, 1884).

VOIGT, CYNTHIA. *Dicey's Song.* New York: Random House, 1982.

WHITE, E. B. *Charlotte's Web.* New York: Harper, 1952.

WILDER, LAURA INGALLS. *Little House in the Big Woods.* New York: Harper, 1953 (first published, 1932).

YEP, LAURENCE. *Dragonwings.* New York: Harper, 1975.

ZINDEL, PAUL. *The Pigman.* New York: Harper, 1968.

Illustration from *The Elephant's Child*, illustration copyright © 1983 by Lorinda Bryan Cauley. Reprinted by permission of Harcourt Brace Jovanovich, Inc.

Style

Let us now consider the literary element that makes language memorable—its style. Frequently someone asks, "But does the writer know what he or she is doing with words?" Yes. The author has added, subtracted, experimented, and substituted, creating the style that best tells his or her story. The skilled writer chooses words that become setting, plot, character, and theme to make a piece of literature.

Style is basically words, *how* an author says something, as opposed to *what* he or she says. From infinite numbers of words available, the writer chooses and arranges words to create a particular story, the words and arrangement best for that story. Rufus Moffat, for example, on the first day of school:

> . . . felt a slight impulse to run home and play as he used to. Play what? . . . Mud pies? he asked himself sarcastically. Pooh! He was too old for all that business now. He was going to school. Soon he would be going home to lunch.

This is Rufus, his own style—that is, author Estes' choice of the style suited to situation and character. By contrast, O'Dell's formal and restrained language and simple sentence structure constitute the style suited to the setting, conflict, and character in his story *Island of the Blue Dolphins*. The protagonist, who lives a life totally dependent upon nature, says in the opening lines:

> I remember the day the Alcut ship came to our island. At first it seemed like a small shell afloat on the sea. Then it grew larger and was a gull with folded wings. At last in the rising sun it became what it really was—a red ship with two red sails.

O'Dell uses nature comparisons throughout the story. Karana's brother Ramo has eyes "half-closed like those of a lizard lying on a rock about to flick out its tongue to catch a fly." An invader's beard is combed until it "shines like a cormorant's wing." Karana says the enemy's mouth is "like the edge of a stone knife." A swarm of friendly dolphins dives in and out "as if they were weaving a piece of cloth with their broad snouts." The sea elephants have faces "like wet earth that has dried in the sun and cracked." Word pictures and comparisons describe characters, action, and setting, but in a style suited to this story of a protagonist who lives with her antagonist, nature. The styles of *The Moffats* and *Island of the Blue Dolphins* could not be interchanged. In each case the style is right for that particular story.

In fiction, style at its best increases our belief in the characters' reality. We come to know them through the words they say, through the words that describe how they look and how they act. We are eager to believe in the characters' experiences, following the plot and visualizing the action described in the chosen words. Through words, we see, hear, and even smell the setting as we realize its effect upon characters and conflict. Style is the product of all the choices the writer makes.

These choices are, of course, an entirely personal matter, since style and writer are inextricable. Mark Twain's style is no more Ogden Nash's style than Twain is Nash. One writer deals with the nature of reality or fantasy in one way; another expresses his or her vision in quite another way. A writer does, of course, vary her or his own style. Since one story differs from another, styles will differ as the writer suits style to story. Notice how O'Dell's restrained and dignified style in the opening of *Island* differs from his brisk and active language in the opening of *The King's Fifth*. This is not Karana but a different character:

> It was eight bells of the morning watch, early in the month of June, that we entered the Sea of Cortés. On our port bow was the Island of California. To the east lay the coast of New Spain.
>
> I sat in my cabin setting down in ink a large island sighted at dawn, which did not show on the master chart. The day was already stifling hot, so I had left the door ajar. Suddenly the door closed. . . .

Style is not something applied to a finished piece of writing, but it is the writing, conveying both the idea and the writer's view of the idea. Henry James says that each word and every punctuation mark directly contribute to meaning; the content of the story and how it is told are inseparable.[1] Tone, word choice, grammatical structure, devices of comparison, sound, and rhythm are style. All of these elements vary with the author's purpose, as the idea, the incidents, and the characters vary. Style gives the whole work its distinction and makes the story memorable.

Originality and style are not the same but they are related in the sense that a writer is himself or herself an original. Nor should novelty be confused with style, for novelty is sometimes mere gimmickry—as it often is in Paul Zindel's novels, for example—rather than unique and personal expression. If the writer's way of telling the story and its truth is distinctively the writer's own, then that expression has a personal mark, and the style should become the best possible one for a particular work.

DEVICES OF STYLE

The most easily identified element of style is the writer's use of certain specific devices of language. Many of these stylistic devices are listed in dictionaries of literary terms, but our chief concern here is with those most often used in children's literature.

Connotation

Connotation is the associative or emotional meaning of a word. Connotative meaning, when added to dictionary meaning, or *denotation,* adds significance and impact to a term. Charlotte, for example, is not as big as a thimble, nor as small as a fingernail, nor as round as a button—all denotative comparisons which might convey her proper size and shape but which have no emotional impact. Charlotte is, instead, "about the size of a gumdrop." Now there's a reassuring comparison for a bloodthirsty spider. The stomach of gluttonous Templeton is not bulbous, nor enlarged, nor even like a ball. Instead, "as big around as a jelly jar" expresses comparative size and shape, but adds pleasant connotations. No spider egg sac ever had the appeal of Charlotte's; it is neither orange nor pink, but peach-colored and looks like cotton candy. The images of cotton candy, jelly jar, and gumdrop are all favorites with children; each of these comparisons describes size, color, and shape, but adds pleasant and positive emotional meaning.

Imagery

By far the most frequently used device, and the most essential, is imagery. *Imagery* is the appeal to any of the senses; it helps create setting, establish a mood, or show a character. We use imagery in our everyday conversations to describe sounds, smells, and sights. We say the sky is sapphire blue, the carpet is celery green, a jacket is fire engine red; we describe the nature of a sound as clanging, buzzing, humming, or thundering. We say that tastes are bitter, sweet, or salty, that smells are acrid or musty, and that texture is scaly or slimy.

The writer, too, relies on imagery to give the reader impressions of what the writer wishes to depict. But *verisimilitude,* or description to duplicate reality, is not the writer's only goal; suggestion and release of the imagination are important. The writer, by the choice of details and of the words used to describe the details, stirs the reader's imagination; the impact may be recognition or delight.

Charlotte's Web demonstrates the use and effectiveness of imagery. In the opening pages of the third chapter, Wilbur has just come to live in the manure pile of the Zuckerman barn, and we explore the building with him. No barn was ever more real, more suggestive of security and activity. The imagery convinces us as we smell the variety of smells, feel the warmth and coolness, and see the clutter of equipment. We may not settle down snugly in the manure pile, but we are as much at home in the barn as Wilbur is.

White describes the silence of the barn, but by sound imagery of a negative kind. The quiet itself is described by White's noting the absence of the customary noises; animals are so quiet that we hear only the weather-vane:

> The sheep lay motionless. Even the goose was quiet. Overhead, on the main floor, nothing stirred: the cows were resting, the horses dozed. Templeton had quit work. . . . The only sound was a slight scraping noise from the rooftop, where the weather-vane swung back and forth.

When Wilbur first arrives at the Fair Grounds, that setting is created for the reader by imagery. As White lists the senses one by one, a specific image appeals to each:

> . . . they could hear music and see the Ferris wheel turning in the sky. They could smell the dust of the race track where the sprinkling cart had moistened it; and they could smell hamburgers frying and see balloons aloft. They could hear sheep blatting in their pens. An enormous voice over the loudspeaker. . . .

White relies on imagery to make the reader aware not only of setting but also of character and action. When Wilbur gets his buttermilk bath, we see him; he stands with closed eyes, feeling the buttermilk trickling over his sides. When he greedily opens his mouth and tastes the delicious buttermilk, Wilbur's childlike character is revealed. He stands in the pig trough and drools with hunger, while White itemizes the slops, each particle a distinctly visual image with a taste of its own:

> It was a delicious meal—skim milk, wheat middlings, leftover pancakes, half a doughnut, the rind of a summer squash, two pieces of stale toast, a third of a gingersnap, a fish tail, one orange peel . . . the scum off a cup of cocoa, an ancient jelly roll, a strip of paper from the lining of the garbage pail, and a spoonful of raspberry jello.

As we visualize slops, each item has color and shape in our minds. At the same time, White appeals to taste by listing foods a child knows and likes. And finally, the variety has the distinct quality of slops, since it is punctuated by a fish tail and a bit of garbage pail liner. Imagery not only helps create setting, but pictures action and character as well.

Figurative Language

Another device of style is *figurative language.* The writer uses words in a nonliteral way, giving them meaning beyond their usual, everyday definitions, and thereby adding an extra dimension to meaning. Personification, simile, and metaphor are the most common kinds of figurative language in stories for children.

Children's stories often make use of *personification,* the giving of human traits to nonhuman beings or inanimate objects. In *Charlotte's Web* a large cast of nonhuman characters is personified, from Wilbur to the maple trees and even crickets:

> The crickets sang in the grasses. They sang the song of summer's ending. . . .
> The sheep . . . felt so uneasy they broke a hole in the pasture fence. . . .
> The gander discovered the hole and led his family through. . . . A little maple tree . . . heard the cricket song and turned bright red with anxiety.

We hear the crickets singing, rather than chirping. The sheep are "uneasy," the goose "family" eats apples, and nearby the "anxious" maple turns autumn colors. Human qualities are given to everything. Where Salten fails in *Bambi,* White is successful because his personification is fresh, and the story is fantasy, not sentimentalized realism.

One of the simplest figurative devices is the *simile,* a stated comparison between unlike things, using *as, like,* or occasionally, *than.* Straw fluttered down "like confetti" at the exciting news from the Fair loudspeaker. When Charlotte is weary, she is swollen and listless and feels "like the end of a long day." These very specific comparisons are easy to see, since they are directly stated. Their combination of imagery and comparison makes them distinctive enough to stir the reader's imagination.

Implied comparisons are called *metaphors.* They are sometimes so neatly put, so recognizably clear that we scarcely notice them—like the familiar beads of water decorating Charlotte's web. As Charlotte catches and stings her insect fare, she metaphorically "anaesthetizes" them. Templeton hears the Fair is a figurative "paradise," where he'll find a "veritable treasure" of leftovers, enough for "a whole army of rats." Paradise is great happiness, treasure great wealth, and army a vast number; all are metaphors.

Hyperbole

We are so accustomed to exaggeration as humor that we scarcely recognize it as a figure of speech; we often stretch a comparison to create *hyperbole*. When, for example, Mrs. Zuckerman is scared to death, or Wilbur threatens to die of a broken heart, the author uses hyperbole that has become part of our daily conversation. But when Templeton, grousing that he did not come to the Fair to be a newsboy, refuses to "spend all my time chasing down to the dump after advertising material. . . . next thing you'll want . . . is a dictionary," his grumbling and sarcasm are hyperbole. Wilbur uses self-pitying hyperbole when he says, "I'm less than two months old and I'm tired of living." But we may laugh at the words of the sheep whose hyperbole is sheer imaginative extremism. He speaks to Templeton:

> "If Wilbur is killed and his trough stands empty day after day, you'll grow so thin we can look right through your stomach and see objects on the other side."

Understatement

The reverse of exaggeration is *understatement*, or playing down. Like hyperbole, it may be used for comic effect. When Fern bites into a raspberry with a concealed "bad-tasting bug," and gets "discouraged," discouragement seems minimal. When Avery removes from his pocket the frog that has traveled back and forth on the barn swing all morning, scrunched and dried in a tight pants pocket, we read that the frog seems tired from a morning of swinging. Merely tired?

Allusion

One figure of speech, *allusion,* probably has meaning only to the mature reader, since it relies on recognition of a reference to something in our common understanding, our past, or our literature. No adult will miss an allusion, for example, to a disastrous experience, an exam perhaps, when it is called "my Waterloo." White adds an opportunity for pleasure for the adult reader when he alludes to the call of the white-throated sparrow which must have come all the way from Boston, "Oh, Peabody, Peabody, Peabody!" Some adults may recognize reference to the Peabody sisters of Salem, but if not, no meaning is lost; it remains a New Englander's description of the bird song. One of the delights of *Alice in Wonderland* for the Victorian readers was the wealth of allusions they could recognize, although contemporary readers, young and old, may miss them. Allusion is difficult for children to catch, since it relies on a background they lack.

Symbol

A *symbol* is a person, object, situation, or action that operates on two levels of meaning, the literal and the figurative or suggestive. Certain symbols are universal: the dove is the symbol for peace, a flag symbolizes a certain country. Other symbols are particular to a story. Clearly, the necklace of shells Karana gives to Tutok in *Island of the Blue Dolphins* is a symbol of friendship. Less obvious is the Borrowers' emerald watch among all the unneeded and unmissed items borrowed from Aunt Sophie's household. We might call it a symbol for the latent materialism in Pod, and particularly in Homily.

Puns and Wordplay

An imaginative writer who enjoys the pleasure of words is tempted to *echo* words of other literary works. When White says that Templeton has no "milk of rodent kindness," we may recognize an echo from *Macbeth*. Wilbur is lured back to his pen by the promise of slops and the goose warns, "It's the old pail trick, Wilbur. Don't fall for it!" We hear echos of "the old shell game." A sly grammatical error slides in, one that parents frequently correct in their children: "He also has a smudge on one side where he lays in the manure." And instead of correcting the grammar, lies for lays, Zuckerman corrects the facts: "He lays in clean straw." Then White adds a bad *pun*.

> "If that ancient egg ever breaks, this barn will be untenable."
> "What's that mean?" asked Wilbur.
> "It means nobody will be able to live here on account of the smell."

And finally, White plays with words in still other ways. Naive Wilbur uses faultless logic when he argues with the lamb that he is not less than nothing:

> "I don't think there is any such thing as less than nothing. Nothing is absolutely the limit of nothingness. It's the lowest you can go. . . . If there were something that was less than nothing, then nothing would not be nothing. . . ."

Devices of Sound

Many stories for children are meant not only for silent reading, but also for reading aloud. The writer who chooses words with care can increase pleasure and clarity by devices of sound.

Onomatopoeia

One sound device called *onomatopoeia*, or words that sound like their meanings, dominates an occasional paragraph of *Charlotte's Web*. For example, as White describes Wilbur's eating his slops, he uses the onomatopoeic words "swishing and swooshing," which suggest Wilbur's happy gluttony. While these slushy sounds suggest one kind of eating, the explosive sounds of "gulping and sucking" describe another.

Alliteration

Another easily recognized sound device is *alliteration*, repetition of initial consonants: "They *s*ang the *s*ong of *s*ummer's ending." The effect of the sentence is musical, but its movement is slow and the music sad and final. By contrast, the Zuckerman dump becomes exciting as visual imagery rhythmically piles up in interesting debris, layer upon layer. Alliteration then adds to the pleasure of the passage: "*b*roken *b*ottles... *d*iscarded *d*ishmops... last *m*onth's *m*agazines."

Assonance

A device that enhances meaning by the repetition of similar vowel sounds within a phrase is called *assonance*. When we hear the crickets' song, "*a* sad, m*o*n*o*t*o*n*o*us s*o*ng," the neutral *a* and the similarly sounded *o*'s, suggest the feeling of sorrow and sameness. Reading the passage aloud shows how sadness and monotony are here extended by assonance.

Consonance

The close repetition of consonant sounds is called *consonance*. In the phrase "emp*t*y *t*in cans and dir*t*y rags and bi*t*s of me*t*al and broken bo*tt*les," repetition of the abrupt *t*'s emphasizes the idea of ragged remains of unrelated items—junk. Again, reading the sentence aloud is the best test for sound devices, since sound rather than spelling shows how meaning is affected.

Rhythm

So closely is *rhythm*—from the Greek word meaning flow—associated with poetry and verse that we often forget that it is also part of prose. Stories that are read aloud to children can make particularly effective use of rhythm, which in prose is sometimes called *cadence*. White uses the word *and* to create rhythm as he shows the Zuckerman dump, an accumulation of one item after another, each joined to the others by *and*s. Reading aloud is the test for rhythm as it is for other sound devices. Here is:

> . . . an astonishing pile of old bottles and empty tin cans and dirty rags and bits of metal and broken bottles and broken hinges and broken springs and dead batteries and last month's magazines and old discarded dishmops and tattered overalls . . . and useless junk of all kinds, including a wrong-size crank for a broken ice-cream freezer.

The rhythmic list slows to a halt with the last comma, followed by the final, jerking phrase filled with abrupt and explosive consonants: "a *wrong size crank* for a *broken* ice-cream *freezer*." The changed rhythm brings the astonishing pile to an end.

An unusually effective example of cadence occurs in White's description of the rope swing as it flies back and forth. The first phrases of the passage anticipate "and jumped," and then the swinging begins. Again by reading aloud, we hear each of the phrases shorten, as the arc of the swing shortens. Abruptly the words bring the swing to a halt, and the swinger jumps to the ground:

> Then you got up all your nerve, took a deep breath, and jumped. . . .the rope would twist and you would twist and turn with the rope. Then you would drop down, down, down out of the sky and come sailing back into the barn almost into the hayloft, then sail out again (not quite so far this time), then in again (not quite so high), then out again, then in again, then out, then in; and then you'd jump off and fall down and let somebody else try it.

Rhythm ceases completely with the series of short, explosive words and phrases at the end of the paragraph. As the successive phrases shorten, we find pleasure in the description of action as well as in the understanding of the experience. Rhythm is the key.

EVALUATING STYLE IN CHILDREN'S LITERATURE

Trite versus Fresh Style

A story written in cliches is dull, just as a person who thinks in cliches is dull. In *The Moffats* Estes makes an ordinary situation seem unusual by the freshness of her style. Jane Moffat, making a delivery for her dressmaker mother,

> . . . took the package and walked as carefully up the street as though she were carrying a lemon meringue pie. The Cadwalladers lived in a sleepy-looking gray house across the street from Chief Mulligan's. The shingles protruded over each window like languorous, drooping eyelids. "I bet they close like eyes after everyone has gone to bed," thought Jane, grinning to herself as she rang the bell.

Estes' personification of the sleepy gray house, her imagery that makes us see just how Jane carries her package, her figurative comparison of the package itself to a pie—these devices make a girl approaching a doorstep a fresh experience.

By contrast, Judy Blume's books, despite the appeal of their subject matter, are often trite in style. In *Then Again, Maybe I Won't* the first person narrator has just found that his friend is shoplifting:

> The salesman told me the mitt I liked was $37.50. I thought that was a lot of money.... I'd have to think about it.... I walked back to the cash register where Joel was waiting. I wanted to know if he thought $37.50 was too much for a mitt. But I never asked him because he was smiling his crooked smile and humming some tune.
>
> I thought, oh no! Please, Joel. I don't want to be sick again. I don't want to go back to the hospital. I know what you've done. I can tell by just looking at you. What'd you take this time, Joel?

We've heard this before. Or even worse—we feel we must have, even if we know we haven't. There are no surprises. Nothing is vivid. The first person narrator gives us no sense of the person speaking because the words lack individuality and freshness. Similarly, the style of Peter and Connie Roop's writing in *Keep the Lights Burning, Abbie* is monotonous, although the subject—Abbie Burgess, the girl who, left alone in 1856, kept the Maine lighthouse lamps burning—is potentially interesting. Simple sentences repeat words and information unnecessarily, and the reader grows impatient waiting to get on with the action.

Notice, by contrast, the opening of a chapter in *The Bears' House*, Marilyn Sachs' story of Fran Ellen, who is trying desperately to care for her baby sister in a chaotic home:

> I don't know why, but that day I felt scared. As soon as I snuck back into the building at recess, my feet began shaking so, I didn't see how I'd ever get myself home. I shouldn't have gone, but I got to thinking about Flora....
>
> I went on down the stairs through the basement and out the back door. I could hardly get my feet moving. And then I thought I heard somebody else behind me. Quick, I swung around. Nobody there, but that scared feeling got inside my mouth, and made my teeth rattle. Then I ran. My feet didn't shake so hard when I ran....

We know Fran Ellen. In this short section little has happened, and yet this narrator speaks in language both fresh and personal: snuck, shaking feet, rattling teeth, scared feelings inside her mouth. Simple as the diction is, the style is expressive.

Style, the manner of speaking, determines our impression of a personality. Look, for example, at the speech of the ship captain and the passenger on the opening page of Joan Aiken's *The Stolen Lake*. The contrast between proper diction from the captain and slovenly language from Dido immediately sets up the difference in character. "How old are you, child?" asks the captain. "I dunno," is the response. "You do not *know* your own *age*? You do not *look* like a stupid child." "O' course I ain't stupid," Dido replies. "But before I came on board this here ship I were asleep a plaguey long time aboard a whaling vessel . . . Davy Jones alone knows how long." From page one, we are aware of character.

Note, too, the manner in which Jerome Foxworthy in *The Moves Make the Man* talks; his language is clear, descriptive, and that of a young basketball player:

> . . . cradling the ball and at the last minute pulling my left hand away like Oscar Robertson and snapping that lubricated right wrist and knowing, feeling it right straight through from the tips of the fingers that had let fly the ball and touched it all the way to the last, straight down the front edge of my toes just before they hit the ground again, that the shot was true, feeling the swish and tickle of the net cords rushing quick down my nerves, and landing square and jaunty in time to watch, along with everybody else, as the ball popped through the net without a single bit of deceit, so clean it kicked the bottom of the cords back up and looped them over the rim, which is called a bottoms up and means you shot perfect and some people even count them three points in street games.

In *Hatchet*, Brian finds seventeen leathery turtle eggs and knows that to survive he must eat them raw. He sharpens a stick to poke a hole in the shell, widens it with a finger and looks inside to see a yolk of dark yellow. We watch him as he brings the egg to his lips, closes his eyes, squeezes the flexible shell, and swallows as fast as possible. Despite its oily taste, it was an egg. "His throat tried to throw it back up, his whole body seemed to convulse with it, but his stomach took it, held it, and demanded more." The vivid sensory images show Brian's struggle to do what he must to survive.

When a story is no longer protected by copyright laws, publishers may ask writers to retell the story in "simple" language. *Peter Rabbit,* for example, has been retold countless times, sometimes with didactic messages for children or with new and trite illustrations. Hans Christian Andersen's "The Ugly Duckling" is another such example. For instance, a major children's author, who is a previous Newbery Award winner, retells the classic Andersen story in such choppy sentences and drab phrases that it loses all its artistry; sensory appeals vanish with the vanished setting, and characters change to become dull and uninteresting. This is a plot summary, not the story:

> Once upon a time there was a proud Mama Duck. She was sitting on four eggs, waiting for them to hatch.

Every day she said, "Quack! Quack! Just wait till my babies come out of their shells. I always have such beautiful ducklings!" . . .

"Quack! Quack!" the Mama Duck said. "Look at them! How beautiful!"

"Peep! Peep!" the baby ducks said. "Look at us!"

Then the Mama Duck looked at the last egg. "Quack! Quack! What's the matter with you? Why don't you hatch?" . . .

Finally the last shell went *Crack*.

. . . "Quack!" she said. "Oh, no! Something's wrong!" For the last baby duck was not beautiful. He was big and ugly. "Oh, no! How could I hatch an Ugly Duckling?"

Now look at what Andersen actually wrote, as translated by R. P. Keigwin.[2]

Summertime! How lovely it was out in the country, with the wheat standing yellow, the oats green, and the hay all stacked down in the grassy meadows! And there went the stork on his long red legs, chattering away in Egyptian, for he had learnt that language from his mother. The fields and meadows had large woods all around, and in the middle of the woods there were deep lakes.

Yes, it certainly was lovely out in the country. Bathed in sunshine stood an old manor house with a deep moat round it, and growing out of the wall down by the water were huge dock-leaves; the biggest of them were so tall that little children could stand upright underneath. The place was as tangled and twisty as the densest forest, and here it was that a duck was sitting on her nest. It was time for her to hatch out her little ducklings, but it was such a long job that she was beginning to lose patience. She hardly ever had a visitor; the other ducks thought more of swimming about in the moat than of coming and sitting under a dock-leaf for the sake of a quack with her.

At last the eggs cracked open one after the other—"peep! peep!"— and all the yolks had come to life and were sticking out their heads.

"Quack, quack!" said the mother duck, and then the little ones scuttled out as quickly as they could, prying all round under the green leaves; and she let them do this as much as they liked, because green is so good for the eyes.

"O, how big the world is!" said the ducklings. And they certainly had much more room now than when they were lying in the egg.

"Do you suppose this is the whole world?" said their mother. "Why, it goes a long way past the other side of the garden, right into the parson's field; but I've never been as far as that. Well, you're all out now, I hope"—and she got up from her nest—"no, not all; the largest egg is still here. However long will it be? I can't bother about it much more." And she went on sitting again.

Here we see a manor house, a deep moat, enormous dock-leaves so huge children can stand beneath them, a dense, figurative forest all tangled and twisted, an onomatopoeic "scuttling," the nonsensical granting of permission to the ducklings to look all around because green is so good for the eyes, the understatement about the size of the world—right into the parson's fields. The stork speaks Egyptian, and a patient mother continues her lonely vigil waiting for her last egg to hatch.

Our memories of *Tom Sawyer* include adventures and characters, as we recall Tom's runaway trip to the pirate island, his surreptitious night visit to Aunt Polly, and Tom, Huck, and Joe as they attend their own funeral. We remember hunting treasure by moonlight, and getting lost in the cave, but we may not be aware that these memories are so vivid because of Twain's style, his use of the right word in the right place.

Twain meticulously describes Tom's and Becky's wandering farther and farther away from the cave mouth, intrigued by the possibility of exciting discovery. Notice the imagery and the figurative devices in Twain's description:

> Presently they came to a place where a little stream of water, trickling over a ledge and carrying a limestone sediment with it, had, in the slow-dragging ages, formed a lace and ruffled Niagara in gleaming and imperishable stone. Tom squeezed his small body behind it in order to illuminate it for Becky's gratification.

A reteller of *Tom Sawyer* matter-of-factly substitutes monosyllables and clichés and eliminates the allusion to Niagara Falls.[3] While Twain's Tom *squeezes* behind the ruffled Niagara, the reteller's Tom *steps* behind the falls:

> Soon they came to a place where a little stream, carrying limestone matter with it, had formed a falls of beautiful stone. Since Tom was small, he stepped behind the falls with his candle so that Becky might see the lacy stone lighted in all its glory.

Twain's description is filled with imagery; he uses details to describe the cave:

> In one place they found a spacious cavern from whose ceiling depended a multitude of shining stalactites of the length and circumference of a man's leg. They . . . presently left it by one of the numerous passages.

The reteller eliminates the long words; he substitutes for stalactites a trite comparison to ice that fails to create a picture, and he turns the children's awed exploration into a pleasant walk through a hallway:

> In one place they found a cave from whose top hung something that looked like ice. Parts of this were nearly the size of a man's leg, and when Tom held his candle up toward them, they shown in the light. The children walked all about this cave, wondering and admiring, and finally left by one of the halls.

Twain shows the children wondering, admiring, marveling, and being bewitched by turns. He creates mounting suspense, his imagery showing the enormous, endless caverns and corridors of the cave. His verbs change from those of appreciative awe to verbs of vigorous action that show Tom's fear and arouse fear in the reader: seizing, hurrying, darting, striking, chasing, plunging. However, when the reteller substitutes more ordinary verbs—saw, flew, put out, hurried—the action loses its suspense. As for the cave, Twain's is a labyrinth of endless passageways and a limitless lake; we fear that Tom and Becky will never find their way out. In the reteller's version of the story, two children merely come to a small hall.

We might point out many more contrasts in the two versions of *Tom Sawyer,* each one showing how the loss of freshness in style results in the loss of suspense in the action, depth in the characterization, and vividness in the setting. The two stories are vastly different, even though the same events are carefully reported in the retelling. The reason for the difference is not what happens, but how the writer selects and uses words to show what happens. This is style.

Stories of Other Periods and Places

Word choice, or *diction,* should give the reader the flavor of the time, the place, and the events; this the writer does by use of language that seems native to the period and locality of the story.

Walter Edmonds in *Bert Breen's Barn* manages to duplicate rural, colloquial language in a convincing way. He mentions a route: the bridge by Dutch Mill, Miller's hatchery, and the bridge over Crystal Creek, to where the "road's going back to brush." During the barn building, Birdy whistles all the time, not "proper" whistling, because it "came through his teeth, half a tune, half the kind of hiss a man makes currying a horse whose hide is clogged with mud." Drawing a "snorty breath," Birdy slaps on a "dose" of mortar. This is rural Pennsylvania, and these are the terms of rural people, the language of rural life. It includes imagery, simile, metaphor, and personification as well as other devices. The flavor and color are appropriate here, as they apply to time, place, characters, and situation. The same statement can be made of Ozark diction in *Where the Lilies Bloom.* As she works her way wildcrafting through dense weeds high as her head, Mary Call is "alone on this blasted mountain working myself to a frazzle." She thinks she must "have moss growing inside [her] head where [her] brains should be." "Nobody but a poor dement" would take on "three snot-nosed kids to raise." "If I had the sense of a rabbit or even half that much, I'd just take off across that bald over there and go down the other side of it . . . and never look back." Although the times and places of their lives are different from our own, the style of these two novels gives us universal characters in whose experiences we believe.

One final example, *Anpao: An American Indian Odyssey* by American

Indian Jamake Highwater, is written in the style and form of the oral tale. The holy man Wasicong tells the story of Anpao's lengthy and dangerous quest, a task set for him by the beautiful Ko-ko-mik-e-is, whom he wants to marry. With his contrary twin Oapna, he must travel to the Sun and get his permission for the marriage. As we follow Anpao, the storyteller maintains a serious, mystical tone achieved by the evocation of the natural world, the formality of the language, and the long cadences of oral telling.

> Once again the sacred pipe was lighted and, under the new stars and among all the people of the land, it was passed around the great circle where the twins sat with the old swan-woman. The campfire rose into delicately twisting flames and the drums sang. . . .
>
> Oapna had fallen asleep while the old woman told her story, and he lay wrapped in a blanket of swan feathers. But even in his sleep he seemed to ebb and drift in the new light of the Sun.

Note next how unusual comparisons describe character in Paula Fox's *One-Eyed Cat*. Ned thoroughly detests Mrs. Scallop the housekeeper, describing her voice as "sharp and grinding as the woodcutter's saw"; her eyes are like "two blue crayon dots . . . her frizzy hair . . . electrified." Nothing about Mrs. Scallop is bright, "only red and inflamed like skin around a splinter." She reprimands Ned in a "tiny voice, as though her throat had shrunk to the size of a pin." In fact, she "could interfere with you just by glancing in your direction." Given Ned's description, his reluctance to cross Mrs. Scallop seems reasonable.

Stories of other lands and times make special demands upon the writer. Before we can accept other times and places as believable, we must first believe that the characters are human beings like ourselves. To understand the new culture we must see the particular differences between our own lives and those of other people. Style makes the difference.

High Fantasy

Since the most significant struggle in all human experience is that between the forces of good and evil, it seems appropriate that the language of high fantasy have dignity. Spicing her serious tone and elevated diction with occasional humor—in descriptions of her pets, the foltstza and the yerig, for example—Robin McKinley uses long, complex sentences and slow cadences in *The Hero and the Crown*. Here elevated language appears in the final lines of the novel as we read of the years following Aerin's defeat of the dragon Mauer and the ascent of Tor and Aerin to the throne:

> Perhaps the memory of the reek of Mauer's despair made her a little forgetful too, for she began to think of the wide silver lake as a place she had visited only in dreams; for the not quite mortal part of her did sleep, that she might love her country and her husband.

SUMMARY

Few of us are content with a plot summary as substitute for the story itself. What happened to the ugly duckling or to Beowulf was not merely plot, since action alone does not make absorbing hours of reading. Helpful as Charles and Mary Lamb are in *Tales from Shakespeare,* the book is no substitute for Shakespeare, and a quick look at a book of plot summaries reminds us that *Tom Sawyer* or *Little Women* were never like this. Any good story is words, many words, selected and arranged in a manner that best creates character, draws setting, recounts conflict, builds suspense to a climax, and ties it all together with some significance.

Style involves the use of comparisons or figurative language appropriate to the story, imagery that describes for the senses what is happening or how things look, exaggeration or understatement to entertain or to heighten feelings, allusions to people or events already known, wordplay with puns or echoes, and sound devices to give pleasure and to heighten meaning. Appropriateness and freshness—the sense that these words are the best possible words for this particular story—are not only the style of the story; they are the story.

READING AND EVALUATING

1. **Problem realism**   Dip into a story by Judy Blume and note style, imagery, and figurative language. Compare the style with that of Bette Greene's novels, or that of the Cleavers. What effect has style on characterization? On conflict and setting?

2. **Epic**   Read two versions of *Beowulf,* one by Ian Serraillier, and the other by Robert Nye, Rosemary Sutcliff, or Dorothy Hosford. How do they compare in their effect upon you, the reader? Which accounts show Beowulf as a man of more heroic stature? Why? What is the effect of the added details in Nye's version, for example?

3. **Folktale**   Read and compare three versions of one of Grimms' folktales. Which seems to retain the style of an oral tale? Comment on traditional form, brevity of characterization, repeated images, memorable phrases, the use of motif. In oral reading, which flows with the cadence of oral telling? Why?

4. **Other countries**   Read a recent book about a child from another country. What is the importance of imagery in the depiction of setting? Of the way of life? Is imagery essential? Does the style add any special effects to the story? What are they? How are they created?

5. **Social Issues realism**   Read a story about a child from a minority group, or about a social issue like sexism. Is there a difference between the diction of narration and that of dialogue? Does the dialogue disappoint by its emphasis

upon ethnic or sexist language, or does it enrich by adding to character and culture? Does the style seem to make the book preachy about the issue being explored?

NOTES

1 Henry James, *The Art of Fiction and Other Essays*. New York: Oxford University Press, 1948.

2 Hans Christian Andersen, *The Ugly Duckling*, R. P. Keigwin, translator, Adrienne Adams, illustrator. New York: Scribner's, 1965.

3 *Tom Sawyer*, adapted by Albert O. Berglund. Glenview, IL: Scott, Foresman, 1949.

RECOMMENDED BOOKS CITED IN THIS CHAPTER

AIKEN, JOAN. *The Stolen Lake*. New York: Delacorte, 1981.

ANDERSON, HANS CHRISTIAN. *The Ugly Duckling*, translated by R. P. Keigwin. New York: Scribner's, 1965.

BROOKS, BRUCE. *The Moves Make the Man*. New York: Harper & Row, 1984.

CARROLL, LEWIS. *Alice's Adventures in Wonderland*. New York: Macmillan, 1963 (first published, 1865).

CLEAVER, VERA and BILL. *Where the Lilies Bloom*. Philadelphia: Lippincott, 1969.

ESTES, ELEANOR. *The Moffats*. New York: Harcourt, 1941.

FOX, PAULA. *One-Eyed Cat*. Scarsdale: Bradbury, 1984.

HIGHWATER, JAMAKE. *Anpao: An American Indian Odyssey*. Philadelphia: Lippincott, 1977.

MCKINLEY, ROBIN. *The Hero and the Crown*. New York: Greenwillow, 1985.

NORTON, MARY. *The Borrowers*. New York: Harcourt, 1965.

O'DELL, SCOTT. *Island of the Blue Dolphins*. Boston: Houghton Mifflin, 1960.

————. *The King's Fifth*. Boston: Houghton Mifflin, 1966.

PAULSEN, GARY. *Hatchet*. New York: Bradbury, 1987.

SACHS, MARILYN. *The Bears' House*. New York: Doubleday, 1971.

SERRAILLIER, IAN. *Beowulf the Warrior*. New York: Walck, 1961.

TWAIN, MARK. *The Adventures of Tom Sawyer*. New York: Macmillan, 1966 (first published, 1876).

WHITE, E. B. *Charlotte's Web*. New York: Harper, 1952.

Tone

We hear the command from old cowboy movies, "When you say that, smile!" and we know what the speaker means: "If you call me your friend, a smile will say you mean it, a frown will mean the opposite." Although using identical words, friend or enemy can change meaning by adding a smile. The same words spoken by a teacher to a child acquire a different tone for different situations by the change in voice inflection. Pulling a rebellious child into the classroom, a teacher says, "Come on!" Encouraging a child to try out the new word puzzle, the teacher says, "Come on!" Rejecting a long-winded excuse from the child who must clear the work table, the teacher says, "Come on!" Each time the words have different meanings because inflection, or vocal tone, changes meaning.

Just as tone of voice reveals how a speaker feels about his or her subject, *tone* in literature tells us how the author feels about his or her subject. In literature, however, we cannot rely upon inflection in a writer's voice. We rely entirely upon words. Words express the writer's attitude toward his or her work, subject, and readers. Without vocal inflection to help convey tone, the writer must choose words with great care.

The author's *style* is what conveys the tone in literature. Sentence structure, word choice, patterns, arrangements, all influence style. Figures of speech are chosen for their sounds, as well as for their meaning. All these choices create the style and determine the tone of the writing, revealing the attitude of the writer toward both the subject and the reader.

You may feel that tone is too subtle a literary element to be found in children's literature. But this is not so. For example, most readers would agree that Kipling's tone in *Just So Stories* is humorous. Kipling's way of saying "this is the way it all happened—just so" is his own unique combination of matter-of-fact and humor:

So the Elephant's Child went home across Africa frisking and whisking his trunk. . . . When he wanted grass he plucked grass up from the ground, instead of going on his knees as he used to do. When the flies bit him he broke off the branch of a tree and used it as a fly-whisk; and he made himself a new, cool, slushy-squshy mud-cap whenever the sun was hot.

We suspend our disbelief and say wouldn't-it-be-fun-if, toying with the idea that it might really have happened this way. Because we like the pompous Bi-Coloured-Python-Rock-Snake, and the Crocodile with his musky tusky mouth who stretches the mere smear nose into a handy trunk, we play along with Kipling's "facts" about how the elephant got his trunk. The tone here is the feeling resulting from all the elements working together—the mock-serious situation Kipling is reporting, the tongue-in-cheek characterization, the playful language, the deliberately overplayed, pretentious style. The humorous tone results from all of these.

Tone in the *Just So Stories,* like tone in any writing, cannot be isolated from the words of the story. More specifically, words of all kinds, and the sounds of these words, show tone, and tone influences meaning. "Frisking," "whisking," and "plucking" are playful and lighthearted kinds of action expressed in short vowels and quick consonants. Their kinds of action are quite different from the action suggested by, for example, "slamming, banging, and breaking." If the light, rapid sounds of "fly whisk" became "fly swatter," tone would become more serious; if the Elephant Child's "schloopy-sloshy mud-cap all trickly behind the ears" became instead an objectively described "cold, messy, runny mudpie dripping behind the ears," the harsher consonants and the longer vowels would influence and change the tone. Kipling's choice of playful words and quickly moving cadences makes his pretense of factual reporting into humorous spoof.

We have noted the literary meaning of point of view as the mind or minds through which we see the story—the voice telling the story, whether a character or an omniscient author. Tone is different. It is the author's attitude toward story and readers. By the writer's choice of materials, the writer almost inevitably revals something about his or her own personality. If the author were telling the story orally, voice tone would reveal attitude and self; since the author is telling the story in print, the choices of words must be the means of showing attitude.

TONE IN *CHARLOTTE'S WEB*

How do we discover tone? We can often describe a writer's tone but are not aware of how we discovered that tone. Tone seems to creep into our consciousness without our being aware of its coming. However, tone, like the showing of action, depiction of character, and description of setting, is created by the writer's choice of words. If we look carefully at a few passages from *Charlotte's Web,* we may see how White's tone is revealed.

The first pages of the book are filled with kindness and affection: Mr. Arable looks at Fern "with love," and speaks to her "gently." Fern kisses her father and mother, pleased that the runt pig is safe. White describes the setting and the characters in the same kinds of affectionate terms. The action—Wilbur spinning a web, for example, or fainting at his honors—is humorous and yet affectionate.

The chapter "Summer Days" begins with a description of setting:

> The early summer days on a farm are the happiest and fairest days of the year. Lilacs bloom and make the air sweet, and then fade. Apple blossoms come with the lilacs, and the bees visit around among the apple trees. The days grow warm and soft. School ends, and children have time to play and to fish for trouts in the brook.
>
> ... All morning you could hear the rattle of the machine as it went round and round, while the tall grass fell down behind the cutter bar in long green swathes. Next day ... the hay would be hauled to the barn in the high hay wagon, with Fern and Avery riding at the top of the load. Then the hay would be hoisted, sweet and warm, into the big loft, until the whole barn seemed like a wonderful bed of timothy and clover. It was fine to jump in, and perfect to hide in.

In this selection, there are nothing but pleasant sensory images—fragrant lilacs, apple blossoms visited by friendly bees, children fishing for trout. Summer work goes on, but the sights and sounds are pleasant; work is another kind of sensory pleasure—rhythmic "round and round," colorful "long green swathes," sweet smelling clover, soft timothy bed for playing in. The abstract terms "happiest," "fairest," "warm," and "soft" describe the days, while "wonderful," "fine," and "perfect" describe the fun the days bring. Both the abstract words and the vivid appeals to our five senses have pleasant connotations. Summertime is not marred by a single unpleasant image or connotation. Summer fun is also humorous; Avery carries in his pocket a stiff, warm trout to be fried for dinner, or finds a slender grass snake and pockets it. Like the rest of the story, this chapter is filled with descriptions of a serene and pleasant world. White loves the summertime, the farm, the children, and the animals. Although White later builds suspense to a strong climax, his affectionate descriptions of all that summer brings have assured us that he will not permit disaster to come. While his emphasis upon the cycle of seasons prepares us for change, he never suggests in his choice of words that the change will bring tragedy or despair. Summing up White's attitude toward his story, we can best characterize it as humorous affection. As White goes on to compare a gray spider to a gumdrop, the contours of a gluttonous rat to a jelly jar, and to describe a pig as terrific, radiant, and humble, we see affection and humor in all that happens in the story. White's word choices—style—have determined tone.

HUMOR

Humor is an important tone in children's literature. Much of the humor comes from situation, that is, incongruous happenings that make children laugh. The cow jumping over the moon, the barber shaving a pig—these situations are funny to a small child. Situation or action is also the source of humor in *Pippi Longstocking* and *Homer Price*. But these stories are more than pie-throwing cartoons; they have invention and absurdity expressed in straightforward language.

Other stories depend for their humor upon style or unexpected phrasing as well as upon situation. Ludwig Bemelmans' *Madeline,* for example, in which the diction is precise and brief, not only shows a humorous situation, but also describes the situation in fresh and unexpected wording, rhythm, and rhyme. The crack upon the ceiling whose habit it is to look like a rabbit is situation nonsense; it is also humorous absurdity because of the unexpected internal rhyme and the personification that accompanies cracks having habits. The source of humor in *Winnie-the-Pooh* does not lie in the situation alone—sailing off on an overturned umbrella or disguising oneself as a black cloud. The humor rises as much from the quiet, almost solemn wording of conversations and descriptions surrounding the absurdities.

The humor of Barbara Park's *Skinnybones* derives from the consistent point of view of the 13-year-old narrator who calls himself a comedian. And he is. A baseball player who wins the Most Improved Award year after year, he says, "I'm not what you'd call a real good athlete. Actually I'm not even real fair. I'm more what you'd call real stinky." Constant humiliation by the Little League champion pitcher forces Skinnybones to play the clown to divert attention from his poor performance. The story opens with his dumping the cat's Friskies all over the kitchen floor while he searches for the contest entry form, his telling his mother that the cat had done it, his backtracking to blame a neighbor's cat, and finally his sweeping up ahead of the cat who gorges herself on Friskies and then disgorges it all over Skinnybones' shoe. When we repeat in our own words the humor of the story, we lose the delight of Park's fresh language, the understated narration, the exaggerated anger at friend and father. Park sustains the tone extremely well throughout her short novel.

In writing *Ali Baba Bernstein,* Johanna Hurwitz shows clearly how well she knows eight-year-olds. Each chapter begins with a different, exact recitation of David's age: eight years, four months, and sixteen days. Tired of being one of many Davids, he has changed his name to Ali Baba, another gambit common to eight- and nine-year-olds. Ali Baba, who fancies himself a detective, follows every false clue to humorous conclusion. Finally, he invites all of the David Bernsteins in the phone book to his birthday party. The tone is sustained throughout, and there is laughter on every page.

Strong rivalry carries the plot of *Supermouse* by British writer Jean Ure, but humor, in both text and Ellen Eagle's illustrations, is its delight. Long, skinny, smart Nicola is never appreciated, while every little simpering thing her sister Rose does is praised and touted. Because the point of view is Nicola's, we know her resentment and her ways of getting back at Rose. Assigned to walk Ben the dog, Nicola chooses the forbidden building site where she can be alone on the mud mound to act out her fury at Rose.

> Nicola, long-leggity in black wool tights and a red plaid skirt that didn't reach her knees, did a little twirl, tiptoe in the mud.
> "Such a *dear* little girl—such a *sweet* little girl—"
> Primp, preen, simper, simper.
> "Just *see* how she can point her toe! See her curtsy—see her pirouette—"
> Nicola pirouetted vigorously on the top of her mud bank.
> "*See her fall flat on her silly fat face—*"
> *BANG.*
> Slap, thud, into the mud.
> "Nicola *hurt* me, Nicola's been *mean* to me . . . boo hoo! Now I'm all *dirty—*"
> Absorbed in being Rose, Nicola covered her face and roared, dramatically.
> "Yes, and serve you jolly well *right*!"
> With a demonic yell, she sprang off the mound. . . . "Silly, simpering, self-righteous *cow*!"
> Whooping and hallooing, she danced around the mound.

Nicola's long legs are compared to those of a crane; she looks like a heron, her mother says. Her skin is sallow, she has no waist, though Nicola knows "it was there, in the middle of her body, the same as everyone else's."

British writer Helen Cresswell's *Bagthorpes Abroad* is filled with humor. Every page offers us a source of laughter, from the variety of screwball characters and the father's rented haunted house to the kinds of things they say to one another. Wild comparisons are part of the humor. For example, Fosdyke the housekeeper "bangs pots like she was being paid a fiver per decibel." "She would never, even under torture, have admitted to *liking* the Bagthorpes. She was simply addicted to them." When the Bagthorpes reach their rented house in Wales, Fossy sees the kitchen: "a rusty black range of such size and antiquity that it could easily . . . have been raised from the boiler room of the *Titanic*." The place has "resident spiders and cockroaches." The bathroom is "the first ever installed in the whole of Great Britain, a museum piece of plumbing. 'It ought to have a plaque on it,'" says Mr. Bagthorpe. Every page has its humor, each speech characteristic of the particular speaker.

In *The Whipping Boy* by Sid Fleischman, Jemmy is a ratcatcher who is pressed into service to take all the whipping the prince deserves but does not get. In a surprise move, however, it is Prince Brat who decides to run away, and he insists that Jemmy accompany him. Together they meet some strange outlaws, Hold-Your-Nose-Billy and Cutwater, but their exchange of identity fools the outlaws. A trip through the sewer, several kind acts, a king's reward, and a slowly developing friendship between Jemmy and a reformed Prince Brat hold the story together. The story has adventure and suspense and a great deal of humor—particularly the humor of distinctively drawn characters: Prince Brat, who loves to see someone else get his punishment; Hold-Your-Nose-Billy, who pops garlic cloves like peanuts; Cutwater, with his huge oak chest of useless treasures; Betsy and Petunia her dancing bear; and Captain Nips, who sells hot potatoes. In part, humor arises from a story set in a past among characters who use contemporary kinds of diction.

Many stories would not be called humorous in tone, and yet they have moments of humor. In *Jacob Have I Loved,* for example, the Captain takes a swing at the tomcat and yells, "Damn it to hell!" Call is shocked, saying that is against the commandments, but the Captain replies, "Call, I know those blasted commandments as well as you do, and there is not one word in them about how to speak to tomcats." Gleefully, Wheeze screeches through her laughter, "I bet there's not one word in the whole blasted Bible on how to speak to cats."

When we seek out the sources of laughter in children's literature, we may be surprised at our discoveries. For example, in Betsy Byars' *The Summer of the Swans,* when Sara tries to dye her orange sneakers baby blue, it is not only the situation that makes us laugh. It is also the freshness of language. As Sara lifts her sneakers out of the sink between two spoons, she asks her friend if there is a name for the new color.

> "There is," Mary said. "Puce."
> "What?"
> "Puce."
> "Mary Weicek, you made that up."
> "I did not. It really is a color."
> "I have never heard a word that describes anything better. Puce. These just look like puce shoes."

Few writers maintain a humorous yet sympathetic tone as successfully as does Betsy Byars, who has written more than twenty books. Her Blossom family series evokes gentle laughter at eccentrics like Pap and misfits like Junior—who thinks he is a misfit—and it also comments on family strength and loyalty.

We expect children to laugh at situation humor, since it is easy to see. But we underestimate children when we assume that is all that they can find humorous. We limit children's discovery when we limit their exposure to the simplest and most obvious. A double row of beds and a double file of children is the situation humor of *Madeline.* However, "lived twelve little girls in two straight lines" is the sophisticated humor of style. Children deserve this source of humor, too.

Parody

Parody is usually a device for older readers, since it relies on the reader's memory of a known piece of writing or of a way of talking. It retains the form of the original but changes the words and the tone for humorous effect. "An hour of freedom is worth a barrel of slops" is a simple parody of an old saying—an ounce of prevention is worth a pound of cure. A parody reminds us of something known, then gives fresh pleasure by duplicating form which contrasts to new and humorous meaning. A clear parody for children is the bedtime story that Charlotte tells Wilbur. It has the traditional beginning, as well as the fluid phrasing, of folk or fairy tale. Within the folktale parody is a description of the struggling fish trapped in the spider web. Read the paragraph aloud and notice its similarity to a prizefight account:

> "There was my cousin, slipping in, dodging out. . . . dancing in, dancing out, throwing her threads and fighting hard. First she threw a left around the tail. The fish lashed back. Then a left to the tail and a right to. . . . "

And again, try square dancing while Charlotte spins her web:

> "Now for the R! Up we go! Attach! Descend! Pay out line! . . . Whoa, girl! Steady now! . . . Now right and down and swing that loop and around and around! O.K.! Easy, keep those lines together! . . ."

The child catches some of the pleasures of White's parody and wordplay, but the adult catches many more; the result is pleasure for everyone. Carroll's literary parodies are extremely witty—Robert Southey's "The Old Man's Comforts" becomes "You Are Old, Father William," for example. But with the exception perhaps of "Twinkle, twinkle, little bat," they are unrecognized by the child—or by most of today's adults, for that matter. White, however, parodies word patterns from three familiar situations—prizefight, folktale, and square dance. Wit explained loses its wittiness, and the last two, at least, need no explanations.

DIFFERING TASTES IN TONE

We all bring to a story our own backgrounds and experiences, and the story has a personal meaning for us because we respond out of our own emotional history and present feelings. Readers, however, can only take from a story something already put into the story by the writer; tone is the effect of the writer's words. If two readers describe tone differently, it is often the result of personal definitions of their descriptive terms, or the result of differing personal taste and experience.

The tone of *Winnie-the-Pooh* may seem to one reader whimsically affectionate. Pooh and Piglet do not converse in fragments the way we do, but in long, complex sentences filled with "that" clauses. And all the time, what they discuss so gravely is near nonsense.

> "I think that I have just remembered something. I have just remembered something that I forgot to do yesterday and shan't be able to do tomorrow. So I suppose I really ought to go back and do it now."
> "It isn't the sort of thing you can do in the afternoon," said Piglet quickly. "It's a very particular morning thing, that has to be done in the morning, and, if possible, between the hours of—What would you say the time was?"

One reader calls the tone whimsical and playful. Another reader, thinking the playfulness and sentiment excessive, reads Christopher Robin's words, "Oh, Bear . . . how I do love you!" and says this is not a lightly affectionate tone, but sentimentality—an adult talking the way children never talk. The same words are used by the writer; two different readers receive them. The differing opinions might be called a matter of taste. Children, like adults, have their personal preferences. They may not define their reactions in terms of tone, but they may think the Pooh stories are "funny," or "silly," or "boring." On questioning them, we may find that these children are responding to what they see as Milne's attitude toward his material and his readers—in other words, tone.

TONE RELATED TO THE AUTHOR'S CHOICE OF MATERIALS

Any kind of tone can be found in any kind of genre of children's literature. A fantasy, for example, may be serious in tone to fit its serious themes, as Robin McKinley demonstrates in *The Blue Sword,* and Eleanor Cameron does in *The Court of the Stone Children.* Or the tone may be light-hearted as it is in *The Wind in the Willows,* which—with its little universe of peace, its pictures of natural beauty, and its variety of friendly and harmless animal characters in a quiet country setting—shows in its tone Grahame's attitude toward his characters and his story. In gentle and kindly acceptance, Grahame not only observes but enjoys the differences among the characters, their styles of living, their preferences, and their habits. Bountiful leisure, filled with lunches, snacks, picnics, and breakfast extending into lunchtime, and all surrounded by profound good will, occupies a benevolent world.

First, notice how the setting reflects Grahame's tone. Rat loves his river. When the brown flood water:

... all drops away and shows patches of mud that smells like plum-cake, and
the rushes and weeds clog the channels, and I can potter about dry-shod
over most of the bed of it and find fresh food to eat . . . .

That is when Rat loves his river best. "Plum-cake" and "potter about" are
connotative of comfort and happiness. The river is Rat's world and its banks
are covered with his friends. Mole learns to love it, too, to enter "into the joy
of running water." Badger is the perfect host in his house "behind
comfortable-looking doors," a cozy home with "wide hearth," chairs
grouped "sociably," "spotless plates" winking from the shelves, and rafters
hung with stored harvest:

> The ruddy brick floor smiled up at the smoky ceiling; the oaken settles,
> shiny with long wear, exchanged cheerful glances with each other; plates
> on the dresser grinned at pots on the shelf, and the merry firelight flickered
> and played over everything without distinction.

Everything in Badger's house is friendly; each item is personified and made
to smile, to glance cheerfully, to grin, to play and be merry. The settles, or
wooden-backed benches, show by their gloss that they have made many
visitors comfortable before the fire. Mole's home, too, although it is also
underground, has a welcoming front yard which shows love of home and a
hospitable welcome:

> A garden-seat stood on one side of the door. . . . On the walls hung wire
> baskets with ferns in them . . . a skittle-alley, with benches along it and little
> wooden tables marked with rings that hinted at beer-mugs.

Here, also, the setting shows tone: the pleasant game court, lined with
spectator benches and with tables that show evidence—rings hinting of
beer-mugs—of a generous host who serves his friends refreshments in
leisurely comfort.

This same kindness and acceptance appear in the characters' attitudes
toward one another. Of the impetuous braggart Toad, who keeps his friends
in a state of constant concern, Rat says indulgently:

> . . . the best of animals. . . . So simple, so good-natured, and so affectionate.
> Perhaps he's not very clever—we can't all be geniuses; and it may be that he
> is both boastful and conceited. But he has got some great qualities, has
> Toady.

When Mole disappears into the Wild Wood, Rat calls out "cheerfully,"
hunts "patiently," is joyful at hearing Mole's cry, and speaks "soothingly"
when he approaches Mole—despite Mole's having ignored Rat's advice.

When Rat is tempted by the Wayfarer to abandon his home and friends, Mole tactfully leads him back to his beloved River by talk of harvesttime. He slips away for paper and pencil and suggests gently that Rat write some poetry, "have a try at it." These terms, with their positive connotations of acceptance and concern, convey the tone. Among these varied characters there is no bickering nor condemning. Grahame's words instead intensify the strong feeling of community among the very different individuals. Such terms as "accepting," "kindly," "friendly," or "genial" might describe tone, but all spring from the close relationship between the idyllic country setting and the gentle, accepting characters.

Science fiction and high fantasy need carefully controlled tone to persuade us to suspend disbelief willingly. H. M. Hoover is successful in *The Lost Star* in which the protagonist Lian seems at home in the environment of Balthor where her aircar has crashed; familiar with many of the space sights, sounds, and invention, Lian accepts them. Carried by the sense that Lian is comfortable here, and yet that Lian like us wishes her parents were not too busy to rescue her, the reader goes along with each of Lian's discoveries. Throughout the high fantasy *A Wizard of Earthsea,* the elevated language, often with long and sonorous line, emphasizes the seriousness of the struggle between good and evil in the soul of Ged. Le Guin preserves such departure from ordinary language when she describes the otak, a small animal Ged carries with him on his travels. By using inverted word order, she sets the otak apart from earthly animals. "They are small and sleek, with . . . fur dark brown or brindle. . . . Their teeth are cruel and their temper fierce, so they are not made pets of. They have no call or cry or any voice." Although not all high fantasy is written in so formal a tone, such word choice seems highly appropriate.

Ian Serraillier in his retelling of *Beowulf the Warrior* uses the language of today and yet retains the tone and qualities of the folk epic as it was first recorded 1,000 years ago. The intent of the folk epic is serious, since the long narrative centers on a national hero and makes clear the values of a people. Serraillier has respected this intent by maintaining a consistently dignified tone. He keeps the elevated language, the compound synonyms or kennings, the imagery, the alliteration, and the extended metaphors. In the passage below, Beowulf and his band set sail:

> They ran up the white sail. And the wind caught her,
> The biting wind whipped her over the waves.
> Like a strong bird the swan-boat winged her way
> Over the grey Baltic, the wintry whale-road.

The voyage across the sea is no happy, light-hearted sail across the bay; Beowulf and his valiant warriors face a sea worthy of their courage.

Hand-to-hand combat with a monster has a dignity heightened by long, rhythmic lines, richly connotative terms, and alliterative descriptions with long vowels and hard consonants:

Spilling the benches,
They tugged and heaved, from wall to wall they hurtled.
And the roof rang to their shouting, the huge hall
Rocked, the strong foundations groaned and trembled.

The long sounds (extended *a*'s and *oo* sounds, slowly moving consonants— *l*'s, *g*'s, and *r*'s, for example) make the poetic lines move slowly to create a sense of dignity that accompanies the awesome struggle. After Beowulf defeats Grendel, Hrothgar praises Beowulf, and thereby shows his own generous and humble nature. But here shorter vowel and consonant sounds quicken the pace and so lighten the tone:

. . . the grateful King,
All glooming gone, his countenance clear and cloudless
As the sky in open radiance of the climbing sun,
Gave thanks to God for deliverance. "Beowulf," he said,
"Bravest of men, I shall love you now as my son.
All I have is yours for the asking."

In the early lines of Part Three, Beowulf, although he is simply described by the statement "mightiest yet mildest," is not merely an average man doing minor deeds of courage. His character is noble and selfless; he leads, and he is victorious. His life exemplifies valor and sacrifice. The actions of such a character are grand and elevated; the tone of such a tale must be equally grand and elevated.

EVALUATING TONE IN CHILDREN'S LITERATURE

Condescension

When someone looks down upon us, treating us as though we are unintelligent or immature, we call this attitude condescension. In the original writings of the Greeks, Homer, Hesiod, and Pindar, the myths conveyed religious truth; they expressed the depth and seriousness of ancient faith. As Edith Hamilton says, we know Greek mythology best through the Greek writers who believed in what they wrote. One of Hamilton's examples is the story of Perseus and the Gorgon's head, a story that moves us, its brief descriptive phrases giving horror and urgency to the tale:

And they are three, the Gorgons, each with wings
And snaky hair, most horrible to mortals.
Whom no man shall behold and draw again
The breath of life.

By contrast, in Nathaniel Hawthorne's retelling in *A Wonder Book,* the Gorgons become snake-fairy-butterfly concoctions:

Why, instead of locks of hair, if you can believe me, they had each of them a hundred enormous snakes growing on their heads, alive, twisting, wriggling, curling, and thrusting out their venomous tongues, with forked stings at the end! . . . and they looked very dazzling, no doubt, flying about in the sunshine.

By making the Gorgons into cartoonlike characters, Hawthorne has turned the tone of the story almost into ridicule; in descriptions of the hero himself, Perseus who slew the Gorgon Medusa, there is none of the expected dignity. Instead, in casual, quick-paced language Hawthorne describes Perseus as pathetically vulnerable. His turning to stone would be a "very sad thing to befall a young man." Perseus' motives seem selfish and glory-seeking, as he "wanted to perform a great many brave deeds, and to enjoy a great deal of happiness in this bright and beautiful world." Perseus could hardly keep from crying. He felt "greatly ashamed . . . like a timid little school boy." "What would my dear mother do, if her beloved son were turned into stone?" "Dear me . . . I shall be afraid to say a syllable." All grandeur is lost in this version.

The tone in Hawthorne's retelling of the myth is not respectful but condescending. He seems to be saying to the reader, "Now, children, isn't this a silly little story about foolish people?" There is no awe at the size of Perseus' task, no admiration for the courageous and liberating act. The myths of ancient people, myths that have come to us from those who believed in them, were filled with reverence and mystery, since by myth human beings were attempting to explain the wonders of human beings and of nature. Hawthorne, although he may have followed the traditional details, has changed the myth completely by his condescending tone.

A modern example of condescension is Walt Disney's *Wonderful World of Knowledge,* Volume 10, which does include the traditional details of the myths. Although the diction is condescending, it is not as offensive as the illustrations: Pluto is Icarus and King Arthur; Mickey Mouse is Jason, Roland, Sigurd, and Galahad; Tinker Bell is one of the ondines or water sprites from the Norse Eddas. Despite color reproductions of classical art works showing myths, the total effect is destroyed by the cartooned heroes.

Does this condescending tone matter? When a retelling so completely violates the original tone or the spirit in which it was told, the story is changed beyond recognition; a child meeting such condescension may be turned off by tone that talks down, and he or she may never be encouraged or interested enough to find a better version. In original fiction, too, literature that talks to us as "dear little readers" demeans us; we may even be insulted. No one likes condescension, and the child who meets it may reject the pleasures and discoveries of literature.

Sentimentality, or the overuse of sentiment, is a kind of condescension. Thornton W. Burgess, still in print and on the library shelves after sixty-five years, in telling his story *Mother West Wind's Animal Friends* is not only trite in language but also sentimental in tone. Burgess creates talking animals that have few traits to convince us either of their likeness to people or of their animal natures—except that those with wings fly, and those without, walk. Open a Burgess story and find this:

> Then old Mr. Toad picked up his cane and started down the Crooked Little Path to the Green Meadows. There he found the Merry Little Breezes stealing kisses from the bashful little wind flowers. Old Mr. Toad puffed out his throat and pretended that he disapproved, disapproved very much indeed, but at the same time he rolled one eye up at jolly, round, red Mr. Sun and winked.
> "Haven't you anything better to do than make bashful little flowers hang their heads?" asked old Mr. Toad gruffly.

The many capitalized nouns and adjectives, the personification of breezes, flowers, and sun, the repetition of words and phrases ("disapproved, disapproved very much indeed") and the clichés ("anything better to do") do little to convey conflict or to make the story move. Peter Rabbit (a nod to Beatrix Potter) and the "Little meadow people and forest folk" are organizing an Easter Egg Rolling for everyone in the Green Meadows, the Purple Hills, and the Green Forest. The long-winded combination of sentimentality and the omniscient point of view create a coy tone and fail to reveal character or to describe actions. Burgess lacks respect for his readers and his characters; his condescension makes a shallow story.

By contrast, Scott O'Dell in *Island of the Blue Dolphins* never condescends, never demeans Karana's life by sentimentality. Her people have always lived on a windswept island, dependent upon themselves and their own capacities to use what is provided by nature, and avoid death at nature's impersonal hands. A product of this culture, living close to the elements, Karana quietly accepts what faces her. Life is sometimes cruel; humans survive by self-control. Ramo's being killed by wild dogs does not make Karana wild in her grief; we sense instead her feeling of inevitability and of necessity for restraint:

> All night I sat there with the body of my brother and did not sleep. I vowed that someday I would go back and kill the wild dogs in the cave. I would kill all of them. I thought of how I would do it, but mostly I thought of Ramo, my brother.

O'Dell's tone of restraint makes us feel sympathy for and understanding of Karana in her isolation and loneliness; there is no sentimentality here.

Nor is there sentimentality in Katherine Paterson's portrayal of Jess' grief at the death of his friend in the flood waters. In *Bridge to Terabithia* we read that Jess' stomach "felt so odd." And yet, the morning after the news, pancakes doused in syrup taste "marvelous." Jess' sister accuses him of not caring, and he is puzzled: "The coldness curled up inside of him and flopped over." As Jess' mother and sister talk, he "could hear them talking and they were farther away than the memory of a dream." He cannot leave the table, but he doesn't know what to do. Then, his mind a blank, he mumbles, "What little girl?" Paterson's depiction is not sentimental, filled with sighs and tears and sobs; we nonetheless see that Jess is shocked and grief-stricken.

Sensationalism, which we have noted in our discussion of plot, is another kind of tone. In many places *The Slave Dancer* and *My Brother Sam Is Dead,* for example, might have been sensational. The writers, however, have carefully chosen words that convey meaning and control tone, but avoid sensationalism.

Changing Values

Styles in writing change—for children as they do for adults. Sometimes it is tone that forces the retirement of a onetime classic. Such, it seems, may be the case in E. Nesbit's *Five Children and It,* a book that continues to appear on lists of classics but is no longer read by many children. While an occasional child today may still respond to the playful fantasy of *Five Children,* it is perhaps the sentimental and condescending tone that has retired it from the active shelf. Lamb, who is too old to be called a baby today, kisses the gypsy woman, "a very nice kiss, as all his kisses are, and not a wet one like some babies give." Robert asks Lamb to "come and have a yidey on Yobby's back." Sentimental and stereotyped characterization combines with condescension toward gypsies, "Eyetalians," and "Red Indians." Condescension and whimsy also contrast artificially the views of children and adults on what is real and true:

> . . . Grown-up people find it very difficult to believe really wonderful things, unless they have . . . proof. But children will believe almost anything, and grown-ups know this . . . they tell you that the earth is round like an orange, when you can see perfectly well that it is flat and lumpy; and why they say that the earth goes round the sun, when you can see for yourself any day that the sun gets up in the morning and goes to bed at night like a good sun as it is, and the earth knows its place, and lies as still as a mouse.

By contrast, look at Eleanor Estes' *The Moffats,* or Beverly Cleary's *Ramona and Her Father,* two other family stories. We might call the tone of such stories "wonder"—a kind of wonder that says "Aren't everyday, ordinary things remarkable?" Ramona, who has made herself a crown of burs and now must have her hair cut off in order to remove them, begs Daddy not to cut any more than he has to. "Does it look awful?" she asks. And her father replies with humor, "It will never be noticed from a trotting horse." Ramona lets out a "long, shuddery sigh, the closest thing to crying without really crying." When Ramona, whose father has lost his job, wishes she might earn a million dollars like the boy on the hamburger commercials, her father replies:

> I'll bet that boy's father wishes he had a little girl who fingerpainted and wiped her hands on the cat when she was little and who once cut her own hair so she would be bald like her uncle and who then grew up to be seven years old and crowned herself with burs. Not every father is lucky enough to have a daughter like that.

Although the events of *Five Children* are fantastic and those of *Ramona* are humorously everyday, *Ramona* is far more successful in its creation of a sense of surprise. True, the children of *Five Children* live in an era more remote and foreign, but time distance is not the issue, since to a child time has no definition by decade. Possibly, what makes one story old-fashioned and relegates it to book lists and what may keep the other alive and read may be to a great extent tone, or how the authors feel about their subjects and readers. Our tastes in tone change. Baby-talk was more acceptable in Victorian fiction than it is today.

Didacticism

Preaching or teaching, as we have noted, is the function of sermons and textbooks. In literature it is a negative quality. By giving the protagonist a few personal traits and setting him or her into a narrative, the writer may seem to have created a story. (Remember our earlier discussion of *Willie Goes to the Seashore.*) Since pleasure comes from a good story told well, and understanding grows from a discovery about human nature, the story often fails as literature.[1]

Look, for example, at the picture book *I Want to Be a Homemaker*. Jane's mother gives her advice about her doll children. She says that they need good food—milk, eggs, vegetables, meat, and so forth—so they will grow. As Jane pours tea into her doll teacups, her mother adds that some foods will build bones and others muscles. Others give "pep" for running, jumping, and playing. "You see, Jane, we need many kinds of food." Moments later Jane tells a visitor about her doll children who sometimes won't behave, won't brush teeth, often get wet feet, and even run into the street. Mother replies that a good homemaker is a teacher all day long.

Such a story seems to have been conceived only in order to teach. Characters are undeveloped, conflict is nonexistent, and style is dull. All that survives is a didactic message: homemakers, i.e., women, must know about child care. While *Homemaker* is an extreme and unfortunate example of sexist stereotyping, many "stories" seem to have as their purpose the underlining of a moral or the teaching of a lesson. Pleasure and understanding are lost.

Variety of Tone

Some writers vary tone as the situation in the story changes; they use various tones to comment on people as individuals and as social groups. While such a story can often be read as a fast-paced, character-conflict-theme story, the perceptive reader who catches the shifts and shading of tone may find added pleasure in the story. As the readers recognize human manners and behavior, they also discover the author's attitude, and a whole new level of pleasure can be uncovered.

We can note the various tone shifts in Andersen's "The Ugly Duckling." Andersen is sometimes humorous, sometimes tender, often critical, and even, sometimes, almost cynical. The child may read "The Ugly Duckling" often during the early years; because of the range of tone, at each reading the child discovers a new tone and added meaning.

For another example, Alice Childress, as she changes point of view with each chapter in *A Hero ain't nothin' but a Sandwich,* shows each of the speakers with different tone. The principal's tone is resigned: "No matter what I do or don't do there are drug addicts." Benjie is naive when he says of his addiction, "I kicked once and I can kick any time I wanta." Walter the pusher, angry and protesting that anyone who sells anything is a pusher, says he is "pushin' for cops, when you get right down to it. You heard me! When I pay off, what the hell you think I'm payin' with? ... I gotta hustle ten bags before I can pay the fuzz five singles, dig?"

Jean Fritz, too, varies tone. In the foreword to *Homesick: My Own Story,* she says "my story, told as truly as I can tell it."[2] In an accepting and reminiscent tone touched with occasional gentle humor, Fritz observes people and events through the eyes of a child. When Jean's mother takes over her education, she insists upon arithmetic, figuring how long a train takes between Hankow and Peking at x miles an hour, stopping y times on the way. Jean, who hates arithmetic, protests the unnecessary study: "I knew that grown-ups never figured out such problems; they just looked at timetables." When Jean meets American girls and is asked to speak some Chinese, she obliges with Chinese insults, then refuses to translate: They are "worthless daughters of baboons," with big turtles for mothers. But Fritz is often serious. When her nurse Lin Nai-Nai returns from her home in beseiged Wuchan, Jean finds her swaying in her chair, trouser legs rolled, foot bindings gone, "her stumps of feet, hard little hooves with toes bent under," painful from running "like a stumbling duck."

And one further example. Accustomed as we might be to the idea of an omnipotent God speaking in stentorian tones to warn of the flood, it comes as a surprise when Rosemary Harris in *The Moon in the Cloud* describes the voice of God very differently. Speaking conversationally, a still small voice says that "the people are grown exceedingly wild. They worship idols, they take too many wives in marriage and discard those that displease them. They care for nothing and nobody—and they're violent." Noah hears a gentle sighing voice as God describes the coming flood. "A clean sweep . . . I had in mind. Everything mean and small and violent done for." The quiet tone of voice that accompanies God's appearance as rings of brilliant color makes God a benevolent but disappointed creator who wants not to punish but to erase the mistakes of human bahavior.

Few stories have greater variety and complexity in tone than *Tom Sawyer*, a story that offers great excitement on the level of character and plot alone. Mark Twain ranges over human attitudes from tenderness to sarcasm, from delight to cynicism. In his depiction of boyhood and adolescence, Twain admits that life is varied and contradictory; he uses tone to show its complexity and perversity. In checking passages from the novel, notice Twain's distance from, and yet smiling acceptance of, the self-deception and self-absorption of the young:

> *On crushes:* He had been months winning [Amy]; she had confessed hardly a week ago; he had been the happiest and the proudest boy in the world only seven short days, and here in one instant of time she had gone out of his heart like a casual stranger whose visit is done.

> *On ceremony:* The oath was complete. They buried the shingle close to the wall with some dismal ceremonies and incantations, and the fetters that bound their tongues were considered to be locked and the key thrown away.

Twain, in commenting on human behavior, is sly and faintly satirical.

> *On theft:* There was no getting around the stubborn fact that taking sweetmeats was only "hooking," while taking bacon and hams and such valuables was plain simple stealing—

> *On the forbidden:* Huckleberry was cordially hated and dreaded by all the mothers of the town, because he was idle and lawless and vulgar and bad—and because all their children admired him so, and delighted in his forbidden society, and wished they dared to be like him.

Although we remember *Tom Sawyer* as a happy book, Twain is ironic, sarcastic, even cynical at times:

> *On showing off:* [The Sunday school superintendent] by bustlings and activities. [The librarian] by making a deal of the splutter and fuss that insect authority delights in. [The teachers] by bending sweetly over pupils that were lately being boxed.

> *On accusation:* The public are not slow in the matter of sifting evidence and arriving at a verdict.

And finally, on public sentimentality he becomes almost sardonic:

> This funeral stopped the further growth of one thing—the petition to the governor for Injun Joe's pardon . . . a committee of sappy women . . . in deep mourning . . . wail around the governor, and implore him to be a merciful ass and trample his duty underfoot . . . scribble their names to a pardon petition, and drip a tear on it from their permanently impaired and leaky waterworks.

By filling his novel with a great variety of tone, Twain has increased the scope and significance of his story. He has shown what pleasure can come from observing all of life and from taking a stand on any and every aspect of it. By varying tone, yet maintaining an overall attitude of humor and enjoyment of each experience, he has not only managed to create a novel of suspense and excitement, but also one that continues to amaze and delight, no matter what the age of the reader or the number of rereadings.

There are kinds of tone that seem unsuited to children's stories. Satire with its intent to reform is often too intellectual an exercise. It demands breadth of experience and ability to see and interpret exaggeration and understatement. There are books, however, in which the story is so strong that it carries the child's interest and the satire may be missed completely without any loss to the reader—the *Alice* books, for example. As overall tone, sarcasm with its intent to wound is also too complex and thus questionable for children. To children, all experience is a subject for wonder. Condemnation, as well as fear and pessimism, seem to have little place in their literature; without experience to place these negative tones in perspective, they may be overwhelmed and moved to despair.

Children's literature in recent years has taken increasingly honest looks at all areas of life, and part of the result has been more suffering, pain, and futility in stories for young readers. As long as these negative attitudes are not unrelieved, they have their place. However, children are less able than adults to defend themselves against despair and so find the pessimistic messages more meaningful if they are presented within a story in which the tone is basically hopeful.

What matters is that tone for children's literature be, if not optimistic, at least positive, or perhaps objective.[3] For children, all the world is opening up; there is so much to be appreciated and marveled at—and improved upon. If limiting tone to optimism and affirmation narrows tone too much, we may consider only condescension and unrelieved despair as unsuitable. But if we defend these kinds of tone, we must remind ourselves of the functions of literature. Futility and despair do not give pleasure nor necessarily increase understanding; there are dozens of other possible attitudes that may do this for young readers.

SUMMARY

Tone, the author's attitude toward subject and readers, is an integral part of story, since it is created by the writer's choice of words. It is not created by any single, deliberate decision of the author; instead it is the result of all the choices made in telling the story. Tone can make the same story—one of heroes and valiant deeds, for example—either a series of trivial anecdotes or a monument to human valor. Tone can fill us with affection and acceptance, or rouse us to examine and to laugh at ourselves.

READING AND EVALUATING

1. **Myth**   Find three versions of the same myth and compare them. Does the tone demonstrate the purpose of myths? Is the tone consistent with the subject? Is it condescending?

2. **Realism**   Find a realistic novel written before 1940 that recurs on classics lists. What is its tone? Is the novel still being read by children? What significance has tone in the life of the work?

3. **Fantasy**   Read *Mary Poppins* by Pamela Travers or a fantasy by Eleanor Cameron, Susan Cooper, Alan Garner, Margaret Mahy, or another writer, and describe tone. Which situations and characters best support your choice of term descriptive of tone? Explain your reaction to the tone.

4. **Social Issues and Problem Realism**   Read a realistic story from the 1960s or later that deals with a protagonist with some kind of problem. What is the tone? What is the effect of tone upon the characterization? Upon the theme? Upon the conflict?

5. **Humor**   Find at least six easy humorous books and compare them. Which rely only upon situation for humor? Upon illustrations rather than upon language? Which have distinctive literary style? In the book you consider to have the most humorous style, which particular devices does the writer rely upon for the creation of humor?

NOTES

1 Joanna Gillespie, in her article, "Schooling through Fiction" *(Children's Literature,* New Haven: Yale University Press, 1986), quotes from early literature for children, part of the Sunday School movement: "It has been my design . . . to direct the minds of children to subjects of higher importance than those which generally occupy the pages of books put into their hands . . . the silly stories which their fathers read in their childhood will soon be, perhaps in a double sense, 'tales of other times!'" (quoted from writer William M'Gavin, 1849).

2 Jean Fritz has reconstructed her China childhood with true incidents but feels that the possibility of inaccuracy in chronology necessitates calling *Homesick: My Own Story* fiction.

3 Natalie Babbitt in "Happy Endings? Of Course, and Also Joy" *(Children and Literature: Views and Reviews,* Glenview, IL: Scott, Foresman, 1973, pp. 155-59) comments on tone and theme in children's literature. Noting the vast range of subjects and tone, she finds that what can and might happen—joy and optimism— seem to be the special pleasure of stories for children, and rightly so.

RECOMMENDED BOOKS CITED IN THIS CHAPTER

ANDERSEN, HANS CHRISTIAN. *The Ugly Duckling.* New York: Macmillan, 1967.

BEMELMANS, LUDWIG. *Madeline.* New York: Viking, 1939.

BYARS, BETSY. *The Blossoms and the Green Phantom.* New York: Delacorte, 1987.

————. *The Summer of the Swans.* New York: Viking, 1970.

CAMERON, ELEANOR. *The Court of the Stone Children.* New York: Dutton, 1973.

CHILDRESS, ALICE. *A Hero ain't nothin' but a Sandwich.* New York: Coward, McCann, 1973.

CLEARY, BEVERLY. *Ramona and Her Father.* New York: Morrow, 1977.

COLLIER, JAMES LINCOLN and CHRISTOPHER. *My Brother Sam Is Dead.* New York: Four Winds, 1974.

CRESSWELL, HELEN. *Bagthorpes Abroad.* New York: Macmillan, 1984.

ESTES, ELEANOR. *The Moffats.* New York: Harcourt, 1941.

FLEISCHMAN, SID. *The Whipping Boy.* New York: Greenwillow, 1986.

FOX, PAULA. *The Slave Dancer.* Scarsdale, NY: Bradbury, 1973.

FRITZ, JEAN. *Homesick: My Own Story.* New York: Putnam, 1982.

GRAHAME, KENNETH. *The Wind in the Willows.* New York: Scribner's, 1953 (first published, 1908).

HARRIS, ROSEMARY. *The Moon in the Cloud.* New York: Macmillan, 1982.

HOOVER, H. M. *The Lost Star.* New York: Viking, 1979.

HURWITZ, JOHANNA. *Ali Baba Bernstein.* New York: Morrow, 1985.

KIPLING, RUDYARD. *Just So Stories.* New York: Doubleday, 1946 (first published, 1902).

LE GUIN, URSULA K. *A Wizard of Earthsea.* Berkeley: Parnassus, 1968.

LINDGREN, ASTRID. *Pippi Longstocking.* New York: Viking, 1950.

McCLOSKEY, ROBERT. *Homer Price.* New York: Viking, 1943.

McKINLEY, ROBIN. *The Blue Sword.* New York: Greenwillow, 1982.

MILNE A. A. *Winnie-the-Pooh.* New York: Dutton, 1926.

O'DELL, SCOTT. *Island of the Blue Dolphins.* Boston: Houghton Mifflin, 1960.

PATERSON, KATHERINE. *Bridge to Terabithia.* New York: Crowell, 1978.

————. *Jacob Have I Loved.* New York: Harper & Row, 1980.

PARK, BARBARA. *Skinnybones.* New York: Knopf, 1982.

SERRAILLIER, IAN. *Beowulf the Warrior.* New York: Walck, 1961.

TWAIN, MARK. *The Adventures of Tom Sawyer.* New York: Macmillan, 1966 (first published, 1876).

URE, JEAN. *Supermouse.* New York: Morrow, 1984.

WHITE, E. B. *Charlotte's Web.* New York: Harper, 1952.

Illustration from *Frog Went A-Courtin'* copyright © 1955 by John Langstaff and Feodor Rojankovsky and renewed 1983 by John Langstaff, Nina Rojankovsky, and Tatiana Rojankovsky-Kely, reprinted by permission of Harcourt Brace Jovanovich, Inc.

From Rhyme to Poetry

When do children first meet literature? If they are lucky, they meet it in infancy, as early as the time they are making valiant efforts to "pat-a-cake, pat-a-cake, baker's man." Because nursery or Mother Goose rhymes use the elements of literature and the devices of style, and because the rhymes are sources of pleasure and understanding, we can legitimately call them the earliest literature for the youngest child. These *rhymes* are brief stories which have been passed orally from generation to generation, and are the beginning of poetry for children.

NURSERY RHYMES

Few narratives in literature for child or adult are told with the joyful economy of the nursery rhyme. Many of them, like "Pussy cat, pussy cat, where have you been?" are the most tightly constructed stories. "Sing a song of sixpence, a pocketful of rye" tells a complete tale in three short verses. "Three wise men of Gotham" could hardly be more condensed:

> Three wise men of Gotham
> Went to sea in a bowl.
> If the bowl had been stronger,
> My story had been longer.

Small children whose attention spans are limited are introduced to brief fictional tales in rollicking rhythms and rhyming forms. While the rhymes are not poetry, they are the most natural introduction to poetry.

Literary Elements

Many of the Mother Goose or nursery rhymes are the simplest and briefest of stories. The *characters* are the Queen of Hearts who made some tarts, the old woman tossed up in a basket, and Old Mother Hubbard whose cupboard is bare. *Setting,* too, is quickly sketched in some rhymes. Amazingly, the Old Woman lives in a shoe, and Peter Pumpkin Eater's wife lives in a pumpkin shell. The brief narratives have simple *plots.* The crooked man uses his crooked sixpence to buy a crooked cat which "caught a crooked mouse/And they all lived together in a little crooked house" for a happy closed ending. Action in these stories varies from the simplest of tumbles taken by Humpty Dumpty to the more complex involvements of "The House That Jack Built" and "Who Killed Cock Robin?"

Ideas or themes also occur in Mother Goose rhymes, ideas a small child can grasp. Some of the simple rhymes are surprisingly clear in their insights, and oftentimes the short verse-stories have slight *themes.* "Life is a fleeting thing," we discover from "Solomon Grundy":

> Solomon Grundy
> Born on Monday,
> Christened on Tuesday,
> Married on Wednesday,
> Took ill on Thursday,
> Worse on Friday,
> Died on Saturday,
> Buried on Sunday,
> That's the end
> of Solomon Grundy.

Because of Dapple Gray, we know that "A pet is worth more than money":

> I had a little pony; his name was Dapple Gray.
> I lent him to a lady to ride a mile away.
> She whipped him, she slashed him,
> She rode him through the mire—
> I would not lend my pony now
> For all that lady's hire.

A child's understanding is increased in other ways.[1] Curiosity about the environment is roused when the commonplace is made exciting. The trip to the grocery store is no longer ordinary: "To market, to market, to buy a fat pig"; and a walk beside the flower beds is time for "Mistress Mary's garden" with "silver bells and cockle shells and pretty maids all in a row."

Style

In a pleasant, regular beat of rhymes there is *rhythm* that may correspond to breathing and heartbeat within us; rhythm is a way into poetry:

> Hickory, dickory, dock.
> The mouse ran up the clock.
> The clock struck one,
> And down he run,
> Hickory, dickory, dock.

The quick rhythmic movement makes a child jump to a beat:

> Jack be nimble, Jack be quick.
> Jack jump over the candlestick!

Children clap hands to "The Farmer in the Dell," and swing their arms to "London Bridge." Rhythm, which is determined by patterns of accented and unaccented syllables and by long or short vowels, moves the lines quickly and happily.

The variety of *sound effects* in nursery rhymes, although simple, acquaints children with poetic devices and gives pleasure. "A tisket, a tasket," or "Hey, diddle, diddle," "Hickety, pickety," or "Rub-a-dub-dub" use *internal rhymes, assonance,* and *consonance. Alliteration* occurs in "Daffy-down-dilly," or "Peter Piper picked a peck of pickled peppers"; consonant and vowel repetitions exist in "Tommy Snooks and Bessie Brooks went walking out one morning." There is *onomatopoeia* in "Hark, hark, the dogs do bark!" and "Bow-wow-wow, whose dog art thou?" The enjoyable sounds of tongue-twisters are endless challenges. And of course the usual *end rhyme* is pleasing:

> Little Boy Blue, come blow your horn!
> The sheep's in the meadow, the cow's in the corn.
> Where's the boy who looks after the sheep?
> Under the haystack fast asleep!

Figurative language is another stylistic trait of Mother Goose rhymes. Dishes and spoons, ravens and daffodils, cats and mice and ladybugs are excitingly *personified.* "Frogs and snails and puppy dogs' tails" contrast to "sugar and spice and everything nice," *metaphors* for bad and good qualities in the little boys and girls. Jack Sprat and his wife figuratively—or literally if we prefer—"lick the platter clean"; in *simile* form, a snail is "like a little Kyloe cow."

As for *tone,* humor with delight is more prevalent than any other. There is laughter in:

> Barber, barber, shave a pig.
> How many hairs will make a wig?
> Four and twenty, that's enough.
> Give the barber a pinch of snuff.

And there is seriousness in:

> Ding Dong Dell, Pussy's in the well!
> Who put her in? Little Johnny Green.
> Who pulled her out? Little Johnny Stout.
> What a naughty boy was that
> To try to drown poor pussy cat
> Who never did him any harm
> But killed the mice in his father's barn.

There is verbal *irony* in:

> A diller, a dollar,
> A ten o'clock scholar,
> What makes you come so soon?
> You used to come at ten o'clock,
> And now you come at noon.

Wonder at romance and possible adventure are awakened in the melodious "Bobby Shafto's gone to sea," or in "I saw a ship a-sailing." Emotional intensity may be more commonly thought of as a quality of fine lyric poetry, but there is also intensity in children's play and the rhymes that accompany this play. Children chant a teasing rhyme, "Tattle-tale, tattle-tale, hanging on a dog's tail!" Carried along by rhythms and sounds, children sing out variations on names:

> Sally-bum-balley, tee-alley-go-falley,
> tee-legged, tie-legged, toe-legged Sally.

Or in the universal taunts of childhood, they adapt verses to their playmates' names:

> Janie's mad and I'm glad,
> And I know how to please her.
> A bottle of wine to make her shine,
> A bottle of ink to make her stink,
> And all the boys to tease her.

Caught up in what Robert Frost calls the catchiness of rhythm and rhyme, children recite and improvise.

In the nursery or folk rhymes, children also find the intrigue and excitement of riddles. They ask each other rhythmic or rhyming questions:

> What can go up the chimney down,
> But can't go down the chimney up?

They are surprised that "umbrella" is the answer. And children never forget the involved question:

> As I was going to St. Ives,
> I met a man with seven wives.
> Each wife had seven sacks;
> In each sack were seven cats;
> Each cat had seven kits.
> Kits, cats, sacks, wives,
> How many were going to St. Ives?

In addition to the rhymes we commonly call Mother Goose, children are made ready for poetry by many other folk rhymes that may have general similarities and local geographical variations. Children from many parts of the country know the ball-bouncing rhyme, "When Buster Brown was one/He learned to suck his thumb." Some children, perhaps from a particular section of a particular state, seem to share common variations of similar rhymes, like the jump-rope verses with the refrain:

> Here comes the doctor,
>   Here comes the nurse,
> Here comes the lady
>   With the alligator purse.

Other rhymes seem to appear by some magic, known at first only to an inside group on a particular playground. If the rhymes are catchy enough, they are soon carried across the country by a child who moves away, or by a visitor who returns to a hometown. It seems unlikely that those who have jumped rope to this rhyme will forget it:

> Fudge, fudge,
> Call the judge.
> Mama's got a baby.
> Ain't no girl,
> Ain't no boy,
> Just a plain old baby.
> Wrap it up in tissue paper.

Put it on the elevator.
First floor, miss!
Second floor, miss!
Third floor, miss!
Fourth floor—
Kick it out the door.[2]

NONSENSE

Nursery rhymes and sidewalk jingles merge with nonsense; there is no line of demarcation. While each is joyful in itself, both prepare the child for poetry. When the cow jumps over the moon, that's nonsense. Of all the animals that Adam named, the least likely moon-jumper is the stodgy cow. Nonsense plays upon our delight in the illogical and the incongruous, upon our pleasure in words cleverly used or misused, upon some secret yearning to see the immutable laws overturned. The best nonsense can do all of these things. Edward Strachey wrote in 1894 in his introduction to Edward Lear's *Nonsense Omnibus* that nonsense is not "a mere putting forward of incongruities and absurdities, but the bringing out of a new and deeper harmony of life in and through its contradictions." Strachey called nonsense the "true work of the imagination, a child of genius, and its writing one of the Fine Arts."

Children thrive on nonsense. They make up and invert words or make illogical comparisons; one child tells another "It's cold as a bumblebee out!" and both children roll on the floor in glee. They repeat nonsense words in series, just for the pleasure of tasting and hearing their sounds; "Eenie-beenie-pepsi-deenie"; "Hogan-Bogan-Mogan was her name." Nonsense relies upon rhythm, sound patterns, figurativeness, compactness, and emotional intensity—the intensity of laughter that may be repeated, stored in the memory, then shared again and again.

Rhythm and Sound

The *limerick* form, first popularized by Edward Lear in the nineteenth century, is the most traditionally structured nonsense verse. It clearly shows how important to nonsense are rhythm and sound:

> There was an Old Person of Ewell,
> Who chiefly subsisted on gruel;
> But to make it more nice,
> He inserted some mice,
> Which refreshed that Old Person of Ewell.

Suitable to the tone—light-hearted laughter—the rhythm is quick, with the syllables more frequently unaccented than accented. The sounds are short, with happy rather than serious overtones.

Compactness and Surprise

Much of the humor in nonsense verse comes from the surprise of names, events, or words. Look, for example, at Harry Behn's "Circles," which surprises us by the consistency of its plural word endings, all distorted to rhyme with "compasses."

> The things to draw with compasses
> Are suns and moons and circleses
> And rows of humptydumpasses
> Or anything in circuses
> Like hippopotamusseses
> And hoops and camels' humpasses
> And wheels on clownses busseses
> And fat old elephumpasses.

Laura E. Richards, who had a gift for nonsense, confuses an unlikely pair, elephants and telephones, in her verse "Eletelephony." "The Owl and the Eel and the Warming Pan" is made up of perfectly assorted incongruities, since more unlikely characters and events would be hard to assemble.

> The owl and the eel and the warming-pan,
> They went to call on the soap-fat man.
> The soap-fat man he was not within;
> He'd gone for a ride on his rolling-pin.
> So they all came back by the way of the town
> And turned the meeting-house upside down.

The light-hearted treatment of disaster or the slightly macabre are often subjects for nonsense; its verses often comment on current fads, as well, as does X. J. Kennedy in "A Choosy Wolf":

> "Why don't you eat me, wolf?" I asked.
>
> "It wouldn't be much fun to.
> Besides, I'm into natural foods
> That nothing has been done to."

In the rhythm and rhyme of nonsense, ordinary creatures become extraordinary, as this anonymous verse notes:

What a wonderful bird the frog are—
When he stand he sit almost;
When he hop, he fly almost.
He ain't got no sense hardly;
He ain't got no tail hardly either.
When he sit, he sit on what he ain't got almost.

Perhaps Lewis Carroll wrote the most compact and intense nonsense, so witty that not a word is wasted, not a sound is out of place. "The White Rabbit's Verses" from *Alice in Wonderland,* for example, uses over forty pronouns, and yet has only five nouns to which the multitude of pronouns might refer. The twenty-four lines are written in such logical word order—subject, verb, complement—that they thoroughly convince us of their truth. And yet, when we finish the six verses, we have no idea what we are now convinced of. Carroll's most admired nonsense is "Jabberwocky," a mystifying tale of valor.

'Twas brillig, and the slithy toves
    Did gyre and gimble in the wabe;
All mimsy were the borogoves,
    And the mome raths outgrabe.

"Beware the Jabberwock, my son!
    The jaws that bite, the claws that catch!
Beware the Jubjub bird, and shun
    The frumious Bandersnatch!"

He took his vorpal sword in hand:
    Long time the manxome foe he sought—
So rested he by the Tumtum tree,
    And stood awhile in thought.

And as in uffish thought he stood,
    The Jabberwock, with eyes of flame,
Came whiffling through the tulgey wood;
    And burbled as it came!

One, two! One, two! And through and through
    The vorpal blade went snicker-snack!
He left it dead, and with its head
    He went galumphing back.

"And hast thou slain the Jabberwock?
    Come to my arms, my beamish boy!
O frabjous day! Callooh! Callay!"
    He chortled in his joy.

>'Twas brillig, and the slithy toves
>   Did gyre and gimble in the wabe;
>All mimsy were the borogoves,
>   And the mome raths outgrabe.

Perhaps the best-known popularizer of nonsense verse in the past decades has been Ogden Nash, many of whose verses are known by adult and child alike. Nash's nonsense employs rhythm and made-up words. For compactness, one could not improve on:

>Dentists' anterooms
>Give me tanterooms.

POETRY

We move from nursery rhymes and nonsense to poetry with a feeling, perhaps, that now the discussion will become somber and difficult to follow. Not so. Something about the idea of getting meaning beyond amusement from brief groups of words in short lines, each line or phrase usually beginning at the left margin, seems to frighten many readers. Strange to say, we can read along easily in paragraphed pages, but if the same words are placed in stanza form, the meaning seems less quickly apparent, and we are lost.

Prose and Poetry

The difference between poetry and prose is not as great as it may seem. Much of what we encounter in poetry we have already met in rhymes or in prose. Flow or cadence in prose may become more regular in poetry and be called rhythm, or meter. Sound patterns in prose, like alliteration and onomatopoeia, exist in poetry to even greater degree. Connotative meaning in prose acquires heightened significance in poetry. Figurative language that compares unlike things exists in prose, but occurs more frequently in poetry. What seems to take us by surprise and to make us feel that the two forms are totally different lies elsewhere.

The principal difference between prose and poetry is *compactness*. A single word in *poetry* says far more than a single word in prose; the connotations and images hint at, imply, and suggest other meanings. In a sense, the poet distills meaning in brief and vivid phrases. Economy and suggestion evoke our response.

The characteristics of poetry that set it apart from prose are essentially *rhythm, sound patterns, figurativeness, compactness,* and *emotional intensity.* The last two qualities are to a large extent the results of effective use of rhythm, sound patterns, and figurative language to produce compressed expression in words. This compactness in turn results in emotional intensity, a particular quality of poetry.

Analysis of rhythm in such metrical patterns as anapestic or iambic, or of such line patterns as dimeter or tetrameter, seems irrelevant to our discussion of rhythm in poetry for children. We focus here not on naming the forms of meter, but on the use of rhythm.

One question seems in order. What is the difference between poetry for adults and poetry for children? Once again, we say that the difference is not in kind, but in degree. We may arbitrarily divide poetry for adults by theme and subject—love or nature lyrics, death or war lyrics, for example. Adults are also concerned about the passage of time, the inevitability of death, and the changing of relationships. Just as the interests of adults are the subjects of their poetry, the concerns of childhood are the subjects of children's poetry. Since much of childhood is spent in play, or in wonder at what is common and yet not commonplace, what surrounds children in their constantly unfolding world are the subjects of children's poetry.

Some poetry appeals to both children and adults, and it seems impossible and unnecessary to designate it as poetry for either group. However, in discussing rhyme and poetry for children, we *can* be somewhat more concise, although no less arbitrary. Nursery or Mother Goose rhymes are the happy rhythmic verses of early childhood; they can also be said to include riddles, chants, and tongue-twisters. As the inventive rhymes focus more on the incongruous and the surprising or unexpected, they become more nonsensical, and we tend to call them nonsense rather than nursery rhymes. Where the division comes, anyone or no one can say. When nonsense seems masterfully created, we may find ourselves calling it poetry, and yet where poetry and nonsense begin and end—again, anyone and no one can say. What does seem important is that we appreciate the particular qualities of language form that are distinctively poetic. In our discussion of the arbitrary categories—nursery rhymes, nonsense, and poetry—we are focusing in varying degrees upon these qualities. The essential point remains that poetry is poetry, and that poetry for children differs from poetry for adults in degree, but not in kind. Subject matter may differ, but our standards remain the same.

Many have tried to define poetry, and most have found such definitions difficult. A. E. Housman sardonically calls poetry a secretion, "whether a natural secretion, like turpentine in the fir, or a morbid secretion like the pearl in the oyster." Robert Frost calls it simply "a performance of words." Most definitions of poetry, however, return to at least one central idea derived from the Greek origin of the word. A poet is a maker, and poetry is *made*; every word counts.

Unlike the word "created," which implies inspiration and mystery, the term "made" suggests materials and effort. If poetry is made, it does not emerge perfect from the writer's pen. Like anything that is made, poetry follows a pattern of development: conception, effort, technical discipline, and refining and polishing, before the maker is pleased with the thing made. Most likely the poem is written and rewritten; words are crossed out, substituted for, perhaps replaced with earlier words, rewritten, crossed out, substituted for—until the maker-poet feels the poem is finally right. Of course, effort alone does not make a poem, any more than it makes good fiction. Skill, patience, and the critical judgment of the disciplined mind are a more likely combination.

Verse and Poetry

First, let us say that *verse* differs from poetry. What matters is not that we distinguish between them, congratulating the poet for poetry and denigrating the versifier for verse. That is not the issue. Once again, we are aware of a continuum; at one end is trite doggerel and at the other the finest of lyrics. Such distinction may suggest that verse is of a lower order than poetry which is, by one definition, the most imaginative and intense perceptions human beings can express concerning themselves, others, and their relationships to the world outside themselves. Another definition—noble emotions, noble thoughts, expressed by noble minds—seems a forbidding description. Far more inviting is Shelley's statement: "Poetry is the record of the best and happiest moments of the best and happiest minds." Such a definition includes an extensive part of the continuum.

The content of poetry is emotion; its contribution to human beings is significance. Perhaps one person will insist that beauty—and beauty is a matter of preference—must illuminate a familiar object with newness and sensitivity; as Coleridge says, poetry's immediate object "is the communication of pleasure," again an end achieved through a wide spectrum of sources. Or, as Wordsworth says, it is "the spontaneous overflow of powerful feelings recollected in tranquility." Note that these statements suggest both joyful intensity and serene happiness. Such feelings may come to us from what one critic might call verse and another poetry, but the possibility of such emotions arising from the experience of doggerel seems highly unlikely. Emily Dickinson had criteria for poetry that few poets can achieve; her statement surely sets poetry apart. "If I read a book and it makes my whole body so cold no fire can ever warm me, I know that it is poetry. If I feel physically as if the top of my head were taken off, I know that it is poetry."

Given the inevitability of difference of opinion, and perhaps even the irrelevance of making a distinction, it might still be worthwhile to look at how some critics have defined verse. They maintain that while poetry is an end in itself, verse has a specific purpose. Poet-critic T. S. Eliot, for example, who seems almost to dismiss verse as "a superior amusement," describes poetry by contrasting it to verse. He says that while feeling and imaginative power are found in real poetry, verse is merely a matter of structure, formal metrical order, and rhyme pattern. Its structure, furthermore, may seem more important than its meaning. Proverbial wisdom occurs in verses as simple as "A stitch in time/Saves nine." The purpose of other verses is to sell diet drinks and chewing gum; still others convey traditional sentiments. We know what greeting card verse is, and, perhaps without knowing why, have a feeling that it is not poetry. Some of such verse is humorous, some sentimental, and some so incongruous that it may provoke a condescending smile: "To love a father is no fad/When he's a father like my dad."

Verses can be pleasant and entertaining; they can remind us of sentiments and ideas with which we agree, but often their expression is trite and awkward, with rigid metrical structure, ordinary images, obvious rhymes, or phrases twisted to produce rhyme. They are not poetry as T. S. Eliot has described it—the distilled and imaginative expression of feeling. Notice, for example, the pointlessness of Annette Wynne's "I Keep Three Wishes Ready," a verse with an incongruous, marching rhythm that takes over the meaning. Prose would say more clearly and with greater brevity the idea expressed in sixteen lines filled with empty, throwaway words.

> I keep three wishes ready.
> Lest I should chance to meet,
> Any day a fairy
> Coming down the street.
>
> I'd hate to have to stammer,
> Or have to think them out,
> For it's very hard to think things up
> When a fairy is about.
>
> And I'd hate to lose my wishes,
> For fairies fly away,
> And perhaps I'd never have a chance
> On any other day.
>
> So I keep three wishes ready,
> Lest I should chance to meet,
> Any day a fairy
> Coming down the street.

We have a tendency to see the name of a poet, like Robert Frost or John Ciardi, and assume that everything that person writes is fine poetry. That is not the case. Both Frost and Ciardi, as well as many, many other poets, have written verse—some clever and some pedestrian. We assume, too, that Robert Louis Stevenson's *A Child's Garden of Verses* has been around so long, it is all poetry. Or that A. A. Milne who delights us with his Winnie-the-Pooh tales is writing poetry in *When We Were Very Young*. The division may sometimes be difficult to distinguish, but the difference between verse and poetry lies in intensification of feeling and in distillation of language, not in regular end rhymes and predictable figures of speech. Available to children are large quantities of both verse and poetry. With exposure, children grow in awareness of the pleasure that artful poetry can bring. Greater experience with imaginative poetry can lead children to an awareness and appreciation of Walter de la Mare's "rarest of the best." But children enjoy verse as well; each has its place.

Kinds of Poetry

We sometimes simplify the classification of poetry and say that it is of two kinds: *narrative,* situational or story poetry, and *lyric* or song poetry. Two familiar examples of narrative poems are Alfred Noyes' "The Highwayman" and Robert Browning's "The Pied Piper of Hamelin," found in many anthologies. One type of narrative, the *ballad,* comes to us from traditional or folk literature. Other ballads are of known authorship; both may show supernatural intervention, themes of physical courage and love, and incidents common to ordinary people. Developing the story through dialogue and using little characterization or description, ballads traditionally have abrupt transitions, are frequently incremental in structure, and rely upon refrains. "John Henry," like other folk ballads originally sung, flows with songlike cadence, and exemplifies many ballad qualities.

Other poems are lyrics or songlike poems which use sounds, rhythms, and figurative devices to express emotional response to some brief moment of experience, as does Carl Sandburg's familiar "Fog," or the less familiar "Forms of Praise" by Lillian Morrison.

> Basketball players
> already tall
> rise on springs
> aspiring for the ball,
> leap for the rebound
> arms on high
> in a dance
> of hallelujahs.

Some adult poems are a pleasure to both children and adults and most children's poems can be enjoyed by adults. The intense experience of lyric poetry, however, is often given to children in some kind of situation or story form.

Rhythm

Look now at the characteristics of poetry, several of which are known to children through rhymes and nonsense. The recurrence of stress is called *rhythm*. In our discussion of rhythm in prose, we mention cadence or flow, but when rhythm is set into a more regular pattern as it often is in verse or poetry, we speak of *meter*. The poet uses rhythm to enhance the feeling that the poet's words express. In choosing the rhythm for a poem, whether it be unvarying metrical form or more freely flowing lines, the poet makes several commonsense choices. When we are happy, we speak quickly; when we are sad, or serious, or matter-of-fact, our words come more slowly. In the same way, the poet uses a quickly moving line with many unaccented syllables and short vowels to express light-heartedness in lines that may move as quickly as those of the limerick. When the poet is expressing serious thoughts, the rhythm moves more slowly with longer vowels and a higher proportion of accented syllables. Within the line, rhythm may also vary as the poet wishes to stress an idea or a single word. And within the poem the rhythm slows or quickens to vary the mood or shift the tone.

The best poetry uses rhythm to add meaning to words, as does Robert Francis' "The Base Stealer." The sense of the baseball player poised on base, almost off, back again, teasing with sideways shuffles and teetering motions, is clearly shown by the irregular rhythm and the increasingly quick vowels.

> Poised between going on and back, pulled
> Both ways taut like a tightrope-walker,
> Fingertips pointing the opposites,
> Now bouncing tiptoe like a dropped ball
> Or a kid skipping rope, come on, come on,
> Running a scattering of steps sidewise,
> How he teeters, skitters, tingles, teases,
> Taunts them, hovers like an ecstatic bird,
> He's only flirting, crowd him, crowd him,
> Delicate, delicate, delicate, delicate—now!

As we note the variation in phrase length, the surprise of the longer phrasing of "come on, come on," then the short vowels, the plosive *t*'s and *c*'s, the sibilant *s*'s, we recognize how the quickening rhythm leads up to an admonitory "delicate, delicate, delicate, delicate," and the final emphatic "now!" which concludes the action.

Similarly, in his poem "The Swing," Robert Louis Stevenson uses regular and lilting rhythm to create the movement of the swing arc:

How do you like to go up in the swing,
　　Up in the air so blue.
Oh, I do think it the pleasantest thing
　　Ever a child can do!

Up in the air and over the wall,
　　Till I can see so wide,
Rivers and trees and cattle and all
　　Over the countryside—

Till I look down on the garden green,
　　Down on the roof so brown—
Up in the air I go flying again,
　　Up in the air and down!

But notice, by contrast, the rhythm of "Falling Snow." The words fall into a regular, thumping pattern of beats, a strong accent on every second syllable and a far cry from the gentle and noiseless falling of actual drifting flakes that accumulate so slowly. The hard, rhythmic beat denies the meaning rather than enhances it.

See the pretty snowflakes　/ᴗ/ᴗ/ᴗ
Falling from the sky;　/ᴗ/ᴗ/
On the walk and housetop /ᴗ/ᴗ/ᴗ
Soft and thick they lie.　/ᴗ/ᴗ/

Here regular meter seems more important to the writer than the experience of snow; rhythm in this verse exists for itself, because a marching rhythm cannot describe falling snow.

As Eve Merriam says about "Inside a Poem," rhythm is important:

It doesn't always have to rhyme,　　　　ᴗ/ᴗ/ᴗ/ᴗ/
but there's the repeat of a beat, somewhere ᴗ/ᴗᴗ/ᴗᴗ/ᴗ/
an inner chime that makes you want to　　ᴗ/ᴗ/ᴗ/ᴗ/ᴗ
tap your feet or swerve in a curve;　　　/ᴗ/ᴗ/ᴗᴗ/
a lilt, a leap, a lightning split:—　　　ᴗ/ᴗ/ᴗ/ᴗ/

The quick, changeable beat contributes to meaning, saying that poetry is joyful discovery of meaning, assisted by rhythm. Here the first line is a serious statement about rhyme, and Merriam's rhythm enforces the factual meaning of the line by regularity and uniformity. The first line has four accented syllables, as do all the others. The second line has the same number of accented syllables, but the line's rhythm picks up speed with the use of two additional unaccented syllables, a ratio of six light to four heavier syllables. The more unaccented syllables, the more quickly the line runs, and the more lightness the meaning acquires. Line three also has four accented syllables, but it includes five unaccented ones; in line four the final anapestic foot ($\cup\cup/$) also adds to the lightness and the unexpected quality of the rhythm. Again in line five, there are four accented syllables, but this time the internal punctuation interrupts the rhythm. The scansion looks the same as that of the first line ($\cup/\cup/\cup/\cup/$), but the commas cause us to stop and start, stop and start. The surprise we feel as we pause for the two final *t*'s of "lilt" and "split" and the final *p* of "leap," when added to the short vowels and the plosive consonants, is all part of what Merriam is saying about rhythm: rhythm need not be absolutely regular, but it does suit meaning. The idea of "Inside a Poem"—while a poem need not rhyme, its rhythm exists to clarify meaning—is clear. Note too that while Merriam says a poem need not rhyme, she uses rhyme, but in unexpected places. The sound of "rhyme" reappears in "chime" a bit later; "repeat of a beat" and "swerve in a curve" are not the regular and predictable rhymes occurring in end positions, but rhymes nonetheless. Merriam uses rhyme as she uses rhythm—not as an end in itself as the versifier does—but as a means to enforce meaning.

Sound Patterns

In "Lost," Carl Sandburg uses musical devices and sound patterns that are exceptionally helpful as they add to meaning. The poet personifies the fogbound boat as a lost child, and the harbor as a mother:

> Desolate and lone
> All night on the lake
> Where fog trails and mist creeps,
> The whistle of a boat
> Calls and cries unendingly,
> Like some lost child
> In tears and trouble
> Hunting the harbor's breast
> And the harbor's eyes.

The long sounds of the words "calls and cries" are not the only desolate ones, since every line echoes the feeling of desolation. The long vowels in "lone," "all," "long," "fog," "trails," and "creeps" give added duration to the words. Sandburg calls the vessel a "boat," its long *o* adding to the loneliness far more than would the word "ship" with its short *i* sound. Consonants are largely liquid *l*'s and *r*'s or nasal *m*'s, *n*'s, and *ng*'s held together with sibilant *s*'s. The long vowel duration and the consonants that further pull and stretch the words, called phonetic intensives, create the slow groping of the fogbound ship. The sounds of the two lines dealing with "mother," the protective harbor, are quite different. Because vowels are short and decisive, and the words are spoken more swiftly, the effect of the lines is reassuring.

As for rhythm, stressed syllables in "Lost" are far more frequent than unstressed syllables, and the effect is a slowly moving poem—movement like a fogbound boat. Sound devices combined with imagery and figurativeness have created a visible and audible scene. The short poem has given us a fresh picture, and its sound has strengthened both the meaning and the impact.

Figurativeness

As we noted in our discussion of style, figurative language is a means by which a writer says one thing in terms of another, and by which the writer makes comparisons. It is this quality of which Christopher Fry speaks when he says that poetry "has the virtue of being able to say twice as much as prose in half the time, and the drawback, if you do not . . . give it your full attention, of seeming to say half as much in twice the time."

When a poem makes either implied or explicit comparisons, the images called up may acquire connotative meaning, or may be seen in a fresh way. For example, Dorothy Aldis in "On a Snowy Day" describes a fencepost topped by the little white cylinder of snow; the personified posts wear metaphorical marshmallow hats. The shapes are aptly compared and the metaphor and image are not only vivid, but also connotatively pleasant.

In "Mama Is a Sunrise" Evelyn Tooley Hunt uses figurative language effectively, comparing Mama by implication to the quiet warmth and light of sunrise.

> When she comes slip-footing through the
>   door,
>   she kindles us
>   like lump coal lighted,
>   and we wake up glowing.
> She puts a spark even in Papa's eyes
> and turns out all our darkness.
>
> When she comes sweet-talking in the room,
>   she warms us
>   like grits and gravy,
>   and we rise up shining.
> Even at night-time Mama is a sunrise
> that promises tomorrow and tomorrow.

"Slip-footing" is Mama's quiet step as she sets her children glowing, kindling them just as she kindles the spark in Papa's eyes. Her sweet talk warms the family to make them rise shining. Using tactile and taste imagery, the simile of warming "like grits and gravy" provides pleasant connotations. The final lines state clearly that at night, too, Mama is just as reassuring that all will be well "tomorrow and tomorrow," when another pleasant sunrise is in store. This is not a mother who flips the windowshade to a loud snap and cries out "Rise and shine!" These children are eased happily into the day.

The moon is a favorite object for poets' contemplation; its changes are mysterious to us all, and particularly to the child. Emily Dickinson's poem which notes the moon's changes begins with a figurative picture of the crescent moon:

> The moon was but a chin of gold
> A night or two ago—
> And now she turns her perfect face
> Upon the world below—
>
> Her forehead is of amplest blond;
> Her cheeks like beryl hewn—
> Her eye unto the summer dew
> The likest I have known.

If the crescent moon is "but a chin of gold," then the full moon must be a "perfect face," with forehead, cheeks, and eyes. The metaphor is perfectly suited to the changing shape of the moon.

Vachel Lindsay in his figurative description of the phases of the moon begins with the full moon:

> The Moon's the North Wind's cooky.
> He bites it day by day,
> Until there's but a rim of scraps
> That crumble all away.

A cookie, rich in connotative meaning particularly for children, begins as whole and round, and ends in crumbs.

Like the jigsaw puzzle already put together, the poem with obvious figurative comparisons—the moon is a golden ball—denies the reader the excitement of a personal search and discovery. When the figurative comparisons are ineptly chosen, they confuse meaning rather than reveal it. In the poem "Night," this is the case:

Night is a purple pumpkin,
Laced with a silver web,
And the moon a golden spider,
Wandering through the strands.
At dawn the purple pumpkin,
Rolling slowly around,
Leans against the star-web,
Moving the spider down.
The silver web slides slowly,
Slowly across the sky,
And the spider moon creeps slowly,
Slowly by.
The twinkling stars cease spinning
Their skeins of silver gray,
The spider moon
Crawls down the strands
And night turns into day.

Night itself is compared to a pumpkin that is purple. Can we, in our wildest imaginings, picture a pumpkin that is not orange? Somewhere, sometime, there may be green pumpkins, but every one we recall seeing is orange. Carved, perhaps, or caved-in, or baked in a pie—but orange. The moon is further compared to a gold-colored spider. Was there ever a spider without eight legs? That's the horror of the spider. The moon is golden and round; a spider is neither. The poet adds to the eight-legged moon a crawling movement, and now not only is the glow of the mysterious sphere gone, but the marvel of its imperceptible climb and descent as well. The confusing metaphor has obscured the night, not illumined it.[3]

The poet's use of metaphors may delay our discovery of meaning. However, at the same time, these comparisons make the puzzle more intriguing and the discovery more exciting. Look, for example, at the completely compatible figurative devices that John Updike uses in his poem "October," each one a reference either to autumn weather or to Halloween:

The month is amber,
    Gold, and brown.
Blue ghosts of smoke
    Float through the town.

Great V's of geese
    Honk overhead,
And maples turn
    A fiery red.

Frost bites the lawn.
   The stars are slits
In a black cat's eye
   Before she spits.

At last, small witches,
   Goblins, hags,
And pirates armed
   With paper bags,

Their costumes hinged
   On safety pins,
Go haunt a night
   Of pumpkin grins.

Sometimes we may be puzzled by the figurative language in a poem; the more complex the poem, the more subtle the metaphors may be. The simplest way to check the meaning and suitability of comparisons is by means of simple "this = that" equations. The similes and metaphors in Lilian Moore's "Bike Ride" form a series of figurative comparisons:

Look at us!

We ride a
road
the sun has paved with   sun = paving machines
shadows.   shadows = pavement

We glide
on leaf lace   leaf lace = shadow pattern
across tree spires   spires = steeplelike shadows of
over   tree tops
shadow ropes   ropes = telephone wires
of droopy wires.

We roll
through a shade tunnel   tunnel = overhanging branches
into light.

Look!
Our bikes
spin
black-and-white
shadow
pinwheels.   pinwheels =
                   shadows of whirling bicycle
                   wheels

"We ride through the shadows on the road" is a summary statement of the lines, but surely the experience of these words is not the same as the poem. The rightness of Moore's figurative comparisons has made a fresh experience from what might have been an ordinary one.

Imagery, the appeal to our senses, makes additionally vivid the figurative comparisons, as we clearly see in Dorothy Aldis' "Fourth of July Night":

> Pinwheels whirling round
> Spit sparks upon the ground,
> And rockets shoot up high
> And blossom in the sky—
> Blue and yellow, green and red
> Flowers falling on my head. . . .

Blossoming flowers and pinwheels spitting sparks make the bright display a picture in our minds.

Imagery further stretches our perceptions to see details and figurative comparisons otherwise only vaguely noted. Cats are sleek and fat, plump and thin, make unpleasant screeching noises as well as pleasant humming ones. Rosalie Moore tells us these facts in her poem "Catalog"; she compares their graceful jumping to skin slipping from a grape, and their refusal to move from a sleep spot to the immobility of City Hall. Aileen Fisher also personifies the cat, giving a clear visual metaphor, in her poem "At Night":

> When night is dark
> my cat is wise
> to light the lanterns
> in his eyes.

Kazue Mizumura, a writer of haiku, uses one sharp image to make a familiar scene visible:

> Who tossed those golden coins,
> The dandelions glittering
> On my lawn?

The value of such images is clear when we look at verse which minimizes sensory appeal. As Herbert Read says, "Poetry is not made up of words like pride and pity, or love and beauty. . . . The poet distrusts such words and always tries to use words that have a suggestion of outline and shape, and represent things seen as clear and precise as crystal."[4] For example, although Stevenson, in his poem "The Swing," successfully duplicates the rhythm of the swing, his terms are not sensory. "Rivers," "trees," "cattle," "countryside," and "pleasantest thing" make little appeal to our senses. Although the roof is brown, we do not see truly vivid sights. We do not smell, hear, taste, or touch them, and both reader and poem are the poorer for lack of sensory appeals.

Whispers, on the other hand, are a very common part of life, and might be vaguely described. But whispers are titillating, bringing secrets for cherishing, then for sharing, and perhaps for embellishing. Once whispers were merely audible, but never again, because "Whispers" by Myra Cohn Livingston captures other sensory qualities. Notice, too, the pleasant connotations of the many sensory appeals:

> Whispers
> tickle through your ear
> telling things you like to hear.
>
> Whispers
> are as soft as skin
> letting little words curl in.
>
> Whispers
> come so they can blow
> secrets others never know.

Whispers will never be the same, because not only do we hear them, but we feel whispers when they "tickle," "blow," and are "soft as skin"; we see them as the "words curl in." Because of the connotative meanings of the words, we delight in whispers, feeling their tender softness and seeing their spiral curl headed for listening ears.

The best chosen words for a poem add by *connotations* new dimensions of meaning to words we have always known. However, sometimes the connotations of words are distracting rather than helpful in uncovering the meaning of the poem. This is the case in "Feeding the Fairies," where fairies are compared to hens and roosters:

> Fairies, fairies, come and be fed,
>   Come and be fed like hens and cocks;
> Hither and thither with delicate tread,
>   Flutter around me in fairy flocks.

First, the title deceives us. Instead of finding ourselves in a quiet grove or a magic circle where we might hope and expect to find fairies, we are taken to the barnyard where clucking, pecking chickens live their unmagical lives. Next the chickens' "flutter" and "delicate tread" (an incongruous phrase because *delicate* connotes the opposite of *tread*) have connotations incompatible with the fragile appearance and delicate movement of fairies. The connotations are wrong for this comparison.

Compactness

Poetry exists for itself, an end in itself. It has no mission nor message beyond discovery, beyond the emotion and thought of the reader as he or she explores the lines. A poem is best said in few and artfully chosen words; it follows that if we change a word, we change the poem. Nothing can be altered in Langston Hughes' simple yet eloquent lament for a lost friend:

> I loved my friend.
> He went away from me.
> There's nothing more to say.
> The poem ends,
> Soft as it began—
> I loved my friend.

Hughes' purpose is not to instruct or to inform us, but through his words to make us experience profound loss. Change a single word and we change the experience. "I miss my friend" is no substitute for these six lines; the poem says far more than that. Even the repeated last line does not repeat the first idea, but adds to it. So compact is the poem that it can bear no paraphrase; it says twice as much in half the time.

Poems are brief and condensed. The poet must make the best possible use of each word, often choosing one term to convey many meanings, or relying on connotation to extend our awareness of the experience. The unknown Anglo-Saxon poet of the eighth century who wrote "Frost Shall Freeze" has condensed meaning into a seven-line stanza, but it is not merely the absence of extra words like vague adjectives or unnecessary conjunctions that makes the poem compact. In such phrases as "ice shall bridge,/And roof the waters," the words call up pictures in our minds as we see figurative sights and comparisons:

> Frost shall freeze; fire melt wood;
> Earth shall blossom; ice shall bridge
> And roof the waters, wondrously lock
> Earth's budding growth. One shall unbind
> The fetters of frost, Almighty God.
> Winter shall pass, fair weather return,
> Sun-hot summer and restless sea.

Emily Dickinson compresses the experience of reading a book into a poem of eight lines. To make her poem compact she relies upon three figurative comparisons, each one expanded in meaning by its richness in connotations:

> There is no frigate like a book
> To take us lands away,
> Nor any courser like a page
> Of prancing poetry—
> This traverse may the poorest take
> Without oppress of toll—
> How frugal is the chariot
> That bears the human soul!

Dickinson does not say that a book is like a mere boat, or even a sailboat; she calls up romance by using the term "frigate." Frigates are sailing vessels used by explorers seeking new lands, by pirates pursuing treasure and adventure, by merchants carrying silks and spices from the Orient to farflung shores. A book is like a "courser," not a mere horse. "Courser" connotes knights charging off on missions fraught with danger and the promise of rescue. No car nor wagon could have the mystery of a "chariot," a fragile royal cart flying along behind the hoofs of a thoroughbred. Other words as well, like "prancing," "frugal," and "toll," are rich in connotative meaning. Specific terms with rich meanings expand the ideas in the compact comparisons. By means of these connotations, the total experience of a book becomes adventure, wealth, discovery, suspense, intrigue, danger, romance, and a multitude of other possibilities. This poem, like that which Eve Merriam describes in "How to Eat a Poem," has nothing unnecessary, nothing to throw away—not a seed nor a pit, a stem, a core, nor a rind.

Emotional Intensity

Like fiction at its best, poetry at its best lets us enjoy an old experience with new insight or understand one that we have never met. However, unlike the writer of fiction, the poet condenses the experience. Poetry attempts to capture the reader where he or she is, and to involve the reader briefly but intensely.

The successful poem is an intense emotional experience. "There Is No Frigate" is an experience of a book. It is not a description of a book, nor of the feelings a child might have while reading a book. By its richly connotative words and its varied sensory images, the poem becomes an intense emotional experience. The same can be said of McCord's "Pickety Fence"; the poem is not a prosy description of a fence nor the sounds a child might hear when drawing a stick along a picket fence. Because of its sounds and rhythms, the poem is an emotional experience of a picket fence. The poem has used the devices of poetry—rhythm, sound, compactness—to give us insight into the experience.

We have noted how rhythm, sound, and figurative language contribute to compactness, and compactness to emotional intensity. Langston

Hughes' poem "Dream Deferred" has emotional intensity, intensity created particularly by his skillful use of unusual figurative comparisons and sensory appeals:

> What happens to a dream deferred?
> Does it dry up
>   like a raisin in the sun?
>
> Or fester like a sore—
> And then run?
> Does it stink like rotten meat?
> Or crust and sugar over—
>   like a syrupy sweet?
>
> Maybe it just sags
> like a heavy load.
>
> *Or does it explode?*

From the poem we have an intense emotional experience of frustration. A festering sore, stinking meat—these are ugly images causing us to experience the emotions that accompany frustration. The images connote neglect, usefulness turned to decay. What was a simple sore is now painfully infected; what was edible meat is now stinking uselessness.

Negative Qualities in Poetry

The negatives of literature, *didacticism, sentimentality,* and *condescension,* make their appearances in poetry, too, but only in poor poetry. These qualities are often expressed in words with distracting connotations, in trite comparisons, commonplace imagery, repetitious and unvaried beat, or in sound unsuited to meaning and tone. Kipling's didactic verse "If" is representative of the preaching verse adults often hear in the so-called inspirational speech. But children are even more often subjected to verses with preaching purpose, and Abbie Farwell Brown's "A Music Box" is one. The first stanza sets up a metaphor; the two that follow preach a sermon:

> I am a little Music Box
>   Wound up and made to go,
> And play my little living-tune
>   The best way that I know.
>
> If I am naughty, cross, or rude
>   The music will go wrong,
> My little works be tangled up,
>   And spoil the pretty song.

I must be very sweet and good
And happy all the day,
And then the little Music Box
In tune will always play.

Intrigued with the metaphor, we are fooled into thinking that "A Music Box" will be a pleasurable experience; then we learn that our sins spoil the song. By the final stanza—"I must be very sweet and good"—we are thoroughly disenchanted, disappointed that what began by intriguing us ends by instructing us to be happy models of perfection.

As for sentimentality and condescension, a poem that speaks to a worm about pain, assuming its pain to be comparable to the pain a person might feel if jumped on by a giant, that poem surely condescends to readers as it tries to rouse our emotions beyond justification:

No, little worm, you need not slip
Into your hole, with such a skip;
Drawing the gravel as you glide
On to your smooth and slimy side.

For my part, I could never bear
Your tender flesh to hack and tear,
Forgetting that poor worms endure
As much as I should, to be sure,
If any giant would come and jump
On to my back, and kill me plump,
Or run my heart through with a scythe,
And think it fun to see me writhe![5]

It is not the subject of the poem that is inappropriate for poetry; it is the sentimental tone. Notice, by contrast, the quality of wonder in Elizabeth Madox Roberts' poem "The Worm," in which the poet duplicates a child-hood experience, relying almost exclusively upon imagery to draw us into experiencing the children's wondering intentness. As the children dig with broken shell, tin, and spade, they find a small clod with a worm inside:

We watched him pucker up himself
And stretch himself to walk away.
He tried to go inside the dirt,
But Dickie made him wait and stay.

The children marvel at the sheen of the soft, wet skin, and they forget to dig their wells. Like children everywhere, they wonder if the worm knows it is a worm:

And while we tried to find it out,
He puckered in a little wad,
And then he stretched himself again
And went back home inside the clod.

Digging up a worm and looking at it intently can be an experience for poetry, an experience so compact that even adults become children once again during their involvement in twenty-four lines. In Roberts' poem there is neither sentimentality nor condescension.

The best poetry is made with care and artistry. Sometimes, in fact, poetry is found in paragraph form; the writer has chosen each word for its imagery and connotative power, asking of the reader concentration and imagination to discover meaning. On the other hand, prose and prosaic writing is sometimes put into the form usually reserved for poetry—irregular lines and stanza arrangement. But by failing to use words rich in connotative meaning, by failing to make figurative comparisons or to use rhythm to enhance meaning, the writer has written prose. Line or stanza arrangement has not made poetry out of prose. The best prose and the best poetry are both written with care and skill. The difference lies primarily in the compactness and the intensity of the expression. Figurative devices, rhythmic flow, and sound patterns occur in prose. There is then no line to be drawn between prose and poetry; the difference is simply in degree. As rhythm becomes more regular, imagery more vivid, and statements more compact, emotions become more intense. The reader feels the increased intensity and becomes aware of the expression as poetry.

SUMMARY

Rhymes and sidewalk jingles are many children's first experience with literature, and surely their first introduction to verse and poetry. The rhymes not only may provide an easy and loving bridge between the parents' childhoods and the new generation, but their simple stylistic devices of rhythm, sound, and comparison, their colorful characters involved in elementary tensions, and their occasional themes about the lives of human beings are sufficient reasons for including them as literature for the youngest child. They may or may not influence children's understanding, but the joy they give is undeniable.

The nursery and nonsense rhymes of childhood contain on different levels many of the elements of literature—of poetry and its style. Rhymes give pleasure through story and sounds. Nonsense delights us by its inventiveness, its unexpected turns and surprises. With its rapid rhythms and unexpected rhymes, and its topsy-turvy, no-sense way of looking at the logic of life, nonsense provides children with a great deal of pleasure—whether the joy is awakened by a patterned limerick, a gem of concentrated wit, or by children's own creations. Nonsense, too, is a way into poetry.

Poetry stands as an experience in itself. Rhythm, sound, and connotation expand meaning; imagery heightens our sensory awareness, and apt figurative comparisons tempt our imaginations. A distilled representation of an experience, poetry at its best permits the reader to participate, but without the burden of didacticism or sentimentality.

Since the whole range from rhyme to nonsense to imaginative poetry is available to children, it seems only fair to introduce them to it all. Led easily from simple rhymes and nonsense to poetry, children, as Herbert Read says, deserve to be enticed and invited, wheedled and persuaded by poetic art. The experience of the best efforts of skillful poets is enlarging; it gives pleasure and promotes understanding. To keep that pleasure forever, let children memorize as they choose.

READING AND EVALUATING

1. Find six editions of the Mother Goose nursery rhymes and compare them for completeness and for attractiveness in format. Which edition focuses on the most familiar rhymes? In the familiar rhymes can you see any pattern that might have made them more familiar—like musical qualities, vivid images, and stories? Which rhymes might give the child some understanding beyond the pure pleasure of sounds and stories? Among the familiar rhymes, are there any you disapprove of? Why?

2. Find a volume of nonsense verse from folk tradition, like *A Rocket in My Pocket* by Carl Withers. Do you see variations that you can expect from folk literature? What accounts for the popularity of folk rhymes with children?

3. Collect from your friends their jump-rope, ball-bouncing, and counting-out rhymes. What devices of style have they in common? How do you account for their popularity?

4. Find a volume of literary nonsense like *What a Wonderful Bird the Frog Are*, edited by Myra Cohn Livingston, or one by Laura E. Richards, Edward Lear, Ogden Nash, or another writer. Why are the rhymes often so brief? What is the effect on the reader when the verses are long? What are the common sources of laughter? What patterns of structure are used?

5. Find a volume of poems by a single poet whose poetry is open to children, like David McCord, Eve Merriam, Aileen Fisher, Harry Behn, Karla Kuskin, Myra Cohn Livingston, or another writer. Have the writings of any of these poets become old-fashioned in tone? Describe each poet in terms of use of imagery, rhythm, figurative language, sound patterns, and use of connotative words. Which poets seem to appeal to older readers? younger readers? Which poets have compressed meaning and feeling to produce emotional intensity? Give examples.

6. Find a large anthology of poetry for children. Select two poems for superior use of connotative language, another two for imagery, for figurative language, sound patterns, and emotional intensity. Check dates of publication of your choices. What conclusion can you reach about aging and agelessness in poetry?

NOTES

1 Myra Cohn Livingston calls attention to occasional new versions of Mother Goose that refuse "to free fancy," but interpolate "didacticism, moralism, and parochialism"; "they destroy the charm to tongue and ear and blind the child's inner eye" ("Don't Cook Mother Goose," *New York Times Book Review*, July 26, 1988.)

2 Francelia Butler in her study of jump-rope rhymes around the world seems to have discovered more brutality and violence in rhymes from America than in those from other countries. (See "Over the Garden Wall/I Let the Baby Fall: The Poetry of Rope-Skipping." *Children's Literature*, Vol. 3. Storrs, CT: Journal of the Modern Language Association and The Children's Literature Association, 1974.)

3 "Night" is by Patricia Hubbell. You might try a series of figurative equations on Joyce Kilmer's "Trees"; try drawing a picture of the woman that a tree is like.

4 "What Is Poetry? An Afterthought" in *This Way, Delight*. New York: Pantheon, 1956, p. 140.

5 Ann Taylor (1782–1866) published verses during a period when instruction was the only excuse for poetry to be published for children. *Original Poems for Infant Minds,* written by Ann, Jane, and their brother Isaac, was published in 1804.

BOOKS CITED IN THIS CHAPTER*

ALDIS, DOROTHY. *Hop, Skip and Jump.* New York: Putnam, 1934.

ANONYMOUS. "Falling Snow," in *A Book of Children's Literature,* Lillian Hollowell, ed. New York: Rinehart & Co., 1939.

BEHN, HARRY. *The Little Hill.* New York: Harcourt Brace Jovanovich, 1949.

BROWN, ABBIE FARWELL. *Pinafore Palace,* Kate Douglas Wiggin and Nora Archibald Smith, eds. New York: Doubleday, 1907.

CARROLL, LEWIS. *Alice's Adventures in Wonderland.* New York: Macmillan, 1963 (first published, 1865).

DICKINSON, EMILY. *The Complete Poems of Emily Dickinson.* Boston: Little, Brown, 1960.

FISHER, AILEEN. *Out in the Dark and Daylight.* New York: Harper & Row, 1980.

FRANCIS, ROBERT. *The Orb Weaver.* Middletown, CT: Wesleyan University Press, 1948.

HUBBELL, PATRICIA. *The Apple Vendor's Fair.* New York: Atheneum, 1963.

HUGHES, LANGSTON. *Selected Poems of Langston Hughes.* New York: Knopf, 1926.

HUNT, EVELYN TOOLEY. *The Lyric.* 1972.

KENNEDY, CHARLES W., ed. *Anthology of Old English Poetry.* London: Oxford University Press, 1960.

KENNEDY, X. J. *The Phantom Ice Cream Man: More Nonsense Verse.* New York: Atheneum, 1979.

LEAR, EDWARD. *Nonsense Omnibus.* New York: Frederick Warne, 1943.

LINDSAY, VACHEL. *The Congo and Other Poems.* New York: Macmillan, 1914.

LIVINGSTON, MYRA COHN. *What a Wonderful Bird the Frog Are.* New York: Harcourt Brace Jovanovich, 1973.

————. *Whispers and Other Poems.* New York: Harcourt Brace Jovanovich, 1958.

MERRIAM, EVE. *Inside a Poem.* New York: Atheneum, 1962.

MIZIMURA, KAZUE. *Flower Moon Snow: A Book of Haiku.* New York: Thomas Crowell, 1977.

MOORE, LILIAN. *Think of Shadows.* New York: Atheneum, 1980.

MORRISON, LILLIAN. *The Sidewalk Racer.* New York: Lothrop, Lee & Shepard, 1968.

*Because of their very nature, anthologies and collections of poetry are not always consistent in their quality. Therefore, the list here is a list of books cited in the chapter, but not necessarily a list of recommended books.

NASH, OGDEN. *The Face is Familiar*. Garden City, NY: Garden City Publishers, 1941.

RICHARDS, LAURA E. *Tirra Lirra: Rhymes Old and New*. Boston: Little, Brown, 1955.

ROBERTS, ELIZABETH MADOX. *Under the Tree*. New York: Viking, 1930.

SANDBURG, CARL. *Chicago Poems*. New York: Harcourt Brace Jovanovich, 1944.

STEVENSON, ROBERT LOUIS. *A Child's Garden of Verses*. New York: Watts, 1966 (first published, 1885).

UPDIKE, JOHN. *A Child's Calendar*. New York: Knopf, 1965.

WYNNE, ANNETTE. *More Silver Pennies*. New York: Macmillan, 1938.

Illustration by John Schoenherr reprinted by permission of Philomel Books from *Owl Moon* by Jane Yolen, illustrations copyright © 1987 by John Schoenherr.

icture Books

Over 50,000 books for children are currently in print, Bowker statisticians assert, and a quick glance at the many on library shelves shows clearly that illustration is growing in importance. We might call a book illustrated when it includes merely a pictorial dust jacket, a cover picture, a frontispiece, or three or four pictures throughout, but the profusely illustrated picture book is the genre most clearly dependent upon illustration. Thanks to a more affluent society, to increased awareness of the importance of childhood, to courses in children's literature and its critical evaluation, and very importantly to the growing significance of awards given to children's books, as well as to publishers' profits accompanying such winning books, and to the attractive packaging of many more, we seem to be continuously blessed with well-illustrated children's literature. This is not to say, of course, that poorly illustrated books do not abound, but instead that artistic excellence is increasingly apparent and appreciated.

Perhaps because illustration has historically been tied to text, it has often in the past been regarded as a lesser art. Although at one time Degas, Daumier, and Roualt all illustrated for the public, they are more appreciated now for their other art. Howard Pyle and N. C. Wyeth, who spent their professional lives making books beautiful, were not taken as seriously as other artists, but as printing processes improved and publishers employed art editors, successful artists like Leo and Diane Dillon, Chris Van Allsburg, Maurice Sendak, and others were attracted to illustrating children's books.

Because illustration has the characteristics of an art form, however, it should be regarded as art. Illustrators use the techniques of representation, expressionism, impressionism, and surrealism, of cubism and pointillism, of naive, folk, and collage styles as well as photography. Like other art forms, illustration uses symbolic language for communication. It has both meaning and content created from visual and usually verbal symbols as well. It creates its own illusions of reality often dissimilar to those of the practical world, and by use of figurative devices of all kinds, it opens for us an imaginary vision. Successful art takes us away from our current world to a level of understanding deeper and wider than our limited lives, maybe to a world more ugly or more beautiful, more humorous or more somber, more simple or more complex. And like the best of any art form, it forces us to confront the depths of our secret selves.[1] Unlike looking at the natural world to take it in and to appreciate it, looking at a picture book involves associational meaning, connecting picture with text, or in the wordless book relating what we see through the whole of the story.[2]

It is said that picture books for the younger child require simpler composition than those for older readers. But real artistry means that complexity may be appropriate for any age, as it is in *Anno's Journey* by Mitsumasa Anno, for example.

In any composite of verbal and pictorial storytelling, we see the picture's contents all at once, but we are exposed to the verbal story a little at a time in linear progression. Joseph Schwarcz comments that we remember, assemble, and associate the elements of the verbal story, keeping them in mind as we simultaneously acquire new information. In a similar but reverse way we look at a picture to see it as a whole, then absorb the details little by little, noting how they compose the whole. We may wander over the picture, lingering here and skipping there, absorbing, assimilating, connecting details, colors, and shapes, until we have observed all of the picture. As Schwarcz says, "Following an illustrated text is, then, a complex activity." Despite complexities, however, and more likely because of them, children never weary of the intimately interwoven visual and verbal arts, demanding to see and hear new illustrated stories as well as being excited by the continuing discoveries in the familiar ones.

Since finding the earliest records of pictorial art in cave drawings, we have assumed drawings were made to accompany verbal storytelling, that one complements the other. "Associates in a partnership" is the term used by B. W. Alderson to describe the relationship of the writer and illustrator of a picture book. No matter what terms we use, it is clear that the two artists who work separately and in differing media together create a whole. Pictures make the verbal visible and extend the texual meaning; they permit the artist to add personal interpretation while staying within the story, but they do not overwhelm the text. "Their responsibility is to reflect truly the imaginative tenor of the text (or, in the case of books without text, of the subject) and to create a sequence or group of pictures which add up to a consistent whole." Alderson says further:

Among the virtues of the traditional approach to book illustration is its care for the details of a picture's narrative content and design. This is not to say that there is always necessarily something going on in the illustrations, but that there is nearly always a nuance of detail for the eye to feed upon and one which in the best work will be in complete harmony (and may even be visually integrated) with the printed text.[3]

Decrying both artwork that is trite and that which distracts and seems to exist for the sake of showing off the artist's skill, Alderson reminds us of the technique, artistry, and versatility that have existed throughout the history of illustration, from Howard Pyle to present-day illustrators.

We note such partnership somewhat differently when we examine pictures made of dolls and puppets in a photograph. There is an interdependence of several artists: the writer, the doll or puppet creator, the designer of the stage, and the director of the whole. Although one person may act in two or more capacities, the result is a compiled effort. Despite photographic techniques of long shots and close-ups, these illustrations convey a sense of still life and seem to be a moment from a play captured by the photographer.

THE ILLUSTRATIVE ELEMENTS OF THE PICTURE BOOK

Designing the Book

Although illustration and other two-dimensional art have much in common, designing an entire picture book is not like designing other works. Publication requires that the illustrator's work be reproducible in mass, and that requirement determines the whole book design, including size, shape, single- or double-page pictures and the placement of the gutter, end papers, title page, cover, and dust jacket (whether it uses a wraparound illustration or separate pictures for front and back). Some pages call for decoration, some are best left "silent," and others may be framed or unframed or may fill the page, edge to edge. All this requires decisions about placement of pictures and text, to create formality or informality, to suit the tone or pace of the story or poem.

The illustrator puts into visual form what the words say, or sometimes what they merely suggest. In *The Snowy Day,* Ezra Jack Keats needs many words to describe Peter's trek through the fresh snow, "with his toes pointing out, like this," dragging "his feet s-l-o-w-l-y" or dragging the "something" and making a third track. In *Fish is Fish,* Leo Lionni, who like Keats is both author and illustrator, tells in pictures what would take a page of verbal description. When the frog returns to tell of the wonders on land, the fish can picture only fish bodies: birds as fish with wings, people as fish in clothes, and fish-cows with horns, four legs, and "pink bags for milk." The illustrator has not only put into visual form what the words say, but he has successfully added to the text, creating incongruous humor and commenting on how we see others in terms of ourselves.

Occasionally an illustrator will use the technique we frequently see in comics, continuous narrative, which is the depiction of action through the repeated picturing of the character in different places or motions all within the same illustration. Using this technique in *A Whistle for Willie*, Keats shows in one illustration two separate actions. Willie, disappointed that he cannot whistle for his dog, tries to distract himself from his feeling of discouragement first by walking the sidewalk cracks, then by trying to run away from his shadow.

Picturing Figurative Language

Figurative language is inherent in human speech. As children add new experiences and experiment with language, they speak figuratively, exploring how this and that are surprisingly like or unlike. Perhaps one of the most interesting ways in which an illustrator enlivens and complements the text is by picturing figurative language. The most common is the personification of animals, as in Robert McCloskey's *Make Way for Ducklings*, or of inanimate objects, as in Virginia Lee Burton's *The Little House*. Greater subtlety occurs in Keats' *Apt. 3;* the blind harmonica player's music becomes "purples and grays and rain and smoke." Another familiar picture book whose broad humor appeals to children is *Amelia Bedelia*, in which "dusting the furniture" and "drawing the drapes" are taken literally. Although this confusion might not properly be called metaphor, children delight in knowing other meanings and in seeing foolish Amelia Bedelia pictured. Sometimes, however, the illustrator may try a literal picturing of the metaphor, and the mood changes. For example, the moon's kiss on the face of a drowsy child awakens our sense of wonder at the luminous moon. Literally picturing the moon descending into the bedroom to touch the child's face totally destroys the mood. In *The Elephant's Child*, Lorinda Bryan Cauley avoids showing the elephant's nose as "no bigger than a boot"; the comparison is convincing as she pictures it but would be distracting if illustrated literally.

Amplifying the Text

The illustrator clarifies and amplifies text, extending it beyond the words or the reader's imagination. "Form," said Ben Shahn in a lecture at Harvard thirty years ago, "is the visible shape of content."[4] Even in books for older children where illustrations are not as frequent as in picture books, the visual images enhance the text. In Robert McCloskey's *Homer Price,* for example, Uncle Telly's ball of string, "six feet across...biggest ball of string in the world," is funny to read about, but vastly more humorous when we see Homer sprawled across the top, trying to add another yard of string. Pooh, tracking the heffalump, is alarmed at the third set of tracks going round the tree; Ernest Shepard has made us laugh as the illustration solves Pooh's mystery. It is far easier to see the relative size of the Borrowers when Beth and Jo Krush picture them in their home beneath the floor, where postage stamps are hung as pictures, spools are used as stools, and stacked matchboxes serve as chests. The illustration creates a recognizable world and compels us to believe that Borrowers do indeed exist.

In another example, Keats uses somber tones for a picture book when he paints the shadowy tenement of *Apt. 3* with a dark palette. Splotches of dark color give the impression of dinginess, dirty walls, lack of light, and a sense of mystery—what goes on behind these closed doors? This is not physical detail added to text but the mood of the whole. When Sam and Ben invite the blind man to take a walk next day, his harmonica music changes to become quiet and soft, and the double-page spreads change to happier, lighter tones of the earlier colors. The final, lighter-colored spread says nothing about a walk, but silhouetted television aerials and a sky, smoky but blue, answer that question. Here illustrations do not merely extend the text, but the two present a complete and inextricable combination, the creation of a new world. This is what Maurice Sendak, creator of *Where the Wild Things Are,* calls "seamlessness," or the perfect joining of text and pictures.

Changing the Story

The illustrator influences, and in some cases changes, the story—not the text, but the story. The greater the proportion of illustrations to text, the greater the influence the illustrations have in the creation of the composite. In some cases text and pictures seem to provide two stories; the impact of Pat Hutchins' *Rosie's Walk,* for example, is dependent upon recognizing this duality. The text tells us that Rosie walks innocently across the farm; the pictures tell us her life is threatened by the menacing fox. Holding these two stories in mind simultaneously constitutes the delight of the whole. In another example, objective narration, combined with humorous illustration, create a two-dimensional story as pictures provide plot that is unspoken in words. This double story occurs in Nancy Tafuri's *Have You Seen My Duckling?;* we see the absent duckling, although the searching mother cannot.

Illustration may also give more exact information, create a mood and atmosphere by depiction of a setting or action, or make us care about a character because the pictured dress and countenance reveal more of a person than does the text. Thus, illustration not only clarifies and amplifies text, but it extends the text beyond our own imaginations. Pooh's gluttony, as he sits surrounded by water "on his branch, dangling his legs . . . beside him . . . ten pots of honey," is made vivid by Shepard's illustration. By contrast, notice how Gustav Tenngren's illustrations for *Snow White and the Seven Dwarfs* change the story. We assume from the title that this is Snow White's story, but that is not the case. Because the bland beauty of Tenngren's Snow White is no match for the personalities we read on the faces of the seven dwarfs and the wicked witch, this has become their story: *The Seven Dwarfs, the Witch (and Snow White)*. The story has changed, and we do not face so clearly one of its major themes—there is strong temptation to do the forbidden.

When illustrated by different artists, a story becomes many quite different tales, each influenced by the vision of the artist, the episodes selected for picturing, the chosen palette, the rhythm and movement of line, the meticulous detail or the bold sweep of pen or brush. Look, for example, at different versions of the Cinderella story, of which new editions continue to appear. Despite knowing well the text of Charles Perrault and others, the reader still gains very different impressions from the various versions. In Shirley Hughes' retelling with twenty-five pictures, Cinderella herself, whose story this is, appears eighteen times, often in less than central focus, while her wicked stepsisters appear eleven times, and often as the major focus. We see Cinderella being scorned by her stepmother, dressing her stepsisters' hair, scrubbing the floor while the sisters preen, watching wistfully in the doorway while in the foreground they dress for the ball, abjectly weeping while we focus on the fairy godmother, and, in a rear view, watching as the splendid coach appears. Then, at long last, on a full page, we see her dressed in her magical finery. In the next picture, she does not appear at all, and in still others, she shares equal billing with the prince, the townspeople, the godmother, the chamberlain. In ratio of two to three, stepsisters to Cinderella, we meet stepsisters echoing their mother's sneer on the frontispiece, and kneeling in supplication for mercy in the twenty-fourth picture. Because of the strong focus on the stepsisters, the impact of the story is that Cinderella is the victim of their envy but is magically saved.

In Paul Galdone's version, Cinderella appears not as beautiful and good, but as pathetic, as Goldone seizes the opportunity to paint wonderful lizards, mice, horses, town criers, coach, and cartoonlike stepsisters. Plot details seem to carry illustrations; Cinderella herself, though important, still does not illuminate the theme of the good person who yearns for and receives acceptance and appreciation.

In still another version, Errol LeCain's highly stylized illustrations distance us from all the characters. In a palette of low color intensity and in pictures swirling with stylized motion, all characters are strictly fairy-tale-never-happened figures. The illustrator seems to have been carried away with the infinite possibilities for creating elaborate coaches, footmen, ball guests, and an evil-looking witch never mentioned in the text. Since in this book pictures are often unrelated to the accompanying text, they serve more as decorations than as illustrations for the story.

The way in which the pictures portray or add to the textual information creates the information itself, as we might note from Nonny Hogrogian's version of Cinderella. She uses soft pastels in illustrations bathed in a mist of fantasy that enhance the fairy tale qualities. Cinderella, herself a lovely girl not unlike lovely girls we might know, convinces us by her humility and devotion that she is indeed as good as she is beautiful and deserves therefore to be rich and to live happily ever after.

THE LITERARY ELEMENTS OF THE PICTURE BOOK

We are often deceived into thinking that because the text for picture books is brief, the writer of the text need not be judged by the standards of literary excellence. When we see, however, that it is possible to develop surprisingly full characters like Beatrix Potter's Peter Rabbit, to create an engaging plot as Maurice Sendak so skillfully does in *Where the Wild Things Are,* to show with words as well as pictures an integral setting like that in *The Spooky Tail of Prewitt Peacock* by Bill Peet—when we see all this, we realize that a good picture book is not as simple as it looks. Our appreciation grows when we notice that words make comparisons and sound resembles meaning—that style is important. As Perry Nodelman comments: "The excitement of a good picture book is the constant tension between the moments isolated by the pictures and the flow of words that join these moments together. The jumpy rhythm of picture books is quite different from the gradually intensifying flow of stories told by words themselves."[5]

Thus, words as well as pictures—fresh comparisons, vivid sensory appeals, and the writer's intelligence and wit—make the most successful story. Some slight tension holds our interest, and the simplest of thematic ideas, such as "We need food for the spirit as well as for the body" from *Frederick* by Leo Lionni, ties it all together. The elements of literature, then, are important here too, just as they are in other genres. By pinning pictures to words, and words to ideas, the best text can enlarge the child's world in ways that even the most careful observation of pictures cannot do.

Plot

The brevity of text in picture books does not eliminate the necessity for some kind of *plot,* some action or tension, the quality most likely to keep us reading. Peter Rabbit's curiosity and waywardness create the tension in his story; Max's wild behavior in *Wild Things* opens the action, and the exciting roars and threats followed by his taming them all continue the tension. Even the story of Peter's *The Snowy Day* has its quiet surprises, the simplest kind of plot. In *Sam, Bangs & Moonshine,* the *climax* comes on the final page when Sam takes her gerbil over to Thomas and tells him it is his, and its name is "Moonshine!" Sam has resolved the *conflict* in her mind and now knows the difference between harmless and harmful, fantasizing between good and bad moonshine. Such an ending is called *closed.* Occasionally we find a picture book with an *open ending,* such as *The Garden of Abdul Gasazi* by Chris Van Allsburg, which leaves us wondering if Fritz the dog has actually been turned into a duck—temporarily.

Picture books without tension or conflict are less successful. There are many examples. Look at *Hold My Hand* by Charlotte Zolotow, described on the jacket as "a moment of intensity," yet there is no tension, no intensity. For a specific example, consider *Willie Goes to the Seashore,* a picture-story book with little excitement. The family has a small cottage at the beach. In a total of seventy-five printed lines, they unpack, roll in the sand, swim, hunt shells, build a sand castle, rebuild the sand castle, and splash in the water. They hang seaweed around their necks and go to bed. Next day Willie finds an old boat, explores the rocks, sees a crab dart off, collects firewood, and puts weiners on roasting sticks. Willie "never had such fun." Willie does everything—and nothing.

Suppose, instead, that Willie had built an elaborate sand castle, planning it, admiring it, embellishing it, and patting it into shape. Then during the weiner roast, the waves in their regular tidal shifts destroy the castle! Result: tension. Or suppose Willie explored the old boat, found it had oarlocks and a hollow bow, and made an imaginary fishing expedition beyond the point. Now the seashore truly becomes a place to have fun, and some tension or conflict is the cause. Look at *Margaret's Birthday* by Jan Wahl and note the similarities to the random activity of Willie's seashore experience.

Even the simplest stories for children can have conflict or tension. Will Goldilocks be caught? Will the three little pigs survive by the hair of their chinny-chin-chins? Will the troll who lives under the bridge get the Billy Goats Gruff? Suspense builds in each of these stories as a threat is repeated three times, and conflict is climaxed by defeat of the threatener. Goldilocks gets away, the wolf falls into boiling water, and the troll is crushed to bits, body and bones.

Character

One of the surprising discoveries about *character* in fiction is that a round character can emerge from a short story for a small child. Contrast *Peter Rabbit* with *Cowboy Small* by Lois Lenski. What does any child remember from *Cowboy Small*? It might be called "a ho-hum book—soonest read, soonest forgotten."[6]

Cowboy Small has a horse which he keeps in a barn, feeds, waters, brushes, and curries. He saddles, mounts, rides, dismounts, cooks, eats, sleeps under the stars, rides again, rounds up cows, eats again, ropes a calf, helps in branding, plays a guitar and sings, sleeps, rides a bronco, falls off, and rides again. No one action is more important than another; there is no selectivity. All there is to Cowboy Small as a person is his name, and even that is no name. Such a story has been written with a message in mind, namely to acquaint a child with the job description of the mythical American cowboy.

We never come to know Cowboy Small (would Cowboy Small have stuffed himself as Peter Rabbit did?). However, we know Peter Rabbit and the Ugly Duckling; from their actions we know a great deal about their feelings and thoughts. We understand them and come to care about them; we remember them. But we are unaffected by Cowboy Small's actions; we cannot even say that we forget him, since we never really knew him. A sterile relationship exists between a round-faced paper cut-out and the things he does. On the other hand, Ezra Jack Keats, within a shorter text than *Cowboy Small,* shows Peter of *The Snowy Day* as a real boy who is delighted at the snowfall, happy with his angel-making, sad at his snowball's melting, and wistful about not being able to join in a snowball fight; in short, Peter is a character we know and like.

Perhaps at this point it is necessary to digress, since some adults may find rabbits and people difficult to interchange. What matters here is not that Peter, like a rabbit, moves on four legs and lives in a sandbank under the roots of a fir tree, nor for that matter that, like a child, he wears a little blue jacket with gold buttons. What makes Peter a little boy is his childlike personality and behavior.

While adults may find it difficult to attribute to animals the traits of human beings, this is not difficult for most children. The child listening to *Peter Rabbit* has no difficulty seeing Peter as a child, because he is a developed or round character. When an animal in a children's story is a believable human being, the *anthropomorphism* merely creates fantasy. If the fantastic but believable character is involved in action related to character, children feel very much at home with the whole idea.

Character and incident in *Peter Rabbit* are so closely tied to one another that we can see no separation. Peter is mischievous from the start; throughout the story he believes he knows better than he actually does. He is adventuresome, since he crawls under the gate, despite his father's accident which resulted in his being eaten in a rabbit pie. He is greedy: he gorges himself on lettuces, French beans, and radishes. He is frightened and frantic in his flight, and woebegone, he cries. As we hear that this is the second lost jacket and shoes in a fortnight, we know Peter's behavior is consistent. Uncomplaining, Peter accepts the kind nursing of his loving mother; he is a secure child. Peter is no cardboard, two-dimensional rabbit. He is instead a round and believable central character.

Can we say that children re-read *Peter Rabbit* again and again because of curiosity about the outcome of the story? Hardly, since the first reading satisfies both parents and children on that score. There must be other considerations. While detailed, delicately colored illustrations as well as suspenseful action give pleasure to the reader and the listener, the character of Peter Rabbit as the universal child is the magnet that pulls us back to read and re-read. Peter's actions are inherent in his personality. The one produces the other, true to James' views on the interrelatedness of character and action.

Theme

Some stories for young children are both humor-filled and rich with a variety of *themes*, but check the shelf of children's fare in any bookstore and notice how often action or situation humor is its only element. The popularity of books like Hans Rey's *Curious George*, with its exciting action and variety—the monkey's balloon flight which coincidentally ends on top of the traffic light, and his play with the telephone which calls in a fire alarm—seems to suggest that a child can appreciate only coincidence and situation humor. But children love George for a different reason: his curiosity matches theirs.

Curious George is a pleasant narrative for a small child, but there is satisfaction in a story with a theme. The equally simple story *Frederick* by Leo Lionni has not only an interesting situation and a conflict that has climax and resolution, but it has thematic strength as well. Frederick is the mouse who collects—not wheat, corn, straw, and nuts, but sun's rays and periwinkle colors. He brings these out during the dull days of winter to remind others of nature's beauty and of hope for spring's return. Frederick's poetry sustains the spirits of his friends throughout the long winter, showing that food and shelter alone do not support life: the spirit needs nourishment too.

The simplest story can illustrate a significant point. While the effective illustrations in the picture book *Ben's Trumpet* by Rachel Isadora successfully convey the confusion of the inner city, the jaggedness of trumpet sounds, and the intricacies of jazz rhythms, the text demonstrates that kindness rewards persistence. In Maurice Sendak's *Where the Wild Things Are,* we have a character, Max, whom we care about, acting out a conflict that interests us—and all united by an implicit theme which can be stated in several ways: We show love in many ways; or, the best place is where there is love. The story is more than a situation with wonderfully effective illustrations, more than the pleasure of its rhythmic style. The story also has a strong theme.

Many kinds of stories have their place for small children: some offer the listening child laughter from a narrative with physical or situation humor, or the reassurance found in pure, day-to-day routine, the unexciting commonplace. Other stories like Miska Miles' *Annie and the Old One* or Lucille Clifton's *The Boy Who Didn't Believe in Spring* combine freshness in language, imagination in plot, and significance in theme, as well as distinctive illustrations.

Once again we refer to *The Tale of Peter Rabbit,* which has its own implicit theme. Action and suspense race to the point of Peter's flopping down on the nice, sandy floor of the rabbit home, where he shuts his eyes. Mother, who is busy cooking, wonders what he has done with his new clothes, but she does not lecture, nor spank, nor compare naughty Peter to good Flopsy, Mopsy, and Cotton-tail. Although Peter didn't feel very well that evening, there is no hint of "It serves him right. He was naughty." Peter's mother puts him to bed and gives him a dose of camomile tea. Potter does not call it punitive medicine, nor does she describe it as tasting bad. Nor does she call Flopsy, Mopsy, and Cotton-tail's bread, milk, and blackberries reward for goodness.

Is the story didactic? Although we adults see clearly that disobedience and curiosity can get you into trouble, *Peter Rabbit,* after all, is for a small child. The theme is implied, but not didactic. *Peter Rabbit* can become didactic, however, if some reteller adds a single phrase to Potter's final paragraph, saying that Flopsy, Mopsy, and Cotton-tail, "who were good little bunnies," ate bread and milk and blackberries at suppertime. Or when we see another illustrator's picture with an admonitory plaque hanging on the kitchen wall, saying, "Good bunnies obey," or, preaching a more positive lesson, "Obedience is rewarded." It seems doubtful that didactic preachments have made *Peter Rabbit* a favorite with children for several generations. It seems more likely that a possible implied theme, "Even when you're naughty, mother loves and accepts you," has kept it a much-loved story.

Lucille Clifton writes picture book text clearly focused on theme. Her book, *My Brother Fine with Me,* is a simple story of Baggy, the little brother who wants to leave home with his minibike cards and a toothbrush to be independent, to be a Black warrior without parents to make rules. Johnetta, who says she likes it fine at home except for him, doesn't wish to join him. But Johnny finds it lonely without Baggy to bother her, to watch over at the park, to eat the peanut butter and jelly sandwiches she fixes. Thus the theme: My brother's fine with me. *Amifika,* another Clifton picture book, demonstrates a clear theme, too. Amifika, who doesn't remember Daddy, is afraid that since the house will be crowded his mother will "get rid of things" Daddy doesn't remember—like Amifika. But when Daddy holds him and Amifika squeezes his arms around Daddy's neck, "his arms remembered." Family love isn't easily forgotten. Still another Clifton picture book, *Three Wishes,* shows the theme that of all possible wishes, the best is for friends; Zenobia knows, because it is true for her.

A clear theme emerges from John Steptoe's *Stevie,* a story of Robert who has to put up with having younger Stevie staying in his house. The usual conflicts of childhood occur: giving up toys, having private space violated, getting blamed for Stevie's mischief, having to share his mother, having a tagalong "little brother" to care for. But when Stevie moves away, Bobby misses him; "he was a nice little guy." The implicit theme shows that companionship develops from being close to someone, a theme that when stated seems too heavy for such a subtly developed text.

In Evaline Ness' *Sam, Bangs & Moonshine,* Sam the fantasizer must learn for herself the difference between good and bad moonshine. Curling up in her "chariot" to daydream is good moonshine, but sending Thomas off on a dangerous search for Sam's mermaid mother is bad moonshine. Sam discovers the difference when she worries through the rescue of Thomas and the near drowning of Bangs the cat.

Setting

Picture books can and often must be extremely effective in depicting *setting.* The brief text of Cynthia Rylant's *When I Was Young in the Mountains* describes primarily the actions of the child narrator, but the pictured swimming hole, the cabin kitchen, the general store, the backyard pump, and the porch swing are all extensions of the text. We see from pictured setting more than from the words why the child never wanted to go anywhere else.

Contemporary society, as we are reminded by the battering of advertisements, is relying less on words for communication and more upon pictures. The trend toward nonverbal communication is reflected in contemporary picture-story books which often depend entirely upon illustration to create setting. All we know of setting in *Ming Lo Moves the Mountain* is the mountain, for example. Arnold Lobel's pictures do the rest to show the oriental setting. In literature for children, however, word pictures give the child an opportunity to create setting in his or her own mind, a special kind of experience which is one of the delights of literature.

Beatrix Potter's *The Tale of Peter Rabbit* is a classic example of *integral setting.* As both author and illustrator, Potter integrates visual and word pictures; setting is so closely interwoven with character, action, and theme that we are never aware of description as such. On page one the family home appears with its soft, sandy floor—the bank under the roots of a large fir tree. Soon we are under the gate and can see the cucumber frame. In this garden, cabbages and potatoes as well as French beans and lettuces grow not far from the net-covered gooseberry bush and the toolshed, with its watering can and its three flower pots on the windowsill. The stone wall has a gate and a stone step; close by are a pond and a wheelbarrow. We even hear the garden sound of the scritching, scratching hoe. This setting is not a suburban front yard. What happens to Peter is influenced by elements in the garden: the gate, the cucumber frame, the gooseberry bush, the pond, and the toolshed with its three flowerpots. Although she mentions each item in the setting, nowhere does Potter stop the action to describe it, and yet at no point is setting unimportant. In this perfectly integrated picture book, illustration and text work together to create setting.

Point of View

Point of view, or the mind through which the writer chooses to tell the story, also varies in picture books, as it does in all literature. Beatrix Potter wishes to tell a story about a rabbit whose mischievous nature gets him into trouble in a vegetable garden. How should she tell the story? Potter has several choices of point of view. She can be objective, telling just what happens, and saying nothing about the effect of events upon Peter's feelings. If Potter has Mother Rabbit tell Peter's story, we might see a mother weary of Peter's regular disobedience and of buying new jackets and shoes, but loving Peter just the same. If Flopsy, one of the good little bunnies, tells the story, we might see a prim little sister who, because she is always good, thinks Peter really ought to know better. Cotton-tail might tell the story enviously: "If I had any courage, I'd have some excitement, too." But Potter chooses to tell her tale from a point inside Peter's feelings and thoughts. We know Peter's curiosity, his appetite as he munches on, his worry as he asks directions, and his panic as he upsets the flower pots. We are as relieved as Peter when he finds his way home and is not scolded for his adventure. Every element in the story has been affected by Potter's choice of point of view. Peter is the protagonist and Mr. McGregor the antagonist. We know the character of Peter; his conflict is determined by the setting. Because of Peter's adventure and his mother's kind care, we understand the thematic point—that although a child is naughty, he or she is still loved.

There are first-person stories among picture books for the smallest child, such as Dr. Seuss' *If I Ran the Zoo.* The "I" narrator of these stories, however, is of minor significance since the focus is on the sheer nonsense of the doggerel and the delight of the sounds and rhythms, to say nothing of the stories' greatest assets, the inventive illustrations. *And to Think That I Saw It on Mulberry Street* uses first-person point of view effectively; it is not only skillful nonsense, but it also shows a child's imagination creating a fantastic parade. Seuss' stories are among the relatively few successful first-person stories for the small child. Many, like *May I Bring a Friend?* by Beatrice de Regniers, rely more upon illustrations—of royalty accepting guests of unusual proportions and dispositions like a hippo, lions, an elephant, and monkeys, for example—than upon our following the thinking of a child.

We see some successful objective point-of-view narration at picture-book level, like, for example, Ludwig Bemelmans' *Madeline,* in which minimal omniscience is present. Others seem to be inadequate stories—*Cowboy Small,* for example. Characterization is minimal; the story has nothing but action objectively related: eating, sleeping, riding, singing, and guitar playing. On the other hand, Ezra Jack Keats' *The Snowy Day* seems at first glance to be objective. We know that Peter has a happy time in the snow because we see all his fun, and we remember our own similar pleasures. But an omniscient writer also comments that Peter thinks it might be fun to play with the big boys, and he knows he isn't old enough. When Peter cannot find the vanished snowball he had tucked into his jacket pocket the night before, he feels sad. Even this simple and short story makes brief use of an interpretive omniscience. Perhaps, by the process of elimination, we can conclude that either of the omniscient points of view may be successful in stories for the young child.

Style

Picture books, too, need interesting style which awakens the interest of the young child in the nuances of possible meaning. In *Something on My Mind* vivid phrasing accompanies Tom Feelings' pictures: "Talking make-believe," "hanging in the park," "remembering/Grandma filling up this porch/with laughing." Contrast these phrases with the halting style of Clyde Bulla in *Mika's Apple Tree:* "They dressed and went into the house. Supper was ready.

They had cabbage soup with rye bread and butter. They had pancakes with jam." Even combining short sentences would create more vitality in style, and yet, if the early reader were reading alone, it would add no more difficulty to the language.

Look again at *Peter Rabbit*, the imagery describing setting, the blue jacket with brass buttons, the five currant buns. Notice the understatement of father's getting into trouble there, the mock-serious tone of "implored him to exert himself," the onomatopoeia of "scritch-scratch" and "lippety, lippety," the assonance and consonance of "Flopsy, Mopsy, Cotton-tail," and the surprise of the name "Peter." *Peter Rabbit* has style.

A picture book whose text is filled with figurative language is Jamake Highwater's *Moonsong Lullaby.* The moon sings a sweet lullaby to the people beside the campfire, while the rabbit and the fox dream, the hawk praises the moonlight, and the roots burrow into the depths of the earth. The night is a shelter for troubled souls, and the moon caresses them. All of nature is personified, and each image connotes contentment and security.

Owl Moon, Jane Yolen's very successful picture book, achieves a soft silence by her phrasing. Stillness pervades the snowy landscapes painted by John Schoenherr, and stillness is everywhere in the text. The woods are "quiet as a dream," the snow more white "than the milk in a cereal bowl." The child narrator is going owling with Pa. "But I never said a word./If you go owling/you have to be quiet/and make your own heat." When they do sight an owl, they watch silently "with heat in our mouths,/the heat of all those words/we had not spoken." The text and pictures are in quiet, beautiful synchrony.

A very different style is apparent in Judith Viorst's *Alexander, Who Used to Be Rich Last Sunday,* illustrated by Ray Cruz. Alexander is the first-person narrator, telling in a child's diction how little by little, four cents by thirteen, he has spent his grandparents' gift dollar. "Anthony told me to use the dollar to go downtown to a store and buy a new face. Anthony stinks." But instead, Alexander buys fifteen cents' worth of gum, bets away another fifteen, rents a snake for twelve, and is fined ten for "certain words" a boy can't ever say, "no matter how ratty and mean his brothers are being."

Rhythm often appears in picture book narration. Wanda Gág uses it in her refrain in *Millions of Cats:* "hundreds of cats, thousands of cats, millions and billions and trillions of cats." Rhythm occurs in Maurice Sendak's *Where the Wild Things Are* as well: "And when he came to the place where the wild things are they roared their terrible roars and gnashed their terrible teeth and rolled their terrible eyes and showed their terrible claws."

Tone

Tone may vary in picture books, just as it does in books of other genres. The thoughtful tone of Norma Farber's *How Does It Feel to be Old?* or the serious tone of *The Little House* is as appropriate as the mock-serious tone of *The*

Elephant's Child or the joyous one of *Frog Went A-Courtin'*. Like character and point of view, tone too is the choice of the author or author/illustrator. Humor, that important quality that helps us develop a perspective on life's ups and downs and keeps us sane, seems essential in the life of a small child. Many writers and illustrators respond to that need, or perhaps they respond to their own need to see things through the sound of laughter.

By helping to carry a book's text, illustrations become a large part of the book's humor. John Langstaff's *Frog Went A-Courtin'* is filled with personification, cover to cover. Feodor Rojankovsky, who draws characters that are convincingly both animal and human, increases the humor by dressing them in suitable garb for their roles in his book's verses. Beetles of different kinds wearing aprons and chef's caps and carrying spoons and forks, a table-setting moth sporting a fuzzy domestic hairpiece, an insect trio performing atop the wedding cake, a bonneted snake who looks benign rather than fearsome—all of these are part of the pictured humor.

Ray Cruz, who illustrated Judith Viorst's *Alexander, Who Used to Be Rich Last Sunday,* chooses to amplify the humor of Alexander's frittering away his dollar by showing the gleeful antics of his two older brothers. The text itself is effectively understated ("And even when I told my friend Donald I'd sell him all the gum in my mouth for a nickel, he still wouldn't buy it."), while Alexander's cheeks bulge with three packs of gum. The final two illustrations show Alexander, his eye closed by his hand on his chin, squashing his face, contemplating what he has to show for his ventures, and on the last page, he is alone and looking away, holding two bus tokens, just where he started.

Tomie de Paola manages to fill his simple drawings, even those in limited color, with subtle humor, as he does in the illustrations for Steven Kroll's *Fat Magic*. The story opens with Prince Timothy atop his favorite tree, thinking about dessert. The tree is a marvel of tree-ness, a fencepost with four limbs, each one with symetrically balanced branches, but it is clearly a tree. Colored visions of desserts float above Timothy's head, while below him stands the court magician, his pointed cap appropriately adorned with a star, a crescent, and a live crow. When fat Timothy falls and makes a hole in the ice, the giant called to rescue him looks giantlike, but the addition of a fringe of hair on a bald head and the giant's humility in lifting his hat to the hole in the ice is a source of humor. Very little reveals a great deal.

The mock-serious tone of Kipling's *The Elephant's Child* is humor of its own delicious kind, and Lorinda Bryan Cauley's black and white illustrations add to it in a harmonious way. Seeing a family of four elephants marching across the title spread, each one with a nose no bigger than a boot, is a startling verification of Kipling's pourquoi tale: This is the way it was—before. Off goes the Elephant's Child to find out what the crocodile has for dinner, wearing big pouchy saddlebags filled with long purple sugar cane, short red bananas, and green crackly melons. His tracks are littered with rind, "because he could not pick it up." When we come to the crocodile who "winked one eye—like this" and "wept crocodile tears" to show his sincerity, we are delighted with his deceptiveness. The breathless Elephant's Child, kneeling on the bank, his round eyes and open mouth eager for the answer to his question, is truly innocent. Each page has its own textual humor; humorous illustration contributes to an inspired story.

There is verbal humor in Lucille Clifton's *Don't You Remember* as impatient Tate, tired of being put off till later for everything she wants, cries out "It's later now," and "Now is next time," as well as when she explodes with "Dag, double dag!" The quiet verbal humor of Russell Hoban's picture books has merit, too, and yet it is quite unlike the vividly phrased ironic humor in the picture books of Isaac Bashevis Singer who also refuses to give children only slapstick. The humor of Maurice Sendak's *Pierre, a Cautionary Tale,* keeps that story from becoming didactic. Arnold Lobel's *Frog and Toad Together* is funny not only because of situation—they are odd animals for step-ladder climbing—but also because of the understated verbal humor, a surprise in basic vocabulary. Arnold Lobel uses a series of metric limericks for *The Book of Pigericks,* which is illustrated with pigs in all states. Whenever his rhythms falter, departing from the required metrical ana-pests, the humor stalls. When his rhythm works, the pigerick, as well as the humor, works.

SUCCESSFUL FAVORITES

We cannot speak of picture books without looking to Maurice Sendak, his view of the illustrator's function, and his best known and loved book, *Where the Wild Things Are,* the book that Selma Lanes calls "the most suspenseful and satisfying nursery tale of our time."[7] In describing the role of the illustrator, Sendak speaks of the "seamlessness" of the perfectly integrated picture book, distinguishing between the direct approach that puts the facts of the story into clear and simple images and the "illumination" of a text, in which just as the musical composer interprets the words of a poem, the pictures interpret the text, "serving the words" by enlarging and interpret-ing. He goes on to say that the illustrator does not picture exactly the words that are written, but he or she finds a space where pictures can go further than words. In fact, "they each tell two stories at the same time. . . . Words are left out and the picture says it. Pictures are left out and the words say it." Pictures "quicken" text; they are "not something just glued onto the page" beside the words. Liveliness, conviction, vitality, "the touch and smell and *hold* of a book," the "zing" and the animation of the whole—these are Sendak's descriptive terms. As he praises Randolph Caldecott's illustra-tions, Sendak says that words take "on unobvious meanings, colors, and dramatic qualities. He *reads* into things, and this, of course, is what the illustrator's job is really all about," interpreting text as a conductor interprets a musical score.[8]

Sendak's book *Wild Things* was published in 1963. For many adults, *Wild Things* focused their difficulty in acknowledging the anxieties and preoccupations of childhood, wanting children to be happy-happy-happy, to deny all unpleasantness and uncertainty. In addressing this issue, Sendak takes a different view. He marvels "that children manage to grow up," to get through childhood, defeating "boredom, fear, pain, and anxiety." He says that he remembers "sounds, feelings, and images" or the emotional quality of significant childhood moments. He successfully pictures many of these feelings and images in his books.

A brief paragraph of description is inadequate to explain the perfect marriage of text and pictures in Sendak's Caldecott Award-winning book. The first pictures of Max show him as an angry boy, mouth and eyebrows turned down as he stands on books to pound a huge nail into the wall with an adult-sized hammer, thus suspending a clothesline made from knotted cloths. Next, leaping down the stairs and waving an enormous fork, Max pursues his frightened dog. The text merely says that "Max wore his wolf suit and made mischief of one kind and another." When, in boldface capital letters, Max threatens, "I'LL EAT YOU UP!", the picture shows Max sent to his room with the door closed; his scowl is angry, and he stands defiant, with shoulder toward the door and wolf claw on his hip. But when the text says that a forest grew in Max's room that night, Max's body language shows him content and even smug about how things are turning out. Soon his wolf toes curl up in glee, and he cannot seem to suppress a giggle of delight. While the fifteen words of text flatly describe how the "ceiling hung with vines," the next full-page illustration shows Max amidst the exotic foliage with his feet dancing and arms waving in the air. By growing from 4 x 5½ inches to a full 9 x 10-inch page, the first six pictures accelerate the story's pace and create suspense.

A private boat, the ocean tumbling by, and a quiet sail are all the text mentions next, but in his full-sailed boat named *Max* stands smiling Max himself, his relaxed body exuding confidence while his boat makes good progress. When Max reaches the land where the wild things are, he is at first uncertain, then wears a "show me" look, and next, waving his arms in a magician's motion, he gives orders to "BE STILL!" Tamed by his magic trick of staring into their yellow eyes without blinking, the wild things are subdued. In these spreads the wild things first appear surprised, then ferocious in motions like those Max had been punished for, then seated and covering their faces and ears with their arms and legs. Their eyes look out fearfully at Max. But soon they acknowledge Max's superiority—"the most wild thing of all"—and line up to bow and give obeisance while Max, hand on hip, sits on a mound, wears a crown, and waves a scepter. He is "king of all wild things."

Now Max commands the rumpus to start, says the text. For three double-page spreads, the wordless rumpus goes on with Max both wild and commanding as he rides the most fearsome thing of all, then says "Now stop!" and sends them off to bed without supper. Now isolated in his royal tent, Max looks thoughtful: he misses those who love him "best of all." The picture makes that loneliness clear. The wild things entreat Max to stay— they'll eat him up, they love him so—but he sails off with a happy wave while they roar, roll their eyes, show their claws, and reach out to him. Max, returning through time and space, looks calm, satisfied, and quietly pleased when he finds his supper still hot. His final gesture is to push his wolf cap from his head; he is no longer a wild thing but a boy at home where he is loved. Sendak's pictures have indeed created a "seamless" whole, illuminating and filling in the spaces in the text, adding what pictures can do better than words.

Another favorite is *The Tale of Peter Rabbit,* Beatrix Potter's classic story for young children, which was first published in 1902. Its popularity endures among children all over the world. Potter once said that many stories for children are "condescending, self-conscious inventions," but Potter herself was never condescending or self-conscious in either pictures or text. First, Potter insisted on the 4 x 5½-inch illustrations, reminding us of Sendak's comment on the importance of "the touch and *hold*" in a picture book. Pictures alternate with text and are consistently in vignette form, irregular ovals surrounded by white space.

The cover picture of Peter trotting boldly along, ears alert and arms swinging, sets up his character: insouciance, light-hearted nonchalance. Inside, the first page shows the rabbit family in its natural habitat and furry garb. Next, the maternal Mrs. Rabbit hands a berry basket to three identical, pink-coated bunnies; they will no doubt behave identically. Meanwhile, though she admonishes them all to avoid Mr. McGregor's garden, Peter, who is dressed in blue, turns heedlessly away, like the next picture in which Peter receives special buttoning-up attention, foreshadowing his nonconformity. Next Mrs. Rabbit leaves the four on their own as she goes off to the baker's. In the natural habitat which includes birds who are also interested in berries, the good little bunnies lay down their jackets to gather them. The next picture showing Peter squeezing under the gate again contrasts him with the well-behaved sisters.

Peter looks euphoric as he samples the garden vegetables: his ears stand up independently, his feet cross casually, and the sun shines on both Peter and the robin. But the brilliant colors pale when we next observe Peter "feeling rather sick"; his hands hold his tummy, his ears seem to lean against each other, and his feet toe out, showing how unwell he is. Even the robin turns away. Pictures of Peter watching Mr. McGregor curiously, then in flight from the farmer, are followed by a suspenseful picture of the robin staring at the lone shoe lost among the cabbages. A saddened and tearful Peter caught in the gooseberry net appears in the next two pictures, one showing him standing on his head, the other lying prostrate—but encouraged by three sparrows with big vocabularies. Peter's pictured hopelessness is troubling until we next see his renewed energy as he abandons his jacket and leaps from under the sieve. Mr. McGregor is unaware of Peter's presence in the toolshed, but the picture says he is there, and if, in the next picture, we could not see the farmer's boot close behind Peter, we might be unaware of how close a call he has. The pace of the pictured narrative now slows to make us anxious: sitting alone and wondering, Peter is forlorn; then he leans disconsolately against the corner of the locked door, tears rolling, one toe atop the other, hand to mouth to catch his sobs; next, from a safe distance, he cautiously watches the dangerous white cat. When Peter finally spots the gate, it looks to be an impossibly long way off, beyond Mr. McGregor and his hoe. But under the protective eyes of the three friendly sparrows, Peter escapes. His jacket now serves as scarecrow, hanging disconsolately on the cross-post with his shoes dangling bottoms-up below, while five friendly birds, two of them crows, check it out.

The final three pictures show undisturbed domesticity: Mother Rabbit, unsurprised, cooking dinner; Peter tucked with care into bed; and three obedient bunnies eating blackberries. The pictures have verified the narrative, but they have done far more: They have shown a universal garden setting that persuades us of the story's truth, created suspense by slowing or hastening the action, characterized Peter and contrasted him to his conformist sisters, as well as added humor. Potter has avoided what she called "a trivial oversight," a "small incorrect detail that [could give] the whole show away." She has created a seamless picture book.

"It's a good feeling to be able to put down a line and know it is right," Robert McCloskey has said. *Make Way for Ducklings* never fails to give good feelings to its readers as well; it is right in every way. Aside from the accurate picturing of the mallard family, the illustrations have other assets, including humor. The balanced first pages of the book are an effective bird's-eye view of the world. We are up there with Mr. and Mrs. Mallard, looking down in perfect perspective for the right spot to build a nest. The artist has given focus to the mallards by size, placement on the page, depth of tone, and forcefulness of line. Clearly, this will be the mallards' story. Below, in distant and thus more softly shaded areas and incomplete lines, we see the houses, the water, and the woods. As we turn the page, we are still in the air with the ducks, but this time the scene below is clearer, more particular; obviously, we are coming closer to the earth and perhaps to the perfect homesite. Now the page is balanced by the two mallards and a tree strikingly bare in early spring on the left, opposite the diagonal bridge and the little island in the Public Garden on the right side. Noting tiny details, we can count eight children walking with parents along the water's edge, and when we turn the page to see the swanboat's passengers, we count again: seven children and their parents. Along the water's edge five more children play, an emphasis that carries throughout: This is consistently a family story.

When we turn to the spread with the bicyclist speeding past the two ducks, his tie and shirttail flying behind him and his action occupying the whole right page, Mr. and Mrs. Mallard's fear and shock are apparent. Their features and body positions, Mr. Mallard knocked off his feet and Mrs. Mallard tilted back with one foot raised, are expressive. Placing the text at the top of the left page and using a large triangle of white space to duplicate the triangle formed by the startled birds give emphasis to their terror. Shadowy horizontal lines show the bicycle's rapid movement, and diagonal lines show the sudden movement of the startled ducks. The gutter dividing the pages is the right division for the action. Three more spreads effectively show from the air the mallards' search, and then we arrive at ground view, child's-eye height. Now we are looking at stones and weeds and bushes and nest, a domestic scene in a quiet island setting. Next a new figure enters the story in the person of Michael the policeman, benign, hospitable, his kindness and roundness giving us a reassuring sense of safety. Turning the page, we see that the balance is reversed: the focus at left, in the "power position," on a big picture of Mrs. Mallard counting her eggs (we must count them, too) is countered by the right-hand block of text and two triangles, one of vegetation and the other of white space. The next page, as the text tells us, pictures obvious parental pride. On the left again, the imposingly vertical father, dark in color, and on the right, the horizontal line of Mrs. Mallard's back echoing the horizontal lines of the text block, present a pleasing composition. If there is any disappointment, it lies in the hiding of one duckling in the gutter of the spread. Here, as in all other pictures, the parents are confident, dignified adults. Each duckling is different from the others; the identical puffball ducklings of supermarket picture books are boring by comparison.

Each spread is different; each page is an addition to the text; each one begs us to count the ducklings, to notice their differences. Within each picture one or two are mavericks, watching a butterfly, hurrying to catch up, following in proper single file but looking the other way. As they approach the traffic, McCloskey incorporates into the pictures the raucous sounds of cars, ducks, and a police whistle. When we reach the point of Michael's run to save the mallard family, he again dominates the picture. His heavy dark boots, and the diagonal of his outstretched leg continued in the diagonal of his meaty hand raised to stop the traffic, are the focus, yet we never lose track of the mallard family. For the next several pages city activities seem to take over, but the ducklings are always there. They strut down the walk, mere dots in one picture and tiny individuals in another, being noticed and marveled at by passersby. Finally, they are isolated in a big empty space in the midst of traffic stopped in four directions. The ducklings might easily have been lost in the city fray, but McCloskey has kept the focus on them through skillful composition, using white space, dark and light tones, and thin, fat, or shaded lines for solid forms, and, of course, through the placement of pictures close to relevant text. The last few spreads, devoted again to family and security, show the setting in detail, with the family all settling into a serene routine, following the swanboats and the peanut-throwing passengers and returning at night to their island home.

Ducklings is a great favorite with children, and adults do not seem to weary of it either. The pages can be examined again and again, and each time they yield new details. In a perfect union of text and pictures, the uniqueness of the ducklings and their parents, realistic yet individualized, is never lost. The pictures give excitement and vitality to the text, resulting in a new composite whole.

Let's look next at a longtime favorite, Wanda Gág's *Millions of Cats*, first published in 1928. Gág's background is steeped in European folktales, and this original fantasy has the traits of such stories. Thumbnail characters (a very old woman and a very old man), the long cadenced lines of oral tradition, and a repeated rhythmic refrain, "hundreds of cats, thousands of cats, millions and billions and trillions of cats," are some of the folktale elements. The fantasy that all of these cats could eat each other up and leave only one survivor is revealed at the brisk climax and concludes the refrain with a happily-ever-after variation: "and not one was as pretty as this one."

The illustrations in sharp black and white lithographs are as straightforward and unadorned as the text; the design of each page produces emphatic rounded shapes and patterns which move the eye left to right across the spread. Shading and texture create three-dimensional hills, clouds, fields, trees—and cats, trillions of cats. Cats seen close up are individuals; the anonymous crowd stretches over the infinite hills.

On every page the illustration is adjacent to the substance of the relevant text. As the very old man chooses the first cat for his wife, the spread is balanced with a segment of tree branch over his shoulder on the left margin and a similar picture on the far right. Centered beside the gutter and below the text are two views of him choosing cats, each one with a semicircular tree curving protectively around him and the chosen ones. The picture illustrating "And they began to quarrel" is chaotically filled with cats in all positions and contortions; it seems feasible that they might indeed eat each other up. In the final spread Gág utilizes continuous narrative illustration, beginning top left with the skinny survivor cat, picturing it greedily eating in eight additional poses which carry diagonally to the lower gutter and then move to the top right where the plump and contented cat sits. The little figures divide each page into two triangles; within the upper two is the brief text. Of particular note is the way in which Gág has placed her hand-lettered text, often in centered lines, as part of the overall page design. Nothing is placed casually on the page. When we examine *Millions of Cats*, we understand the concept of *designing* a book.

The same feeling of design pervades Virginia Lee Burton's *The Little House*, a favorite since it won the Caldecott Award in 1943. The frontispiece condenses and simplifies the story, the title page is illustrated, the dedication is encircled by a wreath of daisies, and even the page numbers are carefully placed for the sake of design. Text is placed rather consistently on the left page, with pictures on the right. Clouds circle across the first page, the sun, with varying expressions, arches across the next spread, while stars light a swirl of navy blue sky in a third. As seasons change, the hills take on different colors, moving from light to deep green to autumn rust to winter white. In spring a group of robins flies from top left around the shaped text to lower center; in summer daisies follow a similar pattern; in fall leaves drift from top left to lower right; and winter snowflakes follow a similar route.

As the little house is slowly surrounded by encroaching roads, then by other houses, by apartment and tenement houses, the colors become somber browns and grays, on to deep charcoal gray lit by inadequate circles of city street lamps. Cars, trucks, buses, trolleys, and subway and elevated trains surround the drab little house, and by now the rolling, tranquil country landscape has changed into a series of dark and darker buildings surrounded by a frenetic visual clamor. Here Burton's pictures are drab grays of all shades, the only color that of the trucks and train cars, the tiny hurrying pedestrians, and a faded little house. Once the little house begins the move back to the country, the colors become lively again; the sun, moon, stars, leaves, daisies, and snowflakes reappear, and the expression on the face of the house is again cheerful. Throughout the book, the cyclical history of the little house has been illustrated with the circular flow of seasonal images and the swirling lines of the pictured settings.

Perhaps the final picture of the house at night, placed on the left facing a blank page, is unnecessary. We have just read that "Once again she was lived in and taken care of," and that seems sufficient; we need not hear the "never agains" to know that the little house will thrive and be happy. All in all, this is a most satisfactory picture book. The change in time of day, in seasons, in the takeover by city life, and in the little house which remains the same yet changes with its changing surroundings—all these elements are there for endless detailed examination.

WORDLESS PICTURE BOOKS

Like works in any genre or subgenre, wordless picture books vary in quality. What seems important is that they have a focus and a unity created by the pictures themselves and by the format in which they are presented. Unlike wordless object and number books, picture books have some thread of story, but because pictures tell it all, words are unnecessary.

Wordless books provide complexity and detail, as well as continuity and consistency. For example, look at the many qualities in Mitsumasa Anno's book, *Anno's Journey*. The intricacy of the pictures offers enduring pleasure, each complex double-page spread filled with detail shown from above. The shore, woods, farm, village, town, park, city, cathedral square, and festival all show people in characteristic actions. Hours of looking could occupy a child: taking in each of the people, each of their varied actions, the architecture, the foliage, the vehicles—it goes on and on. In addition to the consistency of aerial views, as the journey moves from simple country life to complex city and back to country life, all pictures are spreads; tiny Anno returns to the shore to complete the circle of his journey. The result is a totally successful wordless book.

Similar continuity and consistency characterize *The Secret in the Dungeon* by Fernando Krahn, in which each picture is framed with white space and shows a separate action. Marked by her red dress, a spot of color in the shaded line drawings of the castle, the pony-tailed little girl is always the focus. Lost from the tour group, she wanders through the castle, falls down the water chute, and lands on top of a sleeping dragon whose smoky breath next catapults her through the chimney flue back into the midst of the group. The adults, who, of course, know better because they have listened to the guide, laugh and won't believe her story about the dragon in the dungeon. The final left-hand picture shows her gazing sadly out the back window of the car as the family leaves the castle. The story is successful in the clarity of its thematic content: Though it is common for adults not to believe children, children find it hard to accept. The story line is clear, the humorous tone is consistent, and even without verbal description or comment, the protagonist is still a believable little girl.

In another successful wordless picture book, *Sunshine* by Jan Ormerod, sunshine awakens a little girl, who then awakens her father. They breakfast together, prepare a tray for her mother, and linger in bed for a while. The little girl then gets up to dress for school, leaving her parents to drop back to sleep. When she is dressed and ready to go, she appears in her parents' room with the alarm clock. The ensuing pictures show the parents in various actions—hasty dressing, showering, father leaving—and then the little girl is off to school. Here the pictures vary in size, but with reason and continuity. A series of twelve narrow pictures in one spread, for example, shows the girl removing her nightclothes and putting on one item of clothing after another. The story is simply about getting up and getting out in the morning, but the additional interest lies in the child's relationship with her father, and in her taking responsibility not only for her own readiness but also for that of her parents.

In *Do You Want To Be My Friend?*, illustrator Eric Carle uses characteristic poses for his figures—such as side views of all of the animals—and the cliché of a child's lettering for the title question. Yet in his illustrations he does not resort to mimicking a child's drawing. In deep, bold colors, the pictures show the tiny mouse as he looks for a friend, stopping to ask a horse, an alligator, a lion, a peacock, and others, finally finding a friend in a similar little mouse. The idea is clear; picture continuity occurs as, on the right of the spread, the tail of each animal appears. As we turn the page, we see the entire animal. Another unifying element is a bright green tail circling around the dedication on a front page and continuing as a band at the bottom of each succeeding page, until we meet the owner, a big snake who sends the mouse scurrying to the roots of a tree where the two mice meet. This is a simple story with a thematic idea and unique, unified pictures.

Familiarity with the story of Goldilocks helps but is not needed to carry us through Brinton Turkle's satisfying book, *Deep in the Forest,* the story of a little bear who returns the mischief of Goldilocks. Pictures personify the protagonist, and there are several additions to the old story: The little bear doesn't just sleep in the beds; he bounces, throws covers about, and scatters the pillow feathers to the four corners. He doesn't just sit in the chairs; he rocks the non-rocking chair, sprawls in the cushioned one, and does destructive tricks on the little rocker. Like Goldilocks, he is discovered and chased out. It is autumn, and the colors are rusts, golds, and browns. Plenty of action holds our interest until the little bear returns to his loving family.

In *First Snow* Emily Arnold McCully also tells a simple story without words. None of the mouse characters has a name, but we easily single out the one with the pink scarf (obviously a girl from the color she wears) who is afraid to slide down the hills on her sled. Support from her grandparents (the ones with the glasses who drive the truck) and the fun she has with her friends (cousins, perhaps) are not sufficient encouragement. But when she discovers the great fun for herself, she cannot be stopped. She's off, her sled tracks running up and down the hill, and everyone must wait for her when they reload the truck. The action for the most part is clear, although one of the last pictures shows her to be seemingly terrified, flying downhill on the overturned sled, while the connecting page shows her delighted with her success. The illustrations, which are usually double-page spreads, are somewhat humorous. Having developed that expectation, we are mildly puzzled when two pictures that bleed into the gutter occasionally show different actions.

A highly imaginative wordless picture book is Molly Bang's vividly colorful *The Grey Lady and the Strawberry Snatcher.* Silently pursued by the blue-skinned Snatcher, the Grey Lady evades him through town, into the country, and through the woods, until, distracted by blackberries, the Snatcher gives up. The last spread shows the Grey Lady sharing berries with a happy family in a colorful house complete with baby, cat, and parrot. The story rests on the suspense of pursuit and the intriguing way in which the Grey Lady disappears into the background.

Not all wordless picture books are as successful as these. In *The Birthday Trombone* by Margaret Hartelius, the arrangement of pictures presents a major problem. Most pictures are a single page, but they are without frames of any kind around the separate actions. Once we are accustomed to the lack of white space even in the gutter, which might tell us that each page is separate, we are surprised to find a full spread. Now we must count the tigers, hippos, rhinos, giraffes, lions, and monkeys before deciding that this double page represents one action, one picture. The monkey's birthday trombone startles each of the animals: the zebra hanging up striped socks and shirts, the rhinoceros riding a bicycle, the giraffe rocking her small giraffe, and the lion doing a jigsaw puzzle. When a huge snake suddenly appears, threatening to surround all of these large animals, the monkey uses his trombone for snake-charming, and all is well. The story lacks a point; instead, it seems to be an opportunity for the artist to draw animal pictures.

Wordless picture books, like those with text, require consistency. While the conventional "art" of the cheap, mass-produced book does not hold our interest, a personal vision can. Mere cleverness and facility are not sufficient here any more than in any other kind of children's book.

SUMMARY

Picture books are dependent upon illustration[10]; some involve text and others are wordless. The design of the whole, the entire book, including size, shape, single picture or double-page spreads, end pages, title page, cover, dust jacket, and the placement of the gutter, is important. The illustrator puts into visual form what the words say, and yet, in amplifying the text, conveys more than what the words say. When put into pictures, figurative language can be enhanced. By picturing one element or incident rather than another, illustrations can also change the story so that identical text—for a folk tale, for example—with different pictures creates different stories. Like other stories for children, the text of a picture book is judged by standards of literary excellence[11] in plot, character, theme, setting, point of view, style, and tone. Wordless picture books require focus and unity created by pictures and the format of presentation. Complexity and detail may accompany continuity, consistency, and a unique personal vision.

Children's taste, like that of most adults, is dependent largely upon exposure. While it is important to learn what children like or dislike, we remember that children have had only limited exposure to literature and art. Their taste cannot be the most important criterion for judging which illustrations are acceptable, suitable, or desirable. As Ben Shahn has said, "The popular eye is not untrained; it is only wrongly trained." That training is the responsibility of parents and educators in the arts as well as in literature. Exposure to trite, cliche-ridden illustration, like exposure to trite, cliche-ridden language, does little to move the child along. As we contemplate illustration in leisurely enjoyment as children do, we attend to it as an extension of experience, an additional source of pleasure.

READING AND EVALUATING

1. Without reference to the pictures themselves, the texts of several picture books are mentioned in the section of this chapter entitled "The Literary Elements of the Picture Book." Select one of these books and apply to it the criteria for a picture book in which pictures and text are well integrated.

2. Examine Beatrix Potter's *The Tale of Peter Rabbit,* and compare it with another picture book about personified animals. What do the illustrations add to text regarding character, setting, and tone? Or do they seem merely to duplicate the text?

3. Examine five of Maurice Sendak's picture books, noting whether each seems to be a "seamless" whole, with pictures telling what words cannot, and words telling what pictures cannot.

4. Compare five wordless picture books to see whether pictures alone are sufficient to tell the stories. As you look carefully at each book, is its story quickly and obviously told, because there is little to hold curiosity? Or does it sustain your interest so that you are tempted to examine it carefully?

5. Select at least three retellings of the same folktale in picture book form. Compare them by noting how illustrations shape the story. What happens to character, to theme, and to tone?

6. Compare three picture books that are humorous in tone. What is the source of the humor? Words? Pictures? Both?

NOTES

1 Joseph H. Schwarcz, *Ways of the Illustrator: Visual Communication in Children's Literature.* Chicago: American Library Association, 1982, p. 169.

2 Donald Weisman, *The Visual Arts as Human Experience.* Englewood Cliffs, NJ: Prentice Hall, n.d., pp. 18–21.

3 B. W. Alderson, *Looking at Picture Books.* New York: Children's Books Council, 1973, p. 6.

4 Ben Shahn, *The Shape of Contents.* New York: Vintage Books, 1957, p. 124.

5 See Perry Nodelman, "How a Picture Book Works," in *Image and Maker,* Harold Darling and Peter Neumeyer, eds. New York: Greenwillow, 1984.

6 See Sheila Egoff, *The Republic of Childhood,* New York: Oxford University Press, 1967.

7 Selma G. Lanes, *The Art of Maurice Sendak.* New York: Harvey N. Abrams, Inc., 1980, p. 87.

8 See the interview with Maurice Sendak in *Victorian Color Picture Books,* Jonathan Cott, ed. New York: Chelsea House, 1983.

9 Pop-up books and other novelties are regarded by many as toys masquerading as books, but they have their place. Although Selma Lanes suggests that it "is

wise to look with suspicion on books . . . that can be scratched and sniffed, that float in bathtubs or burst into song . . . an evanescent genre," some reputable author/illustrators are creating them.

10 The move to simplify language recurs although we know how language skills decline for lack of stimulation. The most recent horror in this movement is the version of Peter Rabbit (London: Ladybird Press) in which "It would have been a beautiful thing to hide in, if it hadn't had so much water in it" becomes "Peter hid in the watering can but the watering can had water in it, and suddenly Peter felt a sneeze coming on." The humor of the punchline is gone. (Knight News Service) Illustrations are now stuffed animals with plastic eyes. See also "Ruffles and Flourishes" by Susan Ohanian, *Atlantic Monthly,* September 1987, pp. 20–22.

RECOMMENDED BOOKS CITED
IN THIS CHAPTER

ANNO, MITSUMASA. *Anno's Journey.* New York: Putnam, 1977.

BANG, MOLLY. *The Grey Lady and the Strawberry Snatcher.* New York: Four Winds, 1980.

BEMELMANS, LUDWIG. *Madeline.* New York: Dutton, 1937.

BRIGGS, RAYMOND. *The Snowman.* New York: Random House, 1978.

BURTON, VIRGINIA LEE. *The Little House.* Boston: Houghton Mifflin, 1942.

CARLE, ERIK. *Do You Want to Be My Friend?* New York: Crowell, 1971.

CLIFTON, LUCILLE. *Amifika,* illustrated by Thomas DiGrazia. New York: Dutton, 1977.

————. *Don't You Remember?,* illustrated by Evaline Ness. New York: Dutton, 1973.

————. *My Brother Fine with Me,* illustrated by Monetta Barnett. New York: Holt, Rinehart & Winston, 1975.

————. *The Boy Who Didn't Believe in Spring,* illustrated by Brinton Turkle, New York: Dutton, 1973.

————. *Three Wishes,* illustrated by Stephanie Douglas. New York: Viking, 1974.

DE REGNIERS, BEATRICE. *May I Bring a Friend?* New York: Atheneum, 1964.

EMBERLEY, BARBARA. *Drummer Hoff,* illustrated by Ed Emberley. Englewood Cliffs, NJ: Prentice Hall, 1967.

FEELINGS, TOM, and NIKKI GRIMES. *Something on My Mind.* New York: Dial, 1978.

GÁG, WANDA. *Millions of Cats.* New York: Coward McCann, 1928.

GALDONE, PAUL. *Cinderella.* New York: McGraw Hill, 1978.

HIGHWATER, JAMAKE. *Moonsong Lullaby,* photographs by Marcia Keegan. New York: Lothrop, Shepard and Lee, 1981.

HOGROGIAN, NONNY. *Cinderella.* New York: Greenwillow, 1981.

HUGHES, SHIRLEY. *Cinderella.* New York: Walck, 1970.

HUTCHINS, PAT. *Rosie's Walk.* New York: Macmillan, 1968.

ISADORA, RACHEL. *Ben's Trumpet.* New York: Greenwillow, 1979.

KEATS, EZRA JACK. *A Whistle for Willie.* New York: Viking, 1962.

————. *The Snowy Day.* New York: Viking, 1962.

————. *Apt. 3.* New York: Macmillan, 1971.

————. *Goggles!* New York: Macmillan, 1969.

KIPLING, RUDYARD. *The Elephant's Child,* illustrated by Lorinda Bryan Cauley. New York: Harcourt Brace Jovanovich, 1983.

KRAHN, FERNANDO. *The Secret in the Dungeon.* Boston: Houghton Mifflin, 1983.

KROLL, STEVEN. *Fat Magic,* illustrated by Tomie di Paola. New York: Holiday House, 1978.

LANGSTAFF, JOHN. *Frog Went A-Courtin',* illustrated by Feodor Rojankovsky. New York: Harcourt Brace & World, 1955.

LeCAIN, ERROL. *Cinderella.* Scarsdale, NY: Bradbury, 1972.

LIONNI, LEO. *Fish is Fish.* New York: Random House, 1970.

_____ . *Frederick.* New York: Pantheon, 1966.

LOBEL, ARNOLD. *The Book of Pigericks.* New York: Harper & Row, 1983.

_____ . *Fables.* New York: Harper & Row, 1980.

_____ . *Frog and Toad Together.* New York: Harper & Row, 1972.

_____ . *Ming Lo Moves the Mountain.* New York: Greenwillow, 1982.

McCLOSKEY, ROBERT. *Homer Price.* New York: Viking, 1943.

_____ . *Make Way for Ducklings.* New York: Viking, 1969.

McCULLY, EMILY ARNOLD. *First Snow.* New York: Harper & Row, 1985.

MILES, MISKA. *Annie and the Old One.* Boston: Little, Brown, 1971.

MILNE, A. A. *Winnie-the-Pooh.* New York: Dutton, 1926.

NESS, EVALINE. *Sam, Bangs & Moonshine.* New York: Holt, 1966.

NORTON, MARY. *The Borrowers,* illustrated by Beth and Joe Krush. New York: Harcourt, Brace Jovanovich, 1965.

ORMEROD, JAN. *sunshine.* New York: Lothrop Shepard and Lee, 1981.

PARISH, PEGGY. *Amelia Bedelia,* illustrated by Fritz Siebel. New York: Harper & Row, 1963.

PEET, BILL. *The Spooky Tail of Prewitt Peacock.* Boston: Houghton Mifflin, 1973.

POTTER, BEATRIX. *The Tale of Peter Rabbit.* New York: Warne, 1902.

RYLANT, CYNTHIA. *When I Was Young in the Mountains,* illustrated by Diane Goode. New York: Dutton, 1982.

SENDAK, MAURICE. *Pierre.* New York: Knopf, 1962.

_____ . *Where the Wild Things Are.* New York: Harper & Row, 1963.

SEUSS, DR. *And to Think that I Saw It on Mulberry Street.* New York: Hale, 1937.

TAFURI, NANCY. *Have You Seen My Duckling?* New York: Greenwillow, 1984.

TURKLE, BRINTON. *Deep in the Forest.* New York: Dutton, 1976.

VAN ALLSBURG, CHRIS. *The Garden of Abdul Gasazi.* Boston: Houghton Mifflin, 1979.

VIORST, JUDITH. *Alexander, Who Used to Be Rich Last Sunday,* illustrated by Ray Cruz. New York: Atheneum, 1978.

From *Cathedral* by David Macaulay. Copyright © 1973 by David Macaulay.
Reprinted by permission of Houghton Mifflin Company.

*N*onfiction

Adults range widely in their reading interests, from the financial page of the daily newspaper to a favorite comic strip, and on to particular curiosities, whether they be genealogy or strip mining. In between, they run floods of enthusiasm for "everything *that* writer ever wrote" to "everything I see about diet plans." And yet we are continually surprised at the diversity in children's taste or at their sudden enthusiasms for horses or baseball players. People are alike, and often we find that the interesting adult with a multitude of curiosities is the grown child whose reading may have begun with an omnivorous—and simultaneous—devouring of animal fantasy and atomic fission.

What does interest a child in nonfiction? Of course, older children may go in search of information, but small children frequently find fiction and nonfiction shelved in the same section of their libraries. In search of another good book "like the one last week about the ducklings in the park," they encounter another good book—but this time it is about the color wheel and how one color merges with another to form tones and shades and tints and other colors. Both books may be equally fascinating. At other times children who have moved away from the picture book section may happen upon a shelf where there are numbers on the backs of the books, instead of just the initial *E*. And there, wonder of wonders, are all kinds of books about how animals really live, and eat, and raise their babies, and fight to survive. From this discovery, children may take off on a nonfiction binge. In all of this meandering there seems to be a thread that holds one book or group of books to another—curiosity.

The line between fiction and nonfiction is a fine one in books for children. In a great many story books, there is much information about the world, animals, people, history, nature. After all, we learn about spinnerets and the parts of the spider's legs in *Charlotte's Web.* But when we discuss nonfiction, we are really less interested in how suspense is built and more interested in how facts are presented, less interested in character and more in discovery of the relationship and application of concepts to society or the natural world. Sometimes the writer tells the story of the life of an individual. Sometimes the writer uses a chronological arrangement of some kind, a narrative, that makes the nonfiction resemble fiction. Sometimes the writer speaks of "you" and "we" to make the explanation personal or like a story. However, the fact remains that the functions of fiction and poetry are pleasure and understanding, while the purpose of nonfiction is the discovery of factual or conceptual information. That the two purposes mingle in one book is of course possible, but we look at the two somewhat differently.

In the pages that follow we shall notice that the nonfiction writer is concerned with *facts* first of all. But in addition to facts, the writer tries to show the reader that these facts add up to or lead into a *concept,* just as the facts about chemical composition inside the egg lead us to the concept of how the yolk becomes an embryo and then a chick. Affecting our acceptance of fact and concept is *tone,* the writer's attitude toward the subject and the readers. We shall be concerned with all three.

NONFICTION DEFINED

Anyone who has spent time with a child knows that children have enormous curiosity. They are filled with questions that lead to more questions, which, when answered, lead to still other questions. Many of these questions can be answered by the right nonfiction book, whether it is a book about a single topic like trees, an explanation of a concept like energy, a biography of a person like Amelia Earhart, or a book that awakens awareness to an issue like overpopulation. As Margery Fisher says in *Matters of Fact,*[1] an information book evokes many responses:

> A child uses information books to assemble what he knows, what he feels, what he sees, as well as to collect new facts. His reaction to something as ordinary as a loaf [of bread] may be, at one time or another, one of wonder, excitement, interest, aesthetic pleasure, physical satisfaction, curiosity.

When adults seek answers, they may turn to encyclopedias; a solid page of factual information does not frighten nor confuse them. Their experience helps them sift out the specific items they need from the mass of information; they can extract the essential from the nonessential, the clear from the too complex. The child to whom the world is new and perhaps confusing may also, with the help of a book, recognize order in what he or she already sees or knows. This recognition of order and this assembling and sorting help to organize and stabilize the multitude of surrounding facts. The curious child moves from order to comparison, and on to new understanding of concept. To satisfy such needs, the child must have books that combine individuality with clarity in a combination of words that give color and significance to the subject and make it clear.

Wonder as Motivation

The limited experience of the child poses specific problems for the nonfiction writer. First the writer must satisfy curiosity without squelching a sense of wonder; yet the writer must avoid suggesting miracles. "Wonder" connotes curiosity and interest, while "miracle" connotes mystery and the unknowable. The successful writer of nonfiction opens a door to discovery but does not suggest that any of the facts outside are miraculous or beyond ultimate comprehension. There are facts as yet unknown, and principles as yet undiscovered, it is true, but if the child is to be led to discovery, he or she must feel that the search will be rewarding and will not merely deadend at unknowable mystery.

Adults usually choose their nonfiction for utilitarian purposes; they need to know. However, to a child, for whom everything in the opening world is astonishing, wonder is more often the motivation. Curiosity is the force that leads to discovery of all kinds. It led, for example, to the discovery of electricity; the unexplained needed explanation.

In *How Did We Find Out About Electricity,* Isaac Asimov begins his explanation with a narrative situation very similar to the reader's search for answers. Something piques the boy's curiosity as it does the reader's. Asimov takes us back 2,500 years, to the village of Magnesia on the coast of Turkey, where a shepherd boy used an iron-tipped stick to help him climb. As the iron stuck to a stone, the boy was mystified, but he could find nothing sticky on either surface. The odd rock came to the attention of a wise man named Thales, who was a person we would call a scientist; Thales experimented with the stone and discovered that it attracted only iron. Asimov's account follows a pattern very similar to that which our curiosity follows as it is provoked by the unusual; we notice, we experiment, we seek to discover what we can, and when we need help we go to authority.

While Asimov stimulates wonder in one way, Jean George in *Spring Comes to the Ocean* stimulates wonder in another. Without giving human traits to animals, she makes the hermit crab so distinctive and so unusual that we are curious about it and its problems of changing shells, a very dangerous necessity for the crab:

> First he unhooked the muscle at the spiral end of his old shell. Then he pulled himself out and stood vulnerable, so naked that even a windblown grain of sand could kill him. His exposed belly was so delicate that a nodding grass blade could cut him in half. . . . He slashed his tail through the air and stuck it into the new shell. Backing carefully, he reached his tail down and around until he felt the last coil of the shell. Then he hooked onto it with a grip so strong that few could pull him out. When at last he had a firm hold, he contracted all his muscles and slammed himself deep into the shell.

The meticulous description of the crab's vulnerability and actions during the move sets us wondering at the complexity and variety of nature. What other fascinations may lie ahead in *Spring Comes to the Ocean?*

In the opening paragraphs of *The Sea Around Us,* Rachel Carson, who is writing for more mature readers, rouses wonder by means of surprise. First Carson reminds us that we cannot really know how the oceans were formed, since there were no people there to see and to report:

> Beginnings are apt to be shadowy, and so it is with the beginnings of that great mother of life, the sea. Many people have debated how and when the earth got its ocean, and it is not surprising that their explanations do not always agree. For the plain and inescapable truth is that no one was there to see, and in the absence of eyewitness accounts, there is bound to be a certain disagreement.

Carson goes on to suggest the range of estimated age for rocks found on the earth—2.3 billion to 2.5 billion years, an astonishing figure for us who find a month or a year a long time. As we follow Carson's speculations about the earth changing from a ball of whirling gases to a molten mass, and then to patterns of layered materials, our wonder is aroused, and we are led into Carson's hypothesis about the origins of the oceans.

As for biography, we often turn to the lives of significant people because we wish to discover more about what it was like to be alive and aware in a period of history we have just discovered. Or we may become curious about the "what if" of being a frontier hero—"What if I had been one?" Or a winning sportsman, or a worker in the slums. We may be wondering how people become writers or architects. Or we may have discovered that once people didn't even know about bacteria, and we wish to know about that discovery and its relationship to disease. Curiosity, wonder, the possibility of discovery—a number of related motives may lead us to read about the lives of individuals.

The function of the nonfiction book for children as for adults is to give this desired information. If the book is to stimulate the child to reach for more, it must be written with strict attention not only to factual accuracy, but also to tone and style that attract and lead to discovery.[2] The successful nonfiction book manages to supply information and yet make the reader sense that discovery is open-ended. There is more to be known, and finding out is exciting. Because the attitude of wonder is stimulated, we assimilate the facts and come to understand concept.

INFORMATIONAL BOOKS

Organization and Scope

Common sense tells us that facts cannot be dumped upon a reader all at one time; in that situation we would have to make order out of masses of information, a task for an authority, not for an inquirer. The writer of nonfiction must select the key ideas, put them in simple forms, relate them to facts already known or to concepts already understood, and from this point begin to clarify. Breaking down the ideas into component parts that can be easily understood, the writer arranges them in coherent sequence from *simplest to most complex,* from *familiar to unfamiliar,* or from *early development to later development,* as Peter Spier does in *Tin Lizzie,* for example.

Since this task is not as easy as it sounds, not all writers are successful in finding the natural order. Some writers—like some teachers we may know— have a difficult time communicating concepts to those without backgrounds comparable to their own. These writers may have the understanding, but they lack the capacity to recall what it was like when they were uninformed and needed elementary and orderly explanations.

In an example of simple and coherent ordering of facts, R. J. Lefkowitz leads children from raindrops—which they all know—to the ocean—which they may not know. In *Water for Today and Tomorrow,* he writes:

> When it rains, some of the water goes into the ground. But the earth can't soak up all of the water. Water runs along the ground in tiny rivers, called *rivulets.*
>
> Many rivulets running along the ground come together to make a brook. Then the brook bubbles along until it becomes part of a big stream. Water from many brooks may empty into the stream.
>
> From all over, streams rush across the land toward a meetingplace. They end their journey at a mighty river. The river winds along, taking all the water to the ocean.

The scope of this book is clearly not to tell all that is known about water. The simple vocabulary makes clear the point about how water flows, but without dealing with confluence and estuaries. Another book, perhaps even one by the same writer, may explain in more depth and complexity the water flow, as well as water tables, water pollution, and water treatment. The scope of books depends to a large extent upon the interest and maturity of the reader.

Organizing text from early to later developments is clearly shown in David Macaulay's *Cathedral*. Beginning with the gratitude of the French in Chutreaux for peace, health, and plenty, we learn how in 1252 the clergy hired William of Planz to design a cathedral to the glory of God. We read of the designing of the cathedral, the hiring of master craftsmen who owned shops staffed with apprentices learning trades, the addition of laborers, many just returning from the Crusades. Cutting the timber, quarrying the stone, clearing the site, building workshops and forges, digging the foundation—on to walls, piers, buttresses, temporary wooden frames, then arches, and up, up to beams, vaulted ceilings, and towers, and finally, to sculpture placed in niches. Process, from beginning to end, is a logical plan for organization.

The successful writer of informational books begins the explanation of an unfamiliar concept at the child's level. Mary Lou Clark, for example, manages to introduce us to her subject in *You and Relativity* by beginning where we are, on familiar ground. She suggests that if several persons all want to go to the same place, the third floor of a building, they will not all go up. One, who is on the sixth floor, will have to go down; another on the first floor will have to go up. And she introduces the concept of relativity by saying that "*relative* to the sixth floor, the third floor is down, but *relative* to the first floor, the third is up." Clark prepares us for more complicated ideas; we are on our way to discovery when we begin with this simple and ordinary concept of movement from floor to floor in a building. Order in the explanation of these concepts is from the known to the unknown. Organization has been determined in large part by the amount of information the reader is expected to have.

Narrative Form

In nonfiction for the younger child, the writer may weave information into a narrative. Robert McCloskey in his picture book *Time of Wonder* demonstrates that a slight unifying narrative can convey information about the New England shore. The island has a very old rock at the point, a rock that was hot as fire when it was new to a new world, and as cold as ice when the weight of the glacier ground into it. The seal sniffs, while the fishhawks and eider ducks listen and watch. The colors of the fern change from green to yellow and brown. The robins have flown, and the swallows have left their boathouse nest, but their places are taken by birds that rest in migration as they fly south. Gulls and crows fuss and feud, and hummingbirds find the late petunias. Trees that have fallen during the storm leave jagged holes where their roots have been, and we understand the wind's power. A snow-white heap of shells left long ago by the Indians crumbles at a touch, and we realize that once the Indians lived where we are standing, before the white man came. We have moved down the beach, discovered a bit about geology, seen the effect of the storm on the trees, and then sensed the aging agelessness of the Maine seacoast. These facts have been tied together by the slight narrative.

To cite an example from picture books, *Sugaring Time* by Kathryn Lasky takes us chronologically from trail-breaking through the snow to the sugar maples, cutting runner marks on the trail, tapping trees with drill and bit, then collecting into a gathering tank the maple sap which runs like a river, and finally boiling the sap, and the accompanying tasks of skimming, temperature testing, and fire stoking.

Although Jeanne Bendick does not use a continuous narrative to hold together her book *Why Can't I?*, she does use children to wonder about the things they see. From a series of comparisons, we discover why we can't breathe under water like a fish or walk on the ceiling like a fly. On the bottom of each of the fly's six feet is a pad of stiff and sticky hairs. As the fly walks on a smooth surface, these pads flatten and make the fly stick. Able to hold more than just the fly's weight, they keep him on the ceiling. "The bottoms of *your* feet are smooth and slippery," she points out. "You can make them a *little* sticky by wearing sneakers. But you're still too heavy to walk up a wall or across the ceiling." The relating of the facts to the reader, the "I" of the title and the "you" of the text, makes these facts personal, interesting, and remarkable. Comparisons make the facts understandable, and each comparison has some narrative quality. The young reader is involved in this explanatory situation by the simplest of narrative elements.

Sometimes, however, because the writer is intent upon narrative suspense, he or she may not make the facts clear. In *How People Live in the Big City*, for example, we wander through the city and we learn that some people live in very tall buildings with walls of glass. We read that such buildings sometimes are called glass houses, but we do not discover that they are far more often called apartment houses until the term is used later. We learn that riding on the stairs that move is like "floating up, up, up," but not that these stairs are called an "escalator." Some writers seem to fear that words of more than two syllables will not be understood by children. But children's vocabularies are filled with big words: after all, *hamburger* has three syllables, and *refrigerator* has five.

Sometimes, for the sake of the narrative, information is completely lost or is so distorted that it is untrue. *When the Root Children Wake Up*, for example, is a misleading fairy tale, explaining the coming of spring:

> Wide awake at last, in their root house, the root children work busily on their new Spring dresses. Each chooses the color she loves best—violet, yellow, blue, white, orange, or red—and with needle, thread and thimble, sews happily till her work is done.
>
> The root boys . . . wake up the sleeping insects—the beetles, grasshoppers, lady-bugs. . . . They sponge them and brush them and paint their shells with bright Spring colors. . . .

Personification is not the only cause for distortion here; the writer in her eagerness to interest the reader in an account of the changes brought by spring has replaced facts with additional fantasy.

In writing of the pecking order among hyenas, Alice L. Hopf is accurate without personifying animals. "Hyenas have order and rank in their packs. Because females are larger than males, they stand at the top. Or two females are the leaders in each pack, with others ranged below.... [T]he female ... leads the pack on the hunt ... decides where and when to go. She takes her packmates on a boundary-marking expedition or rushes ahead into battle with the neighboring packs of hyenas." Citing the work of several naturalists, Hopf describes the ways of animals that seem a hybrid combination of dogs and cats. She says that Sir Walter Raleigh did not believe Noah would have saved hyenas in the Ark because he saved only the genetically pure.

Robert McClung is highly successful at weaving facts of nature into narrative form. In a factually accurate narrative called *Possum*, McClung faces the reality of the possum's life. We follow a family of nine babies and discover that they are easy prey; one is caught by a fox, another by a great horned owl, a third by a rattlesnake, another by a giant snapping turtle, and a fifth is run over as it crosses the road. These are the facts of life in the possums' world: nine babies, four survivors. Within the narrative form, *Possum* remains factually accurate. A more ambitious purpose unifies McClung's *Samson, Last of the California Grizzlies*. In this vivid narrative, Samson, to satisfy the frontiersmen's craving for excitement, is pitted against Diablo the bull:

> The crowd roared as the two great beasts tangled again. Samson crouched low trying to seize the bull's head in his huge paws, while Diablo thrust his horns downward in a deadly twisting sweep. As Samson rolled sideways to parry the blow, the tip of one of the bull's horns caught in a link of the chain that held the bear. There was a sudden loud snap as the chain broke, and Samson rolled free.

Here is a verifiable narrative of action on the frontier; there is sympathy for the two struggling animals forced to fight till death, but there is no sentimental distortion.

Style

How the writer uses language is style. In nonfiction, as in fiction or poetry, style is an integral part of meaning, and not merely decoration or embellishment added to explanations and descriptions. Style is part of all written matter. Some writers of nonfiction neglect artistry in language as a means of making their subjects interesting, while others are keenly aware of their responsibility to use language effectively.

Simplicity need not be either trite or banal. Comparisons are one means of making concepts clear to the reader, and some writers use comparisons simply and effectively. Irving Adler in *The Story of Light* uses a reference to the familiar Aladdin story. Aladdin rubbed a lamp to summon the Jinni. We flick a switch to summon light. Adler goes on to remind us of how difficult it is to get rid of light; it streams in through windows and drapes, or through keyholes. Light cannot be held by force; although we try to grab it, it slices through our fingers. But if we learn about its tricks, we can put the energy of light to work. Referring next to a common experience, bumping into things in the dark, Adler then compares light to a messenger.

In *Volcano: The Eruption and Healing of Mount St. Helens,* Patricia Lauber is also successful in her use of comparisons. Explaining how a blast of steam tore the mountain open, she says that the water was heated by the magma rising inside. Then, by means of a comparison, she goes on to tell how this could happen:

> Normally water cannot be heated beyond its boiling point, which is 212 degrees Fahrenheit at sea level. At boiling point, water turns to gas, which we call steam. But if water is kept under pressure, it can be heated far beyond its boiling point and still stay liquid. (That is how a pressure cooker works.) If the pressure is removed, this superheated water suddenly turns, or flashes, to steam. As steam it takes up much more room—it expands. The sudden change to steam can cause an explosion.

Frequent comparisons are particularly helpful in the explanations of complex ideas or startling facts. In one picture book, for example, we read the factual statement that the temperature on the sun's surface is close to 10,000 degrees Fahrenheit, and that the temperatures at the sun's center may be close to 32,000 degrees. But we have no frame of reference for these facts. Referring to familiar temperatures like our body heat of around 98 degrees, or water that boils and steam that scalds at 212 degrees would make such high temperatures with so many zeroes even more startling and somewhat more comprehensible.

Some writers simplify their texts by relying upon the simplest sentence structure—subject, verb, complement. Such writers risk losing the interest of children who may weary of the monotonous rhythm created by repeating word patterns. In *What's Hatching Out of That Egg?,* Patricia Lauber, in describing the many animals that hatch from eggs, is factually accurate, and the picture book format is inviting. The style, however, is jerky and halting. Describing the hatching of a monarch butterfly, she uses short simple sentences: "The young animal will spend its days flying about and feeding. But it will no longer eat leaves." Children, after all, do talk in compound and complex sentences; they are more able to read complex sentence forms than some writers assume. *The First Book of New Zealand* is filled with generalizations that suggest that all New Zealanders are alike—an unjust and inaccurate statement. The style of the book is often monotonous and repetitious as well. We are lulled into boredom and disbelief by its declarative sentences, the drumbeat of omniscient authority:

> The New Zealanders of today are law-abiding, practical, and conscientious people. They dislike extremes of any kind. They usually own their own homes. The houses are surrounded by flower gardens, for New Zealanders like to plant and grow things. . . .
> Maori women practice as doctors and dental assistants; they teach school where both the Maoris and *pakehas* are students. They also work as news commentators on the radio. Maori girls are extremely clever.

Keith Lye's *Take a Trip to Argentina* is filled with informative detail, but its brief sentences make it read haltingly. Its failure to relate or compare details to what readers know about the U.S.A. diminishes the impact of the information. We find ourselves asking questions:

> The picture shows Cordoba, Argentina's second largest city. It was founded in 1573. [When was Boston founded?]. . . . Argentina declared itself independent on July 9, 1816. [How many years after the United States declared its independence?]. . . . It consists of a 254-member House of Deputies [Like our House of Representatives?] and a 46-member Senate. [Like ours?] Argentina is a republic and an elected President is Head of State. [Are we a Republic? We elect our President.]

Under the illusion that they are making their meaning more accessible, other writers simplify their language by breaking up compound sentences into halting and choppy fragments:

> How did the glacier do it?
> A glacier works just like a plow. But instead of one blade, it has a thousand. For every rock frozen into its bottom acts like a plowshare.

By contrast, notice the clear and vivid description in *Gorilla Gorilla*. In this book we have facts, but they are given to us in sentences of varying length, with words and phrases in varying orders:

> The hoots grew louder and faster, faster and faster still. Suddenly the huge leader thrust himself to his short legs. He tore up great clumps of bush and vine, tossed them with a furious heave high into the air, and began to thump his massive chest like a frenzied drummer. The drumming boomed and leapt into the leafy jungle, across the high meadows and jutting cliffs of the rain forest—an increasing chorus of beats. The hoots melted into a blurred growl.

Variety in sentence length and construction gives interest to this passage. Further interest in what Carol Fenner wants us to know about gorillas is created by the use of imagery. We hear the drumming and thumping of the huge gorilla and we see his actions. As the leader is compared in a simile to a "frenzied drummer," the drumming booms and leaps. We see the "leafy jungle" and the "jutting cliffs," and hear the "blurred growl," words chosen to convey precise meaning by creating sight and sound images. The result of Fenner's style is that we learn the facts of the gorilla's hooting, and of his feats of strength. But by seeing and hearing him in his natural habitat, we also discover something about the concept explored in the book: captivity influences gorilla behavior.

Any impression that all dress in early America was extremely simple, sensible, and drab is contradicted in *Colonial Living* in Edwin Tunis' word pictures of the Dutch apparel. Relying upon imagery for clarity, Tunis vividly describes the New Netherlanders' dress:

> In an age of ballooning britches, a Dutchman's outswelled all others. His hat was a big plumed hat, not too well suited to his stocky build. Shoe buckles seem to have been popular. . . . the prosperous among the Dutch clung to the starched ruff. . . .
>
> Ruffs were a great nuisance and a great expense. They had to be laundered by experts. . . . The starched flutes . . . were arranged on "setting sticks" and fixed into shape with hot metal "poking sticks." Even then it was necessary to wear a wire "under-propper" to hold a ruff up.

Detailed imagery may also serve to make action clear. In vigorous language, Robert Leckie shows and explains the process of loading the Revolutionary War guns in *The World Turned Upside Down*. Notice Leckie's use of action verbs in differing forms:

> [The British soldier] bit the cartridge open . . . sprinkled a little powder on the pan of his piece. Then, placing the musket butt-downward, he poured the rest of the powder down the barrel. Next, he pushed in the ball. Crumpling the paper into a wad, he crammed that in afterward. Finally, seizing his rifle rod, he rammed all—powder, ball, and paper—down tight inside the barrel.
>
> To fire the musket, he placed the butt against his shoulder and pulled the trigger. This released a cock which struck its flint against a piece of steel to send a shower of sparks into the pan. When the powder here ignited, it flashed through a touch-hole into the bottom of the barrel and exploded the charge which propelled the bullet down the barrel.

A child reading such a description sees that readying the Brown Bess for action was a slow and complicated process; the child may understand that the war play of "rat-a-tat-tat" doesn't apply to the battles of the American Revolution.

Images and figurative comparisons not only contribute to an interesting style, but they are also the means by which the writer clarifies meaning. To create visual pictures filled with comparisons, Jean George uses color imagery and figurative language. In *The Moon of the Monarch Butterfly,* she expresses wonder at the beauty of the monarch by comparing wings to stained-glass windows and antennae to knotted wands:

> Before sundown she came to rest on a wisteria vine that entwined the porch of a small white house in the country. Clinging to a purple flower, she closed her wings above her back, as butterflies do. Her wing tops were burnt orange, their undersides yellow. Black veins spread through them like lead in a stained-glass window and their edges seemed as if the night and day had been knitted together into sparkles of white and black. Her antennas were like wands, slender, with knots on the ends for sensing the flowers, the winds, and other monarch butterflies.

Scientific details and various kinds of eating equipment are made surprisingly clear and easy to understand when Millicent Selsam makes vivid figurative comparisons. In *How the Animals Eat,* the chapter on dinner in the water has several subheadings and captions, each an image suggesting a comparison. Sea Soup or plankton is a mixture of tiny animals that drift together with tiny plants. In some animals Sea Strainers or gill rakers work as built-in strainers holding the sea soup back for the fish to swallow as water passes out through mouth and gills. A Sea Sword is the upper jaw of the fish grown out into a bony, sharp point; it stabs a hole in a big fish and kills it. A Flexible Snout is a trunklike tube that can poke around among the stones in the mud on the bottom of the sea, picking up little sea animals as the hose of a vacuum cleaner sucks up dirt. Each of the metaphors compares in words the unfamiliar manner of eating to something already known to the child. Each verbal comparison becomes vivid and clear. Style, in such cases, can serve as the agent for stimulating wonder and for starting the child's exploration of a subject.

Illustration

The writer of nonfiction relies upon illustration somewhat differently from the writer of fiction. There is no need for characterization, for example, and only occasionally does text evoke mood. In nonfiction, illustration helps to clarify. Sometimes the book makes use of photographs, but often photographs can be less valuable than drawings or diagrams, since they sometimes seem to oversimplify, catching only the external appearances of objects and concepts. Although illustrations are necessary to nonfiction, the writer who cannot achieve corresponding effects of clarity with the use of words is depriving the child of a discovery that words can tell just as pictures can.[3]

A graphic device that is highly useful in some illustrations is a cross-section or a three-dimensional section shown in a line drawing, a representation far more difficult to make clear in a photograph. Growth and change in a bud or flower, for example, are clearer in a drawing where the changes and stages can be shown by captions designating time lapse. Views of the object are visible from all angles and positions. In *Volcano,* which is filled with beautiful full-color photographs, the artist uses five colored drawings as verification of text: an air view of the area affected in differing ways by the eruption, a globe shown from Antarctica noting the Ring of Fire of active volcanos surrounding the Pacific, two cross-sections showing the earth's plates and what happens when they move, and the last showing how a small plate colliding with the larger one built the Cascade Mountain Range. The illustrative combination is most effective.

Tone

Tone is an important part of nonfiction, just as it is of fiction. Many children involve themselves more easily in a nonfiction account if they feel that a real person is conveying the facts to them. Writers may become persons in their own accounts by using the pronouns "we" and "you." To satisfy further this need for person in the communication, the writer also adopts a particular attitude toward the facts and the readers.

Sometimes the writer of books about nature, science, processes, or other facts names the book—*The Wonderful World of*—and we are startled to discover that our city sewer system is wonderful. Although the word *wonder* is overworked, there are a great many subjects about which it is perfectly reasonable to wonder. But when the writer uses the title *The Mystery of Chlorophyll,* he or she adopts a tone of surprise and intrigue. Science and the natural world are not miraculous, because as we discover more about them, their opening mysteries continue to provoke wonder—but become less mysterious. If books of fact are to stimulate the minds of children to further exploration, the writer's tone or attitude might better say, "Remarkable as all this is, we can know it. If we investigate it, we are amazed and enlightened."

Writers of nonfiction, like those of fiction, sometimes fall into a tone of condescension, oversimplifying, thinking of the readers as dear little things, or guarding their ears from the whole truth. In one book about elephants, for example, we are mystified when we read that usually peaceful males, who do not charge unless threatened, get angry and excitable once a year for a few weeks or months. This is a period known in italics as "musth"; apparently we are being protected from awareness of the mating season. Although this condescension may occur in a purely factual account, it seems to appear more frequently in facts tied together with a slight narrative.

History, and particularly remote history, is sometimes narrated in a pattern of condescension. In discussing *The Land and People of Iceland,* Erick Berry describes the Vikings, using the accounts in the Sagas recorded in about 1000 A.D. Berry makes these warriors' lives ridiculous. In violent and purposeless battle, they cut off each other's heads:

> [At nightfall their heads] were miraculously restored, so that they might all sit down together and feast and drink all night. To resume fighting again next morning. Presumably their morning-after headaches also disappeared by magic.

Berry, however, does go on to explain the Vikings' early governmental bodies whose purpose was to settle disputes; "man-made words sought to wipe man-made violence from the land." The effort at humor seems out of place in a chapter that seriously traces Icelandic history from piracy to democracy.

When Edwin Tunis writes of the American Indian in *Indians,* he manages to treat objectively a subject that is often the victim of intellectual snobbery—superstition. Because of the matter-of-fact tone of the account, we accept the Indians' fears:

> There was no Indian who was even reasonably free from superstition: it covered everything in the world. When every animal and every tree, and every stream and every natural phenomenon was possessed of a spirit, probably malevolent, it took a lot of finger-crossing and wood-knocking to ward off evil. The Indian was afraid of everything . . . of killing snakes and wolves . . . of witchcraft and of the owls he associated with it . . . superstition . . . pervaded all Indian living.

Tone also helps us to believe surprising statements. For example, we may be a bit unsettled to learn on page one of Milton Meltzer's *All Times, All Peoples: A World History of Slavery* that "white, black, brown, yellow, red—no matter what [your] color, it's likely that someone in [your] family way back, was once a slave." We go on to understand why this might be true; his factual tone convinces us:

> It was hard for [the earliest peoples] to feed themselves. . . . That is why, when they raided other people, they killed them instead of taking them prisoner. If the winners had spared the lives of the losers, they would have been unable to feed them.

But as farming and food production grew, and it was possible for conquerors to feed prisoners, they kept them as slaves. The book's powerful illustrations in black and white further reenforce the credibility of Meltzer's factual tone.

In books about animals, condescension often takes the form of *anthropomorphism,* an attitude that suggests a lack of interesting qualities in the animals themselves and a need to jazz up their lives by making them more nearly human. When pets are given human qualities, we are not surprised, but it seems unacceptable and highly unscientific to attribute human qualities to prehistoric beasts. In one book about dinosaurs, a brontosaurus is called "terribly dumb"; the tylosaurus, described as clever, fierce, and cruel, seems vicious rather than—more accurately—carnivorous. In *Here Come the Wild Dogs,* which is about the life of a fox family, the father fox thinks to himself:

> What a fine morning for racing with the dogs!
> Excitement!
> Adventure!
> And yes, even danger!

As we follow the race in which the fox outwits the dogs, we hear the victorious fox say, "What fun!" While these may be reasonable emotions for people, the child reading that the fox has such thoughts and feelings is misled about reality, even led to believe that foxes relish the danger and adventure of being hunted. Animal stories are great favorites with children; it is important that when the child expects a factual report, a factual report is given. Any narrative should be kept within the realm of real possibility. The wild animals of McClung's *Shag, Last of the Plains Buffalo* do not play hide and seek with danger. Their lives are filled with serious battles—with pioneers, blizzards, mountain lions, wolves, and hunger. Although the reality of natural struggle includes terms usually used to describe human behavior, such as "lonely and afraid," "leaping in terror," and "wanting to get away," the book shows far more convincingly than the fox book how an animal responds physically to its natural enemies.

The writer of *Ookie, the Walrus Who Liked People* goes a step further than the writer of the fox book; he regards the walrus as almost totally human.[4] We read that she wasn't much interested in the penguin pool; she didn't think they'd be the sort of creatures that would be fun to play with; the seals, however, were the playmates she liked when she was lonely. The huge and yet sleekly graceful walrus becomes cute and coy, like the cartooned characters of a Disney animation. Wonder and curiosity do not urge us to discover more about walruses; the account stops discovery short by making the walrus neither human nor animal.

While accounts of the animal world are particularly subject to the condescension of anthropomorphism, some writers, Jean George for one, show great respect for their animal subjects. The reader, while absorbing detailed information about the gray wolves, acquires at the same time an admiration for their grace and intelligence. In *The Moon of the Gray Wolves*, we watch the wolf as he watches the caribou herd, and looks for prey:

> The black wolf waited until the main herd passed around the bend of the Toklat. Then, studying the forest and tundra for laggers, he tightened his muscles and sprang into a trot. His narrowly spaced wolf-shoulders gave him the stride of a horse rather than that of a dog, and in the manner of all wolves he glided along the ridge like a thoroughbred. Stiff, long guard-hairs grew beyond his fuzzy underfur and fended off ice and snow. . . .

We further discover that the wolf is an essential predator, since by "harvesting" the weak and the old, the wolf keeps the caribou herd healthy, and their numbers balanced with the available food supply. Here George's tone is objective and respectful, suitable for her description.

Phyllis Borea is even more factual in tone in her account of *Seymour, a Gibbon*. In order to make the descriptions clear, Borea often compares the monkeys' actions to those of people, but she carefully avoids lapsing into personification:

> Gibbons . . . live in family groups—father, mother, one or two youngsters, and sometimes a very old gibbon, perhaps a grandfather or mother . . . only gibbons enjoy this close way of living rather like our own. The family wakes at dawn after a night together in their sleeping tree, because, also like us, the higher primates sleep at night and are up and about during the day.

Although Borea compares gibbon families to human families, the two are said to be "perhaps" similar, but never the same. And since Borea cannot know the reasons for the gibbons' morning cries, she only speculates:

> For an hour or more after waking, they greet the dawn and their neighbors with cries that have been called songs and set down on paper like music. . . . their morning songs may be a way of letting other gibbon families know these particular trees are lived in. The songs may also be just for the fun of it.

Herbert S. Zim is another writer intent upon giving the reader the facts and the facts alone. He makes few human comparisons and he gives only verifiable information. In *Monkeys*, Zim uses a completely objective and matter-of-fact tone:

> Records kept at zoos show that monkeys have a fairly long life span compared to other mammals. A mandrill has been known to live 27 years, a macaque up to 29, and a baboon to 45. But these may be special cases, and wild monkeys, on an average, may not live much over 10 or 12 years.

Didacticism and Propaganda

When a writer chooses a controversial topic such as drugs as a subject for a children's book, he or she is probably impelled by a desire to persuade the readers, or to influence their thinking about the dangers of narcotics or of smoking. As a result, writers may have a difficult time separating their facts from their propaganda. The writer, however, has as a first obligation the presentation of generalizations supported by factual information. Experiments, statistics, descriptions of studies, and references to authorities should be the meat of the book. If the facts are carefully arranged, the evidence gathers and builds to prove the point. Preachment is unnecessary.

If, on the other hand, the book lacks sufficient evidence and relies upon generalizations that the writer knows to be true but has not bothered to support with evidence for the reader's examination, the book then raises questions that have not been answered. How do we know? Who says so? When did that happen? If these questions are left unanswered by the data, the reader says "That's just opinion; it's never proved." The effect on the reader's mind is a quick write-off: "Propaganda. Pure propaganda." Doubt and distrust result.

While some concepts have been well-researched and a variety of experiments has led to the same conclusions—smoking endangers the smoker's health—others are still in the process of being tested and proved. Scientists conduct experiments, note results, and draw hypotheses; they then test these hypotheses in an effort to reach a conclusion. But many of these series of experiments are still in hypothetical stages, insufficiently proved. It is most often these hypotheses that turn into propaganda for unproved theories.

The writer of nonfiction has a responsibility to use and to foster the scientific attitude. It is the writer's obligation when dealing with theory not fully proven to make us aware that there are theories and counter-theories on the subject. Perhaps—if society is lucky—the child-readers will be so intrigued by the puzzlement of scientists that they themselves will wish to find the solution some day.

Adults often seek opinion books because they wish to know a particular expert's opinion or attitude toward a subject. The child, however, not knowing that the facts surrounding a social problem can be interpreted through the individual perspectives of various kinds of experts, approaches a book expecting to find facts and objectivity. The child will then be less likely to detect bias. It seems reasonable to say that children's books that inform should not be propaganda. Freedom to draw our own conclusions from the facts is a precious right. If a writer has a bias, we should expect it to be stated openly at some point.

The confusing of theory with truth concerns the scientist with integrity.

In *The Seeds of Tomorrow* Ben Bova cites the published projections of eminent scientists from the Massachusetts Institute of Technology regarding the disastrous effects of overpopulation. Listing the kinds of information fed to the computer, he mentions pollution, farm production, famished continents, infant mortality and increased longevity, and depletion of natural resources, then contrasts them with expected birth rates. Science and technology, while they have produced many of these "problems," are essential parts of a better future; "they offer a chance to avert the total world collapse that awaits us." Describing the evolution of *homo sapiens,* he credits the curiosity of humankind with solving problem after immediate problem, and points to the use of "second generation technology [that] would feed, cure, and protect us without long-term damage to the environment." He makes no effort to preach family planning, but presents the problem in its complexity.

In *Hunger on Planet Earth,* another writer, Jules Archer, focuses primarily on overpopulation as the source of hunger. Noting that wars are often started over too-many-people-too-little-space, he says that wealthy nations have done little to help because food aid only results in higher birth rates. Using a particularly vivid illustration, he says that "each time your heart beats, three more new hearts start to beat elsewhere on earth and three more mouths must be fed," then cites the hard-nosed views of some scientists: "If people breed like rabbits they must be allowed to die like rabbits." Next, the moral argument is cited, followed by mention of countless efforts to solve overpopulation problems at world conferences, acknowledging at the same time the varied objections to family planning. Titles of his last chapters indicate Archer's emphasis on population control: "New Ideas for Feeding Planet Earth" addresses food production, pest control, plant genetics, irrigation, energy innovation, altered diets, sea harvesting, and a variety of other issues. "Controlling World Population," however, is the topic of one whole chapter. Clearly he sees it as paramount.

BIOGRAPHY

In our discussion of nonfiction books for children we have noted that each of them includes three essentials: facts, a concept that facts relate to, and an attitude toward the subject and the reader. *Biography,* the history of the life of an individual, has similar essentials. First of all, the facts are expected to be accurate, up-to-date, and authentic as they depict the person and the period of his or her life. The objective biographer must include or omit the events and details as they suit the interests and age level for which the biography is intended. As for concept, we assume that the subject of the biography is worth reading about, just as it is worth the writer's time in research and writing. A subject for biography has done something or been something, discovered or demonstrated something that makes her or his life significant—more significant, say, than your life or your sister's or brother's. As for attitude, we assume that the attitude of the writer reflects interest and enthusiasm. If the writer finds the subject worth writing about, she or he finds the subject worth writing about with the skill we call style. The skillful biographer uses words imaginatively, even in the simplest biographies for younger readers. Autobiography, written by the subject, cannot be totally objective because the narrated events are filtered through the writer's consciousness. A particularly moving series of personal accounts can be found in Julius Lester's collected slave narratives, *To Be a Slave.*

The Writer's Obligations

Within our definition of biography—biography is the history of the life of an individual—are two terms, and each presents a separate obligation for the writer. The first term, *history,* implies facts, and biography, like other nonfiction, should be factually accurate. Information about the life of the subject comes from such sources as letters, journals, diaries, court records, newspaper accounts, recorded conversations, and interviews, wherever feasible. Although not all biographies for children include a bibliography, it is a useful addition. A quick glance at the foreword or acknowledgments may also tell something about the writer's research and perhaps suggest other readings to the curious child. A closer look at the text itself will reveal dates, quotations, places, and names as they fit into the narrative. But again, the numbers of such details depend upon the age of the intended readers. Such data make the book seem factually authentic, and we are then ready to take other information on faith.

The term *history* implies another obligation on the part of the writer; history when properly written is reported objectively. The historian neither shows personal bias nor assumes omniscience about thoughts and feelings of historical figures. The conscientious biographer, despite interest in the subject, is bound by similar limitations; he or she does not get into the mind of the subject, but limits the information to verifiable matters and to emotions, fantasies, or thoughts the subject has spoken or recorded. For example, in *The Double Life of Pocahontas,* Jean Fritz is faithful in her documentation; notes and bibliography are complete enough for the child reader. As extensive as her research seems to have been, Fritz could not know what Pocahontas thought as she was being "civilized" by the British at Rock Hall. "Perhaps she thought" she would "become one of them. . . . In her long skirts she may already have felt less like an Indian." John Rolfe and Pocahontas "probably first met at church. . . . Perhaps he was falling in love." Partiality yields to fact and objectivity.

By definition, a biography is about an individual, and here lies a second responsibility. Children who become interested in the lives of presidents, for example, often have difficulty sorting out the life of one president from the life of another, because aside from living in different historical periods, presidents in children's biographies may become stereotypes of all that is good. Their differences are slight; Washington is honest, Lincoln compassionate, Wilson scholarly, Theodore Roosevelt nonconforming but commanding. Servants to society like Jane Addams, Clara Barton, or Florence Nightingale are unselfishly devoted to helping others; freed slaves like Amos Fortune may be cardboard figures of self-denial. The process of writing biography, like that of writing informational books, is a process of constant decision-making: what to select and what to omit. The biographer wishes to show the individual as a believable human being, complete with such flaws as occasional self-interest, irritability, or faulty judgment. Although there is a trend toward showing the less admirable traits in the character of the subject, we still usually ignore socially disapproved behavior. Poor biography, however, often ignores completely any negative qualities and presents only the good. The result is sometimes a book colored by an approving tone that may be disproportionate to the subject's achievements or character and in any case is unrealistic.

In *Christopher Columbus,* Susan Heimann gives him credit for his achievements; nonetheless, she does show him as a believable human being. Columbus, in writing about the Indians in the newly discovered land, says of them: "they ought to be good servants and of good skill . . . they would easily be made Christians, because it seems that they belonged to no religion." Heimann goes on to say that Columbus has revealed in these words that while the first motive for the voyage—bringing religion to the natives—is still important, it now seems to come second to "using" these people as skillful servants. Since children often read biography because of curiosity about a hero to emulate, it seems important that the subject of the biography not be so unreal, or so saintly, that the reader feels emulation is impossible. When honestly described, the subject is real enough to encourage the reader to similar efforts and achievements.

Biography and Fiction

We see the terms "biographical fiction" and "fictional biography" and wonder what they mean. Both admit that the writer has dramatized or invented parts that perhaps cannot be verified, or that the writer wishes to make facts into a story to show how the subject *might* have behaved, given his or her character. The problem for the writer of biography for children lies to a great extent in the answers to two basic questions: How much fact shall I include? How much narrative may I invent?

F. N. Monjo, for example, used some of the facts of Lincoln's life along with a fictional storytelling device: Lincoln's son Tad is the first-person narrator of *Me and Willie and Pa.* Tad tells, among other things, of crawling into Pa's bed when he was lonely after his brother Willie's death. The book uses historical facts, but the child's interest is held by the imaginary narrative. A biography as brief as a picture book can also be effective nonfiction, telling only the most significant events. *The Glorious Flight* by Alice and Martin Provensen tells of Louis Blériot, his five children, and the family's fascination with the clacking flying machine overhead. Blériot's keen interest turns to obsession, and he builds one machine after another, until in 1909 Blériot XI flies the twenty miles across the English Channel. The text does not try to describe differences in the eleven models, but pictures them one by one.

Biography for the older child might fall closer to the factual end of the spectrum; the older child can absorb more facts and may require less story. Too much factual detail makes the page dense with the capital letters of places, people, and events, and the appearance is that of an encyclopedia. The response to such a biography may be, "This is more than I really want to know." And yet, too much dramatization or inclusion of probable dialogue prompts the response, "What can I really believe?" Carl Sandburg, in writing about his biography of Lincoln, stated that he did not invent dialogue or incident to prove a point; he adhered to fact. And yet Sandburg's work, from which *Abe Lincoln Grows Up* is drawn, is unsurpassed as a definitive biography of Lincoln, both for accuracy and interest. It is possible to stick to the facts and to write an interesting book. But if the writer does dramatize, these inventions should be historically true to the times and not merely possible, but probable. Such dramatization often occurs when the subject of the biography is long dead and has left few written records.

The carefully researched *Lincoln: A Photobiography* by Russell Freedman is very convincing, largely because Freedman quotes from Lincoln's hand-written notes and occasional journals. He catches the tone of Lincoln's writing, interpreting what happens in light of the insights gained from personal glimpses. Lincoln's last day, for example, rings true to what we know of his compassion. After lunch he "revoked the death sentence of a Confederate spy." And he pardoned a deserter, signing his name with the comment, "Well, I think this boy can do us more good above ground than under ground!" Members at the last cabinet meeting heard his wish that no retaliatory "bloody work" be done, adding that blood enough had been lost.[5]

People who live active lives are naturally and easily made interesting for children; when adventure is part of the subject's life, the narrative pulls the reader along. However biographies of philosophers, poets, or musicians who lived quietly with little drama or action in their lives are more difficult to make interesting, especially for younger readers. The obligation remains, however, for the biographer to focus upon the nature of the person as well as upon the exciting events of his or her life. Where the subject's achievement is less filled with action or adventure, the writer faces the necessity to hold interest in the subject and yet to keep invented action to a minimum. This dual responsibility is not easy to fulfill, particularly when the subject has left few recorded statements. Invention is sometimes the biographer's compromise.

Tone and Style

The reader of biography ought also to expect suitable tone and appropriate style. In five different accounts of Columbus' landing in what he thought to be the Indies, the biographers refer to the Indians and explorers in different ways. One account seems to call undue attention to the Indians' nakedness, and by using quiet verbs and exotic descriptions creates a romantic, fairytale tone. Notice the effect of "scarlet" instead of red, for example:

> Columbus and his men saw a new beautiful world.
> Here were brown men with no clothes at all. Their bodies were painted red and other bright colors. . . . They were pleased to take gifts of bells and beads and scarlet caps. They were a gentle and friendly people.

A second biographer seems to condescend because he places quotation marks around "talk" and "told," as he describes in minimal terms the sign language used by both the Indians and the explorers:

> Columbus finally managed to "talk" to the Indians by making signs with his hands. The Indians made signs too. They "told" Columbus he was welcome.

A third account by its tone of wonder makes the Indians seem like children and the explorers seem, even to the reader, to be like gods.

> [All Columbus saw] were naked, red-skinned savages. They threw themselves to the ground and worshiped Columbus and his bearded men. . . . They thought that gods had descended from the heavens on white-winged birds. They led the white gods to their homes.

And a fourth writer, Susan Heimann, wins our belief by narrating facts in a convincingly objective tone:

> Curiosity quickly overcame fear on the part of the people of the island, and soon they came out to meet these strange men from another world. These "very handsome people" were Tainos. . . . Columbus called them Indians. He described them as gentle and helpful in every way. They wore no clothes, and many of the men painted their bodies.

Jean Fritz in *Where do you think you're going, Christopher Columbus?* seems to be showing Columbus as a very ordinary man who has miscalculated the distance to the Indies as well as what the "Indians" would look like, his impressions gained from the inaccurate, hearsay descriptions of Marco Polo and Sir John Mandeville.

> . . . the only sign of gold was the gold rings that the natives wore in their noses. Indeed, that was all they wore. The people were as naked, Columbus said, "as their mothers bore them," which of course, was pretty naked. Otherwise, they were normal looking. They didn't have umbrella feet or eyes on their shoulders.

Fritz's description of the Indians retains the light, humorous tone of the whole book, and therefore it does not condescend to the Indians any more than to anyone else. The biography seems essentially accurate, and a thoroughly enjoyable "story" complete with endnotes.

In *Commodore Perry in the Land of the Shogun,* Rhoda Blumberg writes of another encounter between people who are strangers to each other. The Americans, who had expected to find savages as they sailed over the world's edge in the 1800s, were charmed by the Japanese, finding them courteous and hospitable, highly cultured and most civilized. Blumberg does not condescend when she tells of the "ferocious-looking masks . . . designed to scare enemies," but she does go on to explain the closed Japanese society of 1853.

Writers of biography may use all of the devices of style. In *Stonewall,* stylist Fritz describes Jackson as experiencing painfully hard years between the deaths of his father and his mother. She calls this time a figurative "hard knot at the very root of his character." Using imagery and onomatopoeic language, she tells us that he lived with his mother's relatives for a time, where the "rumble of wagon wheels, the slip-slopping of water, the buzzing of machinery formed a background music for all the farmwork." Life on his uncle's farm was rough; men "from all over the country came and . . . bet and drank and smoked and swore and spit and carried on." Using five sentences of repeated subject-verb order, Fritz's style, because here it contrasts with her usual sentence variety, emphasizes Jackson's determination. "He decided . . . he had to find rules for his life and then follow them strictly. He wasn't going to let life just happen to him. He wasn't going to be like his father and slip carelessly into errors and from errors to ruin. He was going to be in charge."

The biographer, facing the necessity to arouse and hold the reader's interest, may be tempted to create sympathy for the subject and to make a tearjerker out of early trials. One biographer of the young composer Beethoven has made from some factual information a sentimental story of Beethoven's being victimized by a tyrannical teacher. He says, "Poor Ludwig!" and describes his day as long, hard, and wearying. Ludwig stumbles off to bed, but is shaken awake in the middle of the night and called a lazy rascal. Then he is made to stay awake and write music. His unreasonable teacher stands over him, thunders at his drowsiness, forces the exhausted boy back to work, then goes to bed leaving the weary boy struggling with fatigue as he finishes the writing. Here again it is not the facts we question so much as the tone.

Paderewski the pianist might have been treated with equal sentimentality as he goes off to the Warsaw Conservatory. However, in *Paderewski,* Charlotte Kellogg is unsentimental:

> More than discouraging was his first experience in a piano class. "Not hands for playing," the teacher declared. "That thumb, that third finger, too short." He gave Ignace a trial, then told him to leave, to take up some other instrument.

Concepts and Didacticism

Concept is needed in biography as it is in other literature; our preoccupation with fact must not blind us to idea. The title *Invincible Louisa* suggests a concept behind the biography; the same can be said for *Carry On, Mr. Bowditch,* or *Up From Slavery.* Other biographies, while they may not indicate the unifying idea in their titles, do have a concept that is implicit within them, perhaps the reasons for the writer's having chosen these people as subjects. Sometimes this leader unified his or her country, this scientist persisted until research bore fruit, this athlete overcame difficulties, or this composer was an innovator. Any of these reasons for writing the biography can unify the account to make it a coherent whole.

Concept unifies Fritz's biography, *Stonewall,* a nickname which characterized Jackson's determination in everything, from his health to his battle plans. "I'm going to make a man of myself if I live. What I will do, I can do." Self-control that dictated posture, prayers, and health maintenance picture Stonewall as standing erect to keep his alimentary canal straight:

> [He put] himself on a diet of stale unbuttered bread and lean meat. No tea, coffee, or stimulants of any kind. And he exercised. Fast walks accompanied by leaps and arm-whirlings. . . . One arm, he decided, was heavier than the other so he developed the habit of thrusting the heavy one up in the air at regular intervals. This way the blood would run back into the body . . . and lighten the arm.

However, having a reason to choose a subject for biography does not give the writer license to preach. Intent upon making a point about the worthiness of the subject, the writer may lapse into didacticism. Writing of Louisa May Alcott's early life, Cornelia Meigs insists that we recognize the idealism behind Bronson Alcott's efforts to form the perfect social community. Such insistence intervenes between the readers and Louisa, the real subject; it shakes a finger at the readers to make them accept Meigs' views.

> We must remember, however, that Bronson and his friends, wise in some ways, mistaken in others, had the courage to find out, by the only possible means, where they were right and where they were wrong. There is only one method of testing a system of living; that is by living it.

Louisa saw Concord soldiers march away to the Civil War, and such a picture is relevant to the biography. But here, too, Meigs intervenes:

> There is no experience in the world that can ever match that of seeing soldiers go away, of seeing the gaiety and the excitement and of knowing the black and hopeless tragedy which is behind it all. There is little that is so terrible as seeing strong, wholesome young men, every one of them beautiful in the flush of their high patriotism, as watching them go and knowing that they are surely to die.

By contrast, there is information coupled with vitality in *Carry On, Mr. Bowditch*. Jean Lee Latham tells of Nathaniel Bowditch's discovery of a new and simpler way to make lunar calculations at sea. Without preaching, she simultaneously explains the process, records the action, and reproduces the excitement of discovery:

> Tonight ought to be a good one for a lunar. The moon was due to pass over a star that was bright enough to see in spite of its nearness to the moon.... Just when the moon neared the bright star, a cloud got in the way. Nat shrugged and sighed. There ought to be a better way to work a lunar! He studied the glittering heavens. Was there another star bright enough tonight—that the moon would pass over? Of course not. He knew that. That one ... the moon would pass below it ... that one ... the moon would pass above it ... that one ...
>
> The idea hit Nat so suddenly that he gasped. He raced below and for the second time that night crashed into Prince's cabin without knocking.

A unifying concept and accurate details about manners, costumes, or the appearance of city streets are not enough. Like all nonfiction, biography, too, should arouse the reader's curiosity to want to know more about the time period, the movements in history, or the subject's life or achievements. If biography is to open the world to children, it should stimulate them as they finish the book to believe not "Now I know all about this person, this period, this vocation," but "I wonder what else I can find out—" The biography will then have served, in Margery Fisher's words, not as a stopper but as a starter.

SUMMARY

The purpose of nonfiction is to help the reader toward knowledge—knowledge as contrasted to mere information or fact. It is natural then that techniques will be subordinated to this end. Within each nonfiction book we expect to find fact, concept, and attitude. Curiosity or wonder, the motivation for children seeking out nonfiction, is stimulated by the quality of what they read, tempting them to wish to discover more about worthy people, foreign lands, far off times, scientific concepts, natural elements and animals, or ways of solving society's problems. Since the order in which facts and concepts are presented influences how well we understand, a narrative structure is sometimes used for younger children. Among effective means of explanation, moving from the known to the unknown is often the most effective.

Biography is obliged by its definition to be factually accurate in depicting a unique individual whose life has unusual value; the biographer faces the necessity to keep the account interesting but truthful. Tone influences nonfiction just as it does fiction. Condescension looks down upon its subject; sentimentality distorts it; and propaganda invalidates it. The best choice of tone always enlivens the subject.

Style, though it must be clear, need not be banal or trite; imagery, figurative language, and varied sentence structure make the writing lively and stimulating. The best nonfiction can prompt a reader's response: I want to know more!

READING AND EVALUATING

1. **Informational Books: Organization** Examine three nonfiction books intended for the same age level or reading maturity and that explore similar topics (e.g., cities, frontier life, Puritan days). Which have narrative order? Which begin with the known and move to the unknown? Is the progress of the explanation clear? Are there other methods of development? Are there unexplained gaps? Is too much information given at one time, without giving the reader opportunity for assimilation or comparisons? Explain your answers.

2. **Tone and concept** Examine three nonfiction books for differing age or reading maturity levels that explore the same concept. Does the book stimulate wonder? What is the tone? Identify any passages you feel are condescending. Is the book so packed with closely related information that the reader feels he or she will never understand? Is it a starter book, one that leads the child to explore? Or is it a stopper, one that makes the child think that is all there is to know on the subject? Explain.

3. **Point of view** Examine three books of natural history for their objective reporting. Does the book make the animal interesting without personifying it?

Does it attribute to animals traits that are observable by actions? Does it suggest that animals are interesting in themselves? Or does it suggest that animals are interesting only if they are made human?

4. **Biography: Concept and point of view**   Compare three biographies of the same person, checking them for evidence of the writer's research. Is any one of them too packed with information, reading more like an encyclopedia than like an interesting personal history? Is the biographer's point of view objective? Give evidence. Or does the biographer, like the writer of fiction, assume omniscience about how the subject feels and thinks? Give evidence.

5. **Style and tone**   What evidence of stylistic artistry do you find in any of three nonfiction books? Are there figurative comparisons and imagery to make appearances and actions clear and interesting? Is sentence structure varied, or does it move haltingly? If the book is historical, does it convince the reader that these were real people rather than stereotypes of a historical period? How? What devices of style are used, and how are they effective?

NOTES

1 Throughout this chapter I am grateful to Margery Fisher for many of my ideas. Her book, *Matters of Fact* (Brockhampton, 1973), is an excellent discussion of what should be expected of nonfiction books for children.

2 Fisher contrasts two terms: A starter makes the child "want to pursue it further. A stopper can be quickly skimmed and will be as quickly forgotten because it gives the deadly impression of being self-contained and yet incomplete" (p. 23).

3 Discovery through words gives the child an opportunity for greater growth. Continuous reliance upon illustration for clarity does not expose children to new words nor develop in them the habit of using words to express themselves.

4 William Bridges' book is classified as nonfiction.

5 See "Abe, Honestly and Otherwise" by Henry Mayer (*New York Times Book Review,* February 12, 1989, p. 24) for a comparison of Lincoln biographies for children.

RECOMMENDED BOOKS CITED
IN THIS CHAPTER

ADLER, IRVING. *The Story of Light.* Irvington-on-Hudson, NY: Harvey House, 1971.

ARCHER, JULES. *Hunger on Planet Earth.* New York: Crowell, 1977.

ASIMOV, ISAAC. *How Did We Find Out About Electricity?* New York: Walker, 1973.

BENDICK, JEANNE. *Why Can't I?* New York: McGraw-Hill, 1969.

BLUMBERG, RHODA. *Commodore Perry in the Land of the Shogun.* New York: Lothrop Lee, 1985.

BOREA, PHYLLIS and RAIMONDO. *Seymour, a Gibbon.* New York: Atheneum, 1973.

BOVA, BEN. *The Seeds of Tomorrow.* New York: David McKay, 1977.

CARSON, RACHEL. *The Sea Around Us.* New York: Oxford University Press, 1961.

CLARK, MARY LOU. *You and Relativity.* Chicago: Childrens Press, 1965.

FENNER, CAROL. *Gorilla, Gorilla.* New York: Random House, 1973.

FREEDMAN, RUSSELL. *Lincoln: A Photobiography.* New York: Ticknor & Fields, 1987.

FRITZ, JEAN. *The Double Life of Pocahontas.* New York: Putnam, 1983.

———. *Stonewall.* New York: Putnam, 1979.

———. *Where do you think you're going, Christopher Columbus?* New York: Putnam, 1980.

GEORGE, JEAN. *The Moon of the Gray Wolves.* New York: Crowell, 1969.

———. *The Moon of the Monarch Butterfly.* New York: Crowell, 1968.

———. *Spring Comes to the Ocean.* New York: Crowell, 1966.

HEIMANN, SUSAN. *Christopher Columbus.* New York: Watts, 1973.

HOPF, ALICE L. *Hyena.* New York: Dodd, Mead, 1983.

KELLOGG, CHARLOTTE. *Paderewski.* New York: Viking, 1956.

LASKY, KATHRYN. *Sugaring Time.* New York: Macmillan, 1983.

LATHAM, JEAN LEE. *Carry On, Mr. Bowditch.* Boston: Houghton Mifflin, 1955.

LAUBER, PATRICIA. *Volcano: The Eruption and Healing of Mount St. Helens.* New York: Bradbury, 1986.

LECKIE, ROBERT. *The World Turned Upside Down.* New York: Putnam, 1973.

LEFKOWITZ, R. J. *Water for Today and Tomorrow.* New York: Parents Magazine, 1973.

LESTER, JULIUS. *To Be a Slave,* illustrated by Tom Feelings. New York: Dial, 1968.

MACAULAY, DAVID. *Cathedral.* Boston: Houghton Mifflin, 1973.

McCLOSKEY, ROBERT. *Time of Wonder.* New York: Viking, 1957.

McCLUNG, ROBERT. *Possum.* New York: Morrow, 1963.

———. *Samson, Last of the California Grizzlies.* New York: Morrow, 1973.

———. *Shag, Last of the Plains Buffalo.* New York: Morrow, 1963.

MELTZER, MILTON. *All Times, All Peoples: A World History of Slavery.* New York: Harper & Row, 1980.

MONJO, F. N. *Me and Willie and Pa.* New York: Simon & Schuster, 1973.

PROVENSEN, ALICE and MARTIN. *The Glorious Flight.* New York: Viking, 1983.

SANDBURG, CARL. *Abe Lincoln Grows Up.* New York: Harcourt Brace, 1931.

SELSAM, MILLICENT. *How the Animals Eat.* Eau Claire, WI: E. N. Hale (n.d.).

SPIER, PETER. *Tin Lizzie.* New York: Doubleday, 1975.

TUNIS, EDWIN. *Colonial Living.* New York: World, 1957.

———. *Indians.* New York: World, 1959.

ZIM, HERBERT S. *Monkeys.* New York: Morrow, 1955.

Children's Book Awards

THE NEWBERY MEDAL

Named in honor of John Newbery (1713-1767), the first English publisher of children's books, this medal has been given annually (since 1922) by the American Library Association's Association for Library Service to Children. The recipient is recognized as author of the most distinguished book in children's literature published in the United States in the preceding year. The award is limited to citizens or residents of the United States.

1922 *The Story of Mankind* by Hendrik Willem van Loon, Liveright
Honor Books: *The Great Quest* by Charles Hawes, Little; *Cedric the Forester* by Bernard Marshall, Appleton; *The Old Tobacco Shop* by William Bowen, Macmillan; *The Golden Fleece and the Heroes Who Lived Before Achilles* by Padraic Colum, Macmillan; *Windy Hill* by Cornelia Meigs, Macmillan

1923 *The Voyages of Doctor Dolittle* by Hugh Lofting, Lippincott
Honor Books: No record

1924 *The Dark Frigate* by Charles Hawes, Atlantic/Little, Brown
Honor Books: No record

1925 *Tales from Silver Lands* by Charles Finger, Doubleday
Honor Books: *Nicholas* by Anne Carroll Moore, Putnam; *Dream Coach* by Anne Parrish, Macmillan

1926 *Shen of the Sea* by Arthur Bowie Chrisman, Dutton
Honor Book: *Voyagers* by Padraic Colum, Macmillan

1927 *Smoky, The Cowhorse* by Will James, Scribner's
Honor Books: No record

1928 *Gayneck, The Story of a Pigeon* by Dhan Gopal Mukerji, Dutton

Honor Books: *The Wonder Smith and His Son* by Ella Young, Longmans; *Downright Dencey* by Caroline Snedeker, Doubleday

1929 *The Trumpeter of Krakow* by Eric P. Kelly, Macmillan
Honor Books: *Pigtail of Ah Lee Ben Loo* by John Bennett, Longmans; *Millions of Cats* by Wanda Gág, Coward; *The Boy Who Was* by Grace Hallock, Dutton; *Clearing Weather* by Cornelia Meigs, Little; *Runaway Papoose* by Grace Moon, Doubleday; *Tod of the Fens* by Elinor Whitney, Macmillan

1930 *Hitty, Her First Hundred Years* by Rachel Field, Macmillan
Honor Books: *Daughter of the Seine* by Jeanette Eaton, Harper; *Pran of Albania* by Elizabeth Miller, Doubleday; *Jumping-Off Place* by Marian Hurd McNeely, Longmans; *Tangle-Coated Horse and Other Tales* by Ella Young, Longmans; *Vaino* by Julia Davis Adams, Dutton; *Little Blacknose* by Hildegarde Swift, Harcourt

1931 *The Cat Who Went to Heaven* by Elizabeth Coatsworth, Macmillan
Honor Books: *Floating Island* by Anne Parish, Harper; *The Dark Star of Itza* by Alida Malkus, Harcourt; *Queer Person* by Ralph Hubbard, Doubleday; *Mountains Are Free* by Julia Davis Adams, Dutton; *Spice and the Devil's Cave* by Agnes Hewes, Knopf; *Meggy Macintosh* by Elizabeth Janet Gray, Doubleday; *Garram the Hunter* by Herbert Best, Doubleday; *Ood-Le-Uk the Wanderer* by Alice Lide and Margaret Johansen, Little

1932 *Waterless Mountain* by Laura Adams Armer, Longmans
Honor Books: *The Fairy Circus* by Dorothy P. Lathrop, Macmillan; *Calico Bush* by Rachel Field, Macmillan; *Boy of the South Seas* by Eunice Tietjens, Coward; *Out of the Flame* by Eloise Lownsbery, Longmans; *Jane's Island* by Marjorie Allee, Houghton; *Truce of the Wolf and Other Tales of Old Italy* by Mary Gould Davis, Harcourt

1933 *Young Fu of the Upper Yangtze* by Elizabeth Foreman Lewis, Winston
Honor Books: *Swift Rivers* by Cornelia Meigs, Little; *The Railroad to Freedom* by Hildegarde Swift, Harcourt; *Children of the Soil* by Nora Burglon, Doubleday

1934 *Invincible Louisa* by Cornelia Meigs, Little
Honor Books: *The Forgotten Daughter* by Caroline Snedeker, Doubleday; *Swords of Steel* by Elsie Singmaster, Houghton; *ABC Bunny* by Wanda Gág, Coward; *Winged Girl of Knossos* by Erik Berry, Appleton; *New Land* by Sarah Schmidt, McBride; *Big Tree of Bunlahy* by Padraic Colum, Macmillan; *Glory of the Seas* by Agnes Hewes, Knopf; *Apprentice of Florence* by Anne Kyle, Houghton

1935 *Dobry* by Monica Shannon, Viking
Honor Books: *Pageant of Chinese History* by Elizabeth Seeger, Longmans; *Davy Crockett* by Constance Rourke, Harcourt; *Day on Skates* by Hilda Van Stockum, Harper

1936 *Caddie Woodlawn* by Carol Brink, Macmillan
Honor Books: *Honk, The Moose* by Phil Strong, Dodd; *The Good Master* by Kate Seredy, Viking; *Young Walter Scott* by Elizabeth Janet Gray, Viking; *All Sail Set* by Armstrong Sperry, Winston

1937 Roller Skates by Ruth Sawyer, Viking
Honor Books: *Phoebe Fairchild: Her Book* by Lois Lenski, Stokes; *Whistler's*

Van by Idwal Jones, Viking; *Golden Basket* by Ludwig Bemelmans, Viking; *Winterbound* by Margery Bianco, Viking; *Audubon* by Constance Rourke, Harcourt; *The Codfish Musket* by Agnes Hewes, Doubleday

1938 *The White Stag* by Kate Seredy, Viking
Honor Books: *Pecos Bill* by James Cloyd Bowman, Little; *Bright Island* by Mabel Robinson, Random; *On the Banks of Plum Creek* by Laura Ingalls Wilder, Harper

1939 *Thimble Summer* by Elizabeth Enright, Rinehart
Honor Books: *Nino* by Valenti Angelo, Viking; *Mr. Popper's Penguins* by Richard and Florence Atwater, Little; *"Hello the Boat!"* by Phyllis Crawford, Holt; *Leader by Destiny: George Washington, Man and Patriot* by Jeanette Eaton, Harcourt; *Penn* by Elizabeth Janet Gray, Viking

1940 *Daniel Boone* by James Daugherty, Viking
Honor Books: *The Singing Tree* by Kate Seredy, Viking; *Runner of the Mountain Tops* by Mabel Robinson, Random; *By the Shores of Silver Lake* by Laura Ingalls Wilder, Harper; *Boy with a Pack* by Stephen W. Meader, Harcourt

1941 *Call It Courage* by Armstrong Sperry, Macmillan
Honor Books: *Blue Willow* by Doris Gates, Viking; *Young Mac of Fort Vancouver* by Mary Jane Carr, T. Crowell; *The Long Winter* by Laura Ingalls Wilder, Harper; *Nansen* by Anna Gertrude Hall, Viking

1942 *The Matchlock Gun* by Walter D. Edmonds, Dodd
Honor Books: *Little Town on the Prairie* by Laura Ingalls Wilder, Harper; *George Washington's World* by Genevieve Foster, Scribner's; *Indian Captive: The Story of Mary Jemison* by Lois Lenski, Lippincott; *Down Ryton Water* by Eva Roe Gaggin, Viking

1943 *Adam of the Road* by Elizabeth Janet Gray, Viking
Honor Books: *The Middle Moffat* by Eleanor Estes, Harcourt; *Have You Seen Tom Thumb?* by Mabel Leigh Hunt, Lippincott

1944 *Johnny Tremain* by Esther Forbes, Houghton
Honor Books: *These Happy Golden Years* by Laura Ingalls Wilder, Harper; *Fog Magic* by Julia Sauer, Viking; *Rufus M.* by Eleanor Estes, Harcourt; *Mountain Born* by Elizabeth Yates, Coward

1945 *Rabbit Hill* by Robert Lawson, Viking
Honor Books: *The Hundred Dresses* by Eleanor Estes, Harcourt; *The Silver Pencil* by Alice Dalgliesh, Scribner's; *Abraham Lincoln's World* by Genevieve Foster, Scribner's; *Lone Journey: The Life of Roger Williams* by Jeanette Eaton, Harcourt

1946 *Strawberry Girl* by Lois Lenski, Lippincott
Honor Books: *Justin Morgan Had a Horse* by Marguerite Henry, Rand; *The Moved-Outers* by Florence Crannell Means, Houghton; *Bhimsa, The Dancing Bear* by Christine Weston, Scribner's; *New Found World* by Katherine Shippen, Viking

1947 *Miss Hickory* by Carolyn Sherwin Bailey, Viking
Honor Books: *Wonderful Year* by Nancy Barnes, Messner; *Big Tree* by Mary and Conrad Buff, Viking; *The Heavenly Tenants* by William Maxwell, Harper; *The Avion My Uncle Flew* by Cyrus Fisher, Appleton; *The Hidden Treasure of Glaston* by Eleanore Jewett, Viking

1948 *The Twenty-one Balloons* by William Pène duBois, Lothrop
Honor Books: *Pancakes-Paris* by Claire Huchet Bishop, Viking; *Li Lun, Lad of Courage* by Carolyn Treffinger, Abingdon; *The Quaint and Curious Quest of Johnny Longfoot* by Catherine Besterman, Bobbs; *The Cow-Tail Switch, and Other West African Stories* by Harold Courlander, Holt; *Misty of Chincoteague* by Marguerite Henry, Rand

1949 *King of the Wind* by Marguerite Henry, Rand
Honor Book: *Seabird* by Holling C. Holling, Houghton; *Daughter of the Mountains* by Louise Rankin, Viking; *My Father's Dragon* by Ruth S. Gannett, Random; *Story of the Negro* by Arna Bontemps, Knopf

1950 *The Door in the Wall* by Marguerite de Angeli, Doubleday
Honor Books: *Tree of Freedom* by Rebecca Caudill, Viking; *The Blue Cat of Castle Town* by Catherine Coblentz, Longmans; *Kildee House* by Rutherford Montgomery, Doubleday; *George Washington* by Genevieve Foster, Scribner's; *Song of the Pines* by Walter and Marion Havighurst, Winston

1951 *Amos Fortune, Free Man* by Elizabeth Yates, Aladdin
Honor Books: *Better Known as Johnny Appleseed* by Mabel Leigh Hunt, Lippincott; *Gandhi, Fighter Without a Sword* by Jeanette Eaton, Morrow; *Abraham Lincoln, Friend of the People* by Clara Ingram Judson, Follett; *The Story of Appleby Capple* by Anne Parrish, Harper

1952 *Ginger Pye* by Eleanor Estes, Harcourt
Honor Books: *Americans Before Columbus* by Elizabeth Baity, Viking; *Minn of the Mississippi* by Holling C. Holling, Houghton; *The Defender* by Nicholas Kalashnikoff, Scribner's; *The Light at Tern Rock* by Julia Sauer, Viking; *The Apple and the Arrow* by Mary and Conrad Buff, Houghton

1953 *Secret of the Andes* by Ann Nolan Clark, Viking
Honor Books: *Charlotte's Web* by E. B. White, Harper; *Moccasin Trail* by Eloise McGraw, Coward; *Red Sails to Capri* by Ann Weil, Viking; *The Bears of Hemlock Mountain* by Alice Dalgliesh, Scribner's; *Birthdays of Freedom*, Vol. 1 by Genevieve Foster, Scribner's

1954 *. . . and now Miguel* by Joseph Krumgold, T. Crowell
Honor Books: *All Alone* by Claire Huchet Bishop, Viking; *Shadrach* by Meindert DeJong, Harper; *Hurry Home Candy* by Meindert DeJong, Harper; *Theodore Roosevelt, Fighting Patriot* by Clara Ingram Judson, Follett; *Magic Maize* by Mary and Conrad Buff, Houghton

1955 *The Wheel on the School* by Meindert DeJong, Harper
Honor Books: *The Courage of Sarah Noble* by Alice Dalgliesh, Scribner's; *Banner in the Sky* by James Ullman, Lippincott

1956 *Carry on, Mr. Bowditch* by Jean Lee Latham, Houghton
Honor Books: *The Secret River* by Marjorie Kinnan Rawlings, Scribner's; *The Golden Name Day* by Jennie Lindquist, Harper; *Men, Microscopes, and Living Things* by Katherine Shippen, Viking

1957 *Miracles on Maple Hill* by Virginia Sorensen, Harcourt
Honor Books: *Old Yeller* by Fred Gipson, Harper; *The House of Sixty Fathers* by Meindert DeJong, Harper; *Mr. Justice Holmes* by Clara Ingram Judson, Follett; *The Corn Grows Ripe* by Dorothy Rhoads, Viking; *Black Fox of Lorne* by Marguerite de Angeli, Doubleday

1958 *Rifles for Watie* by Harold Keith, T. Crowell

Honor Books: *The Horsecatcher* by Mari Sandoz, Westminster; *Gone-Away Lake* by Elizabeth Enright, Harcourt; *The Great Wheel* by Robert Lawson, Viking; *Tom Paine, Freedom's Apostle* by Leo Gurko, T. Crowell

1959 *The Witch of Blackbird Pond* by Elizabeth George Speare, Houghton
Honor Books: *The Family Under the Bridge* by Natalie S. Carlson, Harper; *Along Came a Dog* by Meindert DeJong, Harper; *Chucaro: Wild Pony of the Pampa* by Francis Kalnay, Harcourt; *The Perilous Road* by William O. Steele, Harcourt

1960 *Onion John* by Joseph Krumgold, T. Crowell
Honor Books: *My Side of the Mountain* by Jean George, Dutton; *America Is Born* by Gerald W. Johnson, Morrow; *The Gammage Cup* by Carol Kendall, Harcourt

1961 *Island of the Blue Dolphins* by Scott O'Dell, Houghton
Honor Books: *America Moves Forward* by Gerald W. Johnson, Morrow; *Old Ramon* by Jack Schaefer, Houghton; *The Cricket in Times Square* by George Selden, Farrar

1962 *The Bronze Bow* by Elizabeth George Speare, Houghton
Honor Books: *Frontier Living* by Edwin Tunis, World; *The Golden Goblet* by Eloise McGraw, Coward; *Belling the Tiger* by Mary Stolz, Harper

1963 *A Wrinkle in Time* by Madeleine L'Engle, Farrar
Honor Books: *Thistle and Thyme* by Sorche Nic Leodhas, Holt; *Men of Athens* by Olivia Coolidge, Houghton

1964 *It's Like This, Cat* by Emily Cheney Neville, Harper
Honor Books: *Rascal* by Sterling North, Dutton; *The Loner* by Esther Wier, McKay

1965 *Shadow of a Bull* by Maia Wojciechowska, Atheneum
Honor Book: *Across Five Aprils* by Irene Hunt, Follett

1966 *I, Juan de Pareja* by Elizabeth Borten de Trevino, Farrar
Honor Books: *The Black Cauldron* by Lloyd Alexander, Holt; *The Animal Family* by Randall Jarrell, Pantheon; *The Noonday Friends* by Mary Stolz, Harper

1967 *Up a Road Slowly* by Irene Hunt, Follett
Honor Books: *The King's Fifth* by Scott O'Dell, Houghton; *Zlateh the Goat and Other Stories* by Isaac Bashevis Singer, Harper; *The Jazz Man* by Mary H. Weik, Atheneum

1968 *From the Mixed-Up Files of Mrs. Basil E. Frankweiler* by E. L. Konigsburg, Atheneum
Honor Books: *Jennifer, Hecate, Macbeth, William McKinley, and Me, Elizabeth* by E. L. Konigsburg, Atheneum; *The Black Pearl* by Scott O'Dell, Houghton; *The Fearsome Inn* by Isaac Bashevis Singer, Scribner's; *The Egypt Game* by Zilpha Keatley Snyder, Atheneum

1969 *The High King* by Lloyd Alexander, Holt
Honor Books: *To Be a Slave* by Julius Lester, Dial; *When Shlemiel Went to Warsaw and Other Stories* by Isaac Bashevis Singer, Farrar

1970 *Sounder* by William H. Armstrong, Harper
Honor Books: *Our Eddie* by Sulamith Ish-Kishor, Pantheon; *The Many Ways of Seeing: An Introduction to the Pleasures of Art* by Janet Gaylord Moore, World; *Journey Outside* by Mary Q. Steele, Viking

1971 *Summer of the Swans* by Betsy Byars, Viking
Honor Books: *Kneeknock Rise* by Natalie Babbitt, Farrar; *Enchantress from the Stars* by Sylvia Louise Engdahl, Atheneum; *Sing Down the Moon* by Scott O'Dell, Houghton

1972 *Mrs. Frisby and the Rats of NIMH* by Robert C. O'Brien, Atheneum
Honor Books: *Incident at Hawk's Hill* by Allan W. Eckert, Little; *The Planet of Junior Brown* by Virginia Hamilton, Macmillan; *The Tombs of Atuan* by Ursula K. Le Guin, Atheneum; *Annie and the Old One* by Miska Miles, Atlantic/Little; *The Headless Cupid* by Zilpha Keatley Snyder, Atheneum

1973 *Julie of the Wolves* by Jean George, Harper
Honor Books: *Frog and Toad Together* by Arnold Lobel, Harper; *The Upstairs Room* by Johanna Reiss, Crowell; *The Witches of Worm* by Zilpha Keatley Snyder, Atheneum

1974 *The Slave Dancer* by Paula Fox, Bradbury
Honor Book: *The Dark Is Rising* by Susan Cooper, Atheneum/McElderry

1975 *M. C. Higgins, the Great* by Virginia Hamilton, Macmillan
Honor Books: *Figgs & Phantoms* by Ellen Raskin, Dutton; *My Brother Sam Is Dead* by James Lincoln Collier & Christopher Collier, Four Winds; *The Perilous Guard* by Elizabeth Marie Pope, Houghton; *Philip Hall Likes Me, I Reckon Maybe* by Bette Greene, Dial

1976 *The Grey King* by Susan Cooper, Atheneum/McElderry
Honor Books: *The Hundred Penny Box* by Sharon Bell Mathis, Viking; *Dragonwings* by Lawrence Yep, Harper

1977 *Roll of Thunder, Hear My Cry* by Mildred D. Taylor, Dial
Honor Books: *Abel's Island* by William Steig, Farrar; *A String in the Harp* by Nancy Bond, Atheneum/McElderry

1978 *Bridge to Terabithia* by Katherine Paterson, Crowell
Honor Books: *Anpao: An American Indian Odyssey* by Jamake Highwater, Lippincott; *Ramona and Her Father* by Beverly Cleary, Morrow

1979 *The Westing Game* by Ellen Raskin, Dutton
Honor Book: *The Great Gilly Hopkins* by Katherine Paterson, Crowell

1980 *A Gathering of Days: A New England Girl's Journal, 1830–32* by Joan Blos, Scribner's
Honor Book: *The Road from Home: The Story of an Armenian Girl* by David Kherdian, Greenwillow

1981 *Jacob Have I Loved* by Katherine Paterson, Crowell
Honor Books: *The Fledgling* by Jane Langton, Harper; *A Ring of Endless Light* by Madeleine L'Engle, Farrar

1982 *A Visit to William Blake's Inn: Poems for Innocent and Experienced Travelers* by Nancy Willard, Harcourt
Honor Books: *Ramona Quimby, Age 8* by Beverly Cleary, Morrow; *Upon the Head of a Goat* by Aranka Siegal, Farrar

1983 *Dicey's Song* by Cynthia Voigt, Atheneum
Honor Books: *The Blue Sword* by Robin McKinley, Greenwillow; *Dr. De Soto* by William Steig, Farrar; *Graven Images* by Paul Fleischman, Harper; *Homesick: My Own Story* by Jean Fritz, Putnam; *Sweet Whispers, Brother Rush* by Virginia Hamilton, Philomel

1984 *Dear Mr. Henshaw* by Beverly Cleary, Morrow
Honor Books: *The Sign of the Beaver* by Elizabeth George Speare,
Houghton; *A Solitary Blue* by Cynthia Voigt, Atheneum; *Sugaring Time* by
Kathryn Lasky, Macmillan; *The Wish Giver* by Bill Brittain, Harper
1985 *The Hero and the Crown* by Robin McKinley, Greenwillow
Honor Books: *Like Jake and Me* by Mavis Jukes, Knopf; *The Moves Make the
Man* by Bruce Brooks, Harper; *One-Eyed Cat* by Paula Fox, Bradbury
1986 *Sarah, Plain and Tall* by Patricia MacLachlan, Harper
Honor Books: *Commodore Perry in the Land of the Shogun* by Rhoda
Blumberg, Lothrop; *Dogsong* by Gary Paulsen, Bradbury
1987 *The Whipping Boy* by Sid Fleischman, Greenwillow
Honor Books: *On My Honor* by Marion Dane Bauer, Clarion; *Volcano:
The Eruption and Healing of Mount St. Helens* by Patricia Lauber,
Bradbury; *A Fine White Dust* by Cynthia Rylant, Bradbury
1988 *Lincoln: A Photobiography* by Russell Freedman, Clarion/Houghton
Honor Books: *After the Rain* by Norma Fox Mazer, Morrow; *Hatchet* by
Gary Paulsen, Bradbury
1989 *Joyful Noise: Poems for Two Voices* by Paul Fleischman, Harper
Honor Books: *In the Beginning: Creation Stories from Around the World* by
Virginia Hamilton, Harcourt; *Scorpions* by Walter Dean Myers, Harper

THE CALDECOTT MEDAL

Since 1938, the Association of Library Service to Children of the American Library
Association has annually awarded the Caldecott Medal to the illustrator of the most
distinguished picture book published in the United States in the preceding year. The
recipient must be a citizen or resident of the United States. The medal is named in
tribute to the well-loved English illustrator Randolph Caldecott (1846–1886).

1938 *Animals of the Bible* by Helen Dean Fish, ill. by Dorothy P. Lathrop,
Lippincott
Honor Books: *Seven Simeons* written and ill. by Boris Artzybasheff, Viking;
Four and Twenty Blackbirds by Helen Dean Fish, ill. by Robert Lawson,
Stokes
1939 *Mei Li* written and ill. by Thomas Handforth, Doubleday
Honor Books: *The Forest Pool* written and ill. by Laura Adams Armer,
Longmans; *Wee Gillis* by Munro Leaf, ill. by Robert Lawson, Viking; *Snow
White and the Seven Dwarfs* written and ill. by Wanda Gág, Coward; *Barkis*
written and ill. by Clare Newberry, Harper; *Andy and the Lion* written and
ill. by James Daugherty, Viking
1940 *Abraham Lincoln* written and ill. by Ingri and Edgar Parin d'Aulaire,
Doubleday
Honor Books: *Cock-A-Doodle Doo . . .* written and ill. by Berta and Elmer
Hader, Macmillan; *Madeline* written and ill. by Ludwig Bemelmans,
Viking; *The Ageless Story,* ill. by Lauren Ford, Dodd
1941 *They Were Strong and Good* written and ill. by Robert Lawson, Viking
Honor Book: *April's Kittens* written and ill. by Clare Newberry, Harper

1942 *Make Way for Ducklings* written and ill. by Robert McCloskey, Viking
Honor Books: *An American ABC* written and ill. by Maud and Miska
Petersham, Macmillan; *In My Mother's House* by Ann Nolan Clark, ill. by
Velino Herrera, Viking; *Paddle-to-the-Sea* written and ill. by Holling C.
Holling, Houghton; *Nothing at All* written and ill. by Wanda Gág,
Coward

1943 *The Little House* written and ill. by Virginia Lee Burton, Houghton
Honor Books: *Dash and Dart* written and ill. by Mary and Conrad Buff,
Viking; *Marshmallow* written and ill. by Clare Newberry, Harper

1944 *Many Moons* by James Thurber, ill. by Louis Slobodkin, Harcourt
Honor Books: *Small Rain: Verses from the Bible* selected by Jessie Orton
Jones, ill. by Elizabeth Orton Jones, Viking; *Pierre Pigeon* by Lee
Kingman, ill. by Arnold E. Bare, Houghton; *The Mighty Hunter* written
and ill. by Berta and Elmer Hader, Macmillan; *A Child's Good Night Book*
by Margaret Wise Brown, ill. by Jean Charlot, W. R. Scott; *Good Luck
Horse* by Chih-Yi Chan, ill. by Plao Chan, Whittlesey

1945 *Prayer for a Child* by Rachel Field, ill. by Elizabeth Orton Jones,
Macmillan
Honor Books: *Mother Goose* ill. by Tasha Tudor, Walck; *In the Forest*
written and ill. by Marie Hall Ets, Viking; *Yonie Wondernose* written and
ill. by Marguerite de Angeli, Doubleday; *The Christmas Anna Angel* by
Ruth Sawyer, ill. by Kate Seredy, Viking

1946 *The Rooster Crows . . .* (traditional Mother Goose) ill. by Maud and Miska
Petersham, Macmillan
Honor Books: *Little Lost Lamb* by Golden MacDonald, ill. by Leonard
Weisgard, Doubleday; *Sing Mother Goose* by Opal Wheeler, ill. by Marjorie
Torrey, Dutton; *My Mother Is the Most Beautiful Woman in the World* by
Becky Reyher, ill. by Ruth Gannett, Lothrop; *You Can Write Chinese*
written and ill. by Kurt Wiese, Viking

1947 *The Little Island* by Golden MacDonald, ill. by Leonard Weisgard,
Doubleday
Honor Books: *Rain Drop Splash* by Alvin Tresselt, ill. by Leonard
Weisgard, Lothrop; *Boats on the River* by Marjorie Flack, ill. by Jay Hyde
Barnum, Viking; *Timothy Turtle* by Al Graham, ill. by Tony Palazzo,
Viking; *Pedro, the Angel of Olvera Street* written and ill. by Leo Politi,
Scribner's; *Sing in Praise: A Collection of the Best Loved Hymns* by Opal
Wheeler, ill. by Marjorie Torrey, Dutton

1948 *White Snow, Bright Snow* by Alvin Tresselt, ill. by Roger Duvoisin,
Lothrop Honor Books: *Stone Soup* written and ill. by Marcia Brown,
Scribner's; *McElligot's Pool* written and ill. by Dr. Seuss, Random; *Bambino
the Clown* written and ill. by George Schreiber, Viking; *Roger and the Fox*
by Lavinia Davis, ill. by Hildegard Woodward, Doubleday; *Song of Robin
Hood* ed. by Anne Malcolmson, ill. by Virginia Lee Burton, Houghton

1949 *The Big Snow* written and ill. by Berta and Elmer Hader, Macmillan
Honor Books: *Blueberries for Sal* written and ill. by Robert McCloskey,
Viking; *All Around the Town* by Phyllis McGinley, ill. by Helen Stone,
Lippincott; *Juanita* written and ill. by Leo Politi, Scribner's; *Fish in the Air*
written and ill. by Kurt Wiese, Viking

1950 *Song of the Swallows* written and ill. by Leo Politi, Scribner's
Honor Books: *America's Ethan Allen* by Stewart Holbrook, ill. by Lynd
Ward, Houghton; *The Wild Birthday Cake* by Lavinia Davis, ill. by
Hildegard Woodward, Doubleday; *The Happy Day* by Ruth Krauss, ill. by
Marc Simont, Harper; *Bartholomew and the Oobleck* written and ill. by Dr.
Seuss, Random; *Henry Fisherman* written and ill. by Marcia Brown,
Scribner's

1951 *The Egg Tree* written and ill. by Katherine Milhous, Scribner's
Honor Books: *Dick Whittington and His Cat* written and ill. by Marcia
Brown, Scribner's; *The Two Reds* by Will, ill. by Nicolas, Harcourt; *If I
Ran the Zoo* written and ill. by Dr. Seuss, Random; *The Most Wonderful
Doll in the World* by Phyllis McGinley, ill. by Helen Stone, Lippincott;
T-Bone, the Baby Sitter written and ill. by Clare Newberry, Harper

1952 *Finders Keepers* by Will, ill. by Nicolas, Harcourt
Honor Books: *Mr. T. W. Anthony Woo* written and ill. by Marie Hall Ets,
Viking; *Skipper John's Cook* written and ill. by Marcia Brown, Scribner's;
All Falling Down by Gene Zion, ill. by Margaret Bloy Graham, Harper;
Bear Party written and ill. by William Pène du Bois, Viking; *Feather
Mountain* written and ill. by Elizabeth Olds, Houghton

1953 *The Biggest Bear* written and ill. by Lynd Ward, Houghton
Honor Books: *Puss in Boots* by Charles Perrault, ill. and tr. by Marcia
Brown, Scribner's; *One Morning in Maine* written and ill. by Robert
McCloskey, Viking; *Ape in a Cape* written and ill. by Fritz Eichenberg,
Harcourt; *The Storm Book* by Charlotte Zolotow, ill. by Margaret Bloy
Graham, Harper; *Five Little Monkeys* written and ill. by Juliet Kepes,
Houghton

1954 *Madeline's Rescue* written and ill. by Ludwig Bemelmans, Viking
Honor Books: *Journey Cake, Ho!* by Ruth Sawyer, ill. by Robert
McCloskey, Viking; *When Will the World Be Mine?* by Miriam Schlein, ill.
by Jean Charlot, W. R. Scott; *The Steadfast Tin Soldier* by Hans Christian
Andersen, ill. by Marcia Brown, Scribner's; *A Very Special House* by Ruth
Krauss, ill. by Maurice Sendak, Harper; *Green Eyes* written and ill. by A.
Birnbaum, Capitol

1955 *Cinderella, or the Little Glass Slipper* by Charles Perrault, tr. and ill. by
Marcia Brown, Scribner's
Honor Books: *Book of Nursery and Mother Goose Rhymes*, ill. by Marguerite
de Angeli, Doubleday; *Wheel on the Chimney* by Margaret Wise Brown, ill.
by Tibor Gergely, Lippincott; *The Thanksgiving Story* by Alice Dalgliesh,
ill. by Helen Sewell, Scribner's

1956 *Frog Went A-Courtin'* ed. by John Langstaff, ill. by Feodor Rojankovsky,
Harcourt
Honor Books: *Play with Me* written and ill. by Marie Hall Ets, Viking;
Crow Boy written and ill. by Taro Yashima, Viking

1957 *A Tree Is Nice* by Janice May Udry, ill. by Marc Simont, Harper
Honor Books: *Mr. Penny's Race Horse* written and ill. by Marie Hall Ets,
Viking; *1 Is One* written and ill. by Tasha Tudor, Walck; *Anatole* by Eve
Titus, ill. by Paul Galdone, McGraw; *Gillespie and the Guards* by Benjamin

Elkin, ill. by James Daugherty, Viking; *Lion* written and ill. by William Pène du Bois, Viking

1958 *Time of Wonder* written and ill. by Robert McCloskey, Viking
Honor Books: *Fly High, Fly Low* written and ill. by Don Freeman, Viking; *Anatole and the Cat* by Eve Titus, ill. by Paul Galdone, McGraw

1959 *Chanticleer and the Fox* adapted from Chaucer and ill. by Barbara Cooney, T. Crowell
Honor Books: *The House That Jack Built* written and ill. by Antonio Frasconi, Harcourt; *What Do You Say, Dear?* by Sesyle Joslin, ill. by Maurice Sendak, W. R. Scott; *Umbrella* written and ill. by Taro Yashima, Viking

1960 *Nine Days to Christmas* by Marie Hall Ets and Aurora Labastida, ill. by Marie Hall Ets, Viking
Honor Books: *Houses from the Sea* by Alice E. Goudey, ill. by Adrienne Adams, Scribner's; *The Moon Jumpers* by Janice May Udry, ill. by Maurice Sendak, Harper

1961 *Baboushka and the Three Kings* by Ruth Robbins, ill. by Nicolas Sidjakov, Parnassus
Honor Book: *Inch by Inch* written and ill. by Leo Lionni, Obolensky

1962 *Once a Mouse* . . . written and ill. by Marcia Brown, Scribner's
Honor Books: *The Fox Went Out on a Chilly Night* written and ill. by Peter Spier, Doubleday; *Little Bear's Visit* by Else Holmelund Minarik, ill. by Maurice Sendak, Harper; *The Day We Saw the Sun Come Up* by Alice E. Goudey, ill. by Adrienne Adams, Scribner's

1963 *The Snowy Day* written and ill. by Ezra Jack Keats, Viking
Honor Books: *The Sun Is a Golden Earring* by Natalie M. Belting, ill. by Bernarda Bryson, Holt; *Mr. Rabbit and the Lovely Present* by Charlotte Zolotow, ill. by Maurice Sendak, Harper

1964 *Where the Wild Things Are* written and ill. by Maurice Sendak, Harper
Honor Books: *Swimmy* written and ill. by Leo Lionni, Pantheon; *All in the Morning Early* by Sorche Nic Leodhas, ill. by Evaline Ness, Holt; *Mother Goose and Nursery Rhymes* ill. by Philip Reed, Atheneum

1965 *May I Bring a Friend?* by Beatrice Schenk de Regniers, ill. by Beni Montresor, Atheneum
Honor Books: *Rain Makes Applesauce* by Julian Scheer, ill. by Marvin Bileck, Holiday; *The Wave* by Margaret Hodges, ill. by Blair Lent, Houghton; *A Pocketful of Cricket* by Rebecca Caudill, ill. by Evaline Ness, Holt

1966 *Always Room for One More* by Sorche Nic Leodhas, ill. by Nonny Hogrogian, Holt
Honor Books: *Hide and Seek Fog* by Alvin Tresselt, ill. by Roger Duvoisin, Lothrop; *Just Me* written and ill. by Marie Hall Ets, Viking; *Tom Tit Tot* written and ill. by Evaline Ness, Scribner's

1967 *Sam, Bangs & Moonshine* written and ill. by Evaline Ness, Holt
Honor Book: *One Wide River to Cross* by Barbara Emberley, ill. by Ed Emberley, Prentice

1968 *Drummer Hoff* by Barbara Emberley, ill by Ed Emberley, Prentice
Honor Books: *Frederick* written and ill. by Leo Lionni, Pantheon; *Seashore*

Story, written and ill. by Taro Yashima, Viking; *The Emperor and the Kite* by Jane Yolen, ill. by Ed Young, World

1969 *The Fool of the World and the Flying Ship* by Arthur Ransome, ill. by Uri Shulevitz, Farrar
Honor Book: *Why the Sun and the Moon Live in the Sky* by Elphinstone Dayrell, ill. by Blair Lent, Houghton

1970 *Sylvester and the Magic Pebble* written and ill. by William Steig, Windmill
Honor Books: *Goggles!* written and ill. by Ezra Jack Keats, Macmillan; *Alexander and the Wind-Up Mouse* written and ill. by Leo Lionni, Pantheon; *Pop Corn & Ma Goodness* by Edna Mitchell Preston, ill. by Robert Andrew Parker, Viking; *Thy Friend, Obadiah* written and ill. by Brinton Turkle, Viking; *The Judge* by Harve Zemach, ill. by Margot Zemach, Farrar

1971 *A Story—A Story* written and ill. by Gail E. Haley, Atheneum
Honor Books: *The Angry Moon* by William Sleator, ill. by Blair Lent, Atlantic/Little; *Frog and Toad Are Friends* written and ill. by Arnold Lobel, Harper; *In the Night Kitchen* written and ill. by Maurice Sendak, Harper

1972 *One Fine Day* written and ill. by Nonny Hogrogian, Macmillan
Honor Books: *If All the Seas Were One Sea* written and ill. by Janina Domanska, Macmillan; *Moja Means One: Swahili Counting Book* by Muriel Feelings, ill. by Tom Feelings, Dial; *Hildilid's Night* by Cheli Duran Ryan, ill. by Arnold Lobel, Macmillan

1973 *The Funny Little Woman* retold by Arlene Mosel, ill. by Blair Lent, Dutton
Honor Books: *Anansi the Spider* adapted and ill. by Gerald McDermott, Holt; *Hosie's Alphabet* by Hosea, Tobias, and Lisa Baskin, ill. by Leonard Baskin, Viking; *Snow-White and the Seven Dwarfs* translated by Randall Jarrell, ill. by Nancy Ekholm Burkert, Farrar; *When Clay Sings* by Byrd Baylor, ill. by Tom Bahti, Scribner's

1974 *Duffy and the Devil* by Harve Zemach, ill. by Margot Zemach, Farrar
Honor Books: *Three Jovial Huntsmen* written and ill. by Susan Jeffers, Bradbury; *Cathedral: The Story of Its Construction* written and ill. by David Macaulay, Houghton

1975 *Arrow to the Sun* adapted and ill. by Gerald McDermott, Viking
Honor Book: *Jambo Means Hello* by Muriel Feelings, ill. by Tom Feelings, Dial

1976 *Why Mosquitoes Buzz in People's Ears* retold by Verna Aardema, ill. by Leo and Diane Dillon, Dial
Honor Books: *The Desert Is Theirs* by Byrd Baylor, ill. by Peter Parnall, Scribner's; *Strega Nona* retold and ill. by Tomie dePaola, Prentice

1977 *Ashanti to Zulu: African Traditions* by Margaret Musgrove, ill. by Leo and Diane Dillon, Dial
Honor Books: *The Amazing Bone* written and ill. by William Steig, Farrar; *The Contest* retold and ill. by Nonny Hogrogian, Greenwillow; *Fish for Supper* written and ill. by M. B. Goffstein, Dial; *The Golem* written and ill. by Beverly Brodsky McDermott, Lippincott; *Hawk, I'm Your Brother* by Byrd Baylor, ill. by Peter Parnall, Scribner's

1978 *Noah's Ark*, ill. by Peter Spier, Doubleday

Honor Books: *Castle* written and ill. by David Macaulay, Houghton; *It Could Always Be Worse* retold and ill. by Margot Zemach, Farrar

1979 *The Girl Who Loved Wild Horses* written and ill. by Paul Goble, Bradbury
Honor Books: *Freight Train* written and ill. by Donald Crews, Greenwillow; *The Way to Start a Day* by Byrd Baylor, ill. by Peter Parnall, Scribner's

1980 *Ox-Cart Man* by Donald Hall, ill. by Barbara Cooney, Viking
Honor Books: *Ben's Trumpet* written and ill. by Rachel Isadora, Greenwillow; *The Garden of Abdul Gasazi* written and ill. by Chris Van Allsburg, Houghton

1981 *Fables* written and ill. by Arnold Lobel, Harper
Honor Books: *The Grey Lady and the Strawberry Snatcher,* ill. by Molly Bang, Four Winds; *Truck,* ill. by Donald Crews, Greenwillow; *Mice Twice* written and ill. by Joseph Low, Atheneum; *The Bremen-Town Musicians,* ill. by Ilse Plume, Doubleday

1982 *Jumanji* written and ill. by Chris Van Allsburg, Houghton
Honor Books: *Where the Buffaloes Begin* by Olaf Baker, ill. by Stephen Gammell, Warne; *On Market Street* by Arnold Lobel, ill. by Anita Lobel, Greenwillow; *Outside Over There* by Maurice Sendak, Harper; *A Visit to William Blake's Inn* by Nancy Willard, ill. by Alice and Martin Provensen, Harcourt

1983 *Shadow* by Blaise Cendrars, trans. and ill. by Marcia Brown, Scribner's
Honor Books: *When I Was Young in the Mountains* by Cynthia Rylant, ill. by Diane Goode, Dutton; *A Chair for My Mother* by Vera B. Williams, Greenwillow

1984 *The Glorious Flight: Across the Channel with Louis Blériot* by Alice and Martin Provensen, Viking
Honor Books: *Ten, Nine, Eight* by Molly Bang, Greenwillow; *Little Red Riding Hood* retold and ill. by Trina Schart Hyman, Holiday House

1985 *St. George and the Dragon* retold by Margaret Hodges, ill. by Trina Schart Hyman, Little, Brown
Honor Books: *Hansel and Gretel* retold by Rika Lesser, ill. by Paul O. Zelinsky, Dodd; *Have You Seen My Duckling?* by Nancy Tafuri, Greenwillow; *The Story of Jumping Mouse* by John Steptoe, Lothrop

1986 *The Polar Express* written and ill. by Chris Van Allsburg, Houghton
Honor Books: *The Relatives Came* by Cynthia Rylant, ill. by Stephen Gammell, Bradbury; *King Bidgood's in the Bathtub* by Audrey Wood, ill. by Don Wood, Harcourt

1987 *Hey, Al!* by Arthur Yorinks, ill. by Richard Egielski, Farrar
Honor Books: *The Village of Round and Square Houses* written and ill. by Ann Grifalconi, Little, Brown; *Alphabetics* written and ill. by Suse MacDonald, Bradbury; *Rumpelstiltskin* retold and ill. by Paul O. Zelinsky, Dutton

1988 *Owl Moon* by Jane Yolen, ill. by John Schoenherr, Philomel
Honor Book: *Mufaro's Beautiful Daughters* written and ill. by John Steptoe, Lothrop

1989 *Song and Dance Man* by Karen Ackerman, ill. by Stephen Gammell, Knopf

Honor Books: *Free Fall* written and ill. by David Wiesner, Lothrop; *Goldilocks and the Three Bears* retold and ill. by James Marshall, Dial; *Mirandy and Brother Wind* by Patricia McKissack, ill. by Jerry Pinkney, Knopf; *The Boy of the Three-Year Nap* by Diane Snyder, ill. by Allen Say, Houghton

THE LAURA INGALLS WILDER AWARD

This award was first given in 1954 and was presented every five years from 1960–1980. Since 1980, it has been given every three years. The medal is administered by the Association of Library Service to Children of the American Library Association. The award recognizes an author or illustrator whose books, published in the United States, have over a period of years made a substantial contribution to literature for children.

1954 Laura Ingalls Wilder
1960 Clara Ingram Judson
1965 Ruth Sawyer
1970 E. B. White
1975 Beverly Cleary
1980 Theodore Geisel (Dr. Seuss)
1983 Maurice Sendak
1986 Jean Fritz
1989 Elizabeth George Speare

INTERNATIONAL READING ASSOCIATION CHILDREN'S BOOK AWARD

Given for the first time in 1975, this award is presented annually for a book that was published in the preceding year and written by an author "who shows unusual promise in the children's book field." Sponsored by the Institute for Reading Research, the award is administered by the International Reading Association.

1975 *Transport 7-41-R* by T. Degens, Viking
1976 *Dragonwings* by Laurence Yep, Harper
1977 *A String in the Harp* by Nancy Bond, McElderry/Atheneum
1978 *A Summer to Die* by Lois Lowry, Houghton
1979 *Reserved for Mark Anthony Crowder* by Alison Smith, Dutton
1980 *Words by Heart* by Ouida Sebestyen, Atlantic/Little
1981 *My Own Private Sky* by Delores Beckman, Dutton
1982 *Good Night, Mr. Tom* by Michelle Magorian, Kestrel/Penguin (Great Britain); Harper (U.S.A.)

1983 *The Darkangel* by Meredith Ann Pierce, Atlantic/Little
1984 *Ratha's Creature* by Clare Bell, Atheneum
1985 *Badger on the Barge* by Janni Howker, Greenwillow
1986 *Prairie Songs* by Pam Conrad, ill. by Daryl S. Zudeck, Harper
1987 *The Line Up Book* by Marisabina Russo, Greenwillow
1988 *Third Story Cat* by Leslie Baker, Little, Brown

NATIONAL COUNCIL OF TEACHERS OF ENGLISH AWARD FOR EXCELLENCE IN POETRY FOR CHILDREN

This award is presented by the National Council of Teachers of English to a living American poet in recognition of the poet's aggregate body of work in children's literature. It was given annually until 1982, and now is presented every three years, instead of yearly.

1977 David McCord
1978 Aileen Fisher
1979 Karla Kuskin
1980 Myra Cohn Livingston
1981 Eve Merriam
1982 John Ciardi
1985 Lilian Moore
1988 Arnold Adoff

THE SCOTT O'DELL AWARD FOR HISTORICAL FICTION

The award was established in 1981 by Mr. O'Dell and is administered by the Advisory Committee of the Bulletin of the Center for Children's Books. The book must be historical fiction, have unusual literary merit, be written by a citizen of the United States, and be set in the New World. It must have been published in the previous year by a United States publisher and must be written for children or young adults. In some years, no award may be given.

1984 *The Sign of the Beaver* by Elizabeth George Speare, Houghton
1985 *The Fighting Ground* by Avi [Wortis], Harper & Row
1986 *Sarah, Plain and Tall* by Patricia MacLachlan, Harper & Row
1987 *Streams to the River* by Scott O'Dell, Houghton
1988 *Charlie Skedaddle* by Patricia Beatty, Morrow

BOSTON GLOBE—HORN BOOK AWARDS

These awards have been given annually in the fall since 1967 by *The Boston Globe* and *The Horn Book Magazine*. Through 1975, two awards were given—for outstanding text and for outstanding illustration; in 1976 the award categories were changed to (and currently are) Outstanding Fiction or Poetry, Outstanding Nonfiction, and Outstanding Illustration.

1967 Text: *The Little Fishes* by Erik Christian Haugaard, Houghton
Illustration: *London Bridge Is Falling Down* by Peter Spier, Doubleday

1968 Text: *The Spring Rider* by John Lawson, Crowell
Illustration: *Tikki Tikki Tembo* by Arlene Mosel, ill. by Blair Lent, Holt

1969 Text: *A Wizard of Earthsea* by Ursula K. Le Guin, Houghton
Illustration: *The Adventures of Paddy Pork* by John S. Goodall, Harcourt

1970 Text: *The Intruder* by John Rowe Townsend, Lippincott
Illustration: *Hi, Cat!* by Ezra Jack Keats, Macmillan

1971 Text: *A Room Made of Windows* by Eleanor Cameron, Atlantic-Little, Brown
Illustration: *If I Built a Village* by Kazue Mizumura, Crowell

1972 Text: *Tristan and Iseult* by Rosemary Sutcliff, Dutton
Illustration: *Mr. Gumpy's Outing* by John Burningham, Holt

1973 Text: *The Dark Is Rising* by Susan Cooper, McElderry/Atheneum
Illustration: *King Stork* by Trina Schart Hyman, Little, Brown

1974 Text: *M. C. Higgins, The Great* by Virginia Hamilton, Macmillan
Illustration: *Jambo Means Hello* by Muriel Feelings, ill. by Tom Feelings, Dial

1975 Text: *Transport 7-41-R* by T. Degens, Viking
Illustration: *Anno's Alphabet* by Mitsumasa Anno, Crowell

1976 Fiction: *Unleaving* by Jill Paton Walsh, Farrar
Nonfiction: *Voyaging to Cathay: Americans in the China Trade* by Alfred Tamarin and Shirley Glubok, Viking
Illustration: *Thirteen* by Remy Charlip and Jerry Joyner, Parents

1977 Fiction: *Child of the Owl* by Laurence Yep, Harper
Nonfiction: *Chance, Luck and Destiny* by Peter Dickinson, Atlantic-Little, Brown
Illustration: *Granfa' Grig Had a Pig and Other Rhymes* by Wallace Tripp, Little, Brown

1978 Fiction: *The Westing Game* by Ellen Raskin, Dutton
Nonfiction: *Mischling, Second Degree: My Childhood in Nazi Germany* by Ilse Koehn, Greenwillow
Illustration: *Anno's Journey* by Mitsumasa Anno, Philomel

1979 Fiction: *Humbug Mountain* by Sid Fleischman, Atlantic-Little Brown
Nonfiction: *The Road From Home: The Story of an Armenian Girl* by David Kherdian, Greenwillow
Illustration: *The Snowman* by Raymond Briggs, Random House

1980 Fiction: *Conrad's War* by Andrew Davies, Crown
Nonfiction: *Building: The Fight Against Gravity* by Mario Salvadori, McElderry/Atheneum
Illustration: *The Garden of Abdul Gasazi* by Chris Van Allsburg, Houghton

1981 Fiction: *The Leaving* by Lynn Hall, Scribner's
Nonfiction: *The Weaver's Gift* by Kathryn Lasky, Warne
Illustration: *Outside Over There* by Maurice Sendak, Harper

1982 Fiction: *Playing Beatie Bow* by Ruth Park, Atheneum

Nonfiction: *Upon the Head of the Goat: A Childhood in Hungary, 1939-1944* by Aranka Siegal, Farrar

Illustration: *A Visit to William Blake's Inn: Poems for Innocent and Experienced Travelers* by Nancy Willard, ill. by Alice and Martin Provensen, Harcourt

1983 Fiction: *Sweet Whispers, Brother Rush* by Virginia Hamilton, Philomel

Nonfiction: *Behind Barbed Wire: The Imprisonment of Japanese Americans During World War II* by Daniel S. Davis, Dutton

Illustration: *A Chair for My Mother* by Vera B. Williams, Greenwillow

1984 Fiction: *A Little Fear* by Patricia Wrightson, McElderry/Atheneum

Nonfiction: *The Double Life of Pocahontas* by Jean Fritz, Putnam

Illustration: *Jonah and the Great Fish* retold and ill. by Warwick Hutton, McElderry/Atheneum

1985 Fiction: *The Moves Make the Man* by Bruce Brooks, Harper

Nonfiction: *Commodore Perry in the Land of the Shogun* by Rhoda Blumberg, Lothrop

Illustration: *Mama Don't Allow* by Thatcher Hurd, Harper

1986 Fiction: *In Summer Light* by Zibby Oneal, Viking Kestrel

Illustration: *The Paper Crane* by Molly Bang, Greenwillow

Nonfiction: *Auks, Rocks and the Odd Dinosaur* by Peggy Thomson, Crowell

1987 Fiction: *Rabble Starkey* by Lois Lowru, Houghton

Illustration: *Mufaro's Beautiful Daughters* by John Steptoe, Lothrop

Nonfiction: *Pilgrims of Plimouth* by Marcia Sewall, Atheneum

1988 Fiction: *The Friendship* by Mildred Taylor, Dial

Illustration: *The Boy of the Three-Year Nap* by Diane Snyder, Houghton

Nonfiction: *Anthony Burns: The Defeat and Triumph of a Fugitive Slave* by Virginia Hamilton, Knopf

THE CARNEGIE MEDAL

The British Library Association gives this medal each year to the author of a distinguished children's book written in English and first published in the United Kingdom. The award was established in 1937.

1936 *Pigeon Post* by Arthur Ransome, Cape

1937 *The Family from One End Street* by Eve Garnett, Muller

1938 *The Circus Is Coming* by Noel Streatfield, Dent

1939 *Radium Woman* by Eleanor Doorly, Heinemann

1940 *Visitors from London* by Kitty Barne, Dent

1941 *We Couldn't Leave Dinah* by Mary Treadgold, Penguin

1942 *The Little Grey Men,* by B. B., Eyre & Spottiswoode

1943 No Award

1944 *The Wind on the Moon* by Eric Linklater, Macmillan

1945 No Award

1946 *The Little White Horse* by Elizabeth Goudge, Brockhampton Press

1947 *Collected Stories for Children* by Walter de la Mare, Faber

1948 *Sea Change* by Richard Armstrong, Dent

1949 *The Story of Your Home* by Agnes Allen, Transatlantic
1950 *The Lark on the Wing* by Elfrida Vipont Foulds, Oxford
1951 *The Wool-Pack* by Cynthia Harnett, Methuen
1952 *The Borrowers* by Mary Norton, Dent
1953 *A Valley Grows Up* by Edward Osmond, Oxford
1954 *Knight Crusader* by Ronald Welch, Oxford
1955 *The Little Bookroom* by Eleanor Farjeon, Oxford
1956 *The Last Battle* by C. S. Lewis, Bodley Head
1957 *A Grass Rope* by William Mayne, Oxford
1958 *Tom's Midnight Garden* by Philippa Pearce, Oxford
1959 *The Lantern Bearers* by Rosemary Sutcliff, Oxford
1960 *The Making of Man* by I. W. Cornwall, Phoenix
1961 *A Stranger at Green Knowe* by Lucy Boston, Faber
1962 *The Twelve and the Genii* by Pauline Clarke, Faber
1963 *Time of Trial* by Hester Burton, Oxford
1964 *Nordy Banks* by Sheena Porter, Oxford
1965 *The Grange at High Force* by Philip Turner, Oxford
1966 No Award
1967 *The Owl Service* by Alan Garner, Collins
1968 *The Moon in the Cloud* by Rosemary Harris, Faber
1969 *The Edge of the Cloud* by K. M. Peyton, Oxford
1970 *The God Beneath the Sea* by Leon Garfield and Edward Blishen, Kestrel
1971 *Josh* by Ivan Southall, Angus & Robertson
1972 *Watership Down* by Richard Adams, Rex Collings
1973 *The Ghost of Thomas Kempe* by Penelope Lively, Heinemann
1974 *The Stronghold* by Mollie Hunter, Hamilton
1975 *The Machine-Gunners* by Robert Westall, Macmillan
1976 *Thunder and Lightnings* by Jan Mark, Kestrel
1977 *The Turbulent Term of Tyke Tiler* by Gene Kemp, Faber
1978 *The Exeter Blitz* by David Rees, Hamish Hamilton
1979 *Tulku* by Peter Dickinson, Dutton
1980 *City of Gold* by Peter Dickinson, Gollancz
1981 *The Scarecrows* by Robert Westall, Chatto & Windus
1982 *The Haunting* by Margaret Mahy, Dent
1983 *Handles* by Jan Mark, Kestrel
1984 *The Changeover* by Margaret Mahy, Dent
1985 *Storm* by Kevin Crossley-Holland, Heinemann
1986 *Granny Was a Buffer Girl* by Berlie Doherty, Methuen
1987 *The Ghost Drum* by Susan Price, Faber

THE KATE GREENAWAY MEDAL

The Kate Greenaway Medal, given annually by the British Library Association, recognizes the outstanding illustration of a children's book first published in the United Kingdom in the preceding year.

1956 *Tim All Alone* written and ill. by Edward Ardizzone, Oxford

1957 *Mrs. Easter and the Storks* written and ill. by V. H. Drummond, Faber
1958 No Award
1959 *Kashtanka and a Bundle of Ballads* written and ill. by William Stobbs, Oxford
1960 *Old Winkle and the Seagulls* by Elizabeth Rose, ill. by Gerald Rose, Faber
1961 *Mrs. Cockle's Cat* by Philippa Pearce, ill. by Anthony Maitland, Kestrel
1962 *Brian Wildsmith's ABC* written and ill. by Brian Wildsmith, Oxford
1963 *Borka* written and ill. by John Burningham, Jonathan Cape
1964 *Shakespeare's Theatre* written and ill. by C. W. Hodges, Oxford
1965 *Three Poor Tailors* written and ill. by Victor Ambrus, Hamilton
1966 *Mother Goose Treasury* written and ill. by Raymond Briggs, Hamilton
1967 *Charlie, Charlotte & the Golden Canary* written and ill. by Charles Keeping, Oxford
1968 *Dictionary of Chivalry* by Grant Uden, ill. by Pauline Baynes, Kestrel
1969 *The Quangle-Wangle's Hat* by Edward Lear, ill. by Helen Oxenbury, Heinemann; *Dragon of an Ordinary Family* by Margaret Mahy, ill. by Helen Oxenbury, Heinemann
1970 *Mr. Gumpy's Outing* written and ill. by John Burningham, Jonathan Cape
1971 *The Kingdom Under the Sea* written and ill. by Jan Pienkowski, Jonathan Cape
1972 *The Woodcutter's Duck* written and ill. by Krystyna Turska, Hamilton
1973 *Father Christmas* written and ill. by Raymond Briggs, Hamilton
1974 *The Wind Blew* written and ill. by Pat Hutchins, Bodley Head
1975 *Horses in Battle* written and ill. by Victor Ambrus, Oxford; *Mishka* written and ill. by Victor Ambrus, Oxford
1976 *The Post Office Cat* written and ill. by Gail E. Haley, Bodley Head
1977 *Dogger* written and ill. by Shirley Hughes, Bodley Head
1978 *Each Peach Pear Plum* written and ill. by Janet and Allan Ahlberg, Kestrel
1979 *Haunted House* written and ill. by Jan Piénkowski, Dutton
1980 *Mr. Magnolia* by Quentin Blake, Jonathan Cape
1981 *The Highwayman* by Alfred Noyes, ill. by Charles Keeping, Oxford
1982 *Long Neck and Thunder Foot*, Kestrel; and *Sleeping Beauty and Other Favorite Fairy Tales*, both ill. by Michael Foreman, Gollancz
1983 *Gorilla* by Anthony Browne, Julia McRae Books
1984 *Hiawatha's Childhood* by Errol LeCain, Faber
1985 *Sir Gawain and the Loathly Lady* by Selina Hastings, ill. by Juan Wijngaard, Walker
1986 *Snow White in New York* by Fiona French, Oxford
1987 *Crafty Chameleon* by Adrienne Kennaway, Hodder & Stoughton

THE CANADIAN LIBRARY AWARDS

This award is given each year (since 1947) by the Canadian Library Association to a distinguished children's book authored by a citizen of Canada. A similar medal has been given annually (since 1954) to a significant children's book published in French.

1947 *Starbuck Valley Winter* by Roderick Haig-Brown, Collins
1948 *Kristli's Trees* by Mabel Dunham, Hale
1949 No Award
1950 *Franklin of the Arctic* by Richard S. Lambert, McClelland & Stewart
1951 No Award
1952 *The Sun Horse* by Catherine Anthony Clark, Macmillan of Canada
1953 No Award
1954 No English Award
    Mgr. de Laval by Emile S. J. Gervais, Comité des Fondateurs de l'Eglise Canadienne
1955 No Awards
1956 *Train for Tiger Lily* by Louise Riley, Macmillan of Canada
    No French Award
1957 *Glooskap's Country* by Cyrus Macmillan, Oxford
    No French Award
1958 *Lost in the Barrens* by Farley Mowat, Little
    Le Chevalier du Roi by Béatrice Clément, Les Editions de l'Atelier
1959 *The Dangerous Cove* by John F. Hayes, Copp Clark
    Un Drôle de Petit Cheval by Hélène Flamme, Editions Léméac
1960 *The Golden Phoenix* by Marius Barbeau and Michael Hornyansky, Walck
    L'Eté Enchanté by Paule Daveluy, Les Editions de l'Atelier
1961 *The St. Lawrence* by William Toye, Oxford
    Plantes Vagabondes by Marcelle Gauvreau, Centre de Psychologie et de Pédagogie
1962 No English Award
    Les Iles du Roi Maha Maha II by Claude Aubry, Les Editions du Pélican
1963 *The Incredible Journey* by Sheila Burnford, Little, Brown
    Drôle d'Automne by Paule Daveluy, Les Editions du Pélican
1964 *The Whale People* by Roderick Haig-Brown, William Collins of Canada
    Feerie by Cécile Chabot, Librairie Beauchemin Ltée.
1965 *Tales of Nanabozho* by Dorothy Reid, Oxford
    Le Loup de Noël by Claude Aubry, Centre de Psychologie de Montréal
1966 *Tikta'Liktak* by James Houston, Kestrel
    Le Chêne des Tempêtes by Andrée Mallet-Hobden, Fides
    The Double Knights by James McNeal, Walck
    Le Wapiti by Monique Corriveau, Jeunesse
1967 *Raven's Cry* by Christie Harris, McClelland & Stewart
    No French Award
1968 *The White Archer* by James Houston, Kestrel
    Légendes Indiennes du Canada by Claude Mélancon, Editions du Jour
1969 *And Tomorrow the Stars* by Kay Hill, Dodd
    No French Award
1970 *Sally Go Round the Sun* by Edith Fowke, McClelland & Stewart
    Le Merveilleuse Histoire de la Naissance by Lionel Gendron, Les Editions de l'Homme
1971 *Cartier Discovers the St. Lawrence* by William Toye, Oxford University
    La Surprise de Dame Chenille by Henriette Major, Centre de Psychologie de Montréal

1972 *Mary of Mile 18* by Ann Blades, Tundra
No French Award
1973 *The Marrow of the World* by Ruth Nichols, Macmillan of Canada
Le Petit Sapin Qui A Poussé sur une Étoile by Simone Bussières, Presses
Laurentiennes
1974 *The Miraculous Hind* by Elizabeth Cleaver, Holt of Canada
No French Award
1975 *Alligator Pie* by Dennis Lee, Macmillan of Canada
No French Award
1976 *Jacob Two-Two Meets the Hooded Fang* by Mordecai Richler, Knopf
No French Award
1977 *Mouse Woman and the Vanished Princesses* by Christie Harris, McClelland &
Stewart
No French Award
1978 *Garbage Delight* by Dennis Lee, Macmillan
No French Award
1979 *Hold Fast* by Kevin Major, Clarke, Irwin
No French Award
1980 *River Runners: A Tale of Hardship and Bravery* by James Houston,
McClelland & Stewart
No French Award
1981 *The Violin Maker's Gift* by Donn Kushner, Macmillan of Canada
1982 *The Root Cellar* by Janet Lunn, Lester & Orpen Dennys
1983 *Up to Low* by Brian Doyle, Groundwood
1984 *Sweetgrass* by Jan Hudson, Tree Frog Press
1985 *Mama's Going to Buy a Mockingbird* by Jean Little, Penguin
1986 *Julie* by Cora Taylor, Western
1987 *Shadow in Hawthorn Bay* by Janet Lunn, Scribner
1988 *A Handful of Time* by Kit Pearson, Viking

Each year since 1971, the Canadian Library Association has given the Amelia
Frances Howard-Gibbon medal for excellence in illustration of a children's book
published in Canada. The recipient must be a citizen or resident of Canada.

1971 *The Wind Has Wings* ed. by Mary Alice Downie and Barbara Robertson,
ill. by Elizabeth Cleaver, Oxford
1972 *A Child in Prison Camp* written and ill. by Shizuye Takashima, Tundra
1973 *Au Dela du Soleil/Beyond the Sun* written and ill. by Jacques de Roussan,
Tundra
1974 *A Prairie Boy's Winter* written and ill. by William Kurelek, Tundra
1975 *The Sleighs of My Childhood/Les Traineaux de Mon Enfance* written and ill.
by Carlos Italiano, Tundra
1976 *A Prairie Boy's Summer* written and ill. by William Kurelek, Tundra
1977 *Down by Jim Long's Stage: Rhymes for Children and Young Fish* by Al
Pittman, ill. by Pam Hall, Breakwater
1978 *The Loon's Necklace* by William Toye, ill. by Elizabeth Cleaver, Oxford
1979 *A Salmon for Simon* by Betty Waterton, ill. by Ann Blades, Douglas &
McIntyre

1980 *The Twelve Dancing Princesses* written and ill. by Laszlo Gal, Methuen
1981 *The Trouble with Princesses* by Douglas Tait, McClelland & Stewart
1982 *Ytek and the Arctic Orchid: An Inuit Legend* by Heather Woodall, Douglas & McIntyre
1983 *Chester's Barn* by Lindee Climo, Tundra
1984 *Zoom at Sea* by Tim Wynne-Jones, ill. by Ken Nutt, Douglas & McIntyre
1985 *Chin Chiang and the Dragon's Dance* by Ian Wallace, Groundwood
1986 *Zoom Away* by Tim Wynne-Jones, ill. by Ken Nutt, Douglas & McIntyre
1987 *Moonbeam on a Cat's Ear* written and ill. by Marie-Louise Gay, Stoddard
1988 *Rainy Day Magic* by Marie-Louise Gay, Hodder & Stoughton

THE HANS CHRISTIAN ANDERSEN AWARD

The International Board on Books for Young People awards this honor every two years to a living author whose works have made a substantial and international contribution to children's literature. This award was established in 1956. Since 1966, the Board has also awarded an artist's medal.

1956 Eleanor Farjeon (Great Britain)
1958 Astrid Lindgren (Sweden)
1960 Erich Kästner (Germany)
1962 Meindert DeJong (U.S.A.)
1964 René Guillot (France)
1966 Author: Tove Jansson (Finland)
Illustrator: Alois Carigiet (Switzerland)
1968 Authors: James Krüss (Germany); Jose Maria Sanchez-Silva (Spain)
Illustrator: Jiri Trnka (Czechoslovakia)
1970 Author: Gianni Rodari (Italy)
Illustrator: Maurice Sendak (U.S.A.)
1972 Author: Scott O'Dell (U.S.A.)
Illustrator: Ib Spang Olsen (Denmark)
1974 Author: Maria Gripe (Sweden)
Illustrator: Farshid Mesghali (Iran)
1976 Author: Cecil Bødker (Denmark)
Illustrator: Tatjana Mawrina (U.S.S.R.)
1978 Author: Paula Fox (U.S.A.)
Illustrator: Otto S. Svend (Denmark)
1980 Author: Bohumil Riha (Czechoslovakia)
Illustrator: Suekichi Akaba (Japan)
1982 Author: Lygia Gojunga Nunes (Brazil)
Illustrator: Zbigniew Rychlicki (Poland)
1984 Author: Christine Nostlinger (Austria)
Illustrator: Mitsumasa Anno (Japan)
1986 Author: Patricia Wrightson (Australia)
Illustrator: Robert Ingpen (Australia)
1988 Author: Annie M. G. Schmidt (Netherlands)
Illustrator: Dusan Kallay (Yugoslavia)

AUSTRALIAN CHILDREN'S BOOKS OF THE YEAR AWARDS

Book of the Year

1946 *Karrawingi, the Emu* by Leslie Rees, Sands

1947 No Award

1948 *Shackleton's Argonauts* by Frank Hurley, Angus & Robertson

1949 *Whalers of the Midnight Sun* by Alan Villiers, Angus & Robertson

1950 No Award

1951 *Verity of Sydney Town* by Ruth Williams, Angus & Robertson

1952 *The Australia Book* by Eve Pownall, Sands

1953 *Aircraft of Today & Tomorrow* by J. H. and W. D. Martin, Angus & Robertson
Good Luck to the Rider by Joan Phipson, Angus & Robertson

1954 *Australian Legendary Tales* by K. L. Parker, Angus & Robertson

1955 *The First Walkabout* by H. A. Lindsay and N. B. Tindale, Kestrel

1956 *The Crooked Snake* by Patricia Wrightson, Angus & Robertson

1957 *The Boomerang Book of Legendary Tales* by Enid Moodie-Heddle, Kestrel

1958 *Tiger in the Bush* by Nan Chauncy, Oxford

1959 *Devil's Hill* by Nan Chauncy, Oxford
Sea Menace by John Gunn, Constable

1960 *All the Proud Tribesmen* by Kylie Tennant, Macmillan

1961 *Tangara* by Nan Chauncy, Oxford

1962 *The Racketty Street Gang* by H. L. Evers, Hodder & Stoughton
Rafferty Rides a Winner by Joan Woodbery, Parrish

1963 *The Family Conspiracy* by Joan Phipson, Angus & Robertson

1964 *The Green Laurel* by Eleanor Spence, Oxford

1965 *Pastures of the Blue Crane* by Hesba F. Brinsmead, Oxford

1966 *Ash Road* by Ivan Southall, Angus & Robertson

1967 *The Min Min* by Mavis Thorpe Clark, Landsdowne

1968 *To the Wild Sky* by Ivan Southall, Angus & Robertson

1969 *When Jays Fly to Barbmo* by Margaret Balderson, Oxford

1970 *Uhu* by Annette Macarther-Onslow, Ure Smith

1971 *Bread and Honey* by Ivan Southall, Angus & Robertson

1972 *Longtime Passing* by Hesba F. Brinsmead, Angus & Robertson

1973 *Family at the Lookout* by Noreen Shelly, Oxford

1974 *The Nargun and the Stars* by Patricia Wrightson, Hutchinson

1975 No Award

1976 *Fly West* by Ivan Southall, Angus & Robertson

1977 *The October Child* by Eleanor Spence, Oxford

1978 *The Ice Is Coming* by Patricia Wrightson, Hutchinson

1979 *The Plum-Rain Scroll* by Ruth Manley, Hodder & Stoughton

1980 *Displaced Person* by Lee Harding, Hyland House

1981 *Playing Beatie Bow* by Ruth Park, Nelson

1982 *The Valley Between* by Colin Thiele, Rigby

1983 *Master of the Grove* by Victor Kelleher, Penguin

1984 *A Little Fear* by Patricia Wrightson, Hutchinson

1985 *The True Story of Lilli Stubeck* by James Aldridge, Hyland House
1986 *The Green Wind* by Thurley Fowler, Rigby
1987 *All We Know* by Simon French, Angus & Robertson
Pigs Might Fly by Emily Rodda, illustrated by Noela Young, Angus & Robertson

Picture Book of the Year

1956 *Wish and the Magic Nut* by Peggy Barnard, ill. by Shelia Hawkins, Sands
1957 No Award
1958 *Piccaninny Walkabout* by Axel Poignant, Angus & Robertson
1959–1964 No Awards
1965 *Hugo's Zoo* by Elisabeth MacIntyre, Angus & Robertson
1966–1968 No Awards
1969 *Sly Old Wardrobe* by Ivan Southall, ill. by Ted Greenwood, Cheshire
1970 No Award
1971 *Waltzing Matilda* by A. B. Paterson, ill. by Desmond Digby
1972–1973 No Awards
1974 *The Bunyip of Berkeley's Creek* by Jenny Wagner, ill. by Ron Brooks, Kestrel
1975 *The Man from Ironbark* by A. B. Paterson, ill. by Quentin Hole, Collins
1976 *The Rainbow Serpent* by Dick Roughsey, Collins
1977 *ABC of Monsters* by Deborah Niland, Hodder & Stoughton
1978 *John Brown, Rose and the Midnight Cat* by Jenny Wagner, ill. by Ron Brooks, Kestrel
1979 *The Quinkins* written and ill. by Percy Trezise and Dick Roughsey, Collins
1980 *One Dragon's Dream* by Peter Pavey, Nelson
1981 No Award
1982 *Sunshine* by Jan Ormerod, Kestrel
1983 *Who Sank the Boat?* by Pamela Allen, Nelson
1984 *Bertie and the Bear* by Pamela Allen, Nelson
1985 (Commended) *Home in the Sky* written and ill. by Jeannie Baker and Junko Morimoto, retold by Helen Smith, Collins
1986 *Felix and Alexander* written and ill. by Terry Denton, Oxford
1987 *Kojuro and the Bears* adapted by Helen Smith, ill. by Junko Morimoto, Collins

THE PHOENIX AWARD

The Phoenix Award is given by the Children's Literature Association to a book published twenty years ago that did not receive any major award for excellence.

1985 *Mark of the Horse Lord* by Rosemary Sutcliff, Walck
1986 *Queenie Peavy* by Robert Burch, Viking
1987 *Smith* by Leon Garfield, Constable
1988 *The Rider and His Horse* by Eric Christian Haugaard, Houghton
1989 *The Night Watchman* by Helen Cresswell, Macmillan

THE MILDRED L. BATCHELDER AWARD

This award is given for the best translation of a work published in a language other than English.

1968 *The Little Man* by Erich Kastner, trans. by James Kirkup, ill. by Rick Schreiter, Knoff, 1966

1969 *Don't Take Teddy* by Babbis Friis-Baastad, trans. by Lise Somme McKinnon, Scribner, 1967

1970 *Wildcat under Glass* by Alki Zei, trans. by Edward Fenton, Holt, 1968

1971 *In The Land of Ur: The Discovery of Ancient Mesopotamia* by Hans Baumann, trans. by Stella Humphries, ill. by Hans Peter Renner, Pantheon, 1969

1972 *Friedrich* by Hans Peter Richter, trans. by Edite Kroll, Holt, 1970

1973 *Pulga* by Siny Rose Van Iterson, trans. by Alexander and Alison Gode, Morrow, 1971

1974 *Petros' War* by Alki Zei, trans. by Edward Fenton, Dutton, 1972

1975 *An Old Tale Carved Out of Stone* by Aleksandr M. Linevski, trans. by Maria Polushkin, Crown, 1973

1976 *The Cat and Mouse Who Shared a House* written and ill. by Ruth Hurlimann, trans. by Anthea Bell, Walck, 1974

1977 *The Leopard* by Cecil Bodker, ill. by Gunnar Poulsen, Atheneum, 1975

1978 No Award

1979 *Konrad* by Christine Nostlinger, trans. by Anthea Bell, ill. by Carol Nicklaus, Watts, 1977
Rabbit Island by Jorg Steiner, trans. by Ann Conrad Lammers, ill. by Jorg Muller, Harcourt, 1978

1980 *The Sound of Dragon's Feet* by Alki Zei, trans. by Edward Fenton, Dutton, 1979

1981 *The Winter When Time Was Frozen* by Els Pelgrom, trans. by Raphael and Maryka Rudnik, Morrow, 1980

1982 *The Battle Horse* by Harry Kullman, trans. by George Blecher and Lone Thygesen-Blecher, Bradbury, 1981

1983 *Hiroshima no Pika* written and ill. by Toshi Maruki, Lothrop, Lee & Shepard, 1982

1984 *Ronia, the Robber's Daughter* by Astrid Lindgren, trans. by Patricia Crampton, Viking, 1983

1985 *The Island on Bird Street* by Uri Orlev, trans. from the Hebrew by Hillel Halkin, Houghton Mifflin, 1984, © 1983

1986 *Rose Blanche* by Christophe Gallaz and Roberto Innocenti, trans. by Martha Coventry and Richard Graglia, ill. by Roberto Innocenti, Creative Education, 1985

1987 *No Hero for the Kaiser* by Rudolf Frank, trans. by Patricia Crampton, ill. by Klaus Steffans, Lothrop, Lee & Shepard, 1986

1988 *If You Didn't Have Me* by Ulf Nilsson, ill. by Eva Eriksson, trans. by Lone Thygesen-Blecher and George Blecher, McElderry

1989 *Crutches* by Peter Härtling, Lothrop, Lee & Shepard

Selected Magazines for Children

Child Life
1100 Waterway Boulevard
Indianapolis, IN 46206

Children's Digest
1100 Waterway Boulevard
Indianapolis, IN 46206

Children's Playmate
1100 Waterway Boulevard
Indianapolis, IN 46206

Cobblestone
Cobblestone Publishing, Inc.
20 Grove Street
Peterborough, NH 03458

Cricket
Carus Corporation
Box 300
Peru, IL 61354

Ebony, Jr.
820 S. Michigan Avenue
Chicago, IL 60605

Humpty Dumpty
1100 Waterway Boulevard
Indianapolis, IN 46206

Jack and Jill
1100 Waterway Boulevard
Indianapolis, IN 46206

National Geographic
Department 00289
17th & M Streets N.W.
Washington, D.C. 20036

Prism Magazine
1040 Bayview Drive, Suite 210
Ft. Lauderdale, FL 33304

Ranger Rick (nature)
National Wildlife Federation
1400 16th Street, N.W.
Washington, D.C. 20006

Your Big Back Yard (nature)
National Wildlife Federation
1400 16th Street N.W.
Washington, D.C. 20036

Selected Reviewing Media for Children's Books

Appraisal (science books)

ALA (American Library Association)
  Booklist

The ALAN Review

**Bulletin of the Center for
  Children's Books**

Children's Catalog

**Children's Literature Assembly
  Bulletin (NCTE)**

Elementary English

The Horn Book Magazine

Kirkus Reviews

Library Journal

The New Advocate

Parents' Choice

Publishers Weekly

School Library Journal

Wilson Library Journal

Glossary
of Literary Terms

Allegory: a literary work in which characters and actions represent abstractions
Alliteration: repetition of initial consonant sound
Allusion: indirect reference to something or someone outside the literary work
Antagonist: force in conflict with protagonist; usually designated as self, another person, society, nature
Anthropomorphism: the giving of human qualities to nonhuman animals or objects
Assonance: repetition of vowel sound in phrase

Backdrop setting: generalized or relatively unimportant setting
Biography: the history of the life of an individual
Ballad: verse narrative of love, courage, the supernatural. May be of folk origin

Cadence: rhythmic flow in prose
Character: human being, real or personified animal, personified object taking a role in literature
Character development: filling out a variety of character traits to provide the complexity of a human being
Chronological order: events related in the order of their happening
Classic: literary work that lives to be read and reread
Cliché: overused term which has lost meaning
Cliffhanger: unresolved suspense that concludes a chapter
Climax: action that precipitates resolution of conflict
Closed ending: conclusion leaving no plot questions unanswered
Coincidence: chance concurrence of events
Complication: early action; part of rising plot
Conflict: struggle between protagonist and opposing force

Connotation: associative or emotional meaning of a word
Consonance: repetition of consonant sound in phrase

Denotation: explicit or dictionary meaning
Denouement: final or closing action following climax
Diction: choice of words or wording
Didacticism: in literature, an instructive or moralistic lesson often at the expense of entertainment
Dramatic or objective point of view: third-person narration in which actions and speeches are recorded without interpretation
Dynamic character: one who changes in the course of the story

Echo: words repeated in familiar pattern
Epic: long narrative poem about a heroic figure whose actions reveal the values of the culture
Episodic plot: plot with independent, short storylike chapters linked by characters or theme more than by action
Explicit theme: theme stated clearly in the story
Exposition: presentation of essential information needed for understanding of the action

Fable: very brief story, usually with animal characters, that states a didactic theme or moral
Falling action: final or closing action following climax; denouement
Fantasy: story about the nonexistent or unreal in which action may depend upon magic or the supernatural
Figurative language: devices making comparisons, saying one thing in terms of another
First-person point of view: "I" narration in which a person's experiences, thoughts, and feelings are told by himself/herself
Flashback: return to event that occurred before present scene; retrospect
Flat character: one that is little developed
Foil: a character whose contrasting traits point up those of a central character
Folk epic: long narrative poem passed down by word of mouth; often about a hero
Folk rhyme: rhymes passed down by word of mouth
Folktale: story passed down by word of mouth
Foreshadowing: hints of what is to come

Genre: a kind or type of literature that has a common set of characteristics

High fantasy: a type of fantasy characterized by its focus on good and evil
Hyperbole: exaggeration or overstatement

Imagery: verbal appeals to the senses
Implicit theme: theme implied from the story's context
Inevitability: sense that it had to happen; in literature a sense that the outcome was necessary and inescapable

Integral setting: essential and specific setting which influences character, plot, and theme

Legend: a traditional narrative of a people, often with some basis in historical truth

Limerick: five-line humorous vese with traditional rhythm and rhyme pattern

Limited omniscient point of view: third-person narration in which story is seen through the mind(s) of one or few characters

Lyric poem: songlike poem, compact expression of feeling

Metaphor: implied comparison

Meter: somewhat regular rhythm pattern of stressed and unstressed syllables in a line of poetry

Motif: recurring element in literary work, often found in traditional literature

Myth: story originating in folk beliefs and showing supernatural forces operating

Narrative order: sequence in which events are recounted

Narrative poem: poem that tells a story

Objective or dramatic point of view: third-person narration in which actions and speeches are recorded without interpretation

Omniscient point of view: an all-knowing writer tells the story in third person

Onomatopoeia: words that sound like their meanings, such as *meow, moo*

Open ending: final outcome of conflict unknown

Parody: imitation of known form for comic effect

Personification: giving human traits to nonhuman beings or objects

Picture book: a book that relies upon pictures to enlarge or illuminate the text; the pictures may even provide a correlative story of their own

Plot: sequence of events involving character in conflict

Poetry: distilled and imaginative expression of feeling

Point of view: the mind(s) through which the reader sees the story

Primary theme: major underlying and unifying truth of a story

Progressive plot: plot with central climax

Protagonist: central character in the conflict

Pun: humorous use of a word with several meanings

Realism: story based upon the possible, though not necessarily probable

Resolution: falling action following climax

Rhyme: repetition of identical or similar stressed sound or sounds

Rhythm: recurring flow of strong and weak beats

Rising action: exposition and complications that lead to the climax

Round character: a fully developed or three-dimensional character

Science fiction: story that relies upon invention or extension of nature's laws, not upon the supernatural or magical

Secondary theme: less important or minor theme of a story

Sensationalism: focus upon the thrilling or startling

Sentiment: emotion or feeling

Sentimentality: overuse of sentiment, false arousal of feelings

Setting: the time and place in which the action occurs

Simile: stated comparison, usually using *like* or *as*

Static character: one who does not change in the course of the story

Stereotype: character possessing expected traits of a group rather than being an individual

Stock character: flat character with very little development; found in numerous stories, such as folktales

Style: mode of expression

Suspense: state of uncertainty that keeps the reader reading

Symbol: person, object, situation, or action operating on two levels of meaning—literal and figurative or suggestive

Theme statement giving the underlying truth about people, society, or the human condition, either explicitly or implicitly

Tone: writer's attitude toward his or her subject and readers

Touchstone: example of excellence referred to for comparison

Understatement: reverse exaggeration or playing down

Verse: here used to denote rhyming metrical structure with less emotional intensity than poetry

Vicarious experience: experience available to readers through reading about it rather than living it

Wordless picture book: a book that has no written narrative but tells a story with pictures alone

Acknowledgments

(**p. 5,** *passim*) From *Charlotte's Web* by E. B. White, illustrated by Garth Williams. Copyright 1952, renewed 1980 by E. B. White. Illustrations copyright 1952, renewed 1980 by Garth Williams. Reprinted by permission of Harper & Row, Publishers, Inc.

(**p. 42**) Leon Garfield, *Fair's Fair*. Garden City, NY: Doubleday & Company, Inc., 1983.

(**p. 62**) Ursula K. LeGuin, *A Wizard of Earthsea*. Berkeley: Parnassus, 1968.

(**p. 68,** *passim*) Gary Paulsen, *Hatchet*. New York: Bradbury Press, 1987.

(**p. 69,** *passim*) Excerpts from *The Borrowers,* copyright 1953 by Mary Norton and renewed 1981 by Mary Norton, Joe Krush, and Beth Krush, reprinted by permission of Harcourt Brace Jovanovich, Inc.

(**p. 112**) Excerpts from *Anne Frank: The Diary of a Young Girl* by Anne Frank. Copyright 1952 by Otto H. Frank. Used by permission of Doubleday, a division of Bantam, Doubleday, Dell Publishing Group, Inc. and Vallentine Mitchell & Co. Ltd.

(**p. 125**) Madeleine L'Engle, *A Ring of Endless Light*. New York: Farrar, Straus, & Giroux, 1980.

(**p. 125**) Alice Childress, *A Hero Ain't Nothin' but a Sandwich*. New York: Coward, McCann, 1973.

(**p. 127**) Cynthia Voight, *Dicey's Song*. New York: Random House, 1982.

(**p. 149**) Joan Aiken, *The Stolen Lake*. New York: Delacorte, 1981.

(**p. 149**) Bruce Brooks, *The Moves Make the Man*. New York: Harper & Row, 1984.

(**pp. 149-150**) Reprinted with permission of Macmillan Publishing Company from *The Ugly Duckling* retold by Jean Lee Latham. Copyright © 1962 by Macmillan Publishing Company.

(**p. 150**) From *The Ugly Duckling* by Hans Christian Anderson, translated by R. P. Keigwin. Copyright © 1965 by Adrienne Adams. Used by permission of Flensted Publishers, Odense, Denmark.

(**p. 153**) Jamake Highwater, *Anpao: An American Indian Odyssey*. Philadelphia: Lippincott, 1977.

(**p. 153**) Robin McKinley, *The Hero and the Crown*. New York: Greenwillow, 1985.

(**p. 161**) Jean Ure, *Supermouse*. New York: Morrow, 1984.

(**p. 162**) Katherine Paterson, *Jacob Have I Loved*. New York: Harper & Row, 1980.

(**p. 164**) A. A. Milne, *Winnie-the-Pooh*. New York: Dutton, 1926.

(**p. 165**) Reprinted by permission of Charles Scribner's Sons, an imprint of Macmillan Publishing Company from *The Wind in the Willows* by Kenneth Grahame, illustrated by Ernest H. Shepard. Copyright 1933 by Charles Scribner's Sons; copyright renewed © 1961 by Ernest H. Shepard.

(**p. 185**) "Circles" from *The Little Hill,* Poems & Pictures by Harry Behn. Copyright 1949 by Harry Behn. © renewed 1977 by Alice L. Behn. Reprinted by permission of Marian Reiner.

(**p. 185**) "A Choosy Wolf" from *The Phantom Ice Cream Man* by X. J. Kennedy. Copyright

© 1975, 1977, 1978, 1979 by X. J. Kennedy. Reprinted by permission of Curtis Brown, Ltd.

(p. 187) "Obvious Reflection" from *The Face Is Familiar* by Ogden Nash. Copyright 1931 by Ogden Nash. Reprinted by permission of Little, Brown and Company and Curtis Brown, Ltd.

(p. 190) "I Keep Three Wishes Ready" from *All Through the Year: Three Hundred and Sixty-five New Poems for Holidays and Every Day* by Annette Wynne (J. B. Lippincott). Copyright 1932, 1960 by Annette Wynne. Reprinted by permission of Harper & Row, Publishers, Inc.

(p. 191) "Forms of Praise" from *The Sidewalk Racer* by Lillian Morrison. Copyright © 1977 by Lillian Morrison. Reprinted by permission of the author.

(p. 192) "The Base Stealer" from *Orb Weaver* by Robert Francis. Copyright © 1960 by Robert Francis. Reprinted by permission of Wesleyan University Press.

(p. 193) Excerpt from "Inside a Poem" in *A Sky Full of Poems* by Eve Merriam. Copyright © 1964, 1973 by Eve Merriam. All rights reserved. Reprinted by permission of Marian Reiner for the author.

(p. 194) "Lost" from *Chicago Poems* by Carl Sandburg. Copyright 1916 by Holt, Rinehart and Winston, Inc. and renewed 1944 by Carl Sandburg. Reprinted by permission of Harcourt Brace Jovanovich, Inc.

(p. 195) "Mama is a Sunrise" by Evelyn Tooley Hunt from *The Lyric,* 1972. Reprinted by permission of the author.

(p. 196) "The Moon was but a Chin of Gold" reprinted by permission of the publishers and the Trustees of Amherst College from *The Poems of Emily Dickinson,* Thomas H. Johnson, ed., Cambridge, Mass.: The Belknap Press of Harvard University Press. Copyright 1951, © 1955, 1979, 1983 by the President and Fellows of Harvard College.

(p. 196) "The Moon's the North Wind's Cooky," reprinted with permission of Macmillan Publishing Company from *Collected Poems* by Vachel Lindsay. Copyright © 1914 by Macmillan Publishing Company, renewed 1942 by Elizabeth C. Lindsay.

(p. 197) "Night," reprinted with permission of Atheneum Publishers, an imprint of Macmillan Publishing Company, from *The Apple Vendor's Fair* by Patricia Hubbell. Copyright © 1963 by Patricia Hubbell.

(pp. 197-198) "October" from *A Child's Calendar* by John Updike. Copyright © 1965 by John Updike and Nancy Burkert. Reprinted by permission of Alfred A. Knopf, Inc.

(p. 198) "Bike Ride" from *Think of Shadows* by Lilian Moore. Copyright © 1980 by Lilian Moore. Reprinted by permission of Marian Reiner for the author.

(p. 199) "Fourth of July Night" by Dorothy Aldis reprinted by permission of G. P. Putnam's Sons from *Hop, Skip and Jump,* copyright 1941, renewed 1961 by Dorothy Aldis.

(p. 199) "At Night" from *Out in Dark and Daylight* by Aileen Fisher. Copyright © 1980 by Aileen Fisher. Reprinted by permission of Harper & Row, Publishers, Inc.

(p. 199) "Who tossed those golden coins" from *Flower Moon Snow: Book of Haiku* by Kazue Mizumura (Thomas Y. Crowell). Copyright © 1977 by Kazue Mizumura. Reprinted by permission of Harper & Row, Publishers, Inc.

(p. 200) "Whispers" from *Whispers and Other Poems* by Myra Cohn Livingston. Copyright © 1958 by Myra Cohn Livingston. Reprinted by permission of Marian Reiner for the author.

(p. 201) "I Loved My Friend," reprinted from *The Dream Keeper and Other Poems* by Langston Hughes, by permission of Alfred A. Knopf, Inc. Copyright 1932 by Alfred A. Knopf, Inc. and renewed 1960 by Langston Hughes.

(p. 201) "Frost Shall Freeze" from *An Anthology of Old English Poetry,* translated by Charles W. Kennedy.

(p. 202) "There is no Frigate like a Book" reprinted by permission of the publishers and the Trustees of Amherst College from *The Poems of Emily Dickinson,* Thomas H. Johnson, ed., Cambridge, Mass.: The Belknap Press of Harvard University Press. Copyright 1951, © 1955, 1979, 1983 by the President and Fellows of Harvard College.

(p. 203) "Dream Deferred," reprinted from *The Panther and the Lash: Poems of Our Times* by Langston Hughes, by permission of Alfred A. Knopf, Inc. Copyright 1951 by Langston Hughes.

(pp. 204–205) "The Worm" from *Under the Tree* by Elizabeth Madox Roberts. Copyright 1922 by B. W. Huebsch, Inc., renewed 1950 by Ivor S. Roberts. Copyright 1930 by The Viking Press, Inc., renewed © 1958 by Ivor S. Roberts and The Viking Press, Inc. Reprinted by permission of Viking Penguin Inc.

(p. 245) From *Water for Today and Tomorrow* by R. J. Lefkowitz. Copyright © 1973 by R. J. Lefkowitz. Reprinted by permission of Parents Magazine Press.

(p. 248) Alice L. Hopf, *Hyena.* New York: Dodd, Mead, 1983.

(p. 249) Patricia Lauber, *Volcano: The Eruption and Healing of Mount St. Helens.* New York: Bradbury, 1986.

(p. 249) Patricia Lauber, *What's Hatching Out of That Egg?.* New York: Crown, 1979.

(p. 250) Keith Lye, *Take a Trip to Argentina.* London: Franklin Watts, 1986.

(p. 250) Carol Fenner, *Gorilla, Gorilla.* New York: Random House, 1973.

(p. 254) Milton Meltzer, *All Times, All Peoples.* New York: Harper & Row, 1980.

(p. 258) Ben Bova, *The Seeds of Tomorrow.* New York: David McKay, 1977.

(p. 258) Jules Archer, *Hunger on Planet Earth.* New York: Crowell, 1977.

(p. 263) Jean Fritz, *Where do you think you're going, Christopher Columbus?.* New York: Putnam, 1980.

(p. 263, *passim*) Jean Fritz, *Stonewall.* New York: Putnam, 1979.

Index

M

N

O

P